ONCE WE WERE STRANGERS

Once We Were Strangers

A German Immigrant Family in the Nineteenth-Century Midwest

Roberta Reb Allen

University Press of Kansas

© 2024 by the University Press of Kansas
All rights reserved

Published by the University Press of Kansas (Lawrence, Kansas 66045), which was organized by the Kansas Board of Regents and is operated and funded by Emporia State University, Fort Hays State University, Kansas State University, Pittsburg State University, the University of Kansas, and Wichita State University.

Library of Congress Cataloging-in-Publication Data

Names: Allen, Roberta (Roberta Reb), author.
Title: Once we were strangers : a German immigrant family in the nineteenth-century Midwest / Roberta Reb Allen.
Other titles: German immigrant family in the nineteenth-century Midwest
Description: Lawrence, Kansas : University Press of Kansas, 2024 | Includes bibliographical references and index.
Identifiers: LCCN 2023023571 (print) | LCCN 2023023572 (ebook) | ISBN 9780700636273 (cloth) | ISBN 9780700636280 (paperback) | ISBN 9780700636327 (ebook)
Subjects: LCSH: Leuthold family. | Lodholz, Gottfried, 1830–1892—Family. | German Americans—Kansas—Marshall County—History—19th century. | Immigrants—Kansas—Marshall County—History—19th century. | Marshall County (Kan.)—History—19th century. | Marshall County (Kan.)—Biography. | Ebhausen (Germany)—Biography.
Classification: LCC F687.M35 A44 2024 (print) | LCC F687.M35 (ebook) | DDC 978.1/310922 [B]—dc23/eng/20230926
LC record available at https://lccn.loc.gov/2023023571.
LC ebook record available at https://lccn.loc.gov/2023023572.

British Library Cataloguing-in-Publication Data is available.

Printed in the United States of America

The paper used in this publication is acid free and meets the minimum requirements of the American National Standard for Permanence of Paper for Printed Library Materials Z39.48-1992.

To Everett, Maynard, and Louis — The Preservers

And to my grandson Malachi, my great-niece Lilly, and my great-nephews Alex, Charlie, and Jack — The Future

To tell the history of the West without pursuing . . .
Old World linkages is to miss a simple but powerful truth:
Connections matter. From them came the chief puzzle
facing all frontier communities: whether to reproduce the
ways of the old world or abandon them for the new.
—William Cronon, George Miles, and Jay Gitlin,
"Becoming West"

If I went West, I think I would go to Kansas.
—Abraham Lincoln

Contents

Preface xi

Acknowledgments xiii

Introduction 1

Chapter 1: Coming to Amerika: From Ebhausen to Terryville, Connecticut, 1819–57 5

Chapter 2: The Journey West: Michigan, Illinois, Iowa, Nebraska, and Kansas, 1857–58 45

Chapter 3: Life in Kansas and Connecticut, 1859–61 83

Chapter 4: War, Gold, Growth, Death, and Trouble, 1861–73 133

Chapter 5: Change, Tragedy, and the Female Frontier in Marshall County, 1874–90 167

Epilogue: The Lodholzes, the Rebs, and the German Immigrant Experience: The Story Continues 192

Appendix A. Legal and Illegal Emigration   205

Appendix B. Total Population and German-Born
by County: 1860 Federal Census   208

Appendix C. German-Born Place of Birth by County:
1860 Federal Census   211

Appendix D. German-Born Population, County and
Township Statistics by Category: 1860 Federal Census   215

Appendix E. Number of German-Born by Page:
1860 Federal Census   255

Appendix F. Kansas State Census Non-Population Schedule 2:
Foreign-Born by County and Township for Year Ending
May 1, 1865   264

Notes   275

Index   333

Preface

In 2005 the editors of *Kansas History: A Journal of the Central Plains* asked historian Eleanor L. Turk to write an essay surveying the scholarship on the settlement of Kansas by ethnic Germans, the state's largest group of foreign-born immigrants.[1] Professor Turk pointed out that the majority of scholarly attention had been paid to Germans from Russia, while European Germans were mostly "invisible in a historical sense."[2] She accounted for this in part by citing the lack of primary source material, particularly during the territorial period (1854–61), and, to some extent, issues related to language proficiency.[3] Among the few available primary sources mentioned by Turk was a 1918 article by Clara M. Fengel Shields, describing a settlement in the territorial period,[4] and a family memoir by John Ise focusing on the 1870s, first published in 1936 and still in print.[5]

Given this scant information, Turk recommended further study of all aspects of the lives of European Germans—before emigration, the process of emigration, land use patterns, political life, education, family histories, and generational differences in experience, as well as patterns of assimilation, resistance, persistence, and accommodation.[6] This was obviously a tall order requiring years of patient research, which Turk herself had begun. Unfortunately, since her article was published, there has been little focus on European Germans in Kansas.

The translated letters and documents that are the basis for *Once We Were Strangers* add another set of primary sources addressing many of the topics Turk laid out.[7] Like Ise's *Sod and Stubble*, however, *Once We Were Strangers* is also the story of a family—similar to his, but in many ways different. I hope both scholars and general readers will find much to engage with in this book.

Acknowledgments

I am extremely grateful to a number of people who provided significant assistance during the writing of *Once We Were Strangers*. First and foremost is my brother Richard Reb, who gave unfailing support and located Virginia L. Lewis, professor of German at Northern State University in Aberdeen, South Dakota, to translate the majority of the letters in Old German script. He also did yeoman's duty in proofreading various versions of this work. In addition to Professor Lewis, my thanks to Robert Russell, library director at Northern State University, who supported the translation effort and digitized the original letters and documents.

The first chapter of this book would have been sparse indeed without Sheilagh Ogilvie's extensive research on Ebhausen. Since 2020 she has been the Chichele Professor of Economic History at the University of Oxford, and she graciously spent time reading part of an early version of the manuscript and answering my questions.

In Marshall County, Kansas, I relied on Kay Nester, former research assistant at the Research Library of the Marshall County Historical Society. She not only located family records in the county archives but also found and arranged for me to buy two locally published works that were out of print. The details they provided added much to the book.

Over the course of writing *Once We Were Strangers*, I received encouragement and direction from three editors at the University Press of Kansas: Joyce Harrison, Bethany Mowry, and Kim Hogeland. Each helped mold the book, putting her stamp on it to make it better.

Last, I am keenly aware that I am following in the footsteps of two women who wrote extensively about Marshall County: Emma Forter and Oretha Ruetti. It is an honor to be in their company and a privilege to continue their work.

ONCE WE WERE STRANGERS

Introduction

We are a nation primarily of immigrants. Driven by famine, warfare, religious persecution, and political and economic oppression, many of us came to the United States for a freer life and greater economic security. But some of us were brought here as slaves and found neither freedom nor opportunity. And those of us who were already here lost much in people, land, and way of life as a result of contact with immigrants.

These are the broad generalizations found in standard history books. They are impersonal and breathe no life into the past. They give little idea of the complex layering and interweaving of the various histories that make up the larger story of our nation—the histories of states, townships, and cities; of ethnicities, tribes, nationalities, and religious faiths; of wars and relations with people different from ourselves. Beneath all these histories and others we could name lies what I call history at the ground level—the unique stories of the people who lived through the events so briefly described in most history books.

Once We Were Strangers is one such story. Based on an extensive collection of letters and documents in Old German, it follows the fortunes of the Lodholz family as they journey from Württemberg in southern Germany to the Kansas Territory during the nineteenth century. It is a real-life family saga full of hardship, endurance, joy, and sorrow. The story is not always pretty, and it often causes us to feel uncomfortable, such as when it tells of the family's settlement on land that once belonged to the Kickapoo tribe (*Kickaapoi*). But the Lodholz family story is one with heart, as it chronicles how ordinary people experienced the sweep of American history from the 1850s, through the Civil War, to the nominal end of the frontier in 1890.

The journey starts in the early 1800s in what is now Germany, as fifty-two-year-old widow Anna Maria Lodholz and her two teenage children leave their homeland, sailing in steerage across the stormy Atlantic on the SS *Samuel M. Fox* to join her oldest son in New York City. Besides Anna Maria, readers will meet her three very different sons—Gottfried, Georg, and Jakob Friedrich—and her daughter Anna Regina, as well as their spouses. Gottfried, the eldest and most ambitious, came to America by himself, apparently illegally, at the age of seventeen to make money to support the family back in Württemberg. The wandering Georg was sent west to scout cheap land the family could farm. Covering almost a thousand miles in his travels, he ended up on the seemingly endless tallgrass prairie of eastern Kansas. The high-strung Jakob Friedrich left his family in Kansas and returned to the East, where he did not have to eat the cornbread he despised. The earnings from his job in a lock factory helped the rest of the family survive their early years on the frontier. Like her mother, Anna Regina, deeply loved by her husband Heinrich Reb, was widowed too soon, left to raise six children, the youngest just one year old, by herself.

This is not, however, just another family saga. The story encompasses the larger issues of westward expansion and particularly of European German immigration to Kansas, which has been little studied. In general, much of the research on German immigrants by historians such as Linda Schelbitski Pickle and Jon Gjerde has focused on discrete communities bound by homeland or religion and on the patriarchal German family. In Kansas itself, the research has centered largely on the communities founded by ethnic Germans from Russia in western parts of the state after the Civil War. Given the scarcity of primary sources about German settlement during the territorial period, the letters and accompanying research on which this work is based provide a unique opportunity to study German emigration not only from Württemberg in southern Germany but also from other major German states. It complements the work of Jochen Krebber, who detailed the emigration and subsequent settlement of inhabitants from two areas in Württemberg southwest of Ebhausen.

Historians generally do not characterize Germans as "pioneers"; rather, they are seen as settlers who arrived on the land after it was already improved. However, this was not the case with the Lodholzes and the other German immigrants who moved to Kansas in the early days. They were real pioneers, but they were hardly all of the same mold. Their story is complex, and they adopted diverse solutions to living and working in a world dominated by native-borns. The Lodholz family is a case in point. Its male members were not the patriarchs described by Gjerde and Pickle, and the family chose to take advantage of the many opportunities their new country offered. Through their letters, we can see the process of assimilation unfold. As such, the many Germans who assimilated faded into anonymity, leaving little for scholars to study.

Once We Were Strangers was fueled by my passion for history, sparked when I was a teenager in Beirut, Lebanon, where my father was a diplomat, and we explored Sidon, Tyre, Baalbek, and the great Crusader castle of Krak des Chevaliers. At the time, I was unaware of my heritage or any link to Germans in Kansas. There were no clues—no talk of Germans when, in elementary school, we studied the contributions of various ethnic groups to American society, and no special holidays or traditions to celebrate. The Christmas tree and the kindergarten were never explicitly identified as German legacies. It was only much later that I learned about the virulent anti-German sentiment in many parts of the United States, including Kansas, during World War I that virtually wiped out the speaking and teaching of the German language and made Germans the target of threats and sometimes violence, causing many people of German descent to downplay their heritage.

Both my father and my aunt were interested in genealogy, and I took up the quest, producing a thick book for each of my children and my nieces and nephew that traced the family's male and female lines back, where possible, to our ancestors' first arrival in the United States. There were many German strains—Pennsylvania Dutch, Prussians, Henry Reb from the Palatinate, and, of course, the Lodholzes. I thought I was done, but then my brother and I came into possession of a large number of Old German letters and documents after my father's death, refueling my passion for our family history.

The family seemingly threw nothing out, saving letters so they could be savored through multiple readings. My father had gathered the extensive collection of letters in Old German during his visits to relatives in Kansas. He kept hoping to get them translated, but individuals capable of doing so were few and far between. In the end, he managed to get a significant number translated through the good graces of a personal friend, Freda Murray, who was born and brought up in Germany before World War II, but at his death, most of the collection was still not accessible to my brother and me. When we investigated the possibility of getting more letters translated, we found that the cost was beyond our means. My brother persevered, however, and found Virginia L. Lewis, professor of German at Northern State University in Aberdeen, South Dakota. With the backing of her university, she was willing to take on the translations at a much-reduced cost. So slowly but surely, over a period of months, the letters and documents came alive. Northern State University digitized the collection, and my brother and I donated the originals to the university. They are now housed in the Lodholz/Reb Family Collection, South Dakota Germans from Russia Cultural Center, Williams Library, Northern State University.

In these letters I found a richness of detail that made this period of American history come alive, and I wanted to share what it was like to live through that time. When I include details that are not contained in or cannot be inferred from the family's letters and other documents, I rely on historical sources from the same time and place or on scholarship that relies on such sources. When my familiarity with living in a rural area reflects the family's perspective, I draw on my own personal experiences for descriptions.

In writing this book, I became submerged in the Lodholz family's world. I hope readers will be able to transport themselves back almost two centuries and find pleasure in exploring that world and cease being strangers.

CHAPTER 1

Coming to Amerika

From Ebhausen to Terryville, Connecticut, 1819–57

In 1819 there was no Germany. What was to become Germany was a patchwork confederation of thirty-nine states and four free cities, each regarding itself as sovereign within its own boundaries.¹ One of these states was the Kingdom of Württemberg, where the Lodholz family lived in the midsized village of Ebhausen, population roughly sixteen hundred.²

Ebhausen was snuggled in a river valley among the low mountains of the northern Black Forest. It was surrounded by other Germanic states but not far from the borders of France and Switzerland. It actually consisted of two hamlets—Ebhausen proper, on the rise of the valley, and Wöllhausen some two hundred feet below, straddling the spring-fed Nagold River. The Nagold meandered through a broad valley for some fifty-five miles, and although it was neither wide nor deep, it was a major local transportation route. The village had only small local roads connecting it with neighboring villages and larger urban centers; transportation was mainly on foot or by horse or cart. A state highway was finally built in 1851, but there was no railroad line until 1891.³

The area was strikingly beautiful. The winters were long and cold, and stately snow-laden Scotch pines, some hundreds of feet tall, grew on the upper reaches of the valley. In the warmer months the open meadows and grassy areas surrounding the village were full of dandelions and bright blue

View of Ebhausen today. The current population is almost five thousand, about two and a half times what it was in 1819. (Courtesy Gemeindeverwaltung Ebhause)

cornflowers. Nearer the river, deciduous trees offered shade along the path following the curves of the Nagold, their leaves turning red, orange, and yellow in the warm light of autumn.

The village center in Wöllhausen was dominated by the massive, timbered-framed tower of the parish church that dated back to the thirteenth century, when the congregation was Catholic.[4] During the turmoil and warfare accompanying the Protestant Reformation, the ruler of Württemberg chose to convert from Catholicism to a variant of Lutheranism, and the German Evangelical Church of Württemberg was established.[5] At the time, the inhabitants of a country had to follow the religion of their ruler, so the residents of Ebhausen, including the Lodholzes, were members of the established church.

The Lodholz family lived in a backwater. While the Industrial Revolution was literally gaining steam in western Europe and the United States, Ebhausen's economy rested on cottage crafts, regulated by craft guilds as they had been since the late Middle Ages, and on a semifeudal system of agriculture. The inhabitants of Ebhausen lived constrained and scrutinized lives. Although there were local representatives of the king, village leaders handled many important matters in exchange for providing much-needed political support and economic cooperation, such as enforcing regulations and collecting taxes.[6] This local government was rigidly controlled by a ruling elite of the village's wealthier citizens; the local council filled vacancies in its ranks by co-option and elected the chief administrative officials. The communal law court ruled on such matters as who could be granted citizenship, who could reside in the community on good behavior with no citizenship rights, who could be forced to leave, and who could be granted a permit to marry.[7] The primary criteria were economic (whether the individual could support a family), moral, and religious (no Jews, Catholics, or Calvinists need apply). The parish church also exercised control over the inhabitants through its own court that oversaw the morality and spirituality of the faithful, including church and school attendance.

After completing his schooling at age fourteen, the patriarch of the family, Josef Friedrich Lodholz, like most of his male forebears, pursued a career as a worsted weaver. Weaving the lightweight, coarse-textured woolen cloth had a long tradition in Ebhausen and neighboring villages beginning in the sixteenth century.[8] Merchants in urban centers bought the cloth and resold it on the wider market. Scholars dispute how quickly the craft could be taught, but the guild required an apprenticeship of several years.[9] By 1819, Josef had finished his apprenticeship and entered the journeyman stage of his training, gaining more experience before taking an examination and submitting a sample of his work to the local guild masters. Journeyman were not allowed to practice their craft in the local village and compete with the master craftsmen there. To be accepted into the local guild, Josef was forced to look for work within a prescribed region and find master weavers willing to employ him.

In 1819, at the age of twenty, Josef set off on his journey. It had been just four years since Napoleon's defeat at the Battle of Waterloo seemingly ended the threat of the French Revolution's liberal aim of overthrowing the old social and political order. Officials were still wary of individuals freely roaming the countryside and perhaps spreading unrest, so Josef's movements were monitored by local authorities.[10] He had to carry a *Wander-Buch* (Wanderer's Book), issued by the central office of the Black Forest District. Thanks to this *Wander-Buch*, we know what Josef looked like. In the days before photography, physical descriptions had to do: he was slim of build and had a long, thin face, gray eyes, black hair falling over his forehead, and straight legs.[11]

Only the cover page of Josef's *Wander-Buch* survives, so we do not know exactly where he traveled or for how long. However, we know from similar books that they served as both passports and résumés, as well as letters of

Coming to Amerika

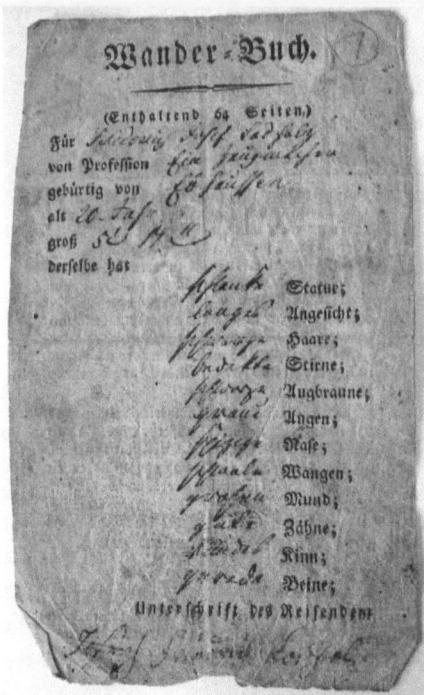

Josef's *Wander-Buch*, front and back cover. The reverse of the cover page gives rules for "wanderers," such as "beware of loitering, begging" and do "not stay over one day, or one night, without permission of the authorities." This gives us an idea of the strictures on Josef's movements and opportunities. (LRFC)

recommendation. Local authorities would stamp the book as evidence of Josef's lawful stay in their village. And any local master considering hiring Josef could read the written comments of all his previous employers about the quality of his work and perhaps his behavior.[12]

Until it was disbanded in 1797, the Calw Worsted Trading Association controlled the export of worsted woolens from the region.[13] Thus, it was in the villages surrounding Calw where Josef would have had the most success in finding masters who were interested in using his services.

By 1825, Josef was once again settled in Ebhausen and had earned the right to set up his own shop there. However, external forces were in the process of rendering his craft obsolete. The disruption of the French Revolution and the subsequent Napoleonic Wars had cut off trade in the Nagold Valley, and consumers' taste for textile goods was changing. The low-quality, cheap worsted woolens produced in Ebhausen were considered "antiquated," and brightly colored cotton prints were becoming fashionable.[14] In addition, with the end of the French blockade, there was an inundation of cheap manufactured goods from England, which particularly hurt the weaving industry.[15] Josef may not have known about changes in fashion, but he would have been aware of the decline in demand with the collapse of the Calw Worsted Trading Association. He and other worsted weavers were free of the association's monopoly, but they themselves now had to find merchants to buy their goods.

The decline in demand was not precipitous, however, and Josef was determined to make a living at his craft. Because there was no abundant supply of raw wool in the area, he had to purchase it elsewhere and take it to the local water-powered spinning mill, Frik and Reichart, which converted it into skeins of wool.[16] Josef then wove the wool on a hand loom in a special craft room in his house. In his determination to make a living at his trade, he sometimes tried to circumvent the rules of the worsted weavers guild. For example, noncitizens had to pay a very high fee to join the guild. So when Josef employed Daniel Friederich Beuttler (probably as a journeyman), who had been born in Walddorf and apparently was not a citizen of Ebhausen, he made Beuttler his "foster son."[17] Josef's ploy allowed Beuttler to become a worsted weaving master at much less expense. Only by being a member of the guild could Beuttler work beside Josef weaving cloth for sale; the guild forbade this task to mere journeymen.[18]

The scant evidence available shows that Josef provided both high-end and coarser types of cloth. Records from 1843 reveal that he sent by messenger a package of very soft, high-quality merino wool cloth to a merchant in Karlsruhe, some forty miles from Ebhausen, and much heavier and coarser shirt flannel to another merchant in Stuttgart, thirty-five miles away.[19] We have no evidence that Josef participated in the annual cloth market in Stuttgart, but we know that in 1837 twenty-five masters from Ebhausen brought 964 pieces of cloth to the market and sold 478.[20] It is instructive to note, however, that the weekly trade journal *Gewerbeblatt aus Württemberg*, catering to businessmen and industrialists, did not mention worsted cloth (*Kammgarn* or *Kammgarntoff*) at all in 1849, its inaugural year of publication. Yet in 1839, 9.5 percent of exported woolens from Germany had come from Württemberg.[21]

Josef had every reason to seek out all potential opportunities and markets, as he had a growing family. In July 1825 he married Anna Maria Schill, three years his junior.[22] They subsequently had six children, described as follows by Anna Maria:

> 1826 20 August, my first child was born, JAKOB FRIEDRICH. This child died 21 Aug. 1835, at 5 PM.
>
> 1829 6 January, my second child was born, GOTTFRIED. He died because it pleased God, on 9 January 1829. God's ways are not our ways.
>
> 1830 10 July. God gave me my 3rd child, GOTTFRIED.
>
> 1833 26 July. My fourth child is born, named JOHANN GEORG. Our, the parents' wish, is that this and all our names would be written in the "book of life" and crossed out again.
>
> 1836 23 September. My 5th child was born, JAKOB FRIEDRICH. God the eternal King. Invisible one and alone in Wisdom, who has created us and through Jesus Christ released us—to whom be praise, honor and praise from eternity to eternity. Amen.
>
> 1838 10 Nov. my sixth children was born, ANNA REGINE. Praise God for his mercy in eternity.[23]

Giving children the names of siblings who died in infancy was a common practice. We do not know the cause of death for nine-year-old Jakob Friedrich, born in 1826. Church records indicate that Gottfried, born in 1829, died of convulsions within three days.[24] Mortality in general was high in Württemberg, but the kingdom also had one of the highest infant mortality rates in Europe, up to three hundred per thousand births.[25] The reasons for this high mortality rate are unclear, but it was not related to income.[26] It may have been due in part to the practice of feeding babies gruel rather than nursing them. The gruel was made from unsterilized water and flour and led to gastrointestinal upsets that often resulted in death.[27]

Anna Maria was a true helpmate to Josef. A wife was permitted to practice a craft under her husband's guild license,[28] so it is likely that Anna Maria not only managed the housework, took care of the children, and tended the garden but also wove cloth.

Like many inhabitants of Ebhausen, Josef was also a part-time farmer. The agricultural system had changed little from the Middle Ages. Although there were no longer any feudal manors in Württemberg and the peasants were not subject to serfdom, the old medieval three-field crop rotation system survived well into the nineteenth century.[29] This system required communal cultivation and harvesting, and the male citizens of Ebhausen kept tight control over agricultural activities through communal assemblies and the watchful eyes of field wardens and inspectors.[30] As a result, Josef had no choice as to what crops to plant and when to plant them.

Anna was by Josef's side in the fields at harvest time. Sickle in hand, she and the other women in the village helped cut the grain. As the Lodholzes' sons grew, they too were expected to help. Typical tasks for young boys included leading the team of sturdy draft horses as they pulled the heavy wooden plow that turned the soil for planting. Later in the year they helped harvest and thresh the grain. They were also in charge of herding the family's cows to and from pasture.[31]

The soil Josef worked was poor. It lacked many nutrients, including iodine, which gave rise to health problems among the inhabitants such as goiter and cognitive impairment. The high altitude meant lower temperatures and a short growing season.[32] Fruit was treasured for the sweetness it added to the diet and for making fruit brandies—schnapps—but an early frost could blight the flowering apple, pear, and plum trees in the orchards, leading to disappointment.

Due to bad weather, crop failures were common, causing great hardship and famine as food prices skyrocketed. A particularly devastating crop failure occurred in 1816–17, the "Hunger Year."[33] The miserable harvest was in fact part of a global phenomenon, but the inhabitants of Ebhausen did not know this. The volcanic eruption of Mount Tambora in Indonesia sent so much ash into the atmosphere that it partially obscured the sunlight, resulting in a significant temperature drop and promoting heavy rains. The hardest hit crops were *Dinkel* wheat (spelt, an ancient type of wheat), oats, and potatoes. Potatoes rotted in the waterlogged soil, and the spelt and oats barely sprouted.[34]

For the residents of Ebhausen (and other southern German states), the ability to obtain sustenance from their strips of land was hindered by inheritance laws. These laws required that any land be divided equally among the decedent's surviving children and/or other heirs, resulting in smaller and smaller parcels of land in each succeeding generation that, in the end, proved inadequate to support a family. Five hectares (approximately twelve and a half acres) was considered the minimum amount of land necessary to sustain a family through its own harvests alone. An 1857 survey showed that 90 percent of the population owned some land, but 75 percent of landowners had less than 3.2 hectares.[35] Complicating matters, this land might be located in other villages some distance from Ebhausen.[36]

They faced hardship and uncertainty, but Josef and Anna knew no other life. They had strong family ties in the community and, as a citizen of Ebhausen, Josef enjoyed a privileged position. For example, he had priority in purchasing any land put up for sale.[37] He also participated in the communal assemblies, which was strictly a male privilege. While Josef was a citizen because of his father's citizenship and having been permitted to marry, Anna Maria was not. Although her father was even more privileged than Josef and was counted among the elite—he held a position on the community council—Anna Maria resided in Ebhausen simply as Josef's wife.[38]

What particularly sustained the Lodholz family and others in Ebhausen was their fervent religious devotion, which created strong bonds among the community. This was not just a go-to-church-on-Sunday type of faith. It was infused with pietism and permeated the inhabitants' everyday lives. Pietism, which had taken root in various German states, including Württemberg, in the mid-seventeenth century, arose in reaction to the influence of the Enlightenment on academic theologians, who produced very cut-and-dried pronouncements on doctrine and theology. Pietism cannot be easily defined, as it had many proponents and took many forms, some more extreme than others.[39] At its core, however, pietism was a religion of the heart, not the head. It emphasized practical piety, reading of the Scriptures by individuals and in small groups, and humility.[40] All these aspects are evident in the Lodholz family documents,[41] perhaps most graphically in an essay Jakob wrote, probably for school:

> A god-fearing countryman was reading aloud from the Bible on a cold winter morning; he was reading from the Gospel of Matthew Chapter 18, where it says: whoever welcomes such a child in my name welcomes me; the father of the household had not been long reading this when someone knocked on the door, and it was opened. There a poor child stepped inside who had lost his parents and was freezing cold, he asked for alms, the countryman looked at his wife and then saw the open Bible, the wife understood what he meant with that, and they said, we want to welcome this child as our own, as the Lord has sent him. The pious country people did just this and took the child in, now the child once again had found a father and mother.[42]

The importance of religion is also evident in the books the family possessed. They had a family Bible, of course, as well as a biblical commentary some five inches thick on the first epistle of John. To this were added books of personal devotion, including *Tägliches Hand-Buch in guten und bösen Tagen*; the full title in English was *Daily Handbook in Good and Bad Days, That Is, Encouragement, Prayer and Singing 1. For Healthy People 2. For the Disabled 3. For the Ill 4. For the Dying with Also Proverbs, Sighs and Prayers to Those Who Are Good Listeners along with Firm Devotions.*

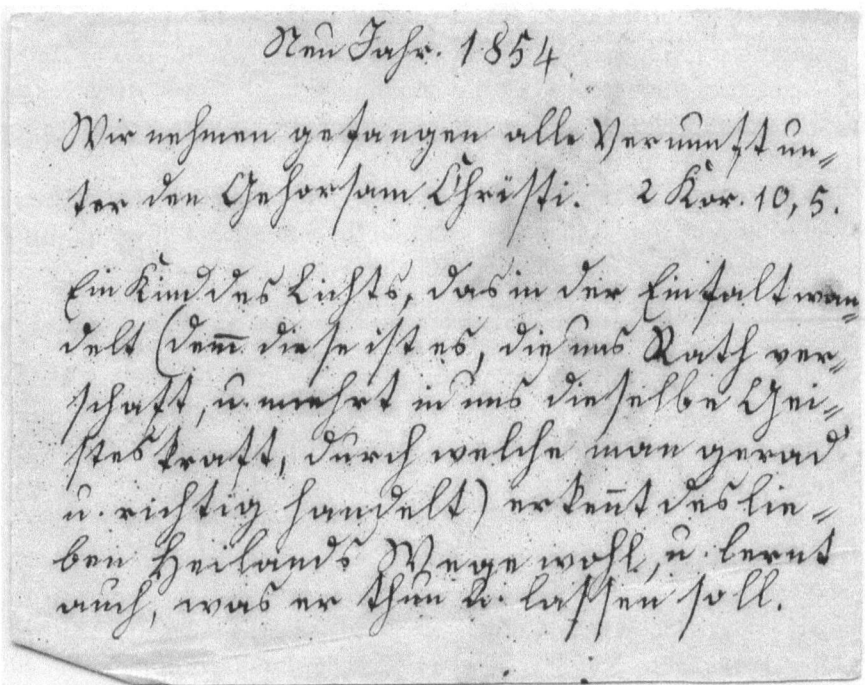

New Year's card from 1854. It quotes from 2 Corinthians 10:5: "We capture all reason beneath obedience to Christ." The rest reads: "A child of the light, who walks in simplicity (for it is this that provides counsel for us, and increases within us the same spiritual power through which one acts in an upright and proper manner), recognizes well the ways of our dear Savior, and learns also what he should do and avoid." (Translated by Virginia L. Lewis; in the family's possession)

Family members even prepared handwritten personal devotional books, often bound with bits of linen thread. These included texts to be read on special religious occasions such as Trinity Sunday and Palm Sunday, responses in preparation for confirmation in the church, and hymnals containing "spiritual songs." Songs were quoted and mentioned often in the Lodholz letters, and they had three copies of a small printed pamphlet of 33 *Missionlieder* (literally, "mission songs"). The fact that the Lodholzes were imbued with pietism would have major consequences when they reached America.

One of the high points of the year for the people of Ebhausen was the Christmas season. The Lodholz house was redolent of spicy ginger as Anna Maria made gingerbread and gingersnaps, a perennial favorite of her children.⁴³ The Christmas tree was decorated with various fruits and aglow in candles.⁴⁴ On New Year's Day, the family exchanged three-inch by three-inch handwritten squares of paper containing biblical quotes. Anna Maria in particular prized these small cards, saving ones from as far back as before her marriage.

Just after the start of 1844, however, the family's familiar routine came to a crashing end. On January 28, 1844, in the bitter depth of winter, Josef died of a lung infection, most likely pneumonia, at the age of forty-five.⁴⁵ Anna Maria and her children mourned Josef's loss.⁴⁶ But grief-stricken or not, Anna Maria had the immediate practical problem of not only supporting her family but also attempting to pay off her husband's debts. We do not know how much he owed, but we do know that debt was common. Statistics for the years 1846 and 1847 reveal that one-sixth of the weavers in Württemberg went bankrupt.⁴⁷ In January 1844 Anna Maria was forty-two years old with four young children. Although widows in Ebhausen did remarry, Anna Maria was somewhat above the median age (37.25 years) for remarriage, based on the closest year for which such statistics are available: in 1850, sixteen widows remarried.⁴⁸ Josef's debts and the four children presumably would have been a deterrent to offers of marriage. So Anna Maria's means of support were meager—whatever could be gleaned from the various strips of land she and her children had inherited from Josef and whatever income she could make from weaving. We have no evidence that her relatives were able to offer any assistance (except for confirmation gifts given to the children). A hope for the future was that Anna Maria's sons would enter a craft and earn money to help support the family. That possibility was some years away, however, as Gottfried, the oldest, was just finishing his schooling and would then begin an apprenticeship in some as yet undetermined craft. Johann Georg was three years younger, and her youngest son was only eight. Anna Regina was six.

The children's schooling came first. Education was the one area in which Ebhausen broke its conservative mold. Children between the ages of seven and fourteen were expected to attend school.⁴⁹ Martin Luther had emphasized the need for individual believers, both male and female, to read and study the Bible, which Luther himself had translated from Greek and Hebrew into German. Gottfried, Johann Georg, Jakob, and Anna Regina attended a church school in Ebhausen, where they learned to read and write as part of their religious training, as well as how to do arithmetic. The catechism book *Auszug der Catechistischen Unterweisung zur Seeligkeit über den Brenzischen Catechismus* (Excerpt from the Catechistic Instruction on the

Soul of the Brenzian Catechism) presented to Gottfried when he was twelve was a formidable read by today's standards.

The topics the students were assigned to write about reinforced church doctrine and religious norms. One of Jakob's essays, reflecting pietism, described an arrogant person:

> Whom does one call a puffed-up person and with what can one compare him. A person who fancies himself to be more than he is, and when one wants to inquire about him, he stands on a step and it is completely different from what he passes himself off as. Thus one can compare him with a weed that has the appearance of being a useful plant, but when one wants to investigate it, it can be totally rotten.[50]

Anna Maria fully supported her children's education. After Josef's death she joined the Association for the Lutheran School, which, in this patriarchal society, was most likely a society of women who had no real say in the running of the school. Her membership card was one of the only documents that used her actual name and did not identify her as Josef Friedrich Lodholz's widow. Membership in the group also provided Anna Maria with the opportunity to socialize and receive moral support from like-minded friends.

We do not know whether Anna Maria considered emigrating at this time. If she did, she eventually decided against it. Certainly immigration to the United States and to other countries, such as Brazil, was taking place. The first wave of German emigration in the nineteenth century occurred during the Hunger Year, when many of the desperately poor attempted to gain passage elsewhere and, lacking the necessary funds, often failed.[51] As the unsuccessful emigrants returned home, they became an object lesson to others, and Anna Maria likely realized she did not have adequate funds to undertake such a journey with her children in 1844. Emigration was in fact officially prohibited, and those who left were considered "stateless," although local officials, seizing an opportunity to rid their villages of a tax burden and avoid possible unrest, often turned a blind eye.[52]

Choosing to remain in Ebhausen, in March 1844 Anna Maria obtained spun wool from Frik and Reichert and began her weaving career.[53] In this, however, she was severely handicapped. The weavers guild allowed wives to continue weaving if their husbands died, but they could not hire apprentices, and their output was restricted.[54] Despite these limitations and the declining worsted wool market, Anna Maria continued to obtain spun wool from the

Etching of a woman working at a loom. (© Can Stock Photo Inc./Morphart)

mill until at least 1847.[55] By then, she was in dire straits. After years of good harvests, famine struck again, caused by an agricultural crisis affecting the potato harvest beginning in 1845.[56] This was followed by poor harvests of wheat, oats, and rye that continued until 1854–55.[57] Anna Maria was faced with less to harvest for her own table as well as rising prices, reminiscent of the hardly forgotten Hunger Year. She possessed a tract titled *Täglich Brot in der Thuerung: Warnung und Trost* (Daily Bread in the Famine: Warning and Consolation) in which the author railed against the population's waning faith and offered the example of a widow with many children who, after praying over the last bit of bread in the house, finds her children rising refreshed from the meal. This simple story resonated with Anna Maria. She could not make enough money from weaving to adequately feed her family. They likely survived on two meals a day with little or no meat. Like many other inhabitants of Württemberg at this time, they had to make do with barely three-quarters of the daily calories they needed, if that.[58]

In 1847 Gottfried was seventeen years old. We do not know whether he had been apprenticed to a craft or what craft that might have been. But years later in America he ordered a loom, so he might have followed in his father's footsteps as a weaver.⁵⁹ If so, he probably did not complete his apprenticeship, as his father had been twenty years old when he began his trek as a journeyman. Given the bankruptcy rate for weavers and the overpopulation of artisans in southwestern Germany, Gottfried saw no future for himself there.⁶⁰ There was general unrest that would soon break out in the revolutions of 1848 that briefly swept France, Italy, and many German states. Letters from earlier German emigrants painted a favorable picture of opportunity in the United States.⁶¹ When his biography was written in 1889, Gottfried told his biographer, "Not being satisfied with his surroundings or prospects in the Fatherland, [he] set out alone in 1847, for America."⁶² The goal was for him to earn enough money to send back home to support the rest of the family. But first, Anna Maria apparently had to go deeper into debt to pay for his passage. An extant promissory note reveals that on October 1, 1847, she borrowed 227 guldens from Josef's "foster son" Daniel Beuttler.⁶³ In normal times, 100 guldens was equivalent to a weaver's average earnings for two years.⁶⁴

There are no records of Gottfried's passage or even that he obtained a passport, so he may well have been traveling illegally.⁶⁵ He presumably left in October 1847 from Le Havre, France, the closest transatlantic port to Ebhausen, for New York City. He was emigrating at the tail end of the second wave of German immigration to America, which consisted of the more prosperous, educated, and skilled inhabitants.⁶⁶ Based on available data, at seventeen Gottfried was younger than the average male emigrant, but he was certainly not unique. When Anna Maria, Jakob, and Anna Regina eventually immigrated to the United States, there were 229 passengers from Württemberg on their ship, 35 percent of whom were single males with an average age of twenty-two. Several, however, were younger—the youngest was fifteen, and four were seventeen.⁶⁷ When Jakob's friend Christian Killinger made his way to America later, the average age of single males from Württemberg on his vessel was twenty-five, although there were one sixteen-year-old and three seventeen-year-olds.⁶⁸

When Gottfried sailed into New York Harbor, there was no Ellis Island to greet him. The US Immigration and Naturalization Service did not exist. The passenger list turned over to the local collector of customs by the ship's captain would have been the only record of his arrival.⁶⁹ His movements were no longer the subject of official scrutiny. He could go wherever he pleased, with no passport needed.

With this freedom came the potential for chaos. We do not know whether Gottfried himself encountered any scam artists, generally called "runners," but they were a plague portside and elsewhere. One earlier German emigrant called his reception a "feeding frenzy."[70] The runners robbed emigrants, seized their luggage, and generally tried to relieve them of their earthly possessions in any way possible. Shabby innkeepers hired them to steer unsuspecting emigrants to their overpriced establishments.[71]

Ebhausen hardly compared with New York City. With a population approaching 700,000, New York was the largest city in the United States. With the exception of a few parks, Gottfried was surrounded not by nature but by rows and rows of stone and brick edifices in myriad architectural styles along endless streets filled with an equally endless muddle of horse-drawn carts and carriages, in between which pedestrians dodged and wove.

The Hudson and East Rivers, which form New York Harbor, made the Nagold River look like a small creek. Instead of rafts transporting lumber there was a jumble of schooners, sloops, and ferryboats. Gottfried found churches of more denominations than he probably ever imagined existed. And he found an ethnic diversity to which he had never been exposed.

It was easy for a stranger to get lost in this melee. Chain migration—with relatives and friends following and joining, even if only temporarily, family and friends who had already settled in America—helped the newcomers adjust to their unfamiliar surroundings and hopefully avoid the scams of the runners. Studies of the phenomenon in Württemberg have shown that chain migration was particularly effective among extended families.[72] But Gottfried was the first in his family to come to America, and we have no evidence that he contacted any previously known acquaintances in New York City. He was, however, resourceful. In fact, all three Lodholz brothers asked questions and sought information about how to take advantage of what America had to offer them. They learned in part by reading newspapers and through an informal camaraderie among German-speaking strangers they met and trusted.[73]

Gottfried had various places to which he could turn for help in New York City. One was the philanthropic German Society, which offered free advice.[74] Another option was to make his way to the area of the city where German emigrants had clustered, called *Kleindeutchland*. There he could mix with former inhabitants of many German states—another new experience for him—and find German-speaking butchers, bakers, doctors, and bankers, as well as churches and numerous societies he could join to widen his local contacts. He could read the German shop signs and local newspapers and communicate in German to find shelter and opportunities for work. Despite the rosy picture painted by some letters home and travel books, it was not easy for young Gottfried, who was alone and apparently had no connections within the German community in New York. He found it difficult to land a job, much less a good-paying one. Gottfried was competing for jobs with the many poor Irish emigrants fleeing famine and death; they at least understood English, even if they could not read or write it. Some German immigrants faltered and returned home, but not Gottfried.

Many of those who arrived in New York made straight for the Midwest, mainly to Ohio, Illinois, and Wisconsin. In 1850, 40 percent of German immigrants lived in the Midwest, compared with 23 percent of the free native-born population.[75] Later letters show that immigrants from Ebhausen were living in Michigan, so there may have been some already there when Gottfried arrived, but he remained near the East Coast, perhaps due to a lack of funds for traveling. The Northeast also had a significant German population that was almost as large as that in the Midwest. Thirty-seven percent of German immigrants lived in the Northeast, but they were concentrated in only two states: New York (20.7 percent) and Pennsylvania (13.7 percent).[76]

Gottfried did not journey to either of these states. Instead, he headed north into New England and sought factory work.[77] Like many of the largely unskilled and poor Irish who became factory workers, Gottfried may have done so at age seventeen because his skill level was inadequate to take up a craft. Through whatever information channels were available to him, he learned of work in Springfield, Massachusetts, where he was employed in a "manufacturing establishment."[78] In 1850 Massachusetts was handling 15 percent of the nation's manufacturing output but had less than 1 percent of the German immigrant population and slightly more than 12 percent of the Irish immigrant population.[79]

Gottfried had never worked in a factory before, with its unrelenting machinery and large numbers of men. He was used to small, home-based craft workshops where one could set the pace of one's own labor. Among his English-speaking coworkers, however, he could pick up English more readily.[80] His earnings were meager, and initially he was unable to send any money to the family.

Meanwhile, back in Ebhausen, Anna Maria had counted too much on Gottfried's anticipated earnings. Upon the completion of Johann Georg's schooling, he was apprenticed to a local baker (the craft her father and brother had taken up), for which he received no pay. With the ongoing grain crisis, this was hardly the best time to embark on such a career, and now her second son could not help support the family by working, for example, as a farm laborer or seeking employment in the city as a wage laborer. For Anna Maria, this may have involved too much loss of social status.

When Anna Maria did not hear from Gottfried by the summer of 1848, she wrote him a pleading letter. Postage was expensive, so she sent it via an acquaintance who was returning to the United States after a visit home. It was, in fact, her second attempt to communicate her plight to her son:

> Ebhausen, 7 August 1848
>
> Beloved Son Gottfried,
>
> As we have an opportunity to send you a letter again through Christian Brenner of Waldorf, who emigrated from America to visit here and is going back to America on 8 August 1848. We already sent you a letter a long time back via Konrad Kempf, Hans Kartle's son, who however did not deliver many of them, therefore we do not know for certain whether you received it.
>
> So we want to report to you once more how things are with us. Thank God we are all well and we would like for our missive likewise to find you in good health. We already described our situation in the previous letter. We've gotten guarantees based on your promise that we can receive some money, now if you do not keep your promise then the guarantors will get to keep our fields and we won't have any fields whatsoever any more. Now you can imagine how things are going with us, there are no earnings, thus things were poorly when you were still with us, but now they are much worse. We beg of you not to go back on your promise and to send money as soon as possible. Your brother Johann Georg is now admittedly doing an apprenticeship with Philipp Jakob Braun, a baker in Wöllhausen. For this reason he can no longer support me.[81]

At this time, Gottfried was still working at the factory in Massachusetts, where he stayed for three years. He then spent one winter in Albany, New York, before ending up at the Eagle Lock factory in Terryville, Connecticut, in 1851.[82] In 1850 Connecticut was providing 4.5 percent of the nation's manufacturing output but, like Massachusetts, had less than 1 percent of the German immigrant population.[83]

It was at this time that, according to the federal naturalization records for Connecticut, Gottfried declared his intention of becoming a US citizen at the Superior Court of Litchfield County. Legally, under the Naturalization

Act of 1802, because Gottfried was only seventeen years old when he arrived, he should have been reported by "his parent, guardian, master or mistress to the clerk of the district court of the district where such alien ... shall arrive."[84] Of course, he had none of these people to report his arrival, and somehow—whether knowingly or unknowingly—he managed to slip through. When he declared his intention to apply for citizenship in 1851, the records stated that he had arrived in 1851 at age twenty-one, the age at which he would have been required to register for himself. Obviously, Gottfried had researched the laws governing US citizenship or was well advised by someone else.

We do not know whether Gottfried was able to provide any financial support to the family during the years he spent in Massachusetts and Albany. If he did, it was not enough. A tax bill for 1850–51 shows that Anna Maria paid only 2 guldens 26 kreuzers out of the 13 guldens 5 kreuzers owed.[85] She became embroiled in a lawsuit with Daniel Beuttler in 1849, which apparently dragged on for several years. A document issued in 1853 reveals that she had many other creditors, including Frik, the owner of the spinning mill. The ruling in the case was that the value of the collateral pledged on Anna's behalf by relatives (several named Schill, her maiden name, and Kempf, the surname of her sister's husband) was insufficient to cover her debts.[86] In the end, she lost all her land. Bankruptcies had become frequent in Württemberg; between 1850 and 1853 one out of every seventy-six families faced foreclosure.[87] But it must have been particularly humiliating for Anna Maria, the daughter of a former member of the community council.

In the midst of her financial troubles, there were other uncertainties. The ideals of the French Revolution did not die with Napoleon's defeat. In 1848 they sparked a series of ultimately unsuccessful revolutions against the ruling powers in several European countries, including Germany. Ebhausen was not subject to an uprising at this time, but the neighboring Duchy of Baden and several other German states were affected. Then, the following year, there was a widespread outbreak of cholera.[88]

Another blow to Anna Maria was the departure of Johann Georg, who left Ebhausen to complete his apprenticeship in Herrenberg, six miles away. It is unclear why he decided to leave, but like Gottfried, he may have seen little future for himself in Ebhausen; in Herrenberg, at least he would not be under the shadow cast by his family's penury. In the future, Johann Georg would prove to be the most unconventional of the brothers, somewhat of a maverick with a love of traveling. He never returned to Ebhausen, and after completing his apprenticeship in January 1852, he found work as a miller's assistant with two masters until the following January.⁸⁹ We have no further information about his whereabouts until 1854. By then, Anna Maria and her remaining children had immigrated to America.

With her two oldest sons no longer in Ebhausen, Anna Maria counted on Jakob for help. In late 1849, at the age of thirteen, he carried on a correspondence with a family friend in Baden who had promised to teach him how to make glass.⁹⁰ Perhaps Jakob hoped to supplement the family's income by this means, but it came to naught. In the same year, Jakob, not Anna Maria, sent a bill to Friedrich Sommer for four shipments of cloth totaling 336 guldens 36 kreuzers.⁹¹ Perhaps they thought that having a male's name on the bill would encourage Mr. Sommer to pay for goods he had already received in June, August, September, and November. In 1850, when Jakob turned fourteen, the age of confirmation in the German Evangelical Church, he received cash gifts of 210 guldens from relatives and family friends in honor of the occasion.⁹² Likewise, when Anna Regina was confirmed in 1852, she received gifts totaling a little more than 283 guldens, including one from the pastor's wife.⁹³ This generosity certainly helped sustain the family. Like her neighbor who grew and sold strawberries, Anna Maria may have earned extra money by selling produce from the small garden attached to her house.⁹⁴ There is no evidence that Jakob was apprenticed in any craft; presumably, he helped his mother in the weaving business. As was traditional for young German women, Anna Regina may have worked as a domestic.⁹⁵

By 1853, Anna Maria was considering emigration. In the three years from 1852 to 1854, some 3 percent of Württemberg's population emigrated.⁹⁶ The only obstacle was obtaining the necessary money. She began to look for the cheapest option and chose to work through an agent, although others in the village did not do so. The sailing ship lines worked with local agents in Europe to recruit passengers, and perhaps Gottfried had suggested that this was the surest and most convenient means of booking travel. In January 1854 Anna Maria received a letter from one such agent, whom the officials in Württemberg would have required to be licensed.⁹⁷

> Mr. Joseph. Fried. Lodholz, widow
>
>   Nagold, 22 January 1854
>
> I hereby inform you that I am currently in the position to accommodate you through Havre at a very competitive price. I believe that an adult person will be able to cover the entire trip from their home with 100 guldens. If she is willing to agree to this, then I think that now is the right time to act.⁹⁸

One hundred guldens was equivalent to approximately $40 at the time.[99] Based on research conducted on fares published in newspapers, the average fare for sailing ships embarking from Bremen was $23 for steerage. Fares for ships leaving from Le Havre were higher but most likely included the cost of traveling to the port. Steamships, which were becoming more common, were smaller than sailing ships, so their passenger fares were more expensive.[100]

Gottfried's earnings at the Eagle Lock Company were now sufficient to pay for his family's journey across the Atlantic,[101] but Anna Maria needed to raise funds to cover their needs as they traveled from Ebhausen to the port of embarkation in Le Havre, France.[102] To do this, she had to sell her possessions. Gottfried, who had washed his hands of Ebhausen, warned her not to waste the money she made from the sale on paying off debts, and he tried to prepare her for life in America. He was counting on his family to assimilate to American ways. He already had in mind a domestic position for Anna Regina and hoped she could develop the skills in Ebhausen to care for fine clothing. He wrote to his mother:

When you sell something, then sell it when the opportunity presents itself and calculate exactly how much you could gather together. If you could bring together enough to be able to undertake the trip to Havre or some other marine city and pay Mr. Killinger from that [probably to transport them and their luggage], then I would arrange for the ship transport here and set things up such that you could leave from your house next July, but not such that, if you have sold, the old debts are paid off with that! For both of us [Gottfried and Georg] have a claim to the money that we've contributed!—If the people had waited, then everything would have been paid off over time, but given that things have come to this point, they must remain this way.

Dear Mother, I'm already rejoicing in the hope of seeing you again soon, assuming God keeps us in good health. Admittedly not everything would be to your liking [in America], . . . and then with the clothing, here everything goes that women who are dressed respectably wear. The woolen skirts and aprons you can't wear here, rather full dresses like for example the parson's wife. It would be very good if dear sister went yet to a fine house so that she could learn how to wash fine clothes and iron them. . . . Now I must close with many greetings to all our friends and acquaintances, and especially to you, dear siblings and you, dear mother.[103]

Once Anna Maria had the money for the trip to Le Havre, she got word to Gottfried, and he sent the required fare via an agent in New York who specialized in such fund transfers.[104] Anna Maria, Jakob, and Anna Regina were about to see Gottfried for the first time in seven years.

The year 1854 was the high-water mark of German immigration to the United States.[105] Some 215,000 Germans arrived at its ports, representing 55 percent of all immigrants that year.[106] According to figures published by the Württemberg government, 14,582 individuals left the kingdom for foreign lands in 1853, the closest year for which figures are available. This constituted somewhat less than 1 percent of the 1,804,140 "souls" counted in Württemberg as of December 1853.[107] The numbers would have been higher the following year.

In 1854 Anna Maria was fifty-two years old, making her one of the oldest female passengers on the ship.[108] According to her emigration passport, she was barely five feet tall, her hair was black (although her eyebrows were graying), and her eyes were blue.[109] Her complexion was described as healthy, but she had sunken cheeks and poor teeth. We have no descriptions of eighteen-year-old Jakob and sixteen-year-old Anna Regina, as the passport indicated only that they were accompanying their mother.[110]

To travel, Anna Maria needed that all-important passport. By using an agent, this apparently became a definite requirement, as her ticket specified that "All passports have to be seen by the police."[111] We do not know the exact procedure for obtaining a passport, but presumably it first involved getting a document from the authorities in Ebhausen vouching for her character and her available funds.[112] Anna Maria's agent worked out of Nagold for the shipping company Chrystie and Schlössmann, which operated sailing vessels that carried passengers between Le Havre, France, and New York City. Nagold, where Anna Maria's emigration passport would be issued, was the district administrative center, seven miles upriver from Ebhausen. Presumably she traveled there on foot or by cart, probably accompanied by her son. She most likely purchased her ticket from the agent first, so that she could show the government officials that she had it in hand when she applied for the emigration passport. Issued on June 26, 1854, the passport specified the date of departure, the route, and the ultimate destination.

The process of obtaining the necessary documentation, however, did not end in Nagold. In a country that tried to control population movement and was not supportive of emigration, there was more red tape.[113] The passport had to be sent to the capital in Stuttgart, some thirty-one miles north of

Nagold, for additional approvals by the Ministry of the Interior, the Ministry for Emigration, and finally the French legation. (No passport or visa was needed to enter the United States.) We do not know exactly how the passport got to Stuttgart and made its way through these agencies.[114] We do know that Anna Maria and her children did not go in person, as they had to wait for the passport to be delivered to them in Kehl, just across the Rhine River from Strasbourg, before they could cross the bridge that marked the border with France.[115] Württemberg was a highly organized, hierarchical state capable of collecting and analyzing the most minute information (for example, about agricultural production), so it is highly likely that there was a fleet of government couriers carrying important documents and instructions throughout the kingdom, similar to Josef's use of nongovernmental couriers to deliver orders.[116]

Meanwhile, Anna Maria returned from Nagold to prepare to leave Ebhausen. July 2 was the specified date of departure from the village, so she and her family had only six days to say their good-byes and pack their necessities, treasured personal items, and enough food to sustain them during the long crossing. It was a hurried, exciting, anxious six days. Anna Maria and her children packed carefully. Chrystie and Schlössmann had specific rules about the construction, size, and overall weight limits of containers. Deciding what to take also involved deciding what to leave behind—forever. They probably used strong, iron-studded chests with good locks, each no bigger than four feet long, two feet wide, and two feet high. Each family member was allowed to bring one hundred kilograms (220 pounds), or twenty English cubic feet, of personal baggage.[117] This amounted to one trunk of the specified maximum dimensions and one smaller trunk measuring no more than four cubic feet. For passengers undertaking such a monumental voyage, this was not very much. Anna Maria, Jakob, and Anna Regina packed clothing and the cooking items they would need to prepare their own meals on the ship, such as utensils and a kettle. They also had to furnish but not pack their own bedding, which consisted of simple palliasses made of a strong, stiff material such as linen and filled with straw.[118] The family also brought items with deep personal meaning, which is why so many of their books, letters, and documents made it to America.

Amidst all the packing, Anna Maria had to obtain 210 pounds of food for each family member, almost the same weight as the personal baggage they were each allotted. The types and amounts of food were spelled out by the shipping company on the ticket: zwieback (a hard, dry bread made from flour, eggs, and sugar), potatoes, rice, flour, butter, smoked ham, salt, and

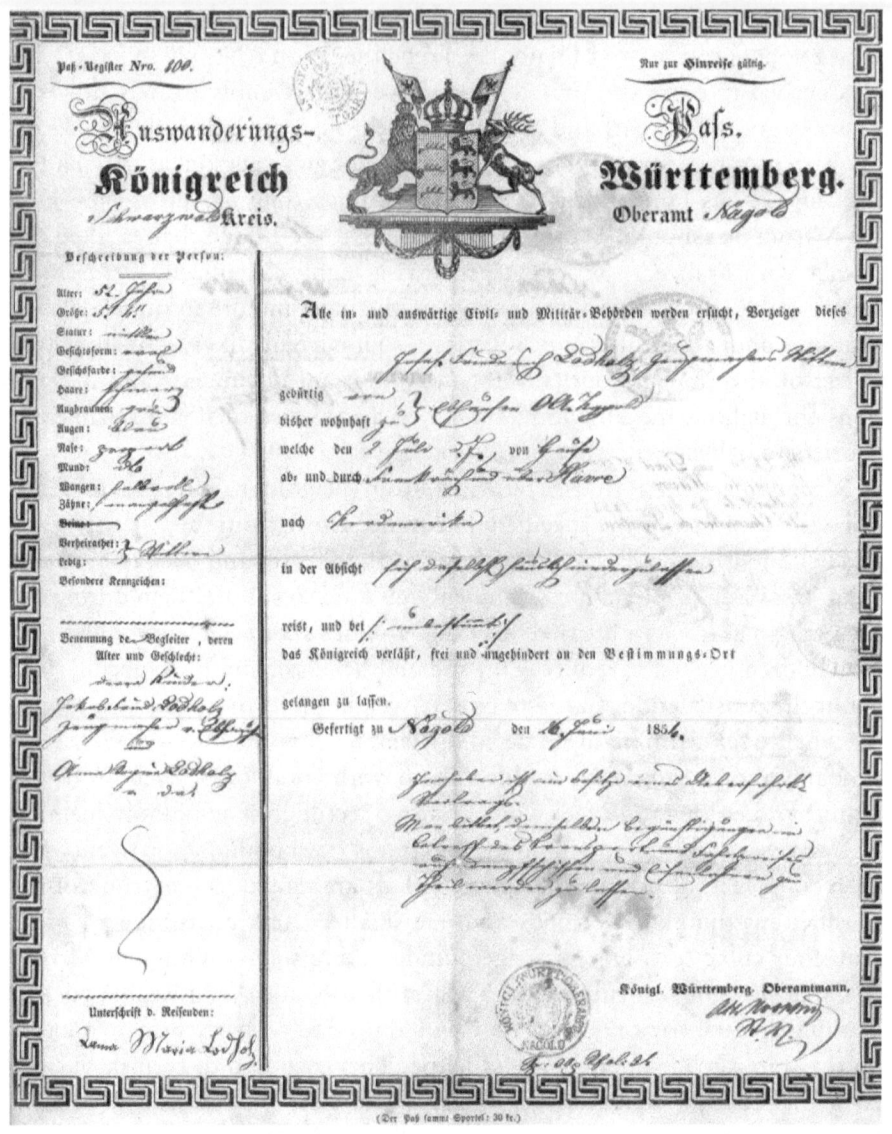

Emigration passport (front and back). (In the family's possession)

Geschehen, Stuttgart den 29. Juni 1854

Aus Auftrag des Ministers des Innern,
für den Kanzlei-Direktor:

Stumpf

N° 10.557. Geschehen, Stuttgart den 30. Juni 1854

Aus Auftrag des Ministers der auswärtigen Angelegenheiten,
der Kanzlei-Direktor:

V. Cotta

VU DE HAVRE

N° 2530 — Droit 2f 50c
Vu pour le Hâvre
Stuttgart, le 30 juin 1854
Le Chancelier de Légation,

L. de Griffon

Vu pour Newyork
sur le navire M. Jon
Havre le 9 juillet 1854
le Commissaire de police Délégué

LÉGATION DE FRANCE
STUTTGART

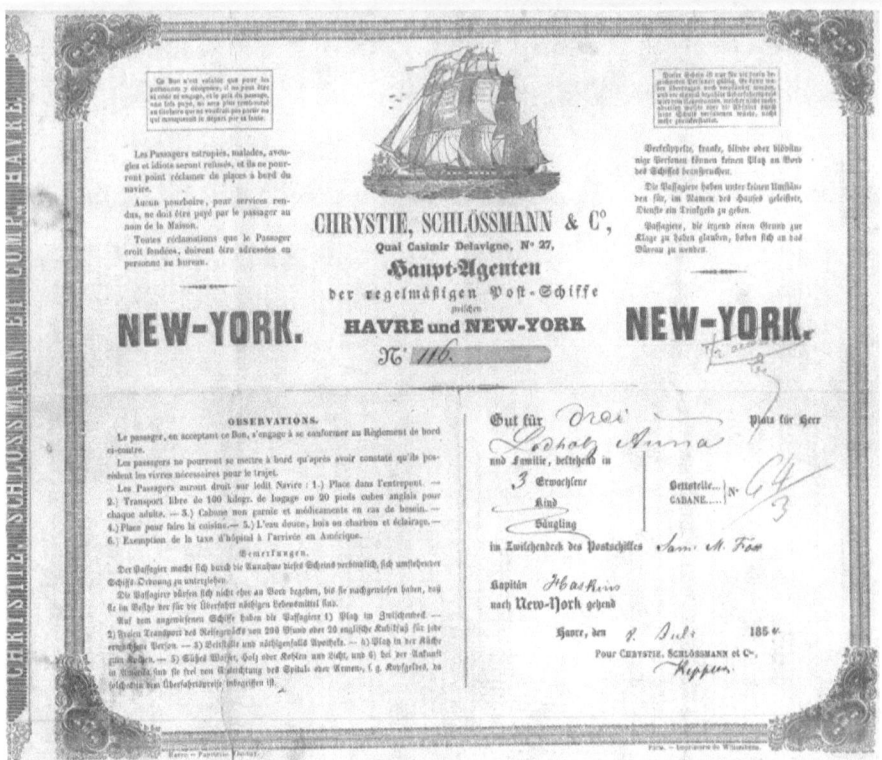

Ticket for the voyage from Le Havre to New York. (In the family's possession)

vinegar.[119] These items were chosen mainly for their long shelf life, as the voyage took an average of thirty-seven days.[120]

Practical matters aside, the leave-taking was emotionally wrenching for everyone. It was particularly hard for Anna Maria to leave her cherished older sister Christina, whom she would never see again. Friends were deeply affected by the loss of the family and wrote farewell letters voicing their love and grief. Anna Maria's good friend Maria Catherina Glaz probably expressed the emotions of many when she wrote:

> What kind of pain is separation for a similarly minded heart? Oh dear sister [in the Lord], we are now experiencing what sort of pain this separation is, as you are leaving our circle so quickly, but . . . we can always come together before the throne of grace. Oh, you know how I loved you, how much this saddened me, but I cannot change it. . . .

Should I not see you anymore, I wish that things might go well. May God's grace protect you.[121]

Jakob later wrote a letter from the United States addressing various relatives and close friends that gives us a sense of the emotions he experienced and the things left unsaid in the hurry to leave:

Dear sister Margretha Barbara Lodholz, I thank you profusely for your love and loyalty which you have shown to me, you once said that you had something else to say to me when I go and then it was forgotten. Please be so kind and let me know it in your next letter, as I am most curious.

Magdalen Lodholz, as I was no longer able to extend my hand to you because of all the work we had to do, don't hold it against me, as I think you will come here yet, so we may well meet each other again, then we will enjoy a happy handshake indeed. . . .

And dear Johannes, that brief hour on Sunday noon comes to mind from time to time and I thank you for that.[122]

Sunday, July 2, came quickly. For some unknown reason, the family's departure was delayed until 8:00 a.m. on Monday, July 3. Jakob kept a notebook where he recorded the date and time they and all their baggage left Ebhausen—alone, except for whoever was driving their cart. They left quietly; perhaps they did not want local officials to know about the delay.[123]

Whatever the feelings of the Lodholz family and their circle of friends and relatives, at least one member of the community was excited at the prospect of going to a new world. One of Jakob's best friends, Christian Killinger, had already written a letter reminding him "to hold to your promise to write to us from America" and answer myriad questions, including, "How do you like it in America? Because I think if you like it, I will too. What do you think, should I come to America or not?"[124]

The high-spirited Christian did not foresee it at the time, but within eight weeks he too would embark for America, but under very different circumstances. We do not know whether the Lodholzes' departure sparked emigration fever in the village, but when Christian left, it was with many other inhabitants of Ebhausen, including several other Lodholzes and one of Jakob's former teachers. They departed on a Sunday with a great deal of fanfare. Christian's farewell to his mother was heartrending:

Coming to Amerika

It was worst for my mother, she had to dry her eyes and cried, then she went to cook. You can imagine how it was when I went and gave her my hand. I thought she would never let go. But the farewell was hard for all my family members. The farewell was harder for the ones who stayed behind than for the ones who leave because we, the ones who went away, whenever we looked at each other we picked up fresh courage.... The number of people who came for the farewells is hard to imagine.[125]

Many accompanied the village group for a while on their journey to Kehl. Unlike Anna Maria and her children, they apparently did not use an agent, and most of them did not have passports (see appendix A).

To reach the French port of Le Havre (known simply as Havre) on the northwestern coast of France, Anna Maria and her children had to travel approximately five hundred miles. The first stage of their journey took them to Kehl in the neighboring Grand Duchy of Baden.[126] As the crow flies, it was fifty-four miles from Ebhausen to Kehl, but because the Lodholzes had to navigate through the forested mountains, their path was a longer, winding one. They stopped briefly at a nearby village where the shipping agent had apparently arranged for them to meet up and travel with two other families. They followed an age-old route and ascended to the Kniebis, a 3,200-foot-high mountain ridge in the Black Forest, where they stayed overnight in a village perched high on the ridge. The next day they left the Black Forest and descended to the valley of the Rhine River. Arriving in Kehl at 4:00 p.m. on Wednesday, July 5, they reported to the office of the shipping company, where they left their trunks and crates for later transport to the dock at Havre.

Anna Maria, Jakob, and Anna Regina spent two long days in Kehl, staying at the Ox Inn and waiting for their passport, which was presumably sent to the shipping company's office by courier. Jakob reported that they picked up the passport at the bridge crossing from Kehl to Strasbourg. Once in France, they left Strasbourg by train at 8:00 p.m. and arrived in Paris the next day at 1:00 in the afternoon. They boarded another train at 10:00 that evening, which got them to Havre by 8:00 the next morning, July 7. Thus, the trip from Ebhausen to Havre took only five days, two of them in Kehl waiting for their passport. They spent a total of twenty-seven hours on trains.

The Lodholzes had never seen a railroad before, much less ridden on one. La Compagnie du Chemin de Fer de Paris à Strasbourg used modern steam locomotives capable of traveling at speeds of 60 kilometers per hour (37 mph).[127] This was a far cry from the pace of a horse- or cow-drawn cart. One earlier passenger reported that the cars were filled beyond capacity and jolted so much that some passengers vomited.[128] The Lodholzes were undoubtedly exhausted by the time they arrived in Havre. However, they had to report immediately to the shipping company's office and to the local police, who dutifully stamped their passport. The French were wary of immigrants on their soil, as many of these travelers were quite destitute.

Havre was a busy cosmopolitan port, sitting on the English Channel at the mouth of the Seine River. It did a wide-ranging business in commercial shipping, transporting coffee, spices, and exotic woods, as well as cotton from the United States destined for factories in Alsace.[129] In other words, it was nothing like Ebhausen. Anna Maria and her children stayed at an inexpensive hostel recommended by the shipping company: the Hotel Suisse, run by François Merki at Quai Barracks No. 2.[130] For the first time in their lives, they were in a foreign land whose native tongue and religion were not their own.

Finally, after a wait of five days, they boarded the *Samuel M. Fox*, an American-built and -owned sailing vessel.[131] It was a packet ship, designed to carry passengers and cargo on a regular basis between two ports—in this case, between New York and Havre. The sturdy vessel's three masts and large, square sails took full advantage of the wind, making it relatively speedy. It was approximately 171 feet long, 37 feet wide at its broadest, and 26½ feet deep.[132] This was almost four times as long as, three times as wide as, and much deeper than the cargo ships used by the Vikings to sail the Atlantic.[133]

According to an ad taken out by Chrystie and Schlössmann in a Leipzig newspaper, the *Samuel M. Fox* was listed at 1,500 tons, but it was actually 1,062 tons.[134] The listing at 1,500 tons may have been a deliberate attempt to imply that the ship could carry more passengers than it legally should have.[135] The Steerage Act of 1819, the first US federal legislation regulating passenger shipping, specified two passengers for every five tons. On paper, at least, the penalties for violation were severe—$150 for each passenger above the legal limit, and forfeiture of the vessel if the overage exceeded twenty passengers—but enforcement required a lawsuit. Tonnage was to be determined by "custom-house measurement."[136] At a tonnage of 1,500, the *Samuel M. Fox* could legally carry 600 passengers; at its actual tonnage, it should have carried only 425. Anna Maria, Jakob, and Anna Regina traveled with a total of 622 steerage passengers plus three above-deck

Ad for the *Samuel M. Fox*. Tonnage is not the weight of a ship but its estimated volume—its cargo-carrying capacity. (Reprinted from J. E. Detraz, "From DESTRAZ to DETRAZ")

passengers: a French woman, her son, and an American, Mr. Allen.[137] We do not know whether the customs official who obtained the passenger list from the captain considered the ship to be in violation, but even if he did, there is no record of any violation being prosecuted.[138] It is worth noting that the federal government's main source of revenue at this time was customs duties, and collecting them was the main function of customs officials.[139]

Shipboard, steerage was the area between the hold, where the cargo and passenger goods were stored, and the upper deck. Its height ranged from five to eight feet.[140] When Anna Maria, Jakob, and Anna Regina descended the ladders from the fore and main hatches, they found no portholes. The space was dusky, and the air was stale. Unless a ship was fitted with ventilating tubes, the only available light and air came from the two hatches.[141] Headroom, particularly in the berths, was minimal. There were likely two tiers of berths down each side of the steerage area, with an aisle about five feet wide between them.[142] The Lodholzes were assigned three spaces in berth 64. Four individuals were often assigned to each berth, and if this was the case on the *Samuel M. Fox*, the fourth spot in their six- by six-foot space would have been occupied by a stranger.[143] We do not know whether they were given an upper or a lower berth. In any case, the berth would have been made of wooden planks with a partition or demarcation to divide one berth from those in front and back. They placed their bedding on these planks. Wealthier first-class passengers had actual cabins on the top deck, and they did not mingle with steerage passengers.

The shipping company transported the family's trunks and crates to the dock, but Anna Maria and her children were responsible for proving to officials that they had the requisite foodstuffs, marking their baggage with the berth number they had been assigned, and getting the trunks and crates on board.[144] We do not know how the family's possessions were loaded onto the ship; sources are silent on this matter, and engravings from the period offer no real clues. Jakob may have carried their small trunks, crates, and palliasses on board and placed them in the passageway next to their berth. But given the weight of the larger trunks and the food—particularly the potatoes and zwieback, destined for the hold—the passengers likely helped one another or paid porters to do the job. The ticket specified that this was not the responsibility of the captain or the emigration agency.[145] The items in the hold were organized by berth number and were probably loaded in that order, making it easier for the passengers to find and retrieve items later in the voyage.

Given the number of people who booked passage, loading must have taken most of a day. Of the 622 steerage passengers, 35 percent were from Württemberg; of these, 60 percent were single males and females. The remainder were traveling as part of a group—families, couples, siblings.[146] It must have been frenzied at times, as passengers were required to have everything on board twelve hours before departure; otherwise, they would not be allowed to sail, and there were no refunds on tickets. The passengers themselves were required to be on board two hours before the scheduled departure.[147]

Finally, at 2:00 p.m. on July 15 1854, the *Samuel M. Fox* set sail.[148] All the passengers were required to come on deck and then return to steerage as each person's name was called.[149] Anyone left would be considered a stowaway and would be taken back to shore by the pilot after he had guided the ship out of the harbor. Perhaps Anna Maria and her children fortified themselves by reading some of the verses in the small handwritten book a friend had given them, "The Farewell Poem for the Trip to North America, Dedicated in Remembrance from a Few Loyal Friends":

> When He is with you on the ship,
> What harm can the sea and its waves do?
> Should storm and billows strike,
> No accident can cast you down;
> And even should death menace you,
> And your heart quake full of fear—Sink into the Savior's lap,
> Then you shall die and fare well.

> The Savior himself was
> A stranger and a traveler,
> He could claim no property,
> No house, not even a bed;
> He also rode by ship
> And slept there calmly and well
> Choose him for your helmsman,
> Then you shall travel and fare well.[150]

It is 3,515 miles from Havre to New York City. The trip took thirty-two days, which was less than the average.[151] It was smooth sailing out of the harbor, but then the family faced the hazards of the open sea. Theirs was a risky venture in many ways. Unbeknownst to Anna Maria, she was sailing during the prime hurricane and cyclone season in the North Atlantic. Between 1847 and 1851, close to sixty ships carrying emigrants were wrecked at sea. However, packet ships like the *Samuel M. Fox* had a better record.[152]

Conditions varied considerably from ship to ship. The worst were the so-called coffin ships carrying poor Irish emigrants trying to escape the potato famine, only to die at sea. Their landlords, many of whom paid their passage as a way to force them off the land, and the British ship owners and crews who transported them thought of them as nuisances at best and subhuman at worst.[153] Many of the ships were poorly built, overcrowded, unsanitary, and inadequately stocked with provisions to feed the passengers, and as a result, death stalked the passage. Dysentery and outbreaks of typhus, cholera, measles, smallpox, and yellow fever occurred. An average death rate of 10 percent was considered normal.[154] The record of the *Samuel M. Fox* was much better. During the Lodholzes' voyage, five people died, including a nine-month-old baby—a death rate of less than 1 percent.[155]

Another indication that the *Samuel M. Fox* was one of the better-run ships is that each morning the steerage passengers were required to straighten and clean their berths and the aisle next to them. Only then were they allowed into the hold to fetch any groceries they needed and then, weather permitting, await their turn to use the "kitchen" on deck, which consisted of an enclosed galley with a smoke vent and a cooking grate over a bed of soil or rocks, with wood as the fuel.[156] With so many passengers sharing the space, Anna Maria and her children were lucky if they got one cooked meal a day.

But even on a well-run ship, conditions in steerage were grim. It was crowded, dark, and damp; lice, fleas, bedbugs, and other insects infested the ship and plagued the passengers. Sleeping three or possibly four abreast

Engraving of a packet ship from an 1851 edition of an English magazine. It depicts the *Isaac Webb*, which was very similar in design to the *Samuel M. Fox*. (*Gleason's Pictorial Drawing-Room Companion* 1, 3 [July 19, 1851]: 33)

on a six-foot-wide plank, Anna Maria, Jakob, and Anna Regina had only eighteen to twenty-four inches apiece in the poorly ventilated steerage area, which, in the middle of July, must have been stifling. Turning over at night would have been well-nigh impossible, and with little headroom, it would have been difficult to sit up.

In such conditions, the stench of so many human bodies must have been overwhelming. The opportunity to change clothing was probably rare, if at all. The crew supplied freshwater only for drinking and cooking; the passengers had to use saltwater for washing their cooking utensils and themselves, which made their skin dry and itchy. The toilet facilities in steerage consisted of large buckets, probably with some sort of privacy screen. It is doubtful that any family member used the head at the aft of the ship's main deck.

In writing to his friend Christian Killinger after they had both reached the United States, Jakob did not dwell on the voyage. He simply said: "I don't think I need to mention the conditions on ship. You will know that yourself."[157] In the small notebook in which he wrote about the voyage he was more detailed, focusing on the ship's progress through a frightening storm and becalmed winds and the passengers' seasickness. The first Sunday at sea there were no religious services, and Jakob was affronted by people working—knitting—on the Lord's day:

> On the ship we felt so ill, we had to throw up, because the ship fairly ran on the first day, then the next day, the Sunday, . . . I saw people who were knitting. . . . When one wants to get through and not be blemished by the doings and forces of the world, one must collect one's seeds and thoughts effectively and refresh oneself in the spirit and consider the goods of grace that are prepared for us in heaven.
>
> Then the first week began on the ship, . . . Tuesday night when, on 18 July, we had a storm, but it wasn't exactly dangerous. But then a bunch of things fell down the staircase, which made a loud noise, and a lantern fell down. We were terrified at that moment, but we commended our souls to God to do as he willed.
>
> Then things proceeded in an orderly manner until Thursday, the 20th. That same night things began swaying again, we were lying at this time in our beds. When we are healthy, we have all sorts of thoughts regarding who is doing more badly than the other. Then followed the second Sunday, and on this day it was said more than once, today is Sunday, today is the Lord's day. And the captain distributed some instructions for the celebration and several hundred [illegible], but then on the other hand on this evening a wild shuddering was heard on the rear deck.
>
> And now this week the ship has run extremely well. So then the third Sunday things were sadder, for there was rainy weather. One could not go to the foredeck much.
>
> So how did things go the third week, we again had regular winds until Tuesday morning, when we traveled past the Sandbank,[158] it was a little stormy, and then on the fourth Saturday the ship was standing practically still, because we had barely any wind.
>
> This week we had no dangers until Friday, when on 11 August from 4 in the afternoon until 8 in the evening we had a strong storm and the ship rocked from one side to the other, so that the cushions [presumably palliasses] . . . [159]

The text ends abruptly here. Jakob presumably did not feel up to continuing his chronicle of their travails.

Eight weeks later, Christian Killinger's voyage was likewise a rough one:

Our ship journey was rather bad, but for many people good because our ship got a hole after 15 days so that 24 men had to pump so that 12 men received 50 fl. [florins, i.e., guldens] in New York and the other 12, 55 fl. Many of us would not have been able to go on from N.Y. if they wouldn't have had this money. All of us unmarried men did pump, except me and Johannes Renz because we were sick.[160]

In the same letter, Christian reported that it took forty-nine days to reach New York, and upon arrival, the emigration party immediately began to scatter. He was headed to his brother's in Ann Arbor, Michigan, and eight others were traveling to the unidentified community of Liniete.[161]

The completion in 1825 of the Erie Canal, connecting the Hudson River at Albany, New York, to Lake Erie at Buffalo, New York, led many New Englanders to buy public lands in southern Michigan, which attained statehood in 1837.[162] But even before then, many families from Württemberg had settled in and around Ann Arbor, and in 1833 they obtained their own Evangelical Lutheran pastor who offered church services in their native Swabian dialect.[163] So Christian's journey was a case of "chain migration."

In a letter to Jakob, Christian reported that he had parted from Sara Lodholz in Buffalo.[164] He also mentioned that two members of the original party, Johann Georg Lodholz and Johannes Renz, were headed for Norwich Falls, most likely referring to the Norwich mine in the Upper Peninsula of Michigan, where copper mining had begun in 1850, although it was a short-lived venture.[165] The two men were among the first immigrants from Württemberg to work in the mines.[166] The fact that news of possible employment there had reached Ebhausen relatively quickly is evidence of an active, informal communications network.

In 1854 there was still no Ellis Island to greet Anna Maria and her children as they sailed into New York Harbor. It was not until the next year that the first immigrant receiving and examination station was set up at Castle Gardens at the tip of Manhattan, succeeded in 1892 by the more familiar Ellis Island.[167]

Before leaving Havre, Anna Maria had written to Gottfried, telling him that they were due to embark soon. He planned to meet them in New York City, but he did not know when the *Samuel M. Fox* would actually be leaving Havre, nor did he know how many days the voyage would take. Time was money for Gottfried, and he wanted to miss as little work as possible, so he counted on the assistance of an acquaintance in New York City, John Strohm. Gottfried had lodged with Strohm for several days in May when he was in New York to arrange the transfer of ticket money to his mother in Ebhausen. At that time Strohm had agreed to "take care of things" upon the arrival of Gottfried's family. This type of networking was key to immigrants' ability to navigate their new world. On July 7 Gottfried sent Strohm a letter asking him to

> be so kind and hand this letter over to a respectable innkeeper who could collect the people from the ship when it arrives—it's three people, my mother, brother and sister. Their name is Lodholz. The innkeeper should show them this letter, then the people will trust him. In addition I would like to ask you to let me know immediately of their arrival. I would sincerely appreciate it if you could send me notice as soon as the ship is announced via telegraph.[168]

When the *Samuel M. Fox* docked on August 16, there was no one there to greet the Lodholzes, but they were not alarmed.[169] Passengers had the right to remain on the ship with their baggage for forty-eight hours after arrival.[170] Anna Maria, Jakob, and Anna Regina stayed on board until the next day, when a "Lodholz [apparently no relation] came who was the innkeeper at the 'Golden Swan' in New York, who then hosted us until our dear Gottfried came, namely on 19 August. You can imagine how great our joy was."[171]

Upon Gottfried's arrival, the newly united family started the hundred-mile journey to Terryville, Connecticut, on August 21. The first leg of their journey was by steamboat—another new experience for Anna Maria, Jakob, and Anna Regina.[172] It is highly likely that they traveled on *The City of Hartford*, launched in 1852 and capable of carrying almost a thousand passengers.[173] The steamboat was longer than the *Samuel M. Fox* but narrower, with a tall smokestack and a large, noisy paddlewheel churning through the water at a rate of eight miles an hour.[174] The boat left New York Harbor and headed east in Long Island Sound until it reached the mouth of the Connecticut River and proceeded north. The trip took place overnight, so the Lodholzes could see little out the windows of their quarters. There were two classes of passengers, and although we do not know which accommodations they chose, it is doubtful that they stayed in the fancy staterooms.[175]

The steamboat traveled up the Connecticut River as far as possible and ended up at Hartford. By ten o'clock the next morning, the Lodholzes were boarding the Hartford, Providence, and Fishkill Railroad for the fifty-mile, twelve-hour journey to Bristol, the railway depot nearest to Terryville.[176] In

> **Gantter & Behrens,**
> [früher **Peter Stocky**,]
> empfehlen ihr neueingerichtetes
> **Gasthaus zum goldnen Schwan**
> **No. 141 Cedar-Street,**
> **New-York.**
>
> Auch haben dieselben eine gut eingerichtete Bade-Anstalt in obigem Hause mit ihrer Wirthschaft verbunden.

Business card for the Golden Swan Guesthouse, announcing new ownership and the existence of a bathing establishment in the same building. Its accommodations would have been a far cry from steerage. (In the family's possession)

the late 1820s railroads started to transform America. By 1835, almost one thousand miles of track had been laid by thirty-nine lines. By 1850, there were nine thousand miles of track, although many of the lines were still short and local.[177]

Traveling in daylight, Anna Maria, Jakob, and Anna Regina got their first look at farmland in America, which was very different from farms in Ebhausen. They saw no common open fields. The boundaries of the scattered farms were often clearly marked by low, stacked stone walls. There were forests containing white oaks, maples, walnuts, and sumac shrubs with crimson spikes of fruit, but they saw nothing resembling the Black Forest. The last leg of their journey was by mail post (stagecoach) to Terryville—a jarring but short three-mile trip. They arrived "in good health" on August 22.[178]

The last member of the family, twenty-one-year-old Johann Georg, would soon join them. There is no mention of how he obtained passage; nor does he appear on any extant ships' passenger lists. Once on American shores, the members of the Lodholz family committed themselves to surviving and thriving. Some of their fellow countrymen returned due to homesickness, disappointment, the difficulty of making a living, and myriad other reasons, but Anna Maria, Gottfried, Johann Georg, Jakob, and Anna Regina never

Coming to Amerika

set foot in their homeland again. As Jakob wrote to his friend Christian: "There was a time when we were on board ship, but now we hardly think of that anymore. Now concerning how things are with us at present, we are of course better off than in Germany."[179]

Terryville was one of three villages in the town of Plymouth in Litchfield County in northwestern Connecticut, abutting New York. In 1850 Plymouth had just over twenty-five hundred inhabitants.[180] The village of Terryville had access to water power from the Pequabuck River, and like many New England towns so blessed, it was in the forefront of the Industrial Revolution. Upriver from the village, the huge horseshoe-shaped dam, created in 1851, was nothing short of dramatic. The cascading water plunged straight down, where it was diverted into ponds and then channeled to power the Eagle Lock Company's waterwheels, which in turn powered the lathes, presses, and other machinery used to make its renowned locks for cabinets and trunks. The company, which existed until the 1970s, dominated the village.

Terryville also had a foundry for the manufacture of malleable iron castings, used in hand tools and pipe fittings. In fact, the first German family to settle in Terryville was headed by Württemberg-born Johans Peter Scheuring. The owner of the foundry recruited Scheuring out of New York City in 1850 because he could find no experienced workers locally.[181]

According to the 1850 federal census, twenty-two Germans already worked in the town of Plymouth before Gottfried's arrival in 1851.[182] The census records do not specify where these Germans came from originally. They represented less than 1 percent of the total population and 11 percent of the foreign population, with the Irish constituting 58 percent of the latter. The German-born population included numerous foundry workers as well as two clockmakers, three lock makers, a collier, and two masons. Tellingly, among the twenty-two Germans, there were only two females. This was not a German settlement per se. There were three families, and in two of them, the German husbands had married native-born women. The majority of the German men lived in boardinghouses, grouped not necessarily by ethnicity but by occupation. This pattern of single German males being predominant in a new settlement area would be repeated.

The Lodholzes were fortunate to have an entire rented house to themselves. The three brothers worked at the lock company, which had two plants. Gottfried had arranged for Anna Regina to serve in the household of one of the bosses, Serano Gaylord, and according to Jakob, "she has it very good."[183] Anna Maria managed the Lodholz household. Sources are

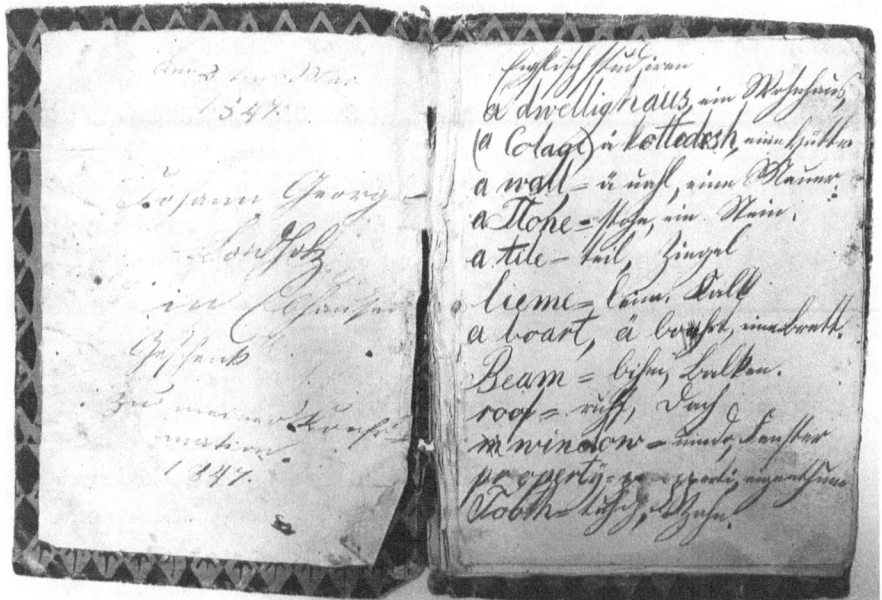

Georg Lodholz's copybook, with English translations of German words. (LRFC)

silent on how common it was for all the members of an immigrant family to stay together, but the fact that the brothers in particular did not go their separate ways was paramount to the family's survival in America. With four incomes, they had options that were unavailable to many of their fellow immigrants.

In terms of size, Terryville was less overwhelming than New York City, but it was still an alien world.[184] This was Puritan country, and the local church was the Congregational Church, born out of the Reformation in England. The Lodholzes had no official edifice where they could gather as a religious community on Sundays, so they most likely met in one another's homes.

While the family spoke German among themselves and with the other Germans in Terryville, they had to learn enough English to communicate with their bosses, shopkeepers, and English-speaking neighbors. Johann Georg kept a little notebook in which he listed English words and their German equivalents. Interestingly, Jakob described an encounter between two neighbors, a Mrs. Baiern and a Mrs. Rayen (probably "Ryan"), whom he presumed were cursing at each other from the yards of their houses. He noted, "I didn't see them for as long as they were cursing, and I didn't understand any of it either."[185] He was obviously keeping his ears open and trying to learn English, which was an important first step toward assimilation.

Jakob felt a deep sense of loneliness and isolation, and he missed the fellowship he had not yet found in America. To Christian Killinger in Michigan, he wrote: "I would like to go back to the times that we spent together in Germany, I think we will be able to have wonderful conversations together, even if it's not right away. If you wanted to visit us from New York [City] it's only a hundred miles, which one can do in half a day."[186] To his friends Michael and Johannes in Ebhausen, he was even more expressive, lamenting the materialism he found in America:

> I often think of the lovely time we spent together, as many a breeze and aroma wafted, granting refreshment and strength to our spirits, as if the true flowers of paradise had come down to earth and refreshed our old limbs. Until now in this land no pure balsamic aroma of the wounds of Jesus has cleansed our souls as was the case there. Ah, therefore it is good for every person to take advantage of such an occasion. They don't come often nor everywhere. I for my part am happy that I could enclose in my memory such pure and clear words which were spoken here and there, as America's external happiness shall take from me my soul's internal happiness, for what the world seeks is transitory and what it has is tainted.[187]

An important event took place after the family was reunited: Gottfried, now nearing his mid-twenties, married Christina Seitz, three years his senior. Christina had traveled on her own from Germany to the United States in 1853 or 1854,[188] joining her sister in Terryville.[189] It proved to be a solid marriage. Over the next two years they had two daughters, Mary and Annie, obviously named after Gottfried's mother.[190] So the Lodholz household was growing.

Jakob, the bean counter of the family, kept a notebook detailing his work and wages. Although his hours varied, he typically worked ten-hour days six days a week, with Sundays off. His wages averaged 50 cents an hour.[191] In 1850 the average *daily* wage for a day laborer in Connecticut was 98 cents, so the Lodholzes were doing better than many.[192] Even so, necessities were not cheap. In nearby Massachusetts, the only state that kept such records at the time, a cord of firewood cost $7 in 1856.[193] Mailing a letter to Germany cost $1, and with so few Germans in Terryville, it was difficult to find someone returning to Germany who could personally carry a letter.[194]

The type of lock the Lodholz brothers would have made at the Eagle Lock factory. (Courtesy The Lock Museum of America, Terryville, Connecticut)

Jakob wrote to Christian Killinger about his dissatisfaction with his income: "I would like it better if I got better wages, as times are somewhat hard, which is why the bosses don't give much in wages."[195]

In fact, by 1856, the economy experienced a major downturn, and panic ensued.[196] The Lodholz brothers were not laid off, but their hours were shortened and they were asked to trust to the future for their pay.[197] Still, they were not desperate. A bill of sale dated May 26, 1857, from a dry goods store in Hartford shows that they were able to indulge in some comparative luxuries. One of the Lodholz brothers made the more than twelve-hour trip to buy two pairs of gloves, a parasol, and some fabric.[198] He purchased an amount of cotton gingham, a popular fabric at the time, that was suitable for making a dress. He also bought poplin and ticking, strong, durable materials used to make mattresses that would most likely be stuffed with goose feathers (also sold at the store). Women sewed these items meticulously by hand, as sewing machines were not yet readily available. Georg later mentioned their feather beds in a letter.

Coming to Amerika

Nevertheless, the economic uncertainties of factory work were a powerful incentive for a family that had faced hardship in Ebhausen. Like many immigrants, they craved security and stability.[199] At some point in early 1857, the family decided to move to the interior of the country and find land to farm. The fact that they even considered doing this meant that they had accumulated enough money to do so. This decision was not a common one for German immigrants at the time. Although they increasingly took up farming throughout the late 1800s, it required a hefty initial investment of time and money, and the farming population remained heavily native-born. By 1880, only 30 percent of German immigrants were farmers, compared with nearly 50 percent of the native-born population. In the 1880 census, there were more German immigrants in the "manufacturing, mechanical, and mining industries" category than in the farming category.[200]

Because Gottfried was now a family man, it fell to the next oldest brother, Johann Georg, to scout for farmland. By this time, Johann Georg was known as Georg among family members, although he tended to use John publicly. Likewise, Jakob Friedrich had taken his middle name as his given name—a common practice when German males reached adulthood. Hereafter, they are referred to as Georg and Friedrich, respectively.

During his search, Georg planned to work at various places along the way to support himself until he found someplace for them to settle—an uncommon plan for a German immigrant. Although his first major stop was in Ann Arbor, where other individuals from Ebhausen had settled earlier, his goal was to find suitable land, not join a community of fellow immigrants. A group of Germans in Hartford organized in 1856 and made plans to settle in Kansas and create a "christian community" there. Eight made the journey in 1857 and joined an apparently non-German group to found the town named Humboldt in Osage County, farther south than Marshall County, where Georg ended up.[201] Georg was apparently unaware of this group, which had started to organize just as he was heading out. Unlike the Hartford group, which had a specific destination in mind—Kansas—Georg had none. He began his journey in the spring of 1857, shortly after his mother's fifty-sixth birthday, on which occasion he wrote her a letter in which he hoped she would "reap much joy yet from your children."[202]

CHAPTER 2

The Journey West

Michigan, Illinois, Iowa, Nebraska, and Kansas, 1857–58

Spring was traveling season. The ice-clogged waterways had begun to thaw, so river traffic could resume. It was not unheard of for men to scout ahead, looking for land on which their families could settle, but it was unusual for a German immigrant to travel as far as Georg did to find good but cheap land. When he started out, of course, he had no idea how far he would have to travel. Nor, as a recently arrived immigrant, was he aware of the fraught history of land settlement in the United States, intertwined with the treatment of the country's nonwhite populations.

Since the days of the Land Act of 1785—officially entitled An Ordinance for Ascertaining the Mode of Disposing of Lands in the Western Territory (encompassing the future states of Ohio, Indiana, Michigan, Wisconsin, and part of Minnesota)—there was a procedure for distributing public lands, that is, lands that were the property of the federal government rather than the individual states, which had ceded their rather dubious claims—given the presence of Native American tribes in the area—to what was known as the Northwest Territory. At least theoretically, the procedure involved making treaties to purchase land from Native American tribes and then surveying the land before offering it for sale at auction.[1] In practice, the federal government exerted little control over what happened on the frontier. Squatters settled on land they considered vacant and were rarely forced to move from land that rightfully belonged to Native American tribes or that had not yet been put up for sale.² The government accommodated the land hunger of its white population through the Indian Removal Act of 1830 and the practice of preemption.

The Indian Removal Act of 1830 authorized the government to make treaties with the eastern tribes, under which they agreed to vacate lands granted to them by previous treaties and move to unsettled land west of the Mississippi.³ This was not a quick process. It was faster for the southern tribes, the majority of which were quickly dispatched west, the infamous Trail of Tears being one of the consequences. But even in the South, there were holdouts that preferred to stay put on smaller amounts of land. In 1852 the US government was in the process of making a treaty with the Chickasaw to cede four square miles in Tennessee.⁴

The process took longer with the northern tribes, leading to a string of treaties with the same tribes or bands within tribes that continually moved them farther west and whittled away at their land. Some tribes went voluntarily, possibly induced by pledges of "perpetual" annuities and vast quantities of land; far more were forced to leave.⁵ Within the tribes there were fierce divisions on this issue. The fact that there were already other Native American tribes acclimated to life on the Great Plains, where the eastern tribes were sent, did not matter to the federal government. Twenty-six tribes made treaties between 1829 and 1851, many of them signing more than one treaty.⁶

Preemption gave squatters a quasi-legal right to the land vacated by the tribes, which then became public land. Heads of families, men older than twenty-one years of age, widows who were citizens,⁷ and foreigners who declared their intention to become citizens could lay claim to 160 acres of land and buy it at the minimum government price ($1.25 per acre), if they did so before the land was offered at public auction. If they could not raise the money by then, the land would be sold to the highest bidder. At first, preemption applied only to land already surveyed; it was later extended to unsurveyed land.⁸ The Lodholzes eventually secured their land by means of preemption.

Georg's immediate destination, however, was not the frontier. He was heading through settled land to the area around Ann Arbor, Michigan, where many of the family's friends from Ebhausen and other villages in Württemberg were living. Christian Killinger had written to Friedrich that during Christmastime "there were 20 together, and all from Ebhausen, you can imagine our joy."⁹

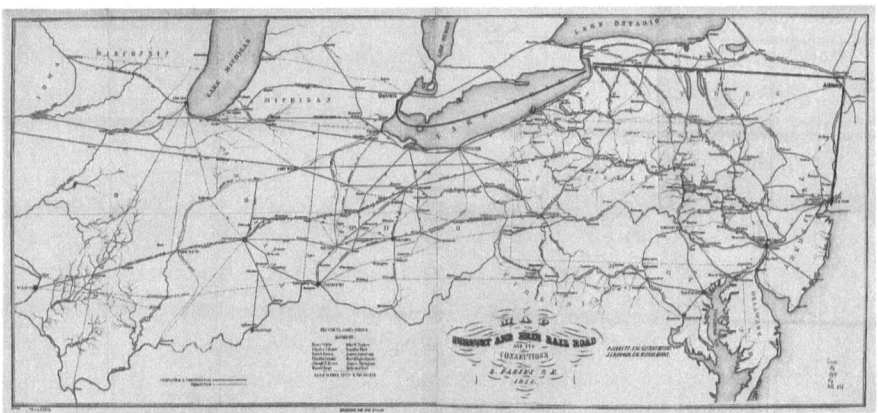

Map of Georg's route to Detroit. ("Map of the Sunbury and Erie Rail Road and its connections," Library of Congress, http://hdl.loc.gov/loc.gmd/g3711p.rr005730)

Georg followed the route taken earlier by Christian. He was traveling light, as his own feet were the only means of transportation he could consistently count on. Presumably he headed west from Plymouth to one of the towns on the Hudson River where he could catch a steamboat to Albany; from there, he boarded a train to Buffalo. The era of the Erie Canal was short-lived. It was already being replaced by the speedier iron horse. By canal, it took eight to fourteen days to reach Buffalo; by railroad, it was a one-day trip.[10] Georg then took another steamboat ride across Lake Erie to Detroit.

Coming from the small village of Terryville, Georg was dazzled by Detroit, which had a population of more than twenty-five thousand in 1851.[11] He informed his family that the city had mainly four-story houses, and "in Detroit one can buy anything one can only imagine. Every day is market [day]."[12] This was hardly surprising. Whereas many New England towns had a religious foundation—the first major building in Plymouth was the Congregational Church[13]—cities farther west such as Detroit and Chicago were commercial, starting out as fur trading outposts. German immigrants had been coming to Detroit since the Erie Canal was completed in 1825. They were the first foreign-born residents, followed by the Irish five years later.[14] In his letters, however, Georg makes no mention of any interactions with the German community there.

By May 14, Georg had traveled by train from Detroit to Ann Arbor and then walked five hours south to reach friends in Fredonia: "They all took me in as if I was a brother."[15] From there he wrote a short letter to his family:

The Journey West

> My journey up to here [Michigan] went fine. Our countrymen here are better off than expected. Could not contact old Jacob Spatholz, he died 2 years ago. His son J. G. is doing well. He has some land, 2 cows and pigs, chicken and does some extra work. He gets about 8 [illegible] for flannel, which they use here for underwear. Renz had lots of land. His son is not married and works for a farmer. Beutler is doing well. Magdalena Spatholz and her husband have 80 acres and a quick life. Many Germans live here, mostly from Württemberg and seem to be doing well. They have been here for about 15 y[ears].[16]

But their success meant that buying local land was now beyond the means of the Lodholzes: "When they came the land was cheap, now it is valuable. Cultivated land with fences costs $20–30 per acre." Even so, their block houses were only a step up from log cabins—long, single-story clapboard residences with a door square in the middle and one or two windows on each side. They were very different from the colonial and Georgian-style homes back in Connecticut, and as Georg noted, they were "simply furnished."[17]

Georg was able to find work to support himself, although he did not say what kind of work it was, mentioning only that the "pay is better than in Terryville." He did not, however, plan to linger. After visiting friends in Ypsilanti and seeing Christian Killinger in Ann Arbor, he planned to "move on inland" in the hope of finding cheaper land.[18]

Georg's second letter to his family was a long one detailing his many-mile journey from Michigan to Nebraska. After a five-hour trek from Fredonia back to Ann Arbor, he took the train seven miles east to Ypsilanti, where he found that his friends there were not doing so well. One worked in a bakery for a dollar a day, which meant he was earning 10 cents an hour for a ten-hour day. Another member of the family helped load and unload freight cars. Georg wrote that a third friend, who was boarding with the family, "was ill when I stayed here. He has not had much luck in this country so far. When he is healthy he helps at the railway. None of his parents or siblings is over here." He also reported, "Tailor Zinnweg's daughter is still unmarried and works as a maid. Her sister Magdalena is in Amerika but nobody knows where. Johannes Lodholz is supposed to be in Canada."[19] The Michigan community of settlers from Ebhausen was losing cohesiveness.

Back in Ann Arbor, Georg finally met up with Christian Killinger, who worked at a wool mill three miles west of town for $17 a week plus board.[20] The two men must have had much to reminisce about, and Christian would have been eager to learn how Friedrich was doing and what the family's plans were.

Ann Arbor, located along the Huron River amidst good agricultural land, had a population of about five thousand residents living along spacious tree-lined streets.[21] The University of Michigan had been established there some twenty years earlier.[22] The land was far more settled than Georg had expected. In Ann Arbor Georg and Christian saw "Schaalweather's Fritz. Fritz and someone from Rohrdorf [a village not far from Ebhausen] started a small business. They set up a loom where they are weaving rugs by hand. One of them weaves while the other one prepares."[23] They and Christian were relying on transplanting their knowledge of the textile industry from the Nagold Valley—the other two men in the time-honored fashion and Christian in a factory. If the Lodholzes ever considered such a possibility, they did not pursue it.

From Ann Arbor, Georg reached Chicago by train and was again overwhelmed. Chicago was one of the fastest growing cities in the world. In 1855 it had more than eighty thousand residents—three times the size of Detroit.[24] Georg described Chicago as "a big city with large houses and developing fast. They say that 12 to 14 railroads will run into it."[25] It was a rough-and-tumble city with small stockyards scattered along the rail lines and periodic outbreaks of cholera and typhoid.

Chicago had a large German-speaking community making up approximately one-sixth of the population.[26] By the time Georg arrived, the German community had become politically active in defending its way of life and its interests. Roughly three-quarters of the Germans there voted Democratic and supported Illinois senator Stephen A. Douglas until 1854, when he proposed the Kansas-Nebraska Act, which was to play a role in the Lodholzes' life.

With increasing immigration in the 1840s and early 1850s, nativism began to take hold in many parts of the United States, including Chicago. The short-lived Native American Party, more commonly known as the Know-Nothing Party, was initially a secret society whose members were instructed to say "I know nothing" when asked for details about it.[27] It was anti-immigrant and especially anti-Catholic.[28] The Know-Nothings were opposed to popery and believed America should be governed by "Americans." The liberal Germans who emigrated in 1848 also raised the Know-Nothings' ire by suggesting governmental reforms such as abolishing the use of the Bible for taking oaths. For a few short years in the 1850s the Know-Nothing Party became a major political force and was the main opposition to the

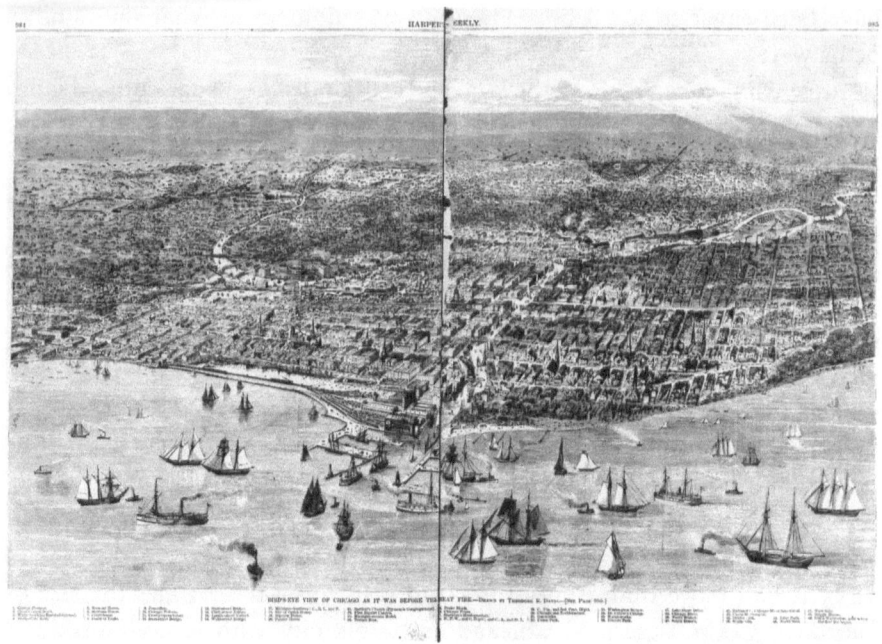

Chicago before the great fire of 1871. (*Harper's Weekly* 15, 773 [October 14, 1871]: 984–985)

Democratic Party, around which Irish and German immigrants tended to rally. The Whig Party, the former opposition, was already in disarray over the slavery issue. Know-Nothing candidates or at least supporters of the party's position captured mayoralties, governorships, and state legislatures and won seats in Congress. But, like the Whigs, it too disintegrated over the slavery issue.[29]

There were Know-Nothing councils in Connecticut, but the Lodholz letters do not mention them. In fact, Connecticut was one of the states that withdrew from the national party over the slavery issue.[30] Even so, signs of friction within the Know-Nothings' state organization were evident when the Connecticut Grand Council evicted a local council, which in turn published "a manifesto denouncing the Order and recommending the people of Connecticut to unite for the purpose of overthrowing 'Americanism' in that State."[31]

In Chicago, enmity arose between the native-born residents—both whiskey drinkers and teetotalers—and the beer-loving Germans. At least some of the latter spent part of their one day of leisure—Sunday—in saloons or marching through the city, accompanied by "blaring bands," and congregating in picnic areas, where they drank large quantities of their favorite beverage.[32] In 1855, two years before Georg's arrival, a small coalition of Know-Nothing Party members and a temperance-minded coterie managed to elect, with low voter turnout, a descendant of Daniel Boone as the mayor. He took aim at the city's German and Irish populations by raising the cost of liquor licenses and ordering the strict enforcement of the law that required taverns and saloons to close on Sunday. Arrests were made, but the German saloon keepers and brewers were determined to resist, turning first to the courts. Several test cases were due to be tried, but when the police arrested a number of men gathered outside the courthouse, the resistance—later known as the Lager Beer Riot—turned violent.[33] When an armed group marched downtown to try to rescue the prisoners, the mayor raised the drawbridge over the Chicago River, halting their advance until he could assemble the police force. Once the drawbridge was lowered, the shooting started, but it ended quickly when the mayor called in additional reinforcements. The outcome, however, was to mobilize German voters in the 1856 election. The mayor was ousted, along with his policies.[34]

Georg makes no mention of politics in his letter describing Chicago, but he might well have been uneasy there. He had just come from an area that welcomed German immigrants to a city where some of the native-born inhabitants would not have been happy to see him.[35] Georg apparently knew no one in the German-speaking community; nor did he report making any acquaintances or mention where he stayed. Prior to 1870, the majority of immigrants were from northern Germany, particularly Prussia, and relatively few from the southern state of Württemberg.[36] Immigrants of all nationalities tended to seek their own kind, but sharing the same religion also played an important role, especially for German immigrants. Prussia was more religiously diverse than Württemberg, which had Catholic enclaves ceded to the ruler by Napoleon to seal their alliance in the early 1800s.[37] But as far as we know, Georg had never been to any. In Prussia, Catholic, Lutheran, and Reformed (Calvinist) churches were permitted. The Prussian ruler was Calvinist, while most of his subjects were Lutheran, and he attempted to create a unified Lutheran and Reformed Church to strengthen the state. However, this ended up creating turmoil and divisions when he tried to impose a common liturgy on all the Protestant churches.[38]

We do not know how the Prussians in Chicago viewed these religious matters. If many of them were Catholic, Georg might have felt uncomfortable in their presence.[39] We do know that the city contained enough German Catholics to support two German Catholic churches.[40] In addition, Georg might have found it confusing that several German evangelical churches were affiliated with different national religious bodies, and one had even split into two congregations over their allegiance.[41] Although Georg never mentioned attending services, he did keep up with his reading of religious material, particularly the newspaper *Der Christliche Botschafter*, published by the German Evangelical Association, which he asked his family to send him.[42]

Georg seemed to dislike city living and did not want to stay in Chicago. He was intent on a rural existence and was fortunate that the Lodholz family had the means to attain this. For an immigrant arriving in New York City, the capital needed for such a venture was estimated at between $750 and $1,200. In 1860 most German-born men older than twenty congregated in cities like Chicago; only about one-third were engaged in agriculture.[43]

Georg's long letter twice mentioned that he could have found enough work in Chicago but decided against it:

> [I] thought to take up work there until I knew the district but when I arrived I didn't feel like it since I learned that the land prospects were the same as in Michigan. . . . I could have had enough work but I didn't want to. The farther I went inland, the better I liked it. But I didn't want to go further north since it was quite cold even here.[44]

This last statement is ironic, considering the climate of his birthplace.

Georg headed south. Given the speed with which he traveled, he undoubtedly went by rail, traversing the roughly 150 miles to Moline, just across the Mississippi River from Davenport, Iowa. Continuing by train, he crossed the newly built railroad bridge and traveled an additional fifty miles to Iowa City in the southeastern part of the relatively new (1846) state. Iowa City was the state capital and already had a major university. Georg was traveling on the state's first railroad line, built just one year earlier.[45] He told his family nothing about this leg of his journey; he was focused on finding cheap land and saw none.

Georg decided to head west from Iowa City, but his means of transportation was now limited. The railroad tracks extended no further, and travelers had to depend on a network of stagecoach lines.[46] He was getting closer to the frontier, and travel was expensive—according to Georg, $10 a mile by stagecoach. He had started looking for work to earn the necessary cash when he had a fortuitous encounter with fellow German immigrant Adam Müller, who was in Iowa City to pick up his brother, recently arrived from

This 1857 map of the Pennsylvania Railroad shows that it had only one line reaching Kansas—at the Missouri River town of St. Joseph, south of where Georg landed. Note the spelling *Kanzas*, referencing the Native American Kanza peoples. ("Pennsylvania Rail Road and Its Connections, Office of the Pennsylvania Railroad Company Philadelphia, November 3d, 1857," Library of Congress, http://hdl.loc.gov/loc.rbc/rbpe.15603000)

Europe.[47] Adam lived in the small town of Austin in Fremont County, three hundred miles southwest.[48] Georg wrote to his family:

> [Fremont] is at the border of the state, at the Missouri River, and it is supposedly one of the best counties of Iowa state. I talked to this man about his district and he praised it. . . . He had a good team & wagon with 2 mules. So I joined them and we drove through Iowa for 12 days. It would have been cheaper if I had gone to St. Louis on the Missouri River but I wanted to travel overland to see how things are.
>
> The state of Iowa seems to have good soil, usually quite black and much better than we could imagine. Only it has not much forest. But this county of Fremont has more forest; especially this Village of Austin is a nice place. I have never seen a nicer scenery. Land costs about from $6 to 16 per acre. The land for 16 has a house and barn and is partly fenced in and if 100 acres are purchased about ½ of it will be fenced, at 200 acres about 90 [acres] will be fenced in. It depends a lot how and where land is situated. Whether there is forest. We can also buy land for $6–8 with [a] house and partly fenced but it will be removed from the Village. But even land like this would cost $20–30 in Michigan and the

[$]16 would be [$]50 in Michigan. There are no fruit trees here yet but one can plant grapes.[49]

Georg arrived in Austin on June 3, but he could find no work there.[50] So he walked five hours north and ferried across the Missouri River on a steamboat to Nebraska City in the Nebraska Territory, officially organized in 1854.[51] He had traveled more than a thousand miles and was on the eastern edge of what was then the frontier.

The area of the country where Georg had landed was beginning a major transformation both of the land itself and of its political fortunes. For years after Thomas Jefferson's 1803 purchase of the Louisiana Territory from France, the immense area of the Great Plains, stretching from the Mississippi River to the Rocky Mountains, was regarded as unsuitable for European habitation. The winters were bitter cold, the summers were blisteringly hot, water and timber were scarce, and the soil was so difficult to plow that it broke farming tools. It was labeled the "Great American Desert" on maps.[52] It was also Indian country—the region where many of the eastern tribes had been relocated.

In their own phrasing, the tribes' new home was supposed to be theirs "as long as the grass grew or the waters run."[53] This phrase appeared later in the treaties the Confederate States of America made with nine of the tribes, but it was never used in any of the treaties between the US government and the Native American peoples.[54] That does not mean that the tribes were wrong about the promises made; the treaties used terms such as "forever" and "permanent," especially those treaties made during the 1830s in the wake of the Indian Removal Act.[55] As the late 1840s approached, more ambiguous wording became common, capable of different interpretations by the parties involved: "to be held as Indians' lands are held."[56]

In the areas supposedly granted to the tribes in perpetuity, white inhabitants were limited to missionaries; Indian agents, who represented the federal government on the reservations; a few owners of trading posts, who did business with the Native Americans; individuals passing through to areas beyond the Rockies; and military personnel based at forts located at strategic points along the routes west to help travelers and to keep peace with the Native Americans. No white settlement was allowed.

Thus, settlers searching for land and opportunity looked to the Far West and Southwest, even though most of the region was not yet part of the United States. What would become Texas was the first area to draw settlers. In the early 1820s, after winning its independence from Spain, Mexico encouraged emigration from the United States to the sparsely settled territory of Mexican Texas, home of the Comanche. Large numbers of Anglos from the South responded and became the most populous group, bringing slavery with them. They revolted and established the Republic of Texas in 1836.[57] During the same period, a much smaller number of Anglos settled in what would become New Mexico.[58]

Beginning in the early 1840s, large numbers of easterners were attracted by the cheap land in Oregon, jointly governed by the United States and Great Britain until its 1848 annexation by the United States after a tense confrontation with the British. In 1846 Mormons, persecuted for their beliefs in the East, began the trek to what would become Utah. In 1848 thousands of people flocked to California after the discovery of gold. Starting out at towns along the Missouri River and passing through what would become Kansas, these groups experienced the unimaginable hardships of traversing the vast Great American Desert. They followed what was originally a Native American path widened to accommodate wagons, which became known as the Oregon Trail; however, there were many different shortcuts, cutoffs, and branches, including the California Trail, the Mormon Trail, and the Santa Fe Trail, depending on the point of departure and the ultimate destination. The Oregon Trail was the longest, stretching some two thousand miles from the Missouri River to Oregon City. But on all the trails, many people turned back, unable to complete the journey, and others died along the way.[59] The hardships Georg endured did not compare.

German and German-speaking immigrants were among the settlers in all these areas, although they did not always take a route across the plains. During the mid-1840s a group of German nobles planned to establish a colony in Texas and recruited up to ten thousand colonists. The mosquito-ridden climate took its toll, and the endeavor was roundly castigated in Germany, but a German presence remained.[60] The first German arrived in California in 1829; Johann Groningen was shipwrecked near what is now Los Angeles and decided to stay.[61] The German-speaking Swiss Johann August Sutter arrived in the Sacramento Valley in 1835; the discovery of gold on his property ruined his life but attracted an avalanche of gold seekers, including young German men who arrived by ship.[62] In Oregon, German-born John Jacob Astor financed an 1811 expedition to establish a fur trading post at Fort Astoria, the first white settlement in the area. In 1850 there were 156 German-born residents at Fort Astoria out of a total foreign-born population of 899. They were outnumbered by the Irish (196), English (207), and British (293). Significantly, however, they were the largest non-English-speaking group (with only forty-five residents from France and two from Sweden). By 1860, the Germans' numbers had increased to 1,061, second only to the Irish at 1,266.[63] New Mexico's 1850 territorial census recorded 224 Germans and 292 Irish, the two largest foreign-born populations.[64]

The Republic of Texas's application for statehood was a primary trigger for expansionist fever in the United States, fostered by the propaganda of many politicians and newspapers.[65] This desire to expand the nation's boundaries came to be called Manifest Destiny. Newspaper editor John O'Sullivan purportedly coined the phrase in 1845 when arguing for the annexation of Texas. He stated that it was inevitable that the country should "overspread the continent allotted by Providence for the free development of our yearly multiplying millions."[66]

Manifest Destiny, however, was hardly a clear-cut vision; its outlines were vague. Proponents disagreed on how far the United States should expand. To the Rocky Mountains, or all the way to the Pacific? Should Canada be included, or perhaps all of North America, meaning Mexico too? Should it be accomplished by means of settlers' free choice, purchase, or even war?[67] It was in fact the threat of war that gained the United States all of Oregon and actual war with Mexico (1846–48) that led to US acquisition of the territory that would eventually become California and large sections of New Mexico, Arizona, Nevada, Utah, and Colorado.

It is unclear how many average American citizens bought into the concept of Manifest Destiny, but the consensus among historians is that it was a widely held belief.[68] Frederick Merk's study did not analyze articles in German-language newspapers, so he presents no evidence of what those readers were being told about the issue. However, Merk determined that the strongest supporters of Manifest Destiny were Democratic and in the Midwest; those in Illinois were particularly belligerent about the issue.[69] This was the German-speaking population's party affiliation and area of major concentration at the time. As he headed west from Connecticut in 1857, Georg may not have been aware of the idea of Manifest Destiny, but he was taking part in the ongoing settlement of the United States.[70]

Once the United States established its continental boundaries in the 1840s, interest in further expansion diminished. Thus, in the 1850s all eyes turned to the Great American Desert, which proved to be less of a desert than originally thought. Having recently signed a string of treaties that would move various eastern Native American tribes to the Great Plains, the US government almost immediately broke faith. On March 3, 1853,

Congress authorized the Bureau of Indian Affairs, established in 1823, to begin negotiations with these tribes to cede their reserves in the Kansas Territory. The commissioner of Indian affairs at the time, George W. Manypenny, was unable to convince these tribes, who thought they had finally found a permanent home in Kansas, to move yet again. However, he eventually got them to agree to cede part of their land in the Kansas Territory in return for money, doled out in annual payments; he envisioned that at least some of this land would be platted and allocated to individual tribe members to farm.[71] As a policy, it was a failure. On May 30, 1854, with no treaties ratified by Congress and no surveys conducted, Congress opened the territories of Nebraska and Kansas to settlement. Two months later, after several treaties had been ratified, Congress for the first time allowed preemption on unsurveyed public lands, and white settlement began in earnest.[72]

In his second letter home, Georg told his family: "I'm sorry not to have written for so long. Forgive me; it was not lack of caring, but I wanted to see where there would be suitable places for our future plans. You'll probably think that I need not have gone so far away, but whoever has not travelled in this country cannot imagine how fast it is being settled."[73] It was in fact a young and restless country. In 1850 one-third of the population was younger than fourteen, and a full 70 percent was younger than thirty.[74] Immigrants like Georg were on the move, but many more native-born Yankees were headed west as well.

Nebraska City provides a microcosm of how swiftly settlement was occurring. In 1882 A. T. Andreas published his *History of the State of Nebraska* in which he describes the city's history in some detail. It was first established as a military outpost in 1844, just fourteen years before Georg's arrival, but was abandoned by 1850. In 1852 there was a log cabin (and a post office) whose owner operated a crude ferry across the Missouri River for those headed west on the Oregon Trail. Several frame houses were built, followed by the first brick house in 1854. That same year, the Nebraska Territory was created and the town was platted. Following the typical procedure on the frontier, a group of men would form a "town company," with each member purchasing at least one share in it. The company would claim title to a large piece of land either by outright purchase or by preemption—dubiously in the case of Nebraska City, as the military had not officially abandoned its claim[75]—staking it out and dividing it into saleable lots, with each shareholder entitled to a portion. Surplus lots would be sold at auction to the highest bidders, and members of the town company would pocket the money. But because they were often residents themselves, they were generally civic-minded about use of the funds. Among the members of the town company for Nebraska City was J. Sterling Morton, editor of the local newspaper and the founder of Arbor Day; his son founded the Morton Salt Company. Morton described the auction as follows:

> There must have been a multitude in attendance, which numbered at least seventeen or eighteen, and about five of them were not members of the town company, and against them every patriotic resident of this hopeful neighborhood—except myself, and I was the auctioneer, and couldn't—bid with great and vehement vigor. That was a proud period in the babyhood of this settlement. It demonstrated the fact that there was some exchangeable value to lots. Everybody began to feel wealthy, and put on the comfortable airs of proprietary and pecuniary plethora. We had lots to sell; the whole world wanted to buy lots, and we could make supply equal to demand, until the plains from the Missouri River to the Rocky Mountains had been chopped into lots.[76]

Morton was obviously a believer in the idea of Manifest Destiny.

The first hotel in Nebraska City was erected in 1854, the same year the brick-making firm of James Decker and Keil Cook was founded. The local court's first term was held in 1855, with a judge originally from Georgia presiding. That same year the First Baptist Church was established, followed by a mighty array of other congregations that often held services in the same building. The appropriately named Pioneer Brewery was also founded that year. The next year the first bank was established in Nebraska City; it was promptly robbed in 1859. Miss Martin (no first name given) set up the first private school in 1857, and in 1858 a freighting firm that had been awarded a government contract selected Nebraska City as the starting point for its trains taking supplies to Utah, New Mexico, and western forts. It employed eleven hundred workers, seven hundred wagons, and almost six thousand yokes of oxen.[77]

Georg reported in June that "someone sent me to Otoe City [just a few miles west of Nebraska City]," where he quickly found work with a blacksmith.[78] His pay was $8 a month more than he had been making in Connecticut, and he paid $4.50 a week for board. But, he lamented, "Everything is expensive. One bushel [of] potatoes: 8.-, 1 bushel corn: 2½. White flour is not too expensive since it is shipped from St. Louis by ship. Costs $12 to 18 per barrel. . . . As soon as I find a special place, I shall write you and you can send your answer."[79] It is unclear what Georg meant by a "special place," but he had certain criteria in mind if not written down. John Hawgood has argued that Germans preferred landscapes similar to those in their native land, particularly wooded or forested areas.[80] Having access to such a place was certainly important to Georg, as was being able to grow fruit.

The fact that Georg and his family in Terryville were able to communicate by letter was a remarkable feat of the US Postal Service. Even when doing so was not profitable, it was committed to extending mail service to remote frontier areas, where the post office might simply be a settler's cabin where a carrier dropped off mail periodically.[81]

Georg lost little time in searching for his special place. He was full of boundless enthusiasm for the land around Otoe City, which he and a friend, telescope in hand, explored on foot. Though sensitive to the land's beauty, he kept a practical eye on its possibilities as viable farmland. He reported on sources of fuel and building materials and the land's suitability for growing fruit trees. Concerned that alarming stories about the untamed West had made it back to Terryville, he assured the family that the major threat was snakes.[82] He did not fear the local Native Americans, probably the Otoes, Missouris, or Pawnees, who had already ceded part of their land to the federal government.[83]

Georg's July 4 letter home was really more of a sales pitch. He wanted the entire family to come west the following spring and detailed how the possibility of owning inexpensive land could become a reality. His plea was particularly urgent because he had seen the great westward wave of migrants in his travels and did not want his family to lose out. Georg obviously expected his letter to be shared among the other Germans in Terryville and hoped to entice some of them to come to the prairie. Like many other German immigrants, he wanted to create a community of his own religious faith. In other words, he hoped for a sort of chain migration, although there was apparently no attempt to encourage relatives still in Ebhausen to join him and the rest of his family. In his hopes to attract more settlers from Terryville, he would ultimately be disappointed. Georg's letter continued:

> Since I've been here for a while, I will write you some more of the surroundings. First—concerning the land. I can't say anything else about it [other than] that it is beautiful, rich land. About 8 days ago I went to explore the country a bit. We went into a small valley with many shrubs. I saw a shrub fully loaded with [wild] plums, within a

short distance I found more rich shrubs, which pleased me very much. It proves to me, that if one planted fruit trees here one could harvest enough fruit within 8 to 10 years' time.

When we had walked about 1.2 hr. we found [a] little forest but mostly [brushwood]. . . . It is flat land mostly, but we found several springs and good water. Very little forest, at some places one can look through a telescope 8–10 kms into the distance. Sometimes one can walk for 4 hours without forest. Very little forest in Nebraska. . . . As far as I've seen so far, I can compare Nebraska's soil with the best soils for root crops in Germany. If it rains, it looks real black.

There are very few stones near the surface, but if you dig lower you'll find stones. But if you need stones for house building one does better to use bricks. 1000 bricks cost about $10. I work in a brick factory at the moment and receive one$ per day plus food. . . .

I have been healthy always, thank God. Now let us get back to the nature of our Heavenly father. What else I can report about that is, that I like it very much here and with very little money one can buy a homestead but we must not lose time since immigration to here is heavy and strong because of all the advantages which the first immigrants have.

For [the] 2 territories, Kansas and Nebraska, the laws are that every white man who is 21 years old, can pick himself 160 acres of land wherever he likes for $1.25 per acre and he has several years to pay it off—but he has to settle on the place immediately and build a house on it and cultivate some land—or if he doesn't do it and leaves the land uncultivated, someone else can come and build a house there and file at the land titles office—then the first one lost the land. And people who arrive first, can pick out the best land and don't need to go so far away, but the ones who come later have to take what's left or have to pay the first owner. On the average the price of land climbs 1½% per acre in one year. If immigration will continue as heavy as at present—land which now costs $1.25 will in 20 years be $50 or 100 per acre. Some people who came a year ago would not want to sell their 160 acres for 3000.

Now, dear mother and brothers, dear sister and friends, we want [to] put this all aside. The land may climb whatever it wants to, or fall—it won't make much difference to me or you. My plan is: for all our best, for our soul and body—if all of you would come here next spring— may it be to Kansas or Nebraska. I shall travel to Kansas next fall to investigate. If I'll like God's nature in Kansas better than here I will prefer Kansas because nights here are quite tough [probably meaning that it got dark and cold quickly].

... At first it isn't too comfortable as you can imagine, what one has to do arriving in a new country where there is nothing done—But as time goes by we could live a good, independent life. And if we took up land we would take such land where a little stream flows through, whose water could help us cook if God keeps us healthy. 3 times 160 acres would be a piece of land of ½ hs^2 and a fortune for a lifetime.[84]

Concerning dangers, may it be from people or animals is of no great importance. As far as white people are concerned I am as safe as in Conn. If I don't harm anyone, no one will harm me. And as for the Indians—there is no danger in my opinion because they sold this land and received their money for it. And there are very few Indians living on the land which they sold. They have withdrawn. They come into the town Nebraska [City] sometimes, which lies about 6 miles from here, and buy whatever they need. They say that 300 of them were there about 8 days and they left [spent] 300.- in one store. I never heard anything that they did any harm to any white person. And if they did—they wouldn't get away with it because of the military.[85]
The most dangerous in my opinion are the snakes, which are in the far West, more than in Nebraska & Kansas, but more in Iowa. I saw some myself and we killed one [that] was about 5 feet long. Rattlesnakes are the most dangerous ones, which sometimes occur, but as far as I found out they flee from people. Unless you step on them, there is not much danger from them. And if the farmer wears boots they won't be able to harm him.

All what I've written so far is not as dangerous as one imagines in Conn. As the way it's written in the newspapers sometimes....

Dear friends, I know that it isn't easy to undertake such a long voyage, but it was a lot easier for me than I ever imagined. For this plan, I wish that you collect this fall as many seeds as possible and, if you don't come here, you could send it to me. Dear mother, if you come here and we become farmers, you will be able to work at whatever you like and whatever pleases you. You don't need to worry about work like in Terryville. Work will come itself. And you 2 dear brothers, the difference between [illegible] cutting wood—housebuilding you can imagine but as time goes by one will be able to harvest what one had planted and we will finally enjoy our good days as God wills.

And you, dear sister Anna, you will be looked after here too and will like it better than with Mr. G. [Gaylord, her employer in Terryville]. And you, dear friend[s], I think you'll like it here too. And who else, God-fearing people who can bring with them $2 or 300 & will come, and I would be happy if we could establish a German Christian Community here. Now dear friends, I hope that this letter reaches you [in as] good health, as I am. And please write to me how you are and if you'll come next spring or not, so I can plan accordingly.[86]

There are two particularly noteworthy pieces of information in this letter. One is that Georg expected the land they settled on to be their permanent home and not purchased for speculation, as many native-born settlers did at the time.[87] Having a permanent piece of land that could be passed down from generation to generation had been part of the family's tradition in Ebhausen. In fact, Georg's emphasis on maintaining a stable home is in keeping with what Hawgood, among other scholars, considered a basic German characteristic.[88] Second, the payments in specie—gold and silver—to Native Americans were an important source of cash flowing into the cash-starved interior of the frontier, where there was little to sell and no transportation to major markets beyond horse and ox carts.[89]

We do not know how long it took Georg to get the news that the rest of the family was planning to join him the following spring, even though he had not yet settled on a piece of land. At the time, Georg was boarding with a settler named Gideon Bennett.[90] This was a common practice and an indication that Georg's English was good enough to make this arrangement with Bennett, who, judging by his surname, did not speak German. Once he received the news of the family's planned arrival, Georg started moving southwest in the Nebraska Territory into the more sparsely settled Gage County, just north of Marshall County in the Kansas Territory. He was now twenty-five miles from the nearest post office at Turkey Creek, where he went to pick up his mail rather than waiting for the weekly delivery by mail carrier. Even so, it took three weeks for letters to reach him.[91]

Georg found a suitable parcel of land being sold by either a speculator or the speculator's agent. Since passage of the Land Act of 1785, speculation in lands in the public domain had been common, as the federal government acquired tracts and put them up for sale. In the era before large corporations, land was the major source of investment for big and small investors alike, and land taxes were the major source of revenue for state and local governments.[92] There was no limit on the amount of land an individual could purchase; wealthy eastern and southern investors, including major political figures such as Daniel Webster, became absentee owners.[93] Land companies and banks, working through their agents, bought thousands of acres of land when it first came on the market and then sold it to newly arriving settlers for a profit. Settlers themselves often bought more land than they needed, usually on credit obtained from what historian Paul Gates termed "loan sharks," who were ubiquitous at auctions, and then tried to resell it later.[94]

George had six weeks to come up with the money to buy the land. He desperately needed his family to send him funds, and he sent two undated letters containing virtually the same instructions for doing so. Sending actual currency was not secure. The express companies—private mail firms such as Wells Fargo and American Express, which transported packages and valuables—did not operate in the Kansas and Nebraska Territories yet. Georg therefore asked his family to send him a check. His letters show a degree of sophistication about the currency situation in the territories; for instance, he stressed the need to obtain insurance and to get a draft from a "good bank"—that is, one with a sound reputation on the frontier. In the virtually unregulated, almost chaotic financial world on the frontier, there were fake banks, wildcat banks, and swindlers, as well as scammers on the East Coast who might take advantage of the Lodholzes. Georg wrote:

> Surely it's not possible to have money sent, as it isn't secure. . . . And package wagons and package ships only are running. This is generally the only secure means: if you want to have a check or a draft sent by a good bank, then the name J. Georg Lodholz must be recorded on the other side, and I can receive my money for that everywhere, and no one else can use it. But I ask that you insure yourselves in case the check should fail to arrive. I ask that you send it as soon as possible.[95]

The family sent him a draft for $270 (equivalent to about $9,000 today).[96] But in a November 3 letter, Georg reported to the family that, after a second visit to the land, he had changed his mind. He was unhappy with the price he had been quoted, and as the seller was willing to take the land back, Georg gladly abandoned the deal. But he was still enthusiastic about prospects in the area: "These 2 Territories have as fine Lands as are in the World and [I] would recommend it to all wishing to travel who can command about $400 when reaching here, as I think that here they can do well but after next spring, those wishing good Land and Timber must go farther away as the Timber here is scarce." In answer to a question posed by Gottfried, he reported: "[Water] is here as good as I have drank anywhere in the World. . . . and should you suppose it [is] here swampy, you are greatly mistaken."[97]

Meanwhile, the Panic of 1857 was reverberating on the Great Plains. In his December 10 letter home, Georg noted that the local banks might not have enough gold to cover the amount of the family's check. In addition, he reported some of the problems of life on the edge of the frontier: "I received your letter with the money draft and will cash it in soon since I'm afraid it might bust. There are so many bank robberies and bad times in USA. Lack of money is severe here and pay for jobs down this winter, but there is enough work available for people who want to work."[98]

Given the scarcity of money, white settlers were amazed at the amounts being disbursed twice a year to Native Americans for ceding their land. In his December 10 letter Georg wrote of "trouble," but it is unclear what that trouble was. Most likely he was referring to uneasiness among the white settlers over the gathering of so many Native Americans, whom they found fearsome:

> Since all the trouble is over since my last letter, I will write again. The trouble was: last Nov 13 the USA paid 705 Indians $13 per head, which they will receive x2 a year for many years to come. There are also other tribes as well who will receive as much for their land. In all my life I never saw so much money! Gold and silver, a big box full of it. It was amazing when one looked at these Indians and many Americans came to look at them from 70 miles.[99]

In his ongoing hunt for the right land, Georg turned south into Marshall County, Kansas, where other Germans had started to settle. The 1855 Kansas Territory census, ordered by the governor to determine who was eligible to vote in the upcoming territorial elections, indicated that Marshall County (not yet officially established) included all or parts of Districts 10 and 11.[100] In District 10 there were three German families comprising twelve individuals who identified themselves as "Bavarian" and, according to the census, came directly from that region.[101] Located east of Württemberg, Bavaria was home to "a special type of Bavarian nationalism" that had developed in the wake of the Napoleonic Wars.[102] In addition, there were fourteen naturalized residents and five declarants (those who had formally filed an intention to become citizens) whose nationality was not specified.[103] There were no Germans listed in District 11, but there were six naturalized residents.[104] Thus, we know that there were at least twelve Germans in the area in 1855, as well as a number of foreign-born whose national origin was not identified—twenty naturalized and five declarants.

Once in Marshall County, Georg's explorations ended. He wrote to his family the day after Christmas:

> As the weather here this winter is particularly nice, I made another small trip to Kansas last week in order to seek out a suitable homestead for us, and in two days' time I found a very nice place that I'm convinced will please you extraordinarily well. It has water, woods, and there is plenty of very lovely, fertile land, and the land can still be bought for $1.25 per acre; this plot of three times 160 acres is 1½ miles long and ½ mile wide, and during the time I was there, I took room and board with the nearest neighbor, and as he has no clock for his room, he wishes as do I for you to bring one along for him, about the same as the one you have, dear brother Gottfried. And a German man with whom I am well acquainted wants to receive the book, namely the *Illustriert Neue Welt*. And you, dear brother Friedrich, I would like to request that you be sure to have your papers available, given that an immigrant is not entitled to 160 acres of Congress [federal] land without these papers.[105]

Georg did not identify his nearest neighbor as German, so apparently he was boarding with another non-German-speaking settler. Presumably his German acquaintance lived in the vicinity. Eleanor Turk argues: "To the extent that they [German settlers establishing individual claims] understood the system for claiming land on the frontier, these Germans already were somewhat 'Americanized.'"[106] The degree of assimilation of the Lodholz family and other early German-born settlers on the Kansas frontier will be addressed in detail later.

This time, Georg was not purchasing land from a speculator. He was taking advantage of preemption to claim an amount of land his family could not have imagined possessing in Ebhausen, and of course, it was not subject to any of its semifeudal constraints or broken into scattered parcels. However, the Lodholzes would need to come up with the money to pay the federal government once the land was formally surveyed and before it was offered for sale at auction.

Georg was fortunate to find this land available. In her history, Emma Forter states that John Wells, who arrived in Marshall County in 1855, got "into land speculation on an extensive scale, buying land for from one

The Journey West

dollar to two dollars an acre until at one time he owned nearly half of Marshall county."[107]

Georg had chosen well when selecting the location of the Lodholz land. Marshall County has abundant water sources. The Big Blue River flows from north to south through the entire county. The Black Vermillion River, which runs east and southeast, and the Little Blue River, which enters the county from the southwest, both empty into the Big Blue. The area east of the Big Blue and north of the Black Vermillion, precisely where the Lodholzes' land was located, is till plain, created by sheets of glaciers that broke off and melted in place, leaving wide river valleys and rolling hills that rarely exceed one hundred feet in height, except near the larger streams. The hills and bluffs along the rivers contained a large variety of building stone, and good timber—both hardwood and softwood—could be found on the banks of the innumerable streams and rivers. The early settlers found this wood invaluable for building their cabins and fences and for fuel. The Lodholzes' land was close to stone quarries and had a creek running through it.[108]

By moving just ten miles south of the Nebraska border, Georg found an entirely different political landscape. For several years, the Kansas Territory had been embroiled in the intense rivalry between North and South over the issue of slavery, which had plagued the nation from its beginning. There had been a series of compromises in an effort to maintain a balance of power between the two sides. The Missouri Compromise of 1820 admitted Maine to the Union as a free state and Missouri as a slave state, but the remainder of the Louisiana Purchase "north of thirty-six degrees and thirty minutes north latitude" was to remain slave free.[109] Texas was admitted as a slave state in 1845. Oregon was eventually admitted as a free state in 1859, but its series of black exclusionary laws did not make it a bastion of abolitionism.[110]

The political negotiations involving the status of the newly acquired territories in the Southwest at the conclusion of the Mexican War were particularly contentious. The Wilmot Proviso, introduced in Congress by Pennsylvania Democrat David Wilmot, specified that slavery should be forbidden in all the territories obtained as a result of that war.[111] Although the Wilmot Proviso never became law, it raised southern hackles and influenced the terms of the Compromise of 1850, which was actually a series of five laws. California was admitted to the Union as a free state, but in determining the terms under which the territories of New Mexico and Utah would become states, the concept of "popular sovereignty" was introduced. This was the idea that the residents of a territory had the right to determine whether they would enter the Union as slave or free. The applicable provision stated: "when admitted as a State, the said Territory. . . . shall be received into the Union, *with or without slavery* [emphasis added], as their constitution may prescribe at the time of their admission."[112] Both territories eventually became states long after the Civil War ended. Statehood was delayed because of the issue of polygamy in Utah and the differing agendas of the Hispanic majority and Anglo minority in New Mexico.[113]

Then came the Kansas-Nebraska Act of 1854. It negated the Missouri Compromise by allowing popular sovereignty in the Kansas and Nebraska Territories, both of which were north of the previously agreed on line. Part of the process of becoming a state involved drawing up a constitution, which had to be approved by Congress, and under the concept of popular sovereignty, the residents of those territories had to decide the slavery question. The Kansas-Nebraska Act included phrasing from the earlier laws pertaining to the territories of New Mexico and Utah, but to gain southern support for the bill, a longer section was added:

> It being the true intent and meaning of this act not to legislate slavery into any Territory or State, nor to exclude it therefrom, but to leave the people thereof perfectly free to form and regulate their domestic institutions in their own way, subject only to the Constitution of the United States: *Provided*, That nothing herein contained shall be construed to revive or put in force any law or regulation which may have existed prior to the act of sixth March, eighteen hundred and twenty, either protecting, establishing, prohibiting or abolishing slavery.[114]

This was a provocation to anti-slavery groups and to many Germans. The German inhabitants of Chicago had supported Stephen Douglas and were content not to interfere with slavery in the South, but they saw the Kansas-Nebraska Act as a "direct attack upon their welfare." The opponents of the act, which included the German press, gave three reasons for their opposition: it threatened the stability of the Union by undoing the earlier compromise on slave versus free states (Compromise of 1820); it degraded manual labor by placing slave labor on the same footing as free labor in the new territories; and the German community wanted a homestead bill that provided public lands to white settlers at no cost. Some in the community were so incensed that they burned Douglas in effigy. This controversy led many Germans to turn to the newly established Republican

Party and Abraham Lincoln.[115] Lincoln recognized the importance of German voters and even purchased a German-language newspaper in Springfield, Illinois.[116]

The Nebraska Territory had the free state of Iowa on its eastern border and attracted little attention. The Kansas Territory, however, was next door to Missouri, an aggressive slave state that did not want a free state on its western border. Pro-slavery Missourians saw the situation both as an economic opportunity to expand the slave economy and, if Kansas were free, as a threat to slavery in Missouri and possibly the rest of the South.[117] "Bleeding Kansas" was the result—a prelude to the Civil War.

At this time, the Kansas Territory stretched all the way to the Rocky Mountains, but the conflict was most intense on its eastern border, where there was a predominance of settlers. In the four years between passage of the Kansas-Nebraska Act and Georg's arrival, the territory had four governors who left in failure, appointed by two presidents (Pierce and Buchanan) who overtly favored or, out of political expediency, supported the pro-slavery cause. Each of the governors had his own views on how popular sovereignty should be implemented, and several were at odds with the president in office at the time.[118] In reality, there was little political control over the animosity between the pro- and anti-slavery forces, manifested by threats and outbreaks of violence.

The position of the pro-slavery faction in Kansas is best summed up in Article VII, section 1, of the Lecompton Constitution, which the pro-slavery territorial legislature presented to Congress when requesting admission as a state. The language is actually much more sedate than the usual strident, often profane rhetoric: "The right of property is before and higher than any constitutional sanction, and the right of the owner of a slave to such slave and its increase is the same and as inviolable as the right of the owner of any property whatever."[119]

The pro-slavery forces engaged in widespread intimidation and voter fraud bolstered by so-called Border Ruffians, individuals from Missouri who crossed into Kansas to vote and wreak havoc but had no intention of settling there permanently.[120] Early on, the Missourians had the upper hand. Pro-slavery towns were established at Leavenworth (near the fort) and at Atchison, both on the Missouri River, bordering Missouri.[121] There, pro-slavery advocates attempted to keep anti-slavery migrants from entering the Kansas Territory, searching steamboats and turning back anyone considered an "abolitionist." They sent appeals to the Deep South for money and migrants, but few came; perhaps they were unwilling to risk bringing their slaves to Kansas before the legal issue had been decided.[122] One group of pro-slavery advocates from South Carolina came to Marshall County and platted the town of Palmetto (named after the tree that flourished in their state), but they had little interest in settling there. They spent most of their time hunting and socializing and made few improvements. They spent the winter in Missouri, and most of them eventually sold out and moved there, so the town of Palmetto was no more.[123]

The pro-slavery faction staked its future on winning elections, and it engaged in massive voter fraud to do so—stuffing ballot boxes, threatening anti-slavery voters and election judges with violence, and calling in Border Ruffians to swell the pro-slavery numbers. Before the first election for the territorial legislature in March 1855, Governor Reeder conducted a census to determine eligible voters, and he ordered that at the polling place, each voter would be required to take an oath attesting to his residency. This attempt at holding a fair and free election was swept aside, and pro-slavery candidates captured the territorial legislature and held on to it until 1857, just as Georg arrived.[124]

Meanwhile, as pro-slavery Missourians mobilized, so did abolitionist groups. Among the most well known was the New England Emigrant Aid Company, which sent settlers to establish communities in Kansas, most prominently Lawrence, near the Missouri border southeast of Marshall County. Abolitionists, however, were not the only ones coming to Kansas; many, like Georg, were attracted by the prospect of cheap land. These settlers, coming mainly from the Midwest—Illinois, Ohio, Iowa, and Indiana—were often anti-black and wanted no competition from slave labor.[125]

It was the blatantly illegal tactics of the pro-slavery party that led these two groups—the abolitionists, mainly from New England, and the midwesterners—to unite and form the Free State Party. They couched their opposition in 1776 rhetoric and argued that they were being made the "slaves" of the Missourians. They denied the authority of the territorial legislature and therefore refused to participate in any elections it called or pay any taxes it levied. In fact, they elected their own territorial legislature and drafted a constitution for submission to Congress that contained a provision excluding free blacks from the territory, similar in spirit to Oregon's exclusionary laws. The pro-slavery party cried "treason" and maintained that it stood for "law and order."[126]

The situation was chaotic; federal troops were called in, and federal and territorial officials arrested prominent Free State leaders, to little effect.[127] Both sides were heavily armed, and individual confrontations led to bloodshed, often creating martyrs to the Free State cause.[128] The violence escalated in 1856. In May a federal marshal and a local sheriff backed by a posse of several hundred men from Missouri attacked Lawrence. They set fire to the Free State hotel, ransacked newspaper offices, and engaged in looting. One pro-slavery man was killed in the assault.[129] Abolitionist John Brown, who had arrived in Kansas in 1855, had grown impatient with the Free State Party's nonviolent resistance.[130] In retaliation, he and his followers attacked a pro-slavery settlement at Pottawatomie Creek and brutally butchered five pro-slavery men, as described in this contemporary account:

> Killed on Saturday night May 24, 1856. 3 men of the name of Doyal— Wm Sherman & Wilkinson [sic]—the latter received 6 wounds each one would have proved fatal old man Doyal was shot through the head & stab[b]ed through the heart & his 2 boys where disherated [sic] cut about the hands—the younger boy's hands were mangled as if he had held up his hands to defend himself from the blows of the saber— Shermans head was cut by a saber blow and other. Five men murdered in one night—enticed from their houses with the promise of being kept from violence, as prisoners of war—led a few rods from their doors then killed. One was flung in the Creek down the bank. [Wilkerson] he was post master—The murderers inquired for Henry, but he was away from home hunting up his cattle this saved his life.[131]

Marshall County, where Georg chose to settle, was north and west of the main area of conflict but still part of the turmoil. When Georg arrived in December 1857, two towns had been platted that would outlive Bleeding Kansas—Marysville and Barrett. They represented the two extremes on the slavery issue. Marysville, closer to the Lodholz claim, was associated with Frank Marshall, for whom the county was named. He was born in Virginia and moved to Missouri, where he was a slaveholder.[132] While on his way to the gold fields in California, he saw a business opportunity and established a ferry to transport settlers and their wagons across a section of the Big Blue River when it was too high to ford—some five thousand to ten thousand a day from April to June, according to his own estimate.[133] Since it was still Indian country at the time, he sought permission from the military authorities at Fort Leavenworth to set up the ferry and a trading post. He was allowed to do so but was warned that warring tribes made it a dangerous area. He later reported having no "serious trouble" with the local Native Americans.[134]

Marshall's ferry was a crude affair made of wooden planks with railings on each side. A rope on a pulley was strung across the river that could be manipulated to use the current to propel the craft.[135] Initially he charged $3 per wagon; when he raised it to $5 in 1856, the Marshall County Board of Commissioners restored the price for a loaded wagon to $3.[136] Near the ferry, Marshall "built a row of rude log cabins; established a blacksmith shop, and opened, with a small stock of foods, a general store. . . . in which low grade tobacco and rot-gut whiskey predominated, and traded with the Indians."[137]

With passage of the Kansas-Nebraska Act, Marshall formed a town company that preempted the land. It became Marysville, named after his wife, and was a pro-slavery stronghold. The South Carolinians who founded Palmetto chose a location north of Marysville because of Marshall's position on slavery, and they sold out to him when they left.[138] The 1855 Kansas Territory census for District 11, the voting district where Marshall lived, showed thirty-five individuals from Missouri and one from Virginia, both slave states.

Meanwhile, Barrett, some twenty-five miles southeast of Marysville, owed its origins to A. G. Barrett of Cadiz, Ohio, where there was a sizable Quaker community opposed to slavery. At a meeting of the Ohio Kansas Company in March 1855, Barrett and four other men were designated to serve as an exploring committee to scout out suitable land for a colony in the Kansas Territory.[139] Arriving in May 1855, the committee found a very desirable, heavily forested area in the Vermillion River Valley near the spot where the Oregon Trail crossed the Black Vermillion.[140] As the land was not yet surveyed, they preempted an area eight miles long and five miles wide, encompassing forty square miles, and returned to Cadiz to report their find to the company.[141] But when it became apparent that there was no guarantee Kansas would be a free state, many decided not to uproot themselves.[142] In the fall of 1855 Barrett returned with a few followers and relatives, and he soon established a sawmill, as Barrett was a businessman as well as an abolitionist. He had owned a sawmill in Cadiz, but as the area became deforested, the business started to falter. In the Kansas Territory, amid its plentiful timber, he started anew. It was an enormous feat to get a disassembled, crated sawmill and the accompanying steam engine from the landing on the Missouri River to the village of Barrett. It took two heavy carts, each pulled by three yokes of oxen, eight days to make the journey.[143] But once in place, his business thrived.

Although A. G. Barrett was a lapsed Quaker—disagreeing with some of the tenets of Quakerism and marrying outside the faith—he was staunchly anti-slavery. The village of Barrett was considered "the most prominent 'Free State' settlement west of the border counties."[144] Barrett himself gave safe harbor to escaped slaves and occasionally hired African Americans to work at his mill, which drew the ire of some Border Ruffians. In the only act of violence reported in Marshall County, Barrett was attacked and tied up by three individuals who were preparing to throw him into the furnace at his mill when an African American worker named Rufe came to his rescue. Using a hefty piece of wood, Rufe bashed the ruffians, knocked the gun out of one attacker's hand, and held the miscreants at gunpoint until more help arrived.[145]

Just as Georg arrived in Marshall County, a major political shift was taking place. The pro-slavery territorial legislature had authorized a constitutional convention, and the aforementioned Lecompton Constitution was the result. Meanwhile, the Free Staters decided to participate in the next election for members of the territorial legislature; they now had the numbers to take control of that body. The pro-slavery constitutional convention subsequently decided to submit its draft constitution to the voters for ratification but to restrict the vote to a constitution either "with" or "without slavery," the latter preventing the *future* addition of slaves.[146] In the subsequent election of state officers, Frank Marshall was running as the pro-slavery candidate for territorial governor, and Marysville became the scene of major voting fraud.[147] William G. Cutler described the situation as follows:

> In the upper rooms of one of [the crude cabins in Marysville] the polls were opened, by setting a soap box on the head of a whisky barrel as the receptacle for ballots. . . . A narrow staircase led to a hole in the ceiling, through which the voter would thrust his hand, holding a ticket, and yell out his name, or the first name he happened to think of, and then would immediately descend, to make room for the next man, absorb a sufficient quantity of "tarantula juice," conjure up a new name and await his opportunity to vote again. Among the twenty-five or thirty voters present, there was a notable personage known by the sobriquet of "Shanghai"—probably so named from his personal appearance.
>
> Long before half the day had passed, "Shanghai," who had become so thoroughly imbued with patriotism for his party, and whisky, that he could not keep a secret, sprang upon a whisky barrel and exclaimed that he had voted twenty-five times, was going to vote twenty-five

more, and would bet any man $100 that he had outvoted anyone in the "outfit.".... No one seemed willing to take up any challenge of the champion voter, and the matter was about to go by default, when it was accepted by one of the [men], the money put up, and a committee appointed to investigate. The result of the investigation showed that "Shanghai" was beaten, the challenged party having deposited nearly one hundred votes. It was shown that he had possession of a St. Louis business directory, and that he was voting in alphabetical order, and had only got half way through the "A" list.

The voting continued briskly throughout the day, and when the shades of evening closed in upon them, the little Spartan band had rolled up a rousing majority of nearly 1,000 votes.[148]

The voting irregularities in Marysville and elsewhere did not go unnoticed. When a commission was subsequently appointed to count the number of voters in the county and investigate potential fraud, it reported that the Marysville precinct had forty-four voters, "yet it has regularly returned about 270 votes for the Pro-Slavery candidates."[149] This was less than the number Cutler projected in telling a good story, but a sizable number nonetheless.

Given the prevailing turmoil, it is startling that Georg never mentioned it in his letters home; nor was there any mention of slavery in subsequent correspondence of Lodholz family members. It certainly must have seemed like a "peculiar institution" to Georg, who had never encountered a slave. There were certainly none in Württemberg.[150] Discrimination against African Americans, both free and slave, had a long history in Connecticut. In the wake of the American Revolution, the state had passed the Gradual Abolition Act of 1784, which freed individuals born into slavery when they reached the age of twenty-five. In effect, the state had abolished slavery by 1848, before the Lodholzes arrived.[151] The last federal census to list slaves in Plymouth Township, the 1840 census, showed that there were five free blacks and only one older slave between the age of fifty-five and one hundred.[152] Georg's entire journey west was through free states, and coming from the Nebraska Territory, he did not pass through any of the towns bordering Missouri.

Certainly the most bitter confrontations were south of Marshall County and nearer the border with Missouri. Focused on finding land, Georg might have had little interest in these events. He was not included in the census of eligible voters conducted at the end of January 1858 for the elections later that year, although, as a naturalized citizen, he would have been eligible. Georg's silence may also reflect the fact that the tide had turned against the pro-slavery faction. Frank Marshall lost the election.[153] In the years ahead the political jockeying continued in Congress, but two referenda on the fate of the Lecompton Constitution were roundly defeated. A new anti-slavery constitutional convention drafted a constitution forbidding slavery, but not until the beginning of the Civil War in 1861, when southerners withdrew from Congress, was Kansas finally admitted as a free state.[154]

The number of people favoring a Kansas without slavery had consistently climbed. One was Georg's future brother-in-law Heinrich Reb, who had settled near Barrett and was a registered voter in 1859.[155] We do not know Georg's views on slavery, but the German Evangelical Association, the denomination to which the Lodholzes belonged in the United States, was decidedly pro-Union.[156] Many Germans coming to Kansas were opposed to slavery, drawn in part by the abolitionist newspaper published out of Atchison, the *Kansas Zeitung, Ein Organ für freies Wort, freien Boden und frie Männer* (an organ for free speech, free soil and free men).[157] In 1857 German settlers were instrumental in the election of a Free State mayor in formerly pro-slavery Leavenworth.[158] In the 1855 territorial census, the largest concentration of Germans and eligible German voters resided in District 16, which included Leavenworth.[159] One must be careful, however, not to paint the position of German immigrants with too broad a brush. William Sherman, one of the men killed during John Brown's Pottawatomie raid, was a German immigrant, and both he and his brother were pro-slavery.[160] Like Georg, many German immigrants came to Kansas for the land, and while they may have been opposed to slavery, they were not ardent abolitionists. There were German settlers in several voting districts where slaves were present, and although this is hardly indicative of the settlers' positions, it suggests a more complicated view of the issue.[161]

Although guerrilla warfare continued in southeastern Kansas in 1858–59, Georg felt no compunction about urging his family to join him there, so he must have sensed little danger.[162] He instructed them what to bring and where to meet him—in Atchison, Kansas, on the Missouri River. Out of concern for his mother and nieces, Georg recommended that they not take the uncomfortable railroad: "I think it would be very hard for our dear Mother to make the trip to St. Louis by Railroad. It is also for you Bro. Gottfried best to come by steamboat on account of the children."[163] Georg advised them to take a steamboat out of Pittsburgh and travel on the Ohio River to where it drains into the Mississippi at the southern tip of Illinois, then take another steamboat north

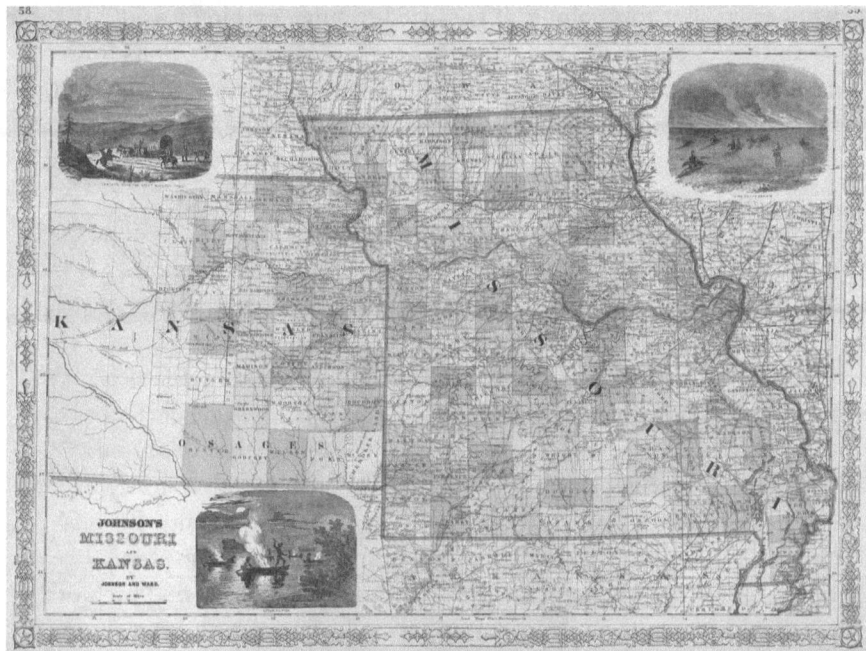

Johnson's 1862 map of Missouri and Kansas shows Marshall County (where Georg preempted land) in the north and the city of Atchison (where Georg met the rest of the family) to the east. ("Johnson's new illustrated (steel plate) family atlas, with descriptions, geographical, statistical, and historical," Library of Congress, http://hdl.loc.gov/loc.gmd/g3200m.gcw0013960)

to St. Louis.[164] That is where the Mississippi River merges with the Missouri River, and the family could catch a third steamboat to Atchison. Steamboats on the Missouri River offered cabin or cheaper below-deck accommodations, and the Lodholzes probably opted for the latter.[165]

Once again, Anna Maria, Anna Regina, and Friedrich had to say goodbye, most likely forever, to their friends—this time, the new friends they had made in Terryville. Once again, they had to sort through their belongings and leave behind many prized possessions, particularly any large, heavy furniture. Anna Maria's precious books, however, made the journey. Even before he found the land in Kansas, Georg advised them what they should bring, including firearms, which they had not needed in Connecticut:

> Dear friends, what I think would be good for you to bring along—bring beds along, as many as possible. Featherbeds are expensive here and hard to find. Here they sleep on corn mattresses on the ground. Further:

The Journey West

bring carpenter tools along. If you need to buy anything I would suggest to do that in St. Louis. You can also buy revolvers there, Colts for $16 or a double barrel gun for $6 to 8. There are many revolvers around, cheaper ones, but those will not hit a target. Also, pack all your house & kitchen utensils and whatever [is] not too heavy. Here most stuff is 30% more expensive than in Conn.

Dear sister, Anna Regina, you want to know about work here, don't be afraid—there is enough work around here. Fabric for clothes is about the same price in St. Louis as in Conn, but here, where we want to settle, things are about 30 [percent] more. So—I would suggest that you bring along all your clothes which do not take up too much room, because a farmer needs a lot of clothes and is glad if one does not have to go in rags. As far as seeds are concerned, buy them in St. Louis, like beans, corn, turnips, potatoes, etc. One can also buy that in Atchison.

I hope that you will arrive in Atchison, Atchison County, Kansas about 15 Apr. 1858. I'm planning to be there [at the] same time. I've heard that the town is not large so we should be able to find each other without difficulty. Should you arrive ahead of me, please wait for me at the lodging house by the river until someone comes to fetch you. Should I be ill I'll send someone to travel with you over land since it is difficult for people who have never handled a team of oxen.

I think if you start out from Terryville about 25 March next year, we would arrive in Atchison at the same time and if someone had to wait, it would be best if it was me because I could work there until your arrival. I would have liked to have it arranged earlier but the Missouri [River] will not thaw up much earlier. For one person it will cost about $50 from N. York to St. Louis or Atchison.[166]

After finding the land, Georg sent a second letter two weeks later, adding to his instructions:

On the 10th of this month I sent my last letter, in which I noted the lake [sic] town in which we want to meet each other first, and I also noted more or less what I think you should take along, but in case the previously sent letter should have failed to arrive, then I want to note once more in this one the most important things, for example I think it's good to bring all the beds that you have and can transport, and I wish for you to take along all your cabinet-making tools, given that such articles are twice as expensive here as in Connecticut. We'll have plenty of firearms left over—if you buy a Colt revolver and a double-barreled gun in St. Louis, otherwise as far as your household items go, I think it will be good if you pack everything up that is easily packed and not terribly heavy in weight.

Dear friends, given that the weather here this winter is so extraordinarily nice and at present we are having many days here like the most beautiful spring days in Connecticut, I think that it will be the best time if you depart from there at the beginning of March, and for the lake [sic] city or Missouri River city where you will land I've chosen Atchison, Atchison County, Kansas, where I too intend to arrive on the first of April 1858 in order to fetch you, assuming the Lord keeps me healthy, and should it be the case that you arrive there before me, then I would like for you to wait in the nearest inn until someone comes and fetches you, but if something bad were to happen to me or in case I should die during this time, then continue your journey into Marshall County, Kansas, at the start of Vermillion Creek KS. But I don't think that our heavenly father will call me from this world before that time, and I hope that we will see each other again first in Atchison. I think everything will come together better than you imagine. . . . now I think that this time I will bring my name to the right place. . . . Dear friends, this year is growing rather long for me and I simply can't wait for the time when I take my trip to Atchison in order finally to see you there; I will most likely arrive there with an ox-driven wagon, and little Maria and Anna will then probably get driven around there for the first time in their life in such a vehicle. Dear friends, if this should be the last letter that you receive before your departure, I wish you all a happy journey and may the Lord accompany you and protect you from all misfortune. And I wish for this missive to find you in good health, just as it is leaving me. I send all of you the friendliest of greetings, John Georg.[167]

Georg's preempted land was six miles north of what would become the town of Beattie in 1870.[168] It was not far from Guittard Station, founded by French immigrant George Guittard in 1857 to provide a stopping place for travelers headed west and to serve as a changing station for the short-lived Pony Express (1860–61).[169] It was also roughly twenty miles from Marysville. To keep claim to the preempted parcels of land, Georg needed to register his intent to settle it with the nearest federal land office, which would have been the Kickapoo Land Office, near Leavenworth.[170] The usual practice was for preemptors to "stake out" their claims by splitting a log to make stakes and writing on them their names and the date of staking.[171] In addition, Georg probably marked his claims by blazing trees on the properties and perhaps crossing four poles to form the foundation of a cabin.[172] Then at the land office he would have described the land as accurately as possible, knowing that once the surveyors did their work, the boundaries might shift.[173]

The conventional narrative of frontier life is one of hard-won heroism by white settlers, but the darker side of settling the Great Plains should never be forgotten. From the point of view of the US government, Georg was acting properly. Four months earlier, Congress had allowed unsurveyed land that had been ceded by treaty to be preempted, and Georg's land had been ceded by the Kickapoo people (*Kickaapoi*). Accustomed to the concept of individual landownership and the buying and selling of land, Georg saw nothing wrong with the Kickapoo people's ceding a major portion of their land to the US government in return for money. But in fact, claims like his and his neighbors' were morally dubious. The treaties signed in the wake of the Indian Removal Act have already been noted, and the succession of treaties between the Kickapoo people and the US government is a forceful example of injustice couched in legalese. With each successive treaty—1795, 1809, 1819, 1820, and 1832—the Kickapoo were forced to move farther away from their hunting grounds around Lake Erie. These treaties granted and then took away land in Indiana, Illinois, and Missouri. Finally, in 1832, the Kickapoo people were placed in the Kansas Territory, where the US government granted them land as a "permanent place of residence as long as they remain a tribe."[174] That land had in fact been wrested from the Kaw Nation by treaty in 1825. In her *History of Marshall County*, Emma Forter provides an absurd reasoning for the government's actions: the Kaw Nation had lived on the land for three hundred years, but "they did not own this land except in a hereditary sense, through having lived on it."[175] Who "owned" the land in the 1500s?

Underlying such a statement, of course, is the general contempt and fear Native Americans aroused in most European settlers, who wanted the land for themselves.[176] In addition, the government in Washington, DC, saw settlement of the Great Plains as promoting national strength and security and even civilization itself, as white Americans defined it.[177] Few were prepared to acknowledge that the Native American peoples had civilizations, albeit very different from their own.

Georg's letters indicate no fear of Native Americans and contain only a vague reference to "trouble" at a large gathering where they received their annuity payments. In fact, there is no mention of the Lodholzes being bothered in any way by the Kickapoo, who numbered only 475 in 1854, or by any other tribe in the area.[178] As far as the family was concerned, Native Americans were apparently nonexistent. This is surprising, as other settlers in Marshall County often mentioned the presence of Native Americans, who still had small reserves in the Kansas Territory under the treaties negotiated by George Manypenny.[179] For example, Joseph Totten, who arrived in Marshall County in June 1858, told his biographer that, upon his arrival, "he found plenty of wild game and Indians. His white neighbors were few and far between."[180] Thomas Waterson, who came to Kansas in 1854, found the Indians "plentiful, many of them being treacherous and hostile, but [as the biographer noted] our subject had no personal trouble with them."[181] Even settlers arriving years later encountered large numbers of Native Americans. William Koeneke, who came to Marshall County with his German-born parents in 1860, stated, "Wild animals were plentiful at the time. . . . , also the Otoe Indians who were. . . . near neighbors, but peaceable and friendly."[182] Forter reported that in 1865 H. Runkle recalled there being "many Indians in the country at the time and there was a huge camp on the home farm."[183] There were, however, some very scary moments. David Miller (Muller), who came to Marshall County in 1858 with his parents, told his biographer about one such event : "When still a child a couple of squaws attempted to steal him, but just as they had got him on a pony, his mother seized him, and after a struggle succeeded in keeping her child. There were numerous alarms of Indian raids during the first year's residence in Kansas, but they never suffered any loss from them."[184]

Once Georg had registered the family's intent to settle on his chosen land, he needed to build some sort of housing to hold on to the claims. He told his family: "I will stay here for a while and build a house on our mother's land so that no one else will establish himself there, and then after that a family house on our 480 acres which I first procured for us three brothers. And with this I then want if possible to stop until you arrive. I bought a very nice wagon with iron axles, it cost $110."[185]

Early settlers on the prairie made their homes out of the materials at hand. Some carved hillside dugouts; in arid western Kansas, many built homes out of clumps of sod. One settler, scouting ahead of his family in Marshall County, lived in a hollow tree one winter.[186] In eastern Kansas, where Marshall County is located, many different types of wood—oak, walnut, hickory, ash, and cottonwood—were available, so Georg built log cabins. Log houses had existed in Germany since medieval times, and the immigrants from Germany built them in Pennsylvania in the 1600s. Log cabins are simple to construct, and despite his lack of experience, Georg could have completed one himself. But he most likely sought advice and help from his neighbors, as raising the heavy logs once the cabin reached a height above his head would have been difficult.[187]

Georg most likely built the family's log cabins out of cottonwood trees, which were plentiful along streams and creeks, one of which conveniently ran through the Lodholz property. Native Americans used cottonwoods (in the poplar family) to make dugout canoes. Because they grow quickly, their wood is relatively weak and thus easier to work with than other hardwoods. Georg probably searched for trees that were not yet fully mature—no more than fifteen inches in diameter, judging from photographs of cabins—and as straight as possible. Their length would depend on the size of the cabin, with many early log cabins measuring ten or twelve feet square.[188] When company came, settlers often had to remove furniture to make room for their guests.[189]

After felling the trees with an ax, Georg would have hacked off the branches and hauled the logs to the building site using his oxen. Leaving the bark intact on the outer and inner portions of the logs helped prevent the wood from decaying, but he may have removed the bark from the top and bottom to ensure a tighter fit. The final preparation was notching the logs at each end.[190] Georg's later letters indicate plans to install a floor, so he would have laid down fieldstone or cross sections of logs before creating a sill of four logs on top. Then the notched logs would be stacked, up to whatever Georg considered a sufficient height.[191] As he referred to this as a "family house," he may have raised the cabin high enough to accommodate a small loft reached by ladder to provide more sleeping room.[192]

Into this large wooden box with no lid, Georg would have cut out a door, perhaps using a blanket to cover the opening.[193] Later, he probably installed a door made of wood slabs swinging outward on wood or leather hinges. If he cut out any windows, they were most likely covered with animal skins.[194]

At each end of one set of walls, he used straight limbs to create triangular gables to hold a ridgepole; then he spaced other limbs along the top sill and the pole, covered it all with more limbs or thinner strips of a log, and placed large pieces of bark over that.[195] The roof leaked in the rain, the floor was packed bare earth, and he stuck whatever insulating materials he could find—small twigs, grass, and clods of mud—in the chinks between the logs to block the wind and cold.[196] However, he could not prevent flies, mosquitoes from the nearby creek, and other insects and small critters from making their way inside.[197] He probably gathered local stones and built a hearth and chimney to provide light, warmth, and a means of cooking. It must have been wearying work, but Georg had stamina. He had to walk twenty to thirty miles just to get paper for writing letters.[198]

Once the building was done, Georg needed to find a paying job, but the Panic of 1857 was in full force:

> Dear friends, I am writing the 2nd time to you about how things are in Kansas. No work anywhere. There are about 30 robbers here who killed a few women and took their money and other things. This is awful.
>
> I worked for 18.- a month. And when I wanted my money he said that he can't pay me. I want to start a small business together with someone. We want to sell spirits. [They would actually be reselling liquor purchased from one of the towns on the Missouri River.] But money is lacking since I haven't earned any yet.[199]

Money was a perennial problem in the early years on the prairie. Georg had already borrowed $140 from Friedrich in September 1857 and would borrow several smaller sums from his brother over the next three years, causing tension in the family many years later.[200]

The family arrived in Atchison on April 1.[201] Georg had bought a horse and wagon, but given the number of people and the amount of goods to be carried almost ninety miles to their new home, it is highly unlikely that just one horse and wagon could have handled the load.[202] Georg most likely used his oxen; a yoked pair of the strong but slow beasts was better suited than horses to pull heavy loads. So Gottfried's children likely got their first ride in an ox-pulled wagon.

The long journey from Atchison took several days, during which the family camped and cooked "by the wayside."[203] The weather was apparently good, and they probably slept in or under their carts. Their route took them onto part of the Oregon Trail. The road was rutted, and the ride was jolting.

The scene that greeted the Lodholz family when they finally arrived at Georg's chosen acreage was both astonishing and daunting. Georg's letters had hardly prepared them. They had traveled from a village in the mountainous Black Forest, with neatly defined fields, to a factory town in the eastern United States. They had never seen anything like the sparsely populated, endless tallgrass prairie of the Great Plains.

The family, especially the women, may have been taken aback by the crudeness of the habitation built by Georg. Compared to their house in Ebhausen or even in Terryville, this log cabin on the Plains was abysmally small and primitive. As Sandra L. Myres states: "The first look at their new homes certainly tested women's courage and fortitude."[204] Weary and relieved that their journey was at an end, Anna Maria, Anna Regina, Friedrich, Gottfried, Christina, Annie, and Mary were no doubt glad to have a roof over their heads and joyful at being with Georg again.

The cabin had no privacy. We do not know how the family's furniture, including the beds, fit into that small space. Perhaps they all slept in just the one room, partitioned by hanging pieces of cloth, or perhaps several slept in the loft, body to body. Through any spaces in the roof, they would have seen the inky black sky, the stars, and the moonlight.

CHAPTER 3

Life in Kansas and Connecticut, 1859–61

In 1860, the year of the first federal census in the Kansas Territory, there were 2,426 people living in the nine hundred square miles of Marshall County, not counting Native Americans on reservations. Of these, 291 were foreign-born.[1] One was Georg Heinrich Reb (sometimes spelled Rebb), the future husband of Anna Regina Lodholz. He arrived by himself in Marshall County in 1857, one year before the Lodholzes. He came not to farm—at least not at first—but to use his highly marketable skills as a blacksmith and wheelwright. With the great stream of settlers heading for California, Utah, and Oregon, such skills were in high demand.[2]

Heinrich Reb was born in Kaiserslautern, Rhenish Bavaria, in 1831—a year after Gottfried.[3] He immigrated to America in 1852, heading first to Michigan, then to Iowa, and finally ending up in Barrett, Kansas, some twenty miles due south of the Lodholzes.[4] There he put down roots among the native-born settlers who had followed A. G. Barrett to found the town.

The reasons for Heinrich's emigration and subsequent settling in Barrett are sheer guesswork. Situated on the left bank of the Rhine just north of France, Rhenish Bavaria, also known as the Palatinate, was more of a battlefield than its distant neighbor of Württemberg. In 1931 Walter F. Willcox wrote a detailed statistical analysis of immigration to the United States and stated: "Hardly any other region in Europe suffered from wars and devastation more often and more severely than the Palatinate."[5] Greatly influenced by the ideals of the French Revolution, the Palatinate's intellectuals as well as its middle and working classes participated in the unsuccessful uprisings against autocratic regimes that swept Europe in 1848. In the wake of their failure, elements in the Palatinate campaigned to secede from Bavaria and form their own republic in 1849. This effort too failed when Prussia intervened militarily.[6] In the succeeding years Prussia and Austria vied for dominance in the region, creating more tension.[7] Given that Heinrich Reb ultimately settled in the liberal-minded town of Barrett, he might have immigrated to America for political reasons. He was certainly civic-minded, registering to vote in 1858.[8] The following year, he and three other bachelors built a fourteen- by twenty-four-foot schoolhouse in Barrett—the first in Marshall County.[9] Each of them donated $10 to pay for nails, windows, and a door; men with families were spared the expense but joined in the labor.[10]

Although Heinrich might have come to Barrett in part because of the settlement's abolitionist stance, both he and its founder were businessmen. Heinrich's blacksmithing business in Greenbush, Iowa, may have been foundering because the town was failing to attract a railroad, which would have impacted its growth.[11] Whatever his reasons, Heinrich was hardly the only Iowan to make his way to Kansas. In 1865 he received a letter from a friend he knew in Greenbush, Jacob Lockridge, who had either accompanied or followed Heinrich to Kansas and eventually settled with his wife in Nebraska.[12] This letter is important because it shows that Heinrich could speak and read English and that he had already made friends among native-born settlers like Lockridge before moving to Kansas, so settling in Barrett would not have been a major departure.

Barrett was near one of the branches of the Oregon Trail, and Heinrich serviced the overlanders' wagons. They were called prairie schooners because their canvas covers, stretched over hoops, resembled the sails of a ship. Wagon trains embarked on the long, arduous, dangerous journey from one of several towns on the Missouri River, where the travelers bought the vast quantities of supplies needed for their trek. The wagons, about twelve feet long, were designed to haul several thousand pounds, so strong oxen were the predominant draft animals. The overlanders needed ropes and spare parts for their wagons; axes, hammers, saws, knives, and shovels; weapons; cooking utensils, mainly cast-iron skillets and Dutch ovens; barrels of water in case they hit a stretch of dry country; and lots of food. They bought hundreds of pounds of dried and cured meats, flour, bacon, rice,

Blacksmith shop, similar to what Heinrich Reb's might have looked like.
(© oscarcwilliams—Can Stock Photo Inc.)

coffee, sugar, beans, hardtack (dried crackers made from flour and water), dried fruits, and other nonperishables.[13]

This heavy load was carried on four large, spoked wooden wheels with metal bands around them. The wagon wheels suffered mightily when traversing the rutted, uneven trails. They sometimes came off, or they weakened and broke. If they were not made of well-seasoned wood, they could shrink and separate from the metal bands.[14] The axles, made of wood or wrought iron, could snap under the weight of the cargo. As a blacksmith and wheelwright, Heinrich would have made new wheels and shaped new metal bands or tightened old ones. He would have repaired broken axles, shoed the overlanders' horses and oxen (a difficult task, as oxen do not like to have their feet lifted), and provided extra shoes for the journey.

Given his occupation, we can assume that Heinrich (known as Henry) was a brawny man. Wearing a leather apron to protect himself from stray sparks, he worked in the heat created by his wood-fired forge, designed to raise the temperature of metal to the point of malleability. The forge was basically a large fireplace built with the hearth at table height and extending out in front, providing a broad work area. Large bellows stoked the fire.

Once the metal was softened, Heinrich could hammer it into the desired shape on an anvil and then cool it in a bucket of water.

Settled into his craft, Heinrich Reb had a relatively secure source of income and, for a time at least, access to a general store in Barrett. The Leavitt family, who arrived in 1855, operated a small store in their home opposite Barrett's mill.[15] Robert Smith set up a store in 1860, but with the population still sparse, "there was little call for his merchandise," so he left two years later.[16] Heinrich might have had to purchase supplies from the overlanders or from one of the larger towns on the Missouri River, such as Atchison or St. Joseph. He probably did not always shop in person, as "neighbors took turns going for they must be gone about three weeks."[17]

In her *History of Marshall County*, Emma Forter called Henry Reb "one of the real pioneers of this county."[18] The same might be said of the Lodholzes. Historian John Hawgood stated: "One of the most salient, if unexpected characteristics of the nineteenth century German settler in the United States is that he was rarely, in the strict sense of the word a pioneer.... Rather did he consolidate and improve what others had won." He attributed this to a combination of factors: love of the "amenities of civilization"; a preference for locating near existing markets and bodies of water; an aversion to speculating in land, with the concomitant desire to settle permanently; and the wish to keep the family together from the beginning. Hawgood does not claim these as exclusively German attributes and concedes that there may have been "an appreciable number of exceptions" to the rule.[19] In fact, there were many exceptions among the thousands of German-born settlers who came to the Kansas Territory between 1855 and 1860, including Heinrich and the Lodholzes. In addition, not all the attributes listed by Hawgood were necessarily deterrents to being a pioneer, such as the Lodholzes' desire to settle permanently.

Hawgood was apparently comparing German settlers to the large numbers of native-born settlers who populated the frontier. However, a comparison with other immigrant groups tells a somewhat different story. According to the 1855 Kansas Territory census, there were 274 foreign-born residents whose place of birth was indicated.[20] Of these, 93 (34 percent) were from Germany, by far the largest foreign-born group. When naturalized citizens and those with no recorded birthplace are included, the foreign-born total increases to 452. Even if none of these additional individuals were born in Germany (which is unlikely), the identified German-born population still constituted 21 percent.

The census listed eighteen families in which one or both spouses were

German-born, including six in which the wife was native-born and one in which the husband was. Of the native-born wives, five were Missourians, and given the large settlement of Germans in Missouri, they might well have been the offspring of German-born parents.[21] All but one of the families gave their occupation as farmers. The vast majority of the German-born, however, were unattached males like Heinrich, and their occupations were about equally divided among farmers, craftsmen such as gunsmiths, mechanics and merchants, and laborers, most likely working on farms.

These figures were comparable to those for the next two largest foreign-born groups in the Kansas Territory at the time: sixty-one English and sixty-five Irish, who were already English-speaking. The 1855 census listed nineteen English families (seven with one native-born spouse and one with a foreign-born spouse) and twenty-three single males. There were eleven Irish families (three with a native-born spouse and one with a foreign-born spouse) and thirty-two single males. These figures would not be substantially altered by taking into consideration naturalized and declarant residents whose place of birth was not indicated, as they included individuals with German surnames. Thus, despite their small numbers, Germans seemed just as willing to be pioneers as other immigrant groups, as evidenced by figures for German settlers in the Far West and Southwest. Recall also that Germans were the first immigrant group to settle in Detroit. Interestingly, this same pattern of just a few families and many single males was present in Terryville, which was not the frontier but represented a relatively new opportunity for German immigrants seeking work.

The majority of German-born individuals residing in the Kansas Territory in 1855 were naturalized citizens or declarants. Significantly, there were four instances in which females in a German family had been naturalized—indicating an awareness of the laws regarding preemption. In contrast, only one English family and no Irish families had a naturalized female member. Prior to 1855 women seldom applied for citizenship because it involved several court appearances and the payment of a fee. Since women could not vote, there was no particular benefit in going through the process. However, in 1855 Congress passed a law tying a woman's citizenship to her husband's, much as it had been in Ebhausen, obviating the need to go through the expense and the legal process required previously.[22] So, in the end, Gottfried's wife Christina and Heinrich's wife Anna Regina became citizens by virtue of their husbands' naturalization. Anna Maria never remarried and never underwent the naturalization process, so she never became a US citizen.

Georg had continually emphasized in his letters how fast settlement was taking place. The 1860 federal census, compiled on the eve of the Civil War, before Kansas was admitted as a state, revealed a major population increase to 107,206, despite the violence and turmoil.[23] Some were lured by cheap land or the drive to abolish slavery, but the lack of security and the poor weather sent others home. For Heinrich's friend Jacob Lockridge, the former was the major reason for his decision to leave: "I have not heard from you since I left you. We left Nebraska on Christmas Day and moved back to Iowa. I liked that country very well but they [sic] was so many Robers [sic] where we was and they was Robing [sic] so many that we was afraid that it would be our turn next and we thought that we would leave in time and not go back til times was settled." If he did not return that fall, he would send the money to Heinrich to pay his property tax.[24] In fact, Jacob never made it back to Kansas.[25] Security was apparently not an issue for Georg. Despite bank robberies and the robbing and killing of "a few women," he did not hesitate to urge his family to come west.[26] Georg also commented on the pleasant weather, but he arrived after the harsh winter of 1856, which convinced many Kansas settlers to depart.[27]

In fact, the frontier was quite fluid. In 1857 J. Cooper Stuck published a map of Douglas County, Kansas, based on plat records and field notes at the surveyor general's office in Lecompton.[28] In the township of Wakarusa, 109 platted properties had been claimed, but by 1860, only twenty-eight were still owned by the original settlers, including one German-born.[29] The three Bavarian families identified in the 1855 territorial census living in the area that became Marshall County no longer appeared anywhere in the Kansas Territory in the 1860 federal census, although other Bavarians had arrived to take their place. This mobility was not exclusive to the Kansas Territory. Many settlers residing in Iowa and Illinois in 1850 were not there in 1860, including some German-born who, contrary to Hawgood's assumption, had settled on unimproved land and then moved on.[30]

A number of circumstances drove the desire for the virgin soil of Kansas. As already noted, the major recession (if not depression) of 1856 led to the Lodholzes' decision to farm rather than rely on factory work, and it may have influenced others to look west for opportunity as well. Not all land in the eastern states was very productive to begin with, and even the best soil became depleted and less productive over time, given the generally poor farming practices in use.[31] In writing about the settlement of Illinois and Iowa, Allan Bogue suggests that among the migrants to those states were those who had failed at farming elsewhere, small farmers who wanted more land but could not afford it where they came from, farm laborers who wanted their own farms, and sons who had no prospect of inheriting a farm.³² The same motivations may have played a role in Kansas.

The 1860 federal census is flawed in many ways (see the introduction to appendix B), particularly as pages scattered throughout the township counts are missing information—most importantly, birthplaces. Nevertheless, it provides a snapshot (albeit somewhat blurred) of the early days of German settlement on the frontier. In 1820, when settlement was in its infancy in places such as Michigan, Illinois, Ohio, and Indiana, census takers collected minimal information; for instance, they did not include any information on ethnicity beyond the racial distinctions made at that time. As explored in this chapter, the German-born settlers on the Kansas frontier were remarkably diverse in many ways, such that Hawgood's model of the typical German settler loses meaning, at least in this time and place. So what were these pioneers like?

Appendix B shows the German-born inhabitants included in the 1860 census, arranged by the counties in existence at that time. By my count, there were at least 4,106 German-born inhabitants, or barely 4 percent of the general population, although the German presence would have been greater due to children born in the United States. There were 1,410 families in which one or both spouses were German-born or that were composed of siblings; in addition, there were 1,066 single individuals (predominantly male) not living in a family. The latter represented a quarter of the German-born settlers, so Heinrich was hardly alone.³³

Of the families, 1,118, or 79 percent, included children, as did Gottfried and Christina's; 223 families, or 16 percent, were couples; and there were 51 groups of siblings (totaling 164 individuals) living together.³⁴ Between families with children and couples, there were 102 other relatives—a mother, father, sister, or brother of the husband or wife—sharing the household.

The couples who migrated to Kansas obviously did not wait to have children or, in the case of older couples, did not bring any children with them or were recently remarried. In looking at the ages of the husbands and wives in counties where couples were particularly numerous—Davis, Douglas, Johnson, Leavenworth, Pottawatomie, and Wyandotte—they were predominantly in their twenties, thirties, and forties, with a few older couples.³⁵

The families with children who migrated to the Kansas Territory tended to be relatively small, like Gottfried and Christina's. Thirty-one percent had just one child, and 24 percent had two, accounting for more than half the families with children; only 14 percent had five or more children. In 1860 the average number of children per family in the United States was 5.21.³⁶

In almost a quarter of the families (268), the oldest or only child had been born in one of the German states. In 1860, 72 percent of these firstborn children were older than ten (192), 27 percent were twenty or older (73), and only 6 percent were five or younger (16). These families tended to be slightly larger than other German families whose first or only child was born in the United States. Forty percent (107) had one or two children, 34 percent (90) had three children, 26 percent (71) had five or more children, but only one family had more than ten children. Of course, these figures are a function of length of a marriage, infant mortality, death of a spouse, and whether the entire family came to the Kansas Territory. The general birth pattern for families whose first child was born in Germany was one child every two to four years, but age gaps documented in the census figures could be considerably wider. For example, one family had two children, one twelve years old and the other three months old. Another had three children aged twenty, twelve, and eight. Such families may have included other members who had not joined the rest of the family on the prairie. This may have been particularly true of families with just one child (52), many of which were headed by widows and widowers. Of forty-eight widows, twenty-eight (58 percent) had just one child in their household—born in Germany. Similarly, of fifty-five widowers, thirty-five (64 percent) had just one child—born in Germany. Although the total number of widow- and widower-headed households was small (103), this demographic pattern deserves more careful scrutiny than is possible here.

Looking at the birthplace of the youngest child in a family, the statistics show that in a quarter of the families whose first child was born in Germany, their last child was born there too (66). With few exceptions, these families, as well as those with a single child born in Germany, apparently stopped having children altogether or experienced a disruption in reproduction. In all but two families, the youngest child was older than five. The cessation of reproduction is underscored by the fact that a significant number of these households were headed by widows and widowers (for ten widows and nine widowers, their first and last children were born in Germany).

With few exceptions, the census can tell us little else about these particular families, beyond what can be inferred from certain facts it provides. For instance, the family whose ten-year-old child was born at sea had apparently been in the United States for a decade. And the families whose one-month-old and three-month-old infants were born in Germany were obviously new arrivals who made their way directly to Kansas.

For other families, we can trace at least part of their journeys to Kansas using the ages and birthplaces of their children.[37] The picture that emerges is one of seasoned settlers who, like many of the native-born people who poured into the Kansas Territory, had already tried their fortunes beyond the East Coast.[38]

There is no standard means of dividing the United States into sections. Here I use the schemata from James R. Shortridge's *Peopling the Plains*, which divides the country into Northeast, North Midland, Upper South, Lower South, West, and Kansas.[39] Of those families whose first child was born in America (819), only 14 percent (113) were from the Northeast, with New York (46) and Wisconsin (40) supplying the largest numbers. (Only eleven families came from Connecticut, so obviously the Lodholzes were outliers.) Most families (274) came from the North Midland (33 percent), with Illinois, Ohio, Pennsylvania, Iowa, and Indiana being the main sources, in descending order. (Heinrich made his way west from Iowa, while the Lodholzes essentially leapfrogged from an eastern factory town directly to Kansas.) The Upper South accounted for 20 percent of the families (163), mainly due to the overwhelming numbers from Missouri (130), which provided more than three-quarters of the settlers from this region. The Lower South and West supplied few. In 252 instances, these families' first child was born in the Kansas Territory (31 percent). In fact, seventy-five had been in the territory long enough to have a second child (57) or even a third (13), fourth (3), fifth (1), and sixth (1).

A similar regional distribution is seen when we look at the states where a family's youngest child was born. Eighteen were born in New York and Wisconsin (Northeast); thirty-four were born in Illinois, Iowa, Ohio, and Pennsylvania and one in New Jersey (North Midland); nineteen were born in the Upper South, with Missouri contributing sixteen; and sixty-five were born in Kansas.

To get an idea of how long some of the families had been living elsewhere, we can look at the 128 families in which the oldest and youngest children were born in the same state other than Kansas. Unless the youngest child was very young, this does not necessarily indicate the state from which the families migrated to the Kansas Territory; they may have been settled elsewhere for some time after their youngest was born. In fact, in twenty of the families, the youngest child was six or older. Before coming to Kansas, these families lived in fourteen different states, with the largest number (68) in the North Midland region—Illinois, Indiana, Iowa, Ohio, and Pennsylvania. Thirty-two lived in the Northeast, with Wisconsin having the largest numbers (19); thirty-three lived in the Upper South, most in Missouri (27);

and one came from Texas. The shortest period of residence was less than a year; the longest, twenty-one years. Almost 50 percent had stayed for at least one to three years, and 13 percent had stayed for at least eleven to twenty-one years.

Not every family, however, stayed put. Starting the count from the first place a child was born in the United States—unless it was a state with a major port of entry: New York, Pennsylvania (Philadelphia), Maryland (Baltimore), Massachusetts (Boston), and Louisiana (New Orleans)—sixty families moved at least once from the state in which they settled initially before coming to Kansas, and ten of them moved twice. All but fifteen of these moves involved a change of residence within or between the North Midland and Upper South regions, and five took place between the North Midland region and the states of Wisconsin and Minnesota in the Northeast. This is not a case of chain migration, with family members following one another, as Christian Killinger did when he first arrived in America; instead, this is step migration, with settlers reaching their presumed final destination in stages. As Jochen Krebber has documented for immigrants from Tuttlingen and Spaichingen in Württemberg, pulling up stakes and moving was an option some Germans took advantage of, although few of these particular immigrants made it to Kansas.[40]

Although some stereotypically large German families migrated to Kansas, they were not preponderant. Like Heinrich and the Lodholzes, the German-born who pioneered the Kansas prairie came primarily as single individuals, couples, and small families. In fact, many started their families after reaching the territory.

The figures in appendix B show that there were Germans in almost every existing county, but as expected, their greatest concentration, as well as the greatest concentration of the population as a whole, was in the counties of Leavenworth, Atchison, and Douglas, where the major cities were located. These cities served nearby farmers and gave those without farms the opportunity to ply their trade, sell merchandise, and obtain work as laborers. In Marshall County, Germans represented just a little over 4 percent of the population, but in other western counties they were a significant percentage of their small populations: Pottawatomie (10 percent), Wabaunsee (18 percent), Dickinson (23 percent), Davis (11 percent).

Use of the term "German" masks the settlers' diverse origins. Although there was no "Germany" yet, the term had meaning, albeit a seemingly amorphous one, for "Germans." For example, the 1838 edition of the *Württembergische Jahrbücher für vaterländische Geschichte, Geographie, Statistik*

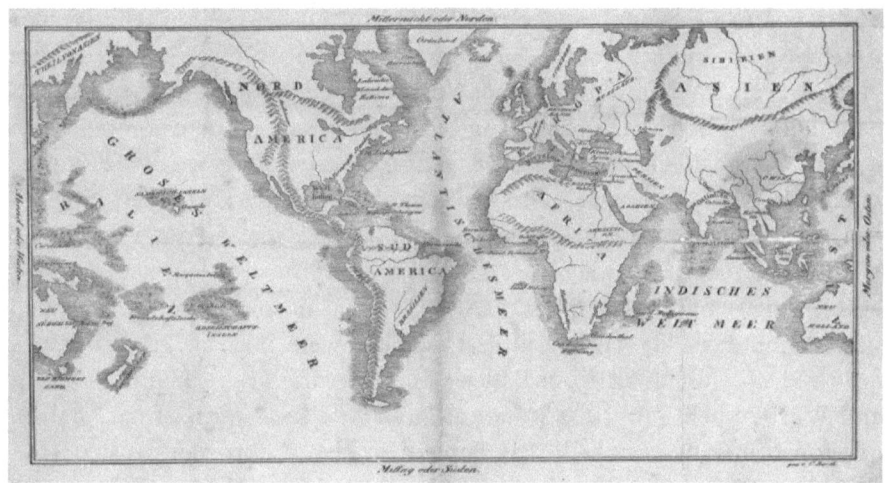

The Lodholz family possessed this world map of unknown origin and date, but most likely from before German unification. It excludes boundaries but identifies Europe as consisting of Spain, France, Russia, Sweden, and Deutschland. (In the family's possession)

und Topographie reported that flu had been widespread in Deutschland.[41] In their letters, the Lodholzes and Christian Killinger reference Deutschland and Deutsch twenty-eight times, Ebhausen twice, and Württemberg just once. "German" seemingly encompassed a shared language (although there were many dialects), as well as shared cultural and historical experiences.[42] The various German states morphed over time, being added to and subtracted from by war and by Napoleon, and many of them had been loosely unified in various confederations as well as the custom union (*Zollverein*) initiated by Prussia after Napoleon's defeat. Even the travels of a journeyman like the Lodholz patriarch Josef helped create a sense of cohesion.[43]

When the opportunity to forge a unified Germany came in 1848 in the midst of a wave of liberal revolutions, the Frankfurt Assembly, charged with drafting a new constitution, came up empty. The representatives could not agree on which states should be included and on what basis. Austria was particularly problematic; it was an amalgam of German-speaking areas and places inhabited by people of several other nationalities, such as Czechs (Bohemians), Slavs, and Croats, who themselves were trying to gain independence.[44]

Using the same schemata as appendix B, appendix C lists the birthplaces of the German settlers. Census takers were given specific written instructions not to enter "Germany" as the place of birth but to specify the particular state.⁴⁵ As appendix C shows, however, this instruction was honored more in the breach.⁴⁶ Whether this was due to the stated preference of the individual inhabitant, the English-speaking census taker's inability to communicate with the German-speaking resident, or some other factor, we do not know. Interestingly, in some cases, one spouse might be listed as being born in Germany, while the other was listed as being born in a specific state.

The 1860 census reveals that settlers were born in the larger states of both southern and northern Germany, as well as in smaller entities in much smaller numbers. By far the largest number were born in Prussia (502), followed by individuals from Baden (151), Bavaria (127), Hanover (121), and Württemberg (105). As it had in Bavaria, a local form of nationalism developed in Prussia, which may explain residents' apparent insistence on recording "Prussia" as their place of birth rather than "Germany."⁴⁷

Appendix C also provides a glimpse of some possible settlement patterns. Relatively large numbers of Prussians were residing in the western counties of Dickinson and Davis. Settlers from Darmstadt-Hesse were concentrated in the northern county of Nemaha, just east of Marshall, and a small group of Westphalians had settled in Riley.

The census takers in only two counties consistently followed directions and listed the actual states where German inhabitants were born. Fortuitously, Marshall was one of them. The count reveals a wide diversity of birthplaces, with no single state predominant. The Lodholzes were among the 15 percent from Württemberg who chose Marshall County as their home. In other counties, enough of the states of birth were identified to create a general picture of inhabitants from almost every German state occupying the same landscape. But as Eleanor Turk, among others, has pointed out, the Germans' "sense of identity was colored by significant religious and regional differences," and sometimes these overlapped.⁴⁸ So there were forces drawing them together—the amorphous sense of being "German," heightened by being strangers in a strange land—and forces pulling them apart.

Regionally, there were differences between northern and southern Germany that involved not only dialects but also politics (e.g., Prussia's heavy-handed involvement in the 1848 uprisings) and religion.⁴⁹ In Marshall County, inhabitants from northern Germany (Prussia, Hanover, Holstein, and Bremen) and southern Germany (Württemberg, Baden, and Bavaria) were equally split. Unlike Württemberg, however, both Baden and Bavaria were predominantly Catholic, creating a possible divide. In fact, religious differences—not only between Catholic and Protestant Germans but also among the many German Protestant denominations competing for adherents on the Great Plains—were probably the most important divisive factor.[50] Protestant German immigrants, coming from a region of state-controlled religions, had no formal organizational structure to turn to when they encountered the separation of church and state in the United States. In Württemberg, the major reformer had been Johan Brenz, who argued strongly in favor of dual roles for church and state in maintaining the "true" religion and restraining the evil impulses of humans.[51] Thus he organized a hierarchical system in the kingdom, interweaving church and state. But, as discussed in chapter 1, pietism had strong roots there. So once the Lodholzes were in the United States, the question arose for them and for many other German immigrants: how to create an organized structure around which like-minded Christians could unite.

There were many choices. The Lodholzes came from a Lutheran kingdom, but it seems that none of the organized Lutheran synods or societies appealed to them. One of the most prominent was the Lutheran Church–Missouri Synod, formally organized in 1841 in St. Louis by a group opposed to the forced merger of the Lutheran and Reformed (Calvinist) Churches in Prussia.[52] They were referred to as "Old Lutherans."[53] At roughly the same time, and also in Missouri, immigrants who favored the merger embodied in the Evangelical Church of the Prussian Union formed the German Evangelical Church Society of the West (*Der Deutsche Evangelische Kirchenverein des Westens*).[54] Given the historical tensions between northern and southern German states that would continue to play out until the unification of Germany in 1871, and given the Lutheran Church–Missouri Synod's rejection of pietism, it is understandable that the Lodholzes were not attracted to either of these camps, which had many faithful in Marshall County.

Based on an unusual document in the Lodholzes' possession, however, it seems that at one point they were investigating Lutheranism in the United States. A twelve-page handwritten booklet contains a report by a Lutheran pastor from Galveston, Texas, who attended the United Lutheran Church General Synod, which was founded in 1820 in Maryland after the merger of four state synods.[55] Pastor Wendt arrived in Galveston in 1851 to serve at the First Evangelical Lutheran Church, and he left in 1856, so the meeting described took place sometime between those years.[56] Two major issues raised at the synod troubled Wendt, who must have been influenced by pietism. He lamented that "our dear German language is completely banned from the general synod. Everything in English." He also objected to the use of the "mourner's bench" or "bench of repentance" for conversion.[57] Placed at the front of the chancel, this bench was where potential converts were subjected to intensive prayers and counseling by church personnel. This was anathema to pietists because it seemed coercive; in their view, conversion should be voluntary and proceed from an interior awakening. So if this was how the Lodholzes perceived Lutheranism in the United States, it is not surprising that they looked elsewhere.

In the end, they chose the German Evangelical Association, a relatively small denomination founded in the early 1800s in Pennsylvania.[58] It had no Lutheran affiliation but a strong affinity with the Methodist Church in both doctrine and hierarchical structure.[59] Significantly, both the German Evangelical Association and the Methodist Church were greatly influenced by pietism, the major difference being that the former saw its mission as preaching in German to its German brethren, while the Methodists initially preached exclusively in English.[60] In 1835 the Ohio Conference of the Methodist Church authorized Wilhelm Nast, a religious leader originally from Württemberg, to establish a German-speaking mission in Cincinnati, and the German Methodist Church was born.[61] It eventually expanded to include some twenty thousand adherents but was still somewhat smaller than the older German Evangelical Association, which continued to evangelize.[62] There is no evidence that the Lodholzes were aware of the German Methodist Church.

In choosing the German Evangelical Association, the Lodholzes were outliers among the settlers in Marshall County, where the association apparently had no organized church.[63] So much of community life centered around religious institutions that their choice denied them the opportunity to socialize with a large group of like-minded Germans. The family undoubtedly set aside Sunday as a day of worship, singing mission songs and reading from the religious books Anna Maria had brought with her.

It is highly likely that the Lodholzes made their choice while still living in Connecticut. During his journey to find land, Georg asked the family to send him *Der Chrisliche Botschafter*, a major publication of the German Evangelical Association. Gottfried may have encountered the association in New York, where it was particularly strong.[64] The family may have even been aware of the association in Württemberg, where it established a foreign mission in 1845.[65] It is interesting to note, however, that the Lodholzes did not seek out settlements where the German Evangelical Association was prevalent, unlike some of the Protestants from two other villages in Württemberg who immigrated to Canada.[66]

Like the Methodists, the German Evangelical Association was organized into conferences, such as the Ohio Conference and the Illinois Conference. Various conferences financed missionaries to Kansas starting in 1858 at the behest of members who had come from the East; the preaching often took place in their homes. Efforts in these early years of settlement were centered in Douglas County, close to Lawrence; in Leavenworth; and in Humboldt in Allen County. There is no evidence that they penetrated the northernmost counties farther west than Nemaha.[67] This reinforces the conjecture that the Lodholzes were already members of the German Evangelical Association when they came to Kansas.

Appendix D provides a more complex picture of German settlement at the township level. It reveals how the forces favoring cooperation and those favoring divisiveness played out, influenced by the degree of assimilation embraced or assumed, perhaps begrudgingly, by the exigencies of circumstance. Relevant scholarship has often focused on discrete settlements of individuals from the same German state or religion; for example, in an unnamed township in Dickinson County, a large concentration of Prussians from Wisconsin lived together. It is noteworthy that this settlement was located in a far western county that was sparsely populated, significantly reducing the pressure to assimilate. In other townships, small groups of Prussians were the only or predominant German settlers, such as Diamond Creek in Chase County and Monroe in Anderson County. Recall that Georg's hope of establishing a religious community in Kansas never came to fruition because moving to the area lost its appeal for the German residents back in Terryville.[68]

There were also concentrations of Germans in which no particular state or religion predominated. All but thirteen of the ninety-two households in Alma Township in Wabaunsee County were German, and twenty of the thirty-six families had a first child born in a German state. According to J. Neale Carman, the settlers were of diverse origins and religions.[69] Eudora in Douglas County was another case in point. As the number of children born in Illinois attests, a town company from Chicago settled there with a mixture of individuals and families from different German states and different religions; even German Jews settled there.[70]

In many cases, spouses were from different German states. Out of 204 families with children in which the specific birth states of the husband and wife are known, forty-three (21 percent) of the spouses were from different states. Similarly, out of sixty-one couples, nineteen (31 percent) of the spouses were from different states. Together, this accounted for roughly

5 percent of all couples and all families with children. There was no pattern to these marriages; that is, former inhabitants of no two particular states were more likely to marry each other. The matches varied considerably, with intermarriage between individuals from almost all the German states. In fact, the majority of marriages involved an individual born in a northern state and an individual born in a southern state. Because the census often recorded an individual as coming only from "Germany," we cannot know how prevalent such marriages were in the Kansas Territory in 1860, but the fact that there were so many indicates that many German settlers found common ground.

The counties and townships in appendix D are listed in the order they appeared in the census records, but given the size of landholdings, families whose properties were listed as next to each other were not necessarily close neighbors by modern standards. A section was one mile square, and a quarter section (160 acres) was half a mile square. In addition, appendix D does not show where couples and single individuals were situated. Germans frequently settled in small groups, and in any given township there might be more than one such group, sometimes all or mainly from one state and sometimes from a mixture of states. For example, in the township of Claytonville in Brown County, there were at least two groups containing Hessians—one situated amid Swiss settlers, with a Swiss wife married to a Hessian and a Hessian wife married to a man from Baden, and the second containing four adjacent families from different German states (Darmstadt-Hesse, Saxony, Württemberg, and Hanover), as well as two Hessian families and a single male from Württemberg nearby. Although such arrangements likely reduced feelings of isolation and allowed German to be spoken beyond the family circle, they were probably not homogeneous and dense enough to forestall assimilation for long.[71] Such groupings were not exclusive to Germans; Claytonville was home to a group of Norwegian families as well as a group of Austrians.

Nevertheless, most German-born settlers were surrounded by a sea of native-born. This is graphically illustrated in appendix E, which lists the numbers of German-born per page of the 1860 census, which presumably meant they were neighbors, albeit perhaps some distance away. For example, in the township of Stranger in Leavenworth County, five pages listed just one German per page, ten listed two to three, and only one listed six to nine. In fact, excluding the cities of Atchison, Leavenworth, and Lawrence, out of a total page count of 3,022, 266 pages listed just one German-born, 253 pages listed two to three Germans, and only 30 pages listed ten or more

German-born. Only ten townships had two or more pages with groups of ten or more Germans. Thus, in general, settlements of the German-born were porous to outside influences.

Some of these German settlers, like the Lodholzes and Heinrich Reb, had undoubtedly started to assimilate before reaching Kansas, but on the frontier there were many avenues beyond having native-born neighbors. One measure of assimilation is the anglicization of surnames, something the Lodholzes and Heinrich never did. Thus the census records include Germans with names such as Franklin Hoover,[72] Joseph Powell,[73] Jacob Rush,[74] and Barney Upjohn.[75] German immigrants also assumed roles serving the larger community. In the city of Atchison, a German settler was a policeman, which presumably required a command of English.[76] Similarly, in the city of Leavenworth, one German was employed as a city clerk,[77] three were constables,[78] one was a policeman,[79] and one was a deputy marshal.[80] Private Charles Smith, a German-born soldier, served among native-born and Irish at Fort Riley in Davis County.[81]

A significant number of German settlers had native-born or non-German foreign-born spouses. This does not mean that they abandoned their native tongue, as their partners might have been from German-speaking countries or second-generation offspring from German-speaking communities.[82] It does, however, indicate a willingness to move beyond the conceptual boundaries of their homeland. In 14 percent of the families with children (158), there was a native-born spouse from one of twenty-four different states, and in 6.5 percent (73), one spouse was foreign-born from one of fourteen different countries. The figures for couples were similar, with a native-born spouse in 17 percent (38) and a foreign-born spouse in 15 percent (33). Overall, these families represented 22.5 percent of the combined totals for families with children and couples.

Not surprisingly, the majority of native-born spouses in these families were from the North Midland region, especially Ohio (37) and Pennsylvania (27), followed by the Upper South, with Missouri supplying the most (19). Such families were generally interspersed in the townships, but in three sparsely settled townships, families with a native-born spouse were in the majority—Emporia in Breckenridge County (where spouses shared a former residency in Indiana), Hartford in Madison County (where spouses shared a former residency in Iowa), and Avon in Coffey County.

Among the foreign-born spouses, Switzerland and France accounted for one-quarter each in families with children (20 and 21, respectively). Parts of Switzerland are German-speaking, so presumably this played a role in spousal selection. France was a predominantly Catholic country, so presumably religion was a factor there. Couples followed a similar pattern. In one couple, the foreign-born spouse was from Austria, and there were three unrelated families from Bohemia in the city of Leavenworth. Thus, although these countries were part of the debate about what constituted a united Germany, the impetus to intermarry was not strong. In fact, more Germans who married foreigners took spouses from English-speaking countries—England, Ireland, Canada, and Scotland—accounting for 22 percent of families with children and 27 percent of couples.

Through their jobs, single German settlers in particular encountered environments that encouraged assimilation. Although many were hired by fellow Germans (162; 5.5 percent), many were employed by native-born (188; 18 percent) and foreign-born (45; 4 percent). Most tellingly, a large number (258; 25 percent) lived or worked in a mixed environment—a hotel or boardinghouse with occupants from diverse backgrounds and families or establishments employing one or more non-German employees. The reverse situation, a German household housing or employing a native-born or foreign-born individual, was rare.

Among single Germans, one-third (351) either lived alone or lived with other unrelated individuals of the same sex.[83] More than 58 percent of these (206) lived alone. In the city of Leavenworth, where one-quarter of the 206 lived, they were craftsmen and businessmen. In rural areas they often farmed alone, but they were not necessarily isolated, as they might be interspersed with German families or reside on adjoining farms. The remaining German singles tended to room together in twos or threes or rarely more, living with other Germans from the same or different German states as well as with native- and foreign-born housemates. These arrangements were usually centered on a business, such as the three bakers from Prussia, Bavaria, and Württemberg,[84] the three shoemakers from Württemberg, Prussia, and Darmstadt-Hesse,[85] the two German and Polish merchants,[86] and the English, Swiss, and Prussian soda manufacturers.[87] It was extremely rare but not unheard of for a female to be on her own, such as a sixty-year-old schoolteacher and three women who worked as bakers and butchers.[88]

How did all this diversity play out at the ground level in Marshall County? What were the Rebs' and Lodholzes' neighbors and fellow pioneers like? In brief, there were different types of settlements and different responses to the pressure to assimilate. Each of the four townships—Blue Rapids, Marysville, Guittard, and Vermillion—had a unique pattern, although there were German-born residents from different German states in each.

In Marysville, there were small clusters based partly on German state of origin and partly on religion. The first German-born settlers came largely from Hanover and were often single males.[89] In many ways, Hanover, in northern Germany, had a different economic experience from Württemberg. The common fields were being enclosed to establish large agricultural estates, and the linen textile industry had declined, forcing many to work for others and creating a sort of "rural proletariat."[90] G. H. Hollenberg, who was born in Hanover, initially settled in Marshall County in 1854 on the Black Vermillion River, where he set up a general store at one of the fords used by the overlanders.[91] Meanwhile, the Brockmeyer family—a widow and her five children—came to Kansas from Hanover in 1856.[92] Hollenberg married one of the daughters and moved west to what he called Cottonwood Ranch in Washington County, just across the county line from Marysville Township.[93] Close by but still in Marysville, families from Württemberg and Baden settled in 1860. Around this nucleus the town of Hanover, Kansas, grew, with most of the settlers belonging to the Missouri Synod.[94]

Another cluster occurred in the township on Horseshoe Creek, a tributary of the Big Blue, where the two Friedrich brothers settled in 1858 and shared a dwelling with H. Lenker, all from Hanover.[95] They too were affiliated with the Missouri Synod.[96] Henry Hepperman and George Goelitz settled that same year at Raemer's Creek, followed in 1860 by brothers Fred and William Raemer, among others.[97] The Raemer brothers were from Prussia and followed the variant of Lutheranism established there.[98] This settlement grew into the town of Herkimer, whereas the Horseshoe Creek settlement became part of Herkimer Township. These nascent clusters survived beyond the frontier days and gave Marysville much of its character. At the time, however, despite the same-named town being the county seat, Marysville was not the most populous township in Marshall County. Of its 481 inhabitants, 87 were foreign-born, with half of them originating from Germany. Based on the occupations listed, the 1860 census indicates that the town of Marysville already had a brewery and a saloon.

Aside from the previously mentioned clusters, German-born residents from various German states were intermingled in Marysville. For example, living in proximity there were couples from Bremen and Baden, a just-married couple from Württemberg and Baden with a one-month-old child, three brothers from Württemberg, and a Polish-Prussian family.[99] An Irishman and a Prussian worked together as masons, and a day laborer from Baden worked with a large number of other day laborers at a mill.[100]

In Blue Rapids (population 640), there were forty-nine foreign-born, half of them German. They lived next to or not far from one another, interspersed with Belgians and native-born. They included neighboring families originally from Bremen, Bavaria, and Holstein, as well as a single farm laborer and a farmer from Württemberg and Baden, respectively, and three farm laborers from Bavaria, Prussia, and Saxony sharing a residence.[101] This clustering would not survive the Civil War, and there is no evidence that any of the Blue Rapids German-born were relatives. The township had a particularly large number of native-born families whose individual members had their own farms, including the Reedys, Abbotts, and Ships, and formed their own clusters.

With a population of 880, Vermillion Township, where Heinrich lived, was the county's most populous. Sixty-four residents (7 percent) were foreign-born. At twenty-seven individuals, the Irish represented the largest group. The fifteen German-born accounted for less than a quarter of the foreign-born and less than 2 percent of the entire township. Except for the families of two Prussian brothers, none of the Germans lived close to one another; they were scattered among the native-born. In those early years, Heinrich's neighbors included Ebenezer Mills (of English ancestry), Eli Puntney (who could trace his roots back to the Revolutionary War), Jacob Parthener (whose great-grandfather emigrated from Germany in 1744), and settlers such as Dan Auld, who followed A. G. Barrett from Ohio to Kansas.[102]

Guittard Township, where the Lodholzes lived, was the most sparsely populated of the four townships (280). One-quarter of the residents were foreign-born. The Irish were the largest ethnic group, with thirty-two, and the nineteen Germans tended to be scattered. The largest cluster of Germans was composed of Gottfried and Georg, with George Watts from Baden on one side of their properties (and John O'Neal from Ireland on the other).[103]

Clearly, this was not a strictly egalitarian society. Gradations of haves and have-nots are apparent from the census's inclusion of real and personal property values.[104] There were farmers whose real and personal property values exceeded those of their neighbors, farmers with more modest real and personal property values (such as the Lodholzes and Heinrich), farmers with real property but no personal property listed, farmers with no real property but personal property listed, individuals identified as farmers with no real or personal property listed, farm laborers regularly employed on a farm, and day laborers. The farmers with no real property values listed were probably tenants.[105]

In Vermillion Township in 1860, there were very few people who were not tilling the soil—a physician, a millwright (Barrett), a Methodist minister, two schoolteachers, four merchants and their clerks, and the county clerk. There were 141 farmers, thirty-five farm laborers who were not the sons of farmers (including two German-born), fifteen day laborers, five female domestics not part of their own family's household, and three not specified. Similarly, in Guittard Township there was one clerk, one schoolteacher, a Pony Express rider and two stagecoach drivers (obviously temporary residents), fifty farmers, eight farm laborers not the sons of farmers, five day laborers, and two unspecified.

Like their neighbors who also came to Kansas to farm, the Lodholzes' immediate challenges were starting a farm from scratch and learning new ways to satisfy their everyday needs, including getting enough food to eat. One of Gottfried's first tasks was to build his own log cabin.[106] A garden would have been prepared near the cabin and planted with the seeds brought from St. Louis—Georg's requested beans, turnips, potatoes, and, most importantly, corn. The corn would have been planted not in the garden but on a very small portion of their land.[107]

They were living amidst the tallgrass prairie, home to some five hundred species of plants, mainly grasses, with different maturation times and heights, many growing from six to almost ten feet tall. Wildflowers added color and gaiety. Milkweed, with its fragrant mop of mauve flower heads, attracted the orange-splashed monarch butterfly. Liatris, commonly known as blazing star, stood erect with its startlingly bright fringes of magenta petals. The deep brown center of the aptly named coneflower protruded from a circle of bright yellow petals. The Maximilian sunflower (smaller than the large-disked, single-bloom sunflower) paraded myriad flowers up and down its tall stalk. It was named after a German prince who explored the Great Plains in the 1830s and first brought the species to the attention of Europeans.[108]

The tallgrass prairie was home to birds and animals the Lodholzes had never seen before—bald eagle, red-tailed hawk, scissor-tailed flycatcher, black-capped chickadee, white-tailed deer, coyote, bobcat, and, of course, buffalo. By the time of the Lodholzes' arrival, however, the buffalo had already migrated farther west, as their habitat was lost to cultivation and they were hunted by settlers for both meat and sport.[109]

The tallgrass prairie must have seemed beautiful but alien to a family from the mountainous, forested region of Württemberg. In the mornings the family could see the sun rise as a blinding yellow sphere, and in the evenings they could watch it sink below the horizon, a burnt orange ball amid a pale

Maximilian sunflowers grow among the grasses of the tallgrass prairie at the Dyck Arboretum of the Plains in Hesston, Kansas. (Courtesy Dyck Arboretum of the Plains)

purple and crimson haze. Even the sun would have looked small against the vastness of the prairie.

On a clear night the huge dome of the sky would be filled with brilliant starlight, and when there was a full moon, its pale reflection could be seen on the grasses. But when the sky was overcast, a deep darkness would engulf the small cabins, and the shrill, frenzied howls of coyotes fighting over their prey and the deep, eerily hollow cries of wolves must have fueled the family's feeling of isolation.[110] The Lodholzes were far from their nearest neighbors.[111]

The tallgrass prairie was not just beautiful; it was hard. It was never meant to be farmed. It was a unique ecosystem designed to survive the extreme weather of the midcontinental climate zone, with cold winters and blistering hot summers. An anonymous writer described it as follows: "Pristine Kansas prairie isn't one kind of grass, or kind of flower. It's hundreds. Meadow rose and wavy-leafed thistle. Bluestem [grass] and sunflower. Leadplant and milkweed. The variety does more than look pretty. It insures against biological calamity. In hot weather, some species wilt—others

2775 Breaking Team near Milbank, S. D. in 1878

This 1878 postcard from South Dakota shows an unusual "breaking team" that combined oxen and horses to break the sod. (In the author's possession)

flourish. When insects and disease strike, some suffer—others thrive. Here's how the prairie bears adversity: diversity."[112]

The tenacious roots of the prairie grasses reached deep underground, searching for water and nourishment. In the winter these grasses withered and died, eventually covering the ground with thatch. Prairie fires, caused by lightning strikes or human carelessness, swept over the plains, ridding it of the thatch and allowing new growth to thrive. Today the tallgrass prairie has almost disappeared. The National Park Service and environmental groups are trying to conserve what remains and to reestablish prairies on small sections of land. What the Lodholzes first saw has now been largely lost through the "breaking of the sod"—the phrase itself indicates the settlers' attitude toward the prairie. It was something wild that needed to be tamed, like breaking a horse, in sharp contrast to the attitude of the Native Americans who inhabited the prairie.

No ordinary wooden plow—the type the Lodholzes were familiar with from Ebhausen—could penetrate the densely matted roots of the grasses.[113] The brothers had to use a breaking plow, a type of steel moldboard plow.[114] It had a coulter in front, a knife-like projection that cut the sod ahead of the plowshare. The plowshare then dug under the sod, and the curved moldboard lifted the sod and turned it over to expose about three inches of the nutrient-rich soil underneath and allow the exposed roots to wither.

Life in Kansas and Connecticut, 1859–61

The plows were walk-behind types with wooden handles. Georg was the brother with the most experience controlling the oxen, so he probably did most of the plowing at first, perhaps another brother helping to drive the beasts. Georg had to bear down hard to keep the plow digging several inches deep as he steered the oxen on a relatively straight path, calling out "gee" and "haw" to direct them right or left.[115] The team plowed for about half a mile and then turned and plowed another furrow next to the first one.[116] In hot weather Georg had to stop frequently to rest the oxen. Once the plowing was done, the brothers dug out any exposed stones and used a stoneboat—a wide wooden sledge—to haul them away. Plowing ten acres was considered enough to supply food for a family of five.[117] The plowed and planted area also had to be protected from their own livestock and strays from neighbors by erecting fences—stakes hewed from trees, driven into the ground, and attached by nailed slats.[118]

The brothers did all the sowing and harvesting by hand. The first year, like many new settlers, they simply dug holes in the furrows with an ax or hatchet, dropped the seeds in, and pushed the soil back with their heels.[119] Those settlers who had no plows had to hoe the soil and plant "sod corn."[120] At harvest time, Gottfried and Georg cut the stalks and bunched them into shocks on the field. Once they were dried, the ears of corn were picked off and shucked, and the kernels were removed—all by hand, using the barest of tools. Mechanization was in the future, and even then, only for those who could afford it.

In the coming years, as Gottfried and Georg broke more sod, they would add wheat and oats as cereal crops. For this, they needed one more step in their soil preparation process to pulverize the broken sod with a harrow—a metal grid three to five feet wide with long, spiked teeth facing downward on horizontal bars. Dragging the harrow was less strenuous than breaking the sod, so horses, which were faster than oxen, could be used.

The harvesting of wheat in Kansas was much the same as it was in Ebhausen. The wheat was cut with a cradle, a modified scythe with a bar extending out and containing four or five long, pointed "fingers" that kept the stalks of grain aligned in the same direction when cut. With a scythe alone, the cut stalks tumbled every which way, which made gathering them into bundles more time-consuming. Once the stalks were sufficiently dry, the brothers laid them on some sort of platform or covering on the ground and threshed them with flails. Flails consisted of two pieces of wood, one longer than the other, connected by a leather strap or chain. The larger end was used as a handle to beat the wheat with the smaller end. The flail knocked the seed heads and their coverings off the stalks, leaving small bits of debris and the denuded stalks, now properly called straw. Some settlers used oxen to trample the wheat rather than flails.[121] The straw was raked off to be used as bedding for animals, and the remaining seed heads and chaff were winnowed—tossed with a pitchfork on a windy day so the lighter chaff blew away, leaving the heavier seed heads.

Wheat and corn had to be taken to a gristmill, such as the one at Barrett, to be made into flour and meal (a coarser consistency than flour). One early pioneer in Marshall County recalled that her husband took their wheat crop to a mill in Table Rock, Nebraska, a four- or five-day trip, while she stayed home alone to do the chores.[122] Traditionally, farmers paid for milling with a portion of the milled grain. In the cash-starved Kansas Territory, there is every reason to believe this was often the case. Benjamin McElroy walked barefoot beside his team of oxen and wagon full of wheat to sell some in Atchison and have the remainder ground into flour. He said, "I didn't mind the walk for I was marketing wheat of my own raising, harvested with a cradle and threshed with a flail."[123] Because there was little money in the local market, farmers like McElroy who had enough of a crop to sell had to haul it elsewhere. The army provided a market for grain at Fort Kearny, some two hundred miles west of Marysville, which was a little over twelve miles from the Lodholzes' farm. Wheat, which sold for 11 cents a bushel in Marysville, brought $1 a bushel at Fort Kearny.[124]

The brothers would have needed to erect a corncrib and a structure to shelter their oxen and horses, the latter necessary to visit neighbors and pick up small amounts of supplies and mail. The animals feasted on prairie grasses and grasses growing near the stream during the summer. Gottfried and Georg had to cut and dry grasses to provide fodder and bedding for the animals during the winter.

Their privy was a crude affair—a hole dug in the ground with two logs across it. Later, it might have been replaced by a raised plank with a hole in it. Chamber pots served during the night and in inclement weather. Toilet paper consisted of leaves, dried corn husks, and corncobs.

The Lodholz brothers had their work cut out for them, but the women made considerable contributions to the family's welfare as well. Probably thanks to Georg's connections in Otoe City, Anna Regina secured a housekeeping job at the Otoe Mission, some distance from the Lodholz land, to earn money for the family. She knew no one there and received her mail in care of Mr. Guthrie, Indian missionary. The prairie was in fact aswarm with missionaries of different faiths competing for souls. Guthrie was probably a

Presbyterian.[125] Anna Regina did not mention having any contact with the Native Americans, but if she did, it would have been friendly. The Otoes lived peaceably with whites and even fought with Company E, Thirteenth Kansas Infantry, during the Civil War.[126]

In a pencil-written letter (most likely a draft of the one she actually sent), Anna Regina described her life to eleven girlfriends back in Ebhausen. Postage to Europe was expensive and money was tight, so she wrote to them as a group, expecting them to pass it around. Though well treated, she was terribly lonely—a stranger in a strange land. She missed the camaraderie of her many friends who shared her religious faith. Her poor command of English probably contributed to her isolation. To the end of her days, she preferred speaking German.

> Beloved sisters in Lord,
>
> I want to write to you, my heart is burning with love, in my mind I am with you, how many hours have we spent with the Holy One and gave each other courage. I wish I could be there when you have your words of God on Wednesdays and Sunday nights. Here I am all alone, there is nobody of my faith. Everyone should love what they like, but I love Jesus.
>
> Otherwise I am well and well treated. I am not working on the fields, but do housework: cooking, baking, washing, ironing, sewing. I hope that we will see each other in Heaven where there are no partings and lovely life is for eternity. To that we shall lift our head and eye.
>
> I am sending you 2 sayings from the choir book. And send you many thousand Greetings.
>
> Your sister in Faith
>
> Anna Regina Lodholz
>
> Please be so good and write how you are.[127]

Before she left Ebhausen, one of Anna Regina's younger friends had called her "a fire woman."[128] To endure the doubly hard separation from friends and family, she had to be.

Gottfried's wife Christina had to shoulder major responsibilities as well.[129] With Anna Regina living elsewhere for the time being, all the housekeeping chores fell to her. She had to keep close watch over her two young daughters, ages four and five, lest they get too close to the fire, lost in the grasses, hurt by one of the animals, or encounter a rattlesnake. Anna Maria, then fifty-six and suffering from a skin rash, likely helped look after the children when she was feeling up to it. Christina's chores included doing the laundry, which was washed in a tub with a corrugated metal washboard, using soft soap Christina made by boiling animal fat with lye extracted from the fireplace ashes. She also mended and patched clothes, weeded the garden, and did whatever she could to make the small, dim cabin more cheerful. Once they had been read, newspapers were probably used to cover the walls. It seems likely that Gottfried and Georg eventually cut out windows to let more light in, but for protection from the elements, the windows would have been covered by greased paper, hindering their usefulness. The brothers likely took logs to a sawmill or stripped logs themselves with an adze to make long, thin planks for flooring.

Perhaps Christina's most important task was cooking over a hot open fire with only basic cooking utensils and many unfamiliar ingredients. The family undoubtedly brought food supplies with them from Atchison, the closest large city, and one of the brothers made the ten- to fifteen-day journey to the Missouri River town once or twice a year.[130] Some supplies would have been available in nearby Marysville, and neighbors might offer items for sale or barter. Many settlers made extra money by opening small stores in their cabins, such as Moses Bennett, who operated a store and a post office on Coon Creek.[131] At one point, Friedrich even suggested that the family set up their own store to earn money.[132] Although there is no mention of bartering with Native Americans in the Lodholz letters, some settlers did. One new arrival obtained cabbage and potatoes from the Otoe tribe.[133]

Cornbread, which the Lodholzes had never eaten before, was now a staple. At first they had to buy cornmeal, but later they had their own supply. The corn had to be shelled by hand and the kernels taken to a gristmill and ground into meal. Some settlers ground corn by hand by punching holes in the bottom of a pail to make a grater. They rubbed the dried ears across the rough surface, releasing and pulverizing the kernels and resulting in a very coarse meal.[134] Christina had no flour or sugar, so her cornbread was actually cornpone. Dense and pancake-like, it was made from a batter of cornmeal, hot water, and salt and fried in animal fat (obtained from the game the brothers shot) in a cast-iron pot over a fire in the fireplace. With her poor teeth, Anna Maria would have found it difficult to eat. Once the settlers had more money, they improved on this recipe and added ingredients to make the fluffier and sweeter cornbread we know today. The family ate their cornpone with soup (perhaps turnip soup) or stews made from the plentiful wild turkeys, rabbits, and prairie chickens, also cooked in a cast-iron kettle hung over the fire. Cooking with cast iron provided female settlers who were menstruating with the iron they needed. Also included in the family's rather monotonous diet was the familiar potato, grown in Ebhausen. In addition, they may have made hominy from dried corn kernels slaked in lye.[135]

To supplement their diet, the family took advantage of the wild nuts and fruits around them. Taking her children with her, Christina collected black walnuts and hazelnuts in the forest, as well as wild plums and wild grapes, preserving some in five-gallon stone jars to use in the cold months.[136]

Coffee was a drink the Lodholzes may have heard of even in Württemberg, where a financier had bought the exclusive privilege of establishing coffeehouses, although it is unlikely there was one in Ebhausen.[137] Coffee was introduced in the United States by Captain John Smith, and the American public, being opposed to the tea-drinking British, particularly after the War of 1812, took up coffee with a vengeance.[138] The Lodholzes had drunk coffee in Terryville. It was one of the staples the westward-heading settlers included in their heavy loads. It would have been available in the towns along the Missouri River, including Atchison, but most settlers did not purchase actual coffee. Initially, at least, the "coffee" they drank was probably made from pulverized, parched corn boiled in water.[139] Once they were able to afford real coffee, they bought whole green beans, which had to be roasted in a skillet and then ground by hand in a coffee mill or, absent a mill, pounded in a bag with a heavy implement. The coarse grounds were added to water and heated, and people drank the brew with the grounds still in the liquid. Heating the water may have saved their lives, as it helped kill harmful bacteria.

At first, the family got their water from the creek on their property, filling large wooden barrels and dragging them home on a stoneboat pulled by their oxen. Set outside the cabin, the barrels were covered with burlap or a washtub to protect the water from dirt blown by the often fierce wind and from animals.[140] But being in eastern Kansas in the midst of a river valley, the men found water not far beneath the surface, and eventually the family had a well lined with stones and operated by a windlass and pulley to lower and raise the bucket.

Once the family bought a "milch" cow and chickens, Christina acquired more chores—milking the cow, churning butter, and collecting eggs. The butter-making process provides a good idea of the amount of work performed by female pioneers. After milking the cow, Christina strained the milk to remove any foreign matter and set the pail in the root cellar, built partially underground to provide a cool place to store provisions for long-term use. Once the cream rose to the top, she skimmed it off and placed it in a churn. The "skimmed milk" left behind spoiled easily, so Christina used it right away to feed the animals, particularly the pigs. It was unpasteurized and hence a possible source of diseases, including tuberculosis. She churned the cream with a wooden paddle until it turned into whipped cream and finally butter. The constant stirring had to be exhausting, and her hands were already tired and red from washing clothes. Not all the cream turned into butter. The heavier butter formed a ring around the walls of the churn, leaving the lighter buttermilk in the middle. Christina had to remove all traces of the buttermilk, or else the butter would spoil. She poured off the buttermilk and saved it to use for baking and perhaps drinking; then she thoroughly washed and salted the butter to preserve it in a crock. Selling or trading extra butter and eggs was an important way for women to help their families financially.

Christina might have been called on to help in the field: plowing, removing stones, casting seeds from a gunny sack hung over her shoulders, and harvesting. As a German woman, she had likely done this type of work back in Württemberg. Recall that Anna Regina expected to have to work in the fields and was relieved that she did not. On the Kansas prairie, females regularly performed typically male tasks.[141] It is little wonder that women in the West obtained the right to vote before their sisters in the East.

During most of 1859, however, Christina was carrying an even heavier burden—literally. She was pregnant with her and Gottfried's third child. The oppressive summer heat and the anxiety about the harvest must have weighed on her, as did all her household tasks. This was undoubtedly why Anna Regina returned in the fall from the Otoe Mission, to help out at home. She and Anna Maria moved in with Georg, so Anna Regina took care of her mother and did the housekeeping chores for her brother. The family's determination to stick together and support one another in hard times was a key factor in their survival on the plains.

This pooling of labor and resources was a basic feature of the family farm for native-born as well as German-born. As Jon Gjerde argues, however, over the course of the nineteenth century, there was a shift in what he calls the "family morality" of native-born Americans, with more of an emphasis on the individual rights of family members, particularly children; in contrast, the German-born maintained a more conservative hierarchical family structure that placed wives and children in a strictly subservient role vis-à-vis the male patriarch.[142] He and other scholars, particularly Linda Schelbitski Pickle, have paid particular attention to the self-effacement of German-speaking women in a patriarchal household, where the husband might assume he had the right to abuse his wife, as he legally did in Europe. Pickle characterizes women's work in the fields in addition to their housekeeping chores as "exploitation."[143] This was a major divide between German- and native-born women.[144] By the mid-nineteenth century, the latter were being relieved of hard labor outside the home.[145] At a time when companionate marriage was taking hold among the native-born, the lack of displays of affection in German-born households created another divide.[146] In these households, sons and daughters were expected to work on the family farm in addition to working for others—daughters as domestics and sons as laborers—with their earnings going to expand the family's landholdings.[147] German-born farmers were buying native-born holdings so that their children—or at least their sons—could have their own farms next to the family homestead.[148] It has been argued that the native-born were only too happy to sell out at a profit and move on. For them, land was a commodity whose sale could fund new ventures, not a patrimony.[149]

As scholars have pointed out, however, such typologies should not obscure the many variations among individual families.[150] They serve here as a point of reference for later descriptions of the behavior and actions of Lodholz and Reb family members, who in most ways did not fit the mold. We have already seen several major differences. Although the society in Ebhausen was highly patriarchal, there was no actual patriarch of the Lodholz family once they immigrated to the United States. As the eldest male, Gottfried played an assertive role, and although the brothers cooperated, they also acted on their own, such as Friedrich's decision to return to Terryville and their choice of different political parties (discussed later). Likewise, the women of the family had comparatively greater freedom to make their own choices. In the "corporate" German family described in the previous paragraph, education was not highly valued, particularly for girls.[151] Yet both Anna Maria and Anna Regina had been educated and could read and write German. Gottfried would later be a strong supporter of public education.[152] Both he and Anna Regina sent their children to the local public schools, and Anna even provided housing for her children's schoolteacher.[153]

In the upper Midwest and in the Norwegian Lutheran and German Catholic communities Gjerde studied, there was a major difference in the demands placed on German and native-born women and children. On the Kansas frontier, this was not necessarily the case, at least not in 1860. The sons and daughters of many native-born settlers were still tied to their families' welfare and survival. In Vermillion Township, among the thirty-six families in which the fathers were born in a wide variety of American states, as well as Ireland and England, fourteen of their teenage daughters worked as domestics, and fifty-one of their teenage sons worked as farm laborers or day laborers. These gendered roles imply a distinction between indoor labor and outdoor labor.[154] We know that Anna Regina, working in a native-born household, was not required to work in the fields. To fully explore this question, however, we would need sources describing the duties of female domestics in native-born and German-born households, particularly whether German-born domestics in German-born households were expected to work in the fields. Many of these teenage domestics and farm laborers in Vermillion Township were living with their families on the family farm, but the census does not tell us whether they were working on the family farm or employed elsewhere. The fact that the census listed these children's occupations indicates their families' attitude about their role in supporting the household. A similar situation existed in Guittard Township.

In addition, Vermillion had two native-born widows who were farming. Forty-three-year-old Eliza Waller from Virginia had four male children aged eleven to twenty-two who presumably helped her on the farm (although the census did not list them as farm laborers).[155] Forty-four-year-old Emily Lathrop from New York had a twelve-year-old son. Presumably she had to work the land herself, as it is doubtful she had the money to hire laborers. The value of her farm and personal property was far below that of her neighbors, which might indicate she had less land or that the land she did have was not improved.[156]

Unlike many of their fellow settlers who left in failure, the Lodholz family was realistic and understood that it would take time to make a go of farming. They knew that, until then, they would need other sources of income—hence Anna Regina's housekeeping job. In November 1858, having had a taste of farmwork on the prairie, Friedrich returned to Terryville, in part to earn money to send back to Kansas. As a consequence, he did not maintain a claim to the land Georg had picked out for him. This decision was not altruistic. Friedrich missed the creature comforts the prairie could not provide. Hawgood was right in his case. It was not uncommon for relatives in the East to send money and provisions to loved ones in Kansas, but among all the biographies consulted for this work, there was no other example of a family member deliberately returning to the East to help support relatives in the West.

Georg accompanied Friedrich as far as Leavenworth, south of Atchison on the Missouri River. It was near the site of a military fort and a haven for slaves escaping from their masters in Missouri. Unlike Georg, Friedrich was appalled by conditions on the prairie. Once he arrived in Terryville he wrote to his family: "I would wish that you'll be able to afford better nourishment [he hated cornbread] and clothes and living space than what you have now because it hurts my heart when I look into your living space and see the need and suffering."[157] Sad as he was to leave his family, he was obviously glad to be back in Connecticut.

At Leavenworth, Friedrich boarded the steamer *Rowina* on November 18, headed for St. Louis. In his first letter from Terryville, he told the family how "low" he had felt upon leaving them, but fortuitously he met a fellow German on board headed for Cincinnati. The trip to St. Louis took six long days. Because of ice on the river, which was particularly dangerous at night, the steamer stopped over each evening.[158] Friedrich may or may not have slept in a cabin. As one traveler with a peevish sense of humor wrote about a similar trip in 1859: "A Missouri River boat is never full as long as there is room to store a man in hold, or cabin, or on deck." He noted that 150 cots, "about as big as door-mats and a trifle thicker," were available to spread on the main cabin floor; they were covered with quilts "about three feet wide and five feet long" and a pillow that could easily be carried off in one's pocket.[159] Friedrich, however, made no complaints about his trip.

Once in St. Louis, at a hostel catering to a German-speaking clientele, Friedrich met another fellow traveler heading to Connecticut. They booked second-class railroad tickets to Buffalo. Then an event occurred that would spook Friedrich for the rest of his life: "We were supposed to travel at 3 PM but were prevented. Our suitcases were already fetched at 2 PM but we had to stay back. But it must have been God's will because the train with our luggage had an accident that night. My suitcase was unharmed."[160] Friedrich later told his family: "I have some resentment toward train travel, because last time it was threatening to me."[161] When he and his traveling companion finally boarded their train, they had a two-day trip ahead of them to Buffalo. Friedrich continued by train to Albany, then to Springfield, Massachusetts, and finally arrived in Terryville by the end of November.

One wonders what Anna Maria, now fifty-six, made of her new life. She had faced hardship in Ebhausen and now faced hardship in America. She had developed a bothersome, persistent rash and was plagued by occasional fevers due to malaria, spread by the mosquitoes that swarmed in the nearby creek. Back in Terryville, Friedrich was concerned about her: "But what causes me worry and care is the illness of dear sweet mother, I would like to hope that dear mother can remain with you another few years yet so that I could speak to her once again."[162]

Tintype of one of the Lodholz brothers, most likely Friedrich, dressed in an outfit from Ebhausen. In Connecticut, Friedrich would have had more opportunities than his brothers in Kansas to engage a photographer, as well as more motivation to send a likeness of himself to his distant family. Interestingly, the subject's visage is close to the description of Josef in the *Wander-Buch*. Tintypes first appeared in the 1850s, but given the subject's relatively young age at the time, it was most likely taken after the Civil War, when tintypes were particularly popular. (In the family's possession)

Friedrich returned to Terryville much thinner than when he had left there.[163] He simply had not been consuming enough calories on the prairie to match his physical exertions. He almost immediately placed himself on a "self-care" regimen to regain his health, which principally involved eating well: "My meals are: early mornings coffee and roasted potatoes, at noon bread and cheese and some fried ham, evenings tea, bread, plum cake and in addition I keep apples around and anything else I enjoy eating, as well as beverages and I am feeling very well."[164] He was enjoying good German fare, while his relatives in Kansas were surviving on strange American food. Friedrich was not alone in his fixation on food; German immigrants' letters to Germany often emphasized the abundance of food in the United States and the practice of eating three good meals a day.[165]

In addition to being thinner, Friedrich suffered from the same bothersome skin rash as Anna Maria. His home remedy was rather drastic: "Since I left you I have taken 20 laxative pills. . . . Dear mother I think if you took those pills you'd get rid of your rash too."[166] Friedrich was overly optimistic about his treatment. He eventually saw a doctor, but surreptitiously, as he found the rash embarrassing.[167] The doctor prescribed an ointment, which Friedrich offered to share with his mother.[168]

In his efforts to find work, Friedrich was bitterly disappointed. He wrote:

> My stay in Terryville will be a source of discontent to me for many years to come. First off, I lost my good position [at the Eagle Lock factory] by going to Kansas, and I have no hope of resuming it here. Further, the pay decreased significantly through the hard times [the financial panic], and now the workers in both factories find themselves under second-rate bosses. Once a man leaves his job, then it's hard to get ahead again.[169]

He found some kind of job with a man named John Peers, but the work petered out. By January 1859, he was working at the local foundry: "Work is very hard in the foundry. Had I known that, I would have stayed in St. Louis. But I have to overcome it and hope for better times."[170] This job was short-lived, and he wrote to his family at the end of February: "I was in bad shape last month, no prospect for making any money." However, things were looking up, as he was back in the employ of the Eagle Lock Company, operating one of the presses.[171] By early September, he had been promoted to the most prestigious location—the upper factory—and bragged to his family: "Until a short time ago I was the only German who received work so quickly in the upper shop."[172] This promotion was most likely based on his mastery of English. However, his stress on being the only German is indicative of ethnic tensions and the feeling of being an outsider amid Americans. There was general animosity at the factory toward the Irish, and with the steam machines now running twenty-four hours a day, the shifts were split by ethnicity to avoid conflict: "During the day Americans and Germans work, and overnight the Irish work in the polishing room."[173] The tension was partly religious, as the Irish were Catholic and the Americans and Germans were generally Protestant, although of differing denominations. Friedrich reported that an "Irish church" was in the offing.[174] There were Catholic Germans, but apparently none in Terryville at the time.

Friedrich was still strongly religious, and sometimes he began or ended his letters with a full page of mission songs. He mentioned no particular sect but let the family know that he attended occasional German church services and Sunday school (which was not just for children) afterward.[175] This probably took place in a private house or some other meeting place. The *History of the Town of Plymouth* makes no mention of a Lutheran or German church, only a Congregationalist, Episcopalian, and Catholic church and an aborted Adventist attempt at establishing a congregation.[176]

Initially, Friedrich boarded with August Martins (full name Augustus Van Martensen), a friend who also worked at the lock company.[177] Martins had been a soldier in Europe and was a sometime fencing teacher in Terryville.[178] This living arrangement was not ideal, however. Martins, who was married to Christina's sister (the widow of the first German to reside in Terryville), owed Gottfried money, and he wanted to charge Friedrich's board against that debt, but Friedrich did not want to "'eat off debt.'"[179]

Taking in borders was a common way for those with sufficient space to earn extra income. As evidenced by his loan from Gottfried, Martins needed money. His wife had been ill during her pregnancy, and he had stayed home from work to take care of her.[180] Martins' house had cost $400, but he could only afford to pay the interest on the loan, nothing on the principal.[181] He was angry when Friedrich moved out, but as Friedrich told Gottfried, "I couldn't stand it there."[182]

Soon after leaving Martins, Friedrich became a boarder in the upper room of another friend, Armbruster, where he was much happier. Armbruster had told Friedrich that "he would go straight away to Kansas if he had enough money to go there," but the impetus to move to Kansas among Terryville's German population had cooled considerably.[183] Friedrich found that nobody wanted to go west, and many were in fact returning.[184] But at the time, he remained committed to going back to Kansas and making his home there. "My love for my very dear blood relations: mother, brother, sister and friends will soon return to me in my home in the far west. . . . I only procure the most essential articles in my little domestic life, so that if I return home I can take everything with me."[185] As a memento, he sent a lock of his hair, a common practice at the time to show one's love and intimacy. Though surrounded by friends in Terryville, Friedrich missed his family very much: "Often I am homesick for you."[186]

Despite missing his family, Friedrich told them, "I shall stay here until you can make money which is necessary for you."[187] With his job prospects much improved, he was able to start sending small amounts of money to his family in Kansas. "I worry about you, that you have such a rough diet, which contributes much to the fever. But if I stay healthy you should cook with more white flour by next fall."[188] He added in another letter, "Corn meal is no fit food for people."[189] And Friedrich was as good as his word. By September, when he was working in the lock company's upper shop, he wrote, "Now so that you can purchase white flour as well as sugar and

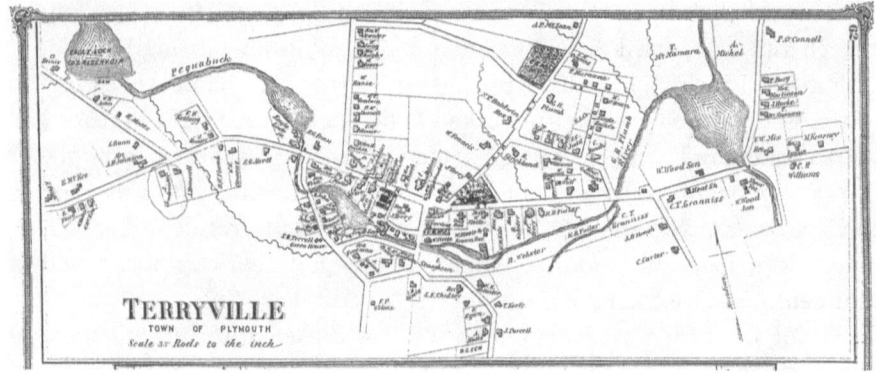

Map of Terryville in 1874 showing Armbruster's house, where Friedrich boarded. It is circled on the left, the last of the four houses in that row. (From a series of maps of Litchfield County, Connecticut, published in 1874 by F. W. Beers & Company)

coffee and clothes, I'm sending to you next week on the 10th of this month about $33 dollars by mail to Marysville under the name George Lodholz, so be sure to visit that post office by the end of September."[190] More money would follow.

At a time when doctors were few and far between, self-medicating was common. Friedrich sent medicines he hoped would relieve some of his family members' pains and illnesses.

> Last Tuesday I sent a box off to you with medicine. It contains Hoffmann's drops, peppermint drops, blood purifying bitters, which are supposed to be a great help against cold fever: mornings and evenings you take a teaspoonful, which cleans your blood, protecting you from noxious air. This salve is very good for healing wounds. . . . Please write to me and let me know if you received the package and how it helps. If you think it useful, then I will soon send something again, even if it's only useful to a small extent, I won't waste a thought on the expense.[191]

Beyond such monetary and medicinal support, Friedrich also played the important role of purveyor of information. He was the recipient and writer of infrequent letters to Ebhausen, which he shared with the family in Kansas and relayed their responses, if any. Knowing they were strapped for cash, he even sent them stamps so they could write back to him.[192] In one such forwarded letter, Anna Maria learned of the death of her sister Christina Magdalena in November 1858, which no doubt caused her sorrow.[193]

Friedrich wrote to the family about purely local goings-on, as well as larger events that might impact their lives. He shared with Anna Regina the news that Mrs. Gaylord, for whom she had done housekeeping in Terryville, had died of consumption (tuberculosis), a common disease at the time, irrespective of social standing. Mr. Gaylord now employed an Irish maid.[194]

Friedrich was fascinated by news of the wider world and an avid reader of newspapers, which he often sent on to Kansas. There were many German-language papers to choose from. Even the popular *Leslie's Illustrated Newspaper* put out a German edition. Friedrich reported that a railroad had been completed to St. Joseph, Missouri, which would be of "enormous value for us, as the Vermillion is a main passage point for travelers from St. Joseph."[195] He thought the Mormon war would speed up the building of railroads west, which would connect the Great Plains to markets in the East and overseas. Friedrich was right about the eventual extension of the railroad to California, but that was several years away. "Congress is considering building [a] railroad to California and we will know soon if it goes by our land or not. The war with the Mormons last year and the troops in Oregon cost the U.S.A. 10,100,000 (millions) dollars. Troops are expensive to keep so far away, that's why they'll build a railroad."[196]

The Mormon war pitted Mormon settlers in Utah against US troops sent by President James Buchanan on the Utah Expedition. Having experienced violent confrontations with Protestant settlers in Missouri and Illinois during which their founder, Joseph Smith Jr., was killed, the Mormons had moved west to Utah under the leadership of Brigham Young. Fearing further violence, they armed themselves and skirmished with the US troops, but fortunately, there were no casualties. However, the attack by a local Mormon militia on an migrant wagon train crossing southern Utah in September 1857, a few months after the troops' arrival, resulted in the Mountain Meadows massacre in which more than one hundred migrants were killed. In the end, a peace was negotiated; all but the perpetrators of the Mountain Meadows massacre were pardoned, and the territorial government was placed in non-Mormon hands.[197]

Friedrich also shared the news that gold fever was heating up in the East. This would eventually sweep up members of the Lodholz family. He wrote, "I think that coming spring many people will go to the Gold mines at Cherry Cr[eek], in Kansas, as is reported in the papers. Once you'll receive my paper every week you'll know what happens in the world. Many thousands will pass by your place on their way to the Goldmines which are about 400 miles west of you."[198]

Gold was discovered in an area close to Pike's Peak, at the eastern edge of the Rocky Mountains and, for the time being, still part of the Kansas Territory. Despite attempts to keep the find at Cherry Creek secret, word got out. Newspapers quickly picked up the story, and none other than *New York Tribune* editor Horace Greeley (famous for the line "Go West, young man, go West") visited one of the finds and reported in the *Rocky Mountain News* that he had seen the gold himself.[199] The rush was on. In the end, though not as lucrative as the California fields, the Pike's Peak gold rush drew thousands of would-be prospectors to the area, including some three hundred German-born, 83 percent of whom were single.[200]

In addition to providing his family with money and timely news, Friedrich actively worked to help them gain title to the land they had preempted but did not yet own. As mentioned in chapter 2, the Lodholzes took advantage of the preemption laws, which allowed them to settle on the land, await the official survey of the area, and then file a written claim within three months of the survey.[201] (Georg had already filed preemption claims, but the boundaries undoubtedly changed once the surveyors had completed their work.) Now they had to come up with a payment of $1.25 per acre; otherwise, the land would be sold at a public auction, which the federal government had scheduled for July 1859.[202] In January Friedrich told his family: "It is good that we went to Kansas although we had so many experiences last year. But we do have good land of our own and I will do all I can so that by next July it will be our own."[203]

This was not a simple task or a foregone conclusion. The Lodholzes' position, like that of many other settlers in the Kansas Territory, was precarious. If they could not come up with the money they needed, their land and any improvements on it would be sold at auction to the highest bidder, which probably would not be them, for two reasons. First, the demand for land as an investment, by both the wealthy and less well-off, was high and fueled speculation. Newspapers in the Kansas Territory—and there were many of them, albeit short-lived—were full of ads from law firms, banks, land agencies, railroad companies (to which Congress had given land grants to defray the cost of running new tracks west), and individuals selling, renting, and otherwise dealing in land. One advertiser, S. N. Wood, guaranteed a return of 50 to 100 percent on an initial investment.[204] The 1860 federal census lists individuals in Marshall County's major cities whose sole occupation was "speculator" or "land dealer"; there were six in Atchison,[205] one in Leavenworth,[206] one in Lecompton,[207] and one German-born in Lawrence.[208] The Lodholzes had no plans to engage in land speculation, but determining how many German-born actually did so would involve a detailed examination of land values and township plats.[209]

Smaller investors might buy a piece of property, make some improvements, and then sell out and move on to the next plot of land.[210] Or they might stay and sell just a portion of the land.[211] Many bought land from the federal government in anticipation of holding on to it until they could make a profit on the sale.[212] The 1860 census lists many "unoccupied" plots in the townships and lots in the cities. Only those who had enough capital to pay the taxes or who rented out their land, taking advantage of the tenants' improvements when the time came to sell, could afford to keep their land off the market for any period of time. Many took out loans to buy land, and if they overextended themselves they could end up in foreclosure, losing everything.[213] The newspapers regularly carried notices of sheriff's sales in which foreclosed land was put up for auction.[214] This was partly the result of the exorbitant interest rates of many loan contracts, which were essentially short-term mortgages—rarely for more than a year or two.[215] The mortgagee was required to pay the monthly interest and then, at the end of the term, pay the principal. The interest might be as high as 4 percent per month or 48 percent per annum.[216] When the territorial legislature passed a usury law setting 10 percent as the maximum legal rate, the *Weekly Leavenworth Herald* commented: "They might as well have passed a law to limit the price of potatoes or eggs."[217] Starting a farm from scratch with no means of getting produce to the big markets to make money to pay off the mortgage was a big risk. If, at the end of the loan term, the farmer could not pay, another mortgage might be drawn up, perhaps at a higher interest rate; the farmer might become a tenant; or the farmer might simply move on, leaving the improved land behind.[218] The capital for these loans came largely from investors in the East, absentee landlords working through local agents; they were more interested in receiving regular interest payments than in holding land.[219]

The second reason the Lodholzes could not afford to buy their land at auction was simple: they lacked the necessary cash. The $270 Georg received while on his scouting journey had obviously been spent; the wagon he bought cost $110 alone. Wisely, the Lodholzes were not trying to hold on to all the land Georg had preempted. At this point, Gottfried and Georg wanted just 160 acres each, but at the government's price, that was $200 per brother—significantly less per acre than other land Georg had priced on his scouting trip, but still a large sum. The federal government no longer sold land on credit; only private investors or their agents extended credit, and of course, they attended the auctions. They might arrange to purchase a farmer's land for him and set up a loan contract, but the Lodholzes seemed determined to avoid this.[220] They had lost their lands to debt in Germany and did not want a repeat.

Thus, the period between January and August 1859, when the Lodholz family finally purchased their land, was nerve-racking for all. Friedrich initially had trouble finding work in Connecticut, and on the prairie, the family was able to raise little money on their own. Overwrought, Friedrich vacillated between abundant optimism and anxious realism. He had law books in his possession (whether in German or English we do not know) that detailed the laws regarding public lands.[221] His efforts on the family's behalf focused on getting military land warrants. Veterans of any war or their heirs were entitled to receive 160 acres of public land subject to sale, and these military land warrants were transferable.[222] Thus, they could be used like cash to pay off money owed for preempted land. Under the law, a preemptor was entitled to 160 acres of public land, and a warrant entitled its owner to 160 acres of public land, so it was an easy trade-off. Speculators and real estate brokers in the East bought warrants for a song from veterans or their widows who had no interest in settling on the frontier and then resold them to settlers or their agents.[223]

In January 1859 Friedrich wrote to the family about the going rate for such warrants. Clearly worried that they might lose the land, he dispensed a lot of mother hen advice as well:

> Lately I inquired about prices of Land Warrants. One can find out in New York. 160 acres cost $120, 120 acres $84; 80 acres $60; 40 acres $40. I think it would be best if you sold some oxen next spring and send me the money by draft. It is most important that we will own our land. If you should distrust to send the land payment I would bring you the land warrants personally [i.e., he would buy the warrants, deliver them to Kansas, and receive payment].
>
> Please save your money and don't buy anything unnecessary. After the land is paid off one can think of other things and doesn't have to worry about credit and interests. I will save whatever I can.[224]

The prices quoted in Friedrich's letter represented a significant savings for the brothers—if they could take advantage of it—but the cost was still too high. Friedrich next explored getting the land warrants on credit but learned that only cash was acceptable.[225]

Then Friedrich got his hopes up about the possibility of buying even cheaper land, only to have them dashed. The practices of speculators, which included many major political figures, led to huge debates fostered by the Free-Soil Party and individuals such as Horace Greeley, whose newspaper gave him a public forum to express his support of land reform. This also led to innumerable bills in Congress proposing one scheme or another. Friedrich wrote:

> It is uncertain whether land in Kansas next July will be given for sale [i.e., whether the federal government would offer public land for sale]. As you might remember Senator Johnson[226] was recommending that the land should be sold to real settlers for low prices. Last week this bill came up in Washington again and it seems promising for the senator. He wants it sold for 10 to 15 cents (!) per acre to real settlers and not to speculators.
>
> I am anxious to see the outcome. Should it come true that land will go for 10 to 15 cents per acre, I will hurry to get some in Kansas. It would be such luck for us.[227]

But nothing came of the bill. It was not until several years later that the Homestead Act was passed.

By May 1859, the family was afraid they would be unable to raise the necessary money in time, so Gottfried, backed up by Friedrich, applied to Mr. Gaillert, a wealthy Connecticut resident, for a loan.[228] He was not German, so they were going outside their circle of friends, who probably had no cash to spare. Gottfried and Friedrich must have hoped the interest rate Gaillert charged would be far less than that in Kansas. Friedrich was initially overconfident about this source of funds:

> Received your letters on 27 April, 4 May, and 14 May. Please forget your worries about paying for the land. I came home from a visit to Mr. Gaillert. He received your letter last night. He is distrustful. But on account of my urgent talks, his heart softened. I told him how much you would appreciate his good heart and explained everything in detail and told him about our decency and honesty. He told me I should visit him again next week. He would let me know by then. He was very friendly when I said goodnight. I shall write you about the outcome.[229]

But then his hopes were dashed again, and Friedrich became rather peevish about Mr. Gaillert:

> About 6 days ago I sent you a letter in which I mentioned that I talked to Mr. Gaillert for the first time, and he was friendly. But when I visited him for the second time tonight he told me that he would not give money away to people far away, because if Gottfried would die, the money would not be worth a cent. He had loaned $400 to someone in the West and lost all. And so he never wanted to loan money so far away.
>
> I talked and told him about our circumstances, but he is a miser and didn't budge. The worry about his money will carry him to an early grave. So, I guess there is nothing else left but to sell your animals and pay for your land until later I can send you some money so you will be able to buy new animals.
>
> Next month I'll send you $50.[230]

After all the ups and downs of searching for funds before the deadline, the Lodholz family was able to buy their land outright with the help of money from Friedrich. Gottfried and Georg obtained their lands with warrants, apparently purchased locally from the widows of two unrelated veterans of the War of 1812, and the Lodholz patents to the land were subsequently recorded by the Bureau of Land Management in Washington, DC. Friedrich was ecstatic. "The treasured news for which I waited so longingly in August has finally arrived, namely your dear letter from 13 August which I received last Tuesday evening. I'm glad that you successfully exchanged the bill, and it means a great deal to me specifically that the beautiful land on the Vermillion is now in your hands as property."[231]

Gottfried and Georg now owned two contiguous quarter sections, numbered 26 and 27, close to the town of Beattie in Guittard Township.[232] The brothers reported to Friedrich that they had a good harvest, but that would have been for their own consumption.[233] The all-important railroads that made commercial farming possible were not yet in place. In 1860 representatives from several counties and towns (but not Marshall) met in Topeka to prepare a plan for land grants to railroads to present to Congress.[234]

Although they now owned their land, the Lodholzes were still not financially secure and self-sufficient. That fall, Georg went to Atchison for supplies and tried to raise cash by selling several oxen to a beer hall keeper.[235] They still depended on Friedrich to send them money, and he advised them to set up a general store: "As to your circumstances . . . I can't say much, except that I want to support you as well as I can. Until next spring you can perhaps set up a little store, as I can do a fair amount of saving this winter if the dear Lord keeps me this healthy. Your worst times are more or less over now. I suspect that you will now rush forwards."[236]

The Lodholzes, however, had a "mercilessly cold" winter that year. With no insulation for their drafty cabins, they were unrelentingly cold and likely stayed near the fire and bundled in the feather beds they had brought from Terryville. With so many people sleeping in such a small space, they could at least share body warmth as the snow blew in through the cracks in the cabins. Water in the water barrels froze, and they had to melt snow over the fire not only for themselves but also for their livestock, which had to be tended no matter what the temperature. Dishes, clothes, and people would have gone unwashed. Friedrich urged: "Please don't be sparing with the wood, and if you should burn up your forest, we can soon get a supply of kindling and coal from Missouri."[237]

Despite the weather, by the end of 1859, life was looking up for the Lodholz family both on the prairie and in Terryville. Though the family had needed to borrow money, Friedrich sent funds so they could pay "the old man out there."[238] One of the Eagle Lock Company's two factories had been destroyed by fire, and while the new plant was being rebuilt, Friedrich worked at a job that was unfamiliar to him, pressing many different types of locks: "At first I was terribly overworked with business; . . . later then it got better because the boss Gaylord wrote all the orders on his board for me . . . and [I] gradually became familiar with many types . . . I did things well."[239] Shortly thereafter he wrote that he was back at the newly restored and much warmer factory: "Today is the third day that I'm working again in the new shop, it's very nice down here now, there is no need to heat up an oven, as the entire shop is heated with little steam pipes that pass along the wall."[240]

The year 1860 likewise began well for Friedrich:

I thank you warmly for all the blessings and wishes for this new year. I must say, it's gotten off to a good start for me. My health at present is good again, but during Christmas I had an infected thumb nail on my left hand which caused me a great deal of pain. . . .

In the month of March I'm thinking of sending you money again, at present I have about 36 dollars saved up for you, but I want to wait another month with it, so that you don't have to travel to the river [where they presumably obtained his draft and cashed it] for nothing.

Life in Kansas and Connecticut, 1859–61

> . . . I continue to live in old Terryville, where the people are so simple that they know of nothing else to say besides how this or that person behaves and acts. We are all just living as free people in a free country. . . . Martin's family is also in good health again, the two boys come frequently here to my house, in fact Willie is just now getting my newspaper. . . . When I come home [to Kansas] I don't believe I'll be using any more foreign words.[241]

Friedrich was obviously looking forward to conversing with his relatives in German.

Over the next few years, however, good fortune would not last in either Kansas or Connecticut. First to feel the pain was the Great Plains. In 1860 Kansas suffered a severe drought, followed by a bitter winter with a large snowfall. The drought led to a national call for aid to the Kansas settlers. Contributions from all over the country came in dribs and drabs to Atchison, where clothing, money, flour, and other provisions were distributed to the settlers. After the severe winter, seed likewise arrived in Atchison, the railroads hauling it for free. Marshall County alone received almost 155,000 pounds of various types of aid.[242] Presumably, the Lodholzes took advantage of some of it. Their situation, however, led to a disappointing decision by Friedrich, who desperately wanted to see his mother again:

> Dear mother, when I said good-bye to you, I didn't think that my stay in the East would be longer than two years; now I realize that I will be living apart from you for four or five years, mainly because this year you have had to suffer poor harvests. I know your main worry regarding me is that I should not risk losing the salvation of my soul.
>
> Dear mother, every time I pray to him who has earned salvation for us, I also think of you—all of you—and I hope that you are also including me in your prayers.[243]

Nature was still not through with the Great Plains. The drought had made tinder of the prairie grasses, and the following year came the dreaded prairie fires, driven inexorably by the wind. A line of light on the horizon was cause for alarm. Friedrich learned about Gottfried's fate from a friend in Terryville to whom his brother had written while Friedrich was working elsewhere:

> It's been quite a long time since I heard from you all, now suddenly friends from Terryville are bringing me sad news. I heard namely that

Gottfried sent a letter to Sam's Terry and wrote there that his house, his belongings and everything in it burned to the ground from a prairie fire. If that is the case, then it would indeed be very sad. Friedrich Egen wrote me that Terry had collected money to send to Gottfried, it's reportedly about $50 that was brought together. Now I wish only that you should report to me regarding the state of things.[244]

Many settlers created firebreaks by burning the vegetation around their cabins, but Gottfried had apparently not done so. He certainly had no experience with prairie fires in Ebhausen and may not have thought to take precautions. He must have seen the furious flames approaching and gotten the family out of harm's way, as fortunately, no one was injured. Other settlers caught up in prairie fires did not fare so well. J. M. Watson "lost one horse, cow, hay, fencing and was caught myself. I lay down and the fire passed over me, burning the clothes off my back. They rolled me in a sack of flour to take out the burns, while they sent twenty miles for a doctor and he was not at home. I was laid up for three months."[245] The Lodholz family's dismay at seeing all their hard work literally go up in smoke must have been intense. There was nothing to do but start again.

Georg's property was apparently untouched, so Gottfried's family could have lived with him temporarily. The collection taken up in Terryville certainly helped, but even two years later, Gottfried was reporting how cold his new cabin was in the depths of winter; it had only a dirt floor because in the freezing weather he could not get timber to the sawmill to make planking.[246]

Adding to Friedrich's concerns for the family was his fear of the Native Americans: "The Pawnee Indians are also very restive, between Fort Riley and Kearney they had a big skirmish."[247] However, his fear was misplaced. First of all, he seemed to be unaware that Forts Riley and Kearny were far to the west of Marshall County. Second, the Pawnee were dependent on farming for part of the season and buffalo hunting for the other, and the tribe was in conflict with the larger, nomadic tribes in the area, including the Sioux and Cheyenne. Decimated by diseases spread by the European settlers, approximately four thousand Pawnee remained in 1860, and it was they who needed protection from their enemies. A special dispatch to the *New York Times* reported in July of that year:

> Another report has been made to the Indian Department by the Agent of the Pawnees, Mr. Gillis, in which he gives the particulars of another attack upon the village of that now comparatively helpless tribe by

the Cheyenne, Sioux and other bands. We gave in the Times a few days since his report of a former attack, in which he prevailed upon the hostile bands to desist, but with a threat to return and renew their attack on a subsequent day i[t] seems that they have carried their threat into execution, although at a time when the Pawnee warriors were absent on their annual hunt, leaving in the village only a few sick and crippled men and squaws. They scalped one of the squaws, burned about twenty lodges, and destroyed all the growing corn and vegetables. It is to be hoped that Government will immediately institute measures for the more efficient protection of these friendly Indians.[248]

It was little wonder that many Pawnee warriors served as scouts for the US Army. The inability of the various tribes to present a united front in negotiations with the federal government was part of the sad story of the Indian wars.

Even in the year of the devastating drought, there were marriages to celebrate on the prairie. On September 10, 1860, Gottfried, acting as justice of the peace for Guittard Township, married his sister Anna Regina to Heinrich Reb and his brother Georg to Wilhelmina Gertrude Wender.[249] There is no credible information about Wilhelmina in the immigration records; nor do we know how they met. Given that Anna Regina was getting married, it is tempting to assume that Georg's marriage was an opportunity to get someone else to keep house for him, as he definitely did not like housekeeping. During his land scouting expedition he had written to his family: "I am again my Cook and Housekeeper which no doubt will appear laughable to you."[250] In this, he was the brother closest in outlook to the typical German male head of household.

Georg's marriage, however, would prove to be ill-fated. By January, he was already writing to Friedrich that it was not going well. Wilhelmina was apparently not the docile housewife he had been expecting. Her brother had been living with them, perhaps with the idea of helping out on the farm, but Georg thought he was a bad influence and sent him packing. With his brother-in-law gone, Georg was getting along better with his wife, at least for the time being.[251]

More enduring and more loving was the marriage of Anna Regina and Heinrich Reb. Again, we do not know how they met. Perhaps Gottfried or Georg used Heinrich's services as a blacksmith and facilitated the match. In sparsely populated Marshall County, the number of eligible German-speaking bachelors who belonged to or were willing to join the German Evangelical

Association would have been very small indeed. There was a Methodist minister in Vermillion Township, and perhaps Heinrich initially belonged to this near relative of the German Evangelical Association.

At the time of their marriage, Heinrich used a military warrant to purchase the approximately thirty acres he had preempted in Barrett; the following spring, he used another military warrant to purchase an adjoining 160 acres.[252] He was still blacksmithing, but by then, he was certainly thinking about farming. Anna Maria joined Heinrich and Anna Regina in the log cabin he built. It was not until the 1880s that a proper frame house was erected.

With both Annas now being supported by Heinrich, this left more of the meager resources for Gottfried's growing family. Back in January 1860, Anna Maria and Anna Regina would have helped Christina give birth to another daughter, also named Christina, in the Lodholz's small log cabin. There was no doctor for miles, and even if there had been one close by, he could not have made it through the huge snowdrifts of that bitterly cold winter. As was the general custom, Anna Maria and Anna Regina would have stayed by Christina's side during labor to encourage her and keep her company. They may have heated water and placed a warm cloth on her perineum to stretch the skin and make tearing less likely. Once the baby was born, they would have cut and tied the umbilical cord, washed the newborn, wrapped her in a warm blanket, and disposed of the placenta somewhere out of sight.[253] Many pioneer women did not have such experienced support and, with their husbands traveling or working in the fields, somehow managed to give birth on their own.[254]

Though not nearly as risky as in Ebhausen, giving birth in America still posed a risk to both mother and child. Obtaining accurate statistics on the dangers of childbirth, however, is well-nigh impossible.[255] The overall infant mortality rate in the United States was 18 percent in 1860.[256] Even if neither mother nor baby died, there could be major complications. In one of this letters, Friedrich wrote: "The old man Friedrich Egen is to be pitied, as his wife has an ailment in her spine since delivering her last baby, so that she can no longer even walk upright, she walks about all hunched over and incapable of getting anything done, which includes more than just sewing. . . . Imagine now such a troubling situation."[257]

Meanwhile, political ferment was building at the national level as conflicts between the North and the South came to a head. The spark was the Kansas-Nebraska Act of 1854, which led to the formation of the new Republican Party. The Republicans called not only for repeal of the

Kansas-Nebraska Act but also for the construction of a transcontinental railroad and free land for western settlers. One early member of the party was Abraham Lincoln. In 1858 he ran against Illinois senator Stephen Douglas, author of the Kansas-Nebraska Act. Lincoln did not win the Senate seat, but the Lincoln-Douglas debates, reported in the newspapers, propelled him into the national spotlight and led to his party's nomination for the presidency in 1860. The traditional political opposition to the Democratic Party, the Whigs, had splintered over the Kansas-Nebraska Act, with many of its members joining other political coalitions, including the Republicans.[258]

It was precisely at this time, in March 1860, that Friedrich proudly became an American citizen and subsequently voted for the first time. Under the Naturalization Act of 1802, "aliens" wishing to obtain citizenship appeared before the clerk of the local state or territorial court, who would record, among other things, the person's name, age, birthplace, and place of intended settlement and issue a certificate of immigration. (Recall that Gottfried did not do this when he first entered the United States.) Three years before naturalization, the immigrant filed a notice of intent, renounced allegiance to any prior sovereign or state, and swore or affirmed his or her support of the US Constitution. Two years later, after a total of five years of residency, the immigrant could apply for citizenship by producing two witnesses who could attest to his or her moral character and attachment to the Constitution. Friedrich wrote to his family:

> Because I am now, as of 30 March 1860, a citizen of the United States, I can't help but share everything with you regarding how it went. Since the Americans here know that I am a Republican, I was made aware of the election last Monday. . . . I could not decide right away whether to go to Hartford just for this. But they gave me no rest, they wanted to have my vote. And the accountant [illegible] paid $5.50 in order to see my witness August Martinsen and me completely free from duty, so that it would cost me nothing to become a citizen.
>
> I must say, Mr. Martinsen conducted himself very respectably in Hartford. When I was entitled to vote in Plymouth, Mr. Baldwin appeared as my witness. Everything went beautifully! The Republicans won in this state![259]

Gottfried, Georg, and Heinrich had preceded Friedrich in becoming citizens.[260]

Despite the happy event of Friedrich's naturalization, in the erratic economic climate of the time, his fortunes took a turn for the worse. He wrote:

My pay is 1.125 a day. It is admittedly frustrating that I had made $1.20 three years ago and must now work more cheaply and harder, but I can do nothing except endure; last year I started at 75 cents per day, then 87, then $1 and since this spring a little more. You can easily imagine here that it cost me the upmost effort to send the money that I did. But I know my homeland is in Kansas and that refreshes my spirit daily.[261]

The Eagle Lock Company was faltering, and Friedrich's wages suffered. In January 1861, just as President Lincoln was being sworn in, Friedrich wrote to Anna Regina and his new brother-in-law: "Wish you a good and happy New Year. Got your address last week through Gottfried. Glad to hear that you are well and that mother is with you. Can't tell you much good from Terryville. The New Year started badly, made only $5 so far. Nobody wants locksmiths. The cause is the war build up in South Carolina and the other Southern States."[262]

With the firing on Fort Sumter, the war was on, and Friedrich had to search for work elsewhere. He finally found a job at the Colt pistol factory in Hartford, Connecticut, twenty-five miles east of Terryville. The plant, noted for its onion dome topped with a bronze pistol designed by Colt himself, supplied firearms for Union troops.[263] The war was a boon to northern factories and businesses. The wartime need for weapons, uniforms, and more spurred the armament, textile, and myriad other industries.

In Hartford, Friedrich was lonely, cut off from family and friends. In 1860 he and his old friend Christian Killinger were still writing to each other and planning to get together.[264] But even the prospect of visiting Christian, who was working in Massachusetts, did not lift his spirits. "I have not yet visited Christian Killinger, and now it is also no longer so important to me."[265] This was the last time the two childhood friends attempted to meet.

In November 1861, however, there was a piece of good news. One year after their marriage, Heinrich and Anna Regina had their first child, George Henry Reb—known as Henry Jr. in his youth. Unaware of his nephew's birth, Friedrich wrote a doleful Christmas letter to his sister and mother:

I have been in Hartford for the past two months and work in Colt's gun shop. The work I have would be all right except that I've been feeling unwell for about three weeks, which has been a disadvantage for me, I grew weak in the limbs. Admittedly now it seems to be getting better again. Today I feel fairly well, otherwise I could not write in a cold room. Write to me also and tell me how the harvest turned out, whether you are doing well and are healthy, as I haven't heard anything at all from you in a long time.

If you want to write to me, then just send the letters to Terryville. Friedrich Egen then sends them here to me, as I don't know exactly how long I'll stay here. When things are better again in Terryville, then I'll go back, as in Terryville I have better friends than in Hartford.

When I'm in a strange place like this, I think very often of you all. A person could sometimes use someone who can sew or mend for him, but I'll just have to do without. But one thinks all the more of one's friends.

Now, mother and sister, in just a few weeks the blessed Christmastime will come, so I would like to wish that we all again will be able to spend this Christmas season of grace in blessedness. If we were together in unity, there would admittedly be more blessedness. But the ruler and guide of all things who reigns all-powerful in heaven and from whom nothing is hidden will also know how to rule and will know when the time will come for us to spend Christmas together!

I remain your loving son, brother, and friend
Friedrich Lodholz[266]

CHAPTER 4

War, Gold, Growth, Death, and Trouble, 1861–73

The Civil War created bitter divisions that went beyond mere sectional rivalries. It divided one state in two when West Virginia split off from Virginia. It divided families, with brother fighting against brother. Religious denominations officially divided on the slavery issue, forming separate northern and southern organizations, long before the war broke out—Presbyterians in 1838, Methodists in 1844, and Baptists in 1845.[1] The Lutheran split, however, did not occur until 1863.[2]

The warfare was devastatingly violent and cruel. Given that Kansas had been admitted as a free state in 1861, it is not surprising that a significant number of Kansans volunteered to serve in the Union forces. Kansas had fewer than thirty thousand men of military age at this time, but twenty thousand served in the Union army, with a casualty rate of approximately 43 percent.[3] African Americans living in Kansas joined the segregated First Kansas Colored Infantry—the first such unit to see action.[4] In 1867 the provost marshal general of the US Army reported that Kansas provided more soldiers in proportion to its population than any other state and likewise suffered the greatest percentage of soldiers killed or wounded.[5]

At the outbreak of the war, Frank Marshall and other pro-slavery supporters still had influence in Marysville. When news of the firing on Fort Sumter first reached the town, only six men there professed loyalty to the

Union.⁶ Soon that would change. Frank Marshall and his family pulled up stakes and headed west to Colorado.⁷ Marysville became a Union recruiting station, and in the end, Marysville and Vermillion Townships supplied most of the Union volunteers from Marshall County.⁸ The first volunteers came from Barrett in Vermillion Township, which Emma Forter singled out as "intensely loyal"; among the Union supporters listed was "honest, old Henry Rebb."⁹ In the fall of 1861 six young men from Barrett headed to Fort Leavenworth after attending church at the schoolhouse the previous evening. One recruit later wrote:

> Since that morning I have had some triumphs and have received honors at the hands of Marshall County people, but never felt as solemnly proud and grateful as on that morning when we bade farewell to the people of Barrett. The warm hand-shake, the tearful eye, and the tremulous "God bless you," told us that we would be always in our careers as soldiers held in affectionate remembrance by these good people.¹⁰

One of these young men, Robert Henderson, was the first Marshall County soldier killed in the line of duty.¹¹ The county had 450 voters and supplied 431 volunteers to the war effort prior to 1865, plus an additional 31 in 1865, including one company from the Otoe tribe.¹²

For the most part, the war itself was waged elsewhere, but the conflict along the border between Kansas and Missouri, particularly in southeastern Kansas, had never really stopped, as Jayhawkers from Kansas and Bushwhackers from Missouri waged guerrilla warfare.¹³ Attempts to launch attacks from slave-owning Missouri into Kansas along the banks of the Missouri River were repulsed. The most devastating attack, however, came not from regular Confederate troops but from the guerrilla group formed by William Quantrill, known as Quantrill's Raiders, which included Jesse James and Cole Younger, who later became well-known outlaws. On August 21, 1863, Quantrill and his men attacked Lawrence, Kansas. Subject to attack earlier in the "Bleeding Kansas" era, it remained a bastion of anti-slavery sentiment and a base for attacks by Jayhawkers. At the time, Quantrill's Raiders were several hundred strong.¹⁴ At dawn they bore down on the unsuspecting city, killing close to 150 men and boys, burning and ransacking homes and businesses, and, by 9:00 a.m., hightailing it out of town.¹⁵ As we know from the 1860 federal census, there were a significant number of German-born residents in Lawrence, and although we have no

Illustration of Quantrill's raid on Lawrence, Kansas, published in *Harper's Weekly* two weeks later. We do not know whether it was based on eyewitness accounts, but it matches the description provided by eyewitness Richard Cordley. (*Harper's Weekly* 7, 349 [September 5, 1863]: 564)

accounts of their experience, some of them must have been caught up in the mayhem. One eyewitness recounted the horror of the raid:

> [Quantrill's Raiders had been] seen approaching by several persons in the outskirts, but in the dimness of the morning and the distance, they were supposed to be Union troops. They passed on in a body till they came to the high ground facing the main street, when the command was given "Rush on to the town." Instantly they rushed forward with a yell. They first came upon a camp of new recruits for the Kansas Fourteenth. These men had not yet been armed, and were waiting for orders. On these the bushwhackers fired as they passed, killing seventeen out of twenty-two. The attack did not check the general advance. A few turned aside to run down and shoot the fugitive soldiers, but the main body rushed on with unslackened speed.... The guerillas rode with the ease and abandon acquired by a life spent in the saddle.... Their horses scarcely seemed to touch the ground and the riders sat with bodies and arms perfectly free, shooting at every house and man they passed, and

yelling at every bound. On each side of the stream of fire, as it poured along, were men falling dead and wounded. . . .

No description can give an idea of the scene in Lawrence after the raiders had left. The business section of the town was entirely destroyed, and a large portion of the dwelling houses. Those homes which were not burned had most of them been ransacked and robbed. . . . The dead were lying everywhere. . . . Massachusetts Street was one long line of blackened walls and cellars filled with ashes and embers. The dead lay along the sidewalks, many of them so burned that they could not be recognized.[16]

In response, on August 25 Thomas Ewing, commander of the District of the Border, issued Order No. 11, which, with few exceptions, ordered the residents of four southwestern Missouri counties on the Kansas border to vacate by September 9. Although not all Missourians supported the Confederacy, many did, and the intent of Order No. 11 was to deprive Bushwhackers of succor and aid from Missourians living in close proximity to Kansas, to allay Kansans' fear of future attacks, and to forestall any acts of retaliation (which it did, for the most part, although troops enforcing the order looted and pillaged).[17]

With so many men absent from Kansas, "the farms were neglected, crops failed and business was poor."[18] The hardship endured by the wives left behind is a story yet to be told, but the biography of Samuel Paul provides a glimpse. He returned home to a wife "who had experienced in many ways the hardships of the war as much as the soldiers on the field of battle. Those three years were filled with many privations in the care of the five children of the family."[19] Few individuals settled in Kansas during the war years.

As the war dragged on and casualties mounted, there were not enough volunteers to meet the needs of the Union army. The North was growing weary of this seemingly endless strife. As a consequence, Congress passed the Conscription Act of 1863, authorizing the second military draft in US history, the first having been instituted by the Confederacy the previous year.[20] It required all men between the ages of twenty and forty-five to register, although exceptions were made for those with dependents requiring financial support and those with physical infirmities. Quotas were set for congressional districts, and if those quotas were not filled by volunteers, men would be drafted by lottery.[21] To avoid serving, individuals could take the legal route, paying a hefty $300 commutation fee or paying a substitute to take their place, or they could outright try to evade the draft.

Men dutifully registered for the draft in Kansas, but it was never implemented there because enlistments surpassed the assigned quotas.[22] Volunteers included German-born men such as George Goelitz, an early settler at Horseshoe Creek, who joined the Union forces to fight "mit Siegel [sic]."[23] He was referring to German-born Franz Sigel, a major general in the Union army who recruited many Germans for the fight. In fact, large numbers of Germans in the United States, whether citizens or not, fought on the Union side.[24]

The Conscription Act was widely unpopular. In New York City its passage led to four days of brutal rioting by white laborers, and judging by the surnames published in the *New York Times*, they were mainly Irish and German. Many rioters, soldiers, policemen, and innocent residents were shot, burned, hung, and clubbed to death, including blacks, whom the workers thought might take their jobs if the slaves were freed. Even the Colored Orphan Asylum was ransacked and burned, resulting in the death of a ten-year-old girl, among others.[25] There was resistance to the draft elsewhere, too. In Ozaukee County, Wisconsin, just north of Milwaukee (where Lincoln had received just 627 of 2,450 votes), a crowd of about a thousand attacked the draft commissioner. The governor found it prudent to use military force not only to quell the uprising but also to superintend the selection of draftees in Milwaukee.[26] There was massive resistance to conscription in Pennsylvania, particularly by Democrats, who considered the law unconstitutional.[27] Desertion and draft dodging were widespread; individuals assigned to apprehend the miscreants were shot at and killed. A German-speaking mob had to be dispersed by soldiers when the group tried to prevent the selection of draftees.[28]

Though Gottfried, Georg, and Heinrich were in no danger of being drafted, twenty-six-year-old Friedrich, single and working at the Colt factory in Hartford, was a prime candidate. There were insufficient volunteers from his district to meet the quota, and although he supported Lincoln, Friedrich did not want to go to war. Luckily, his number was not called. He shared the good news with the family:

Hartford, 1 September 1863

Dearly beloved mother and sister!

Because two months ago I feared I would be drafted, and the time has now passed here, I can now report to you that I have still not become a soldier. Although last month here in Hartford more than a thousand men were drafted, I for my part am quite content to be wound-free, for how long, however, I don't know, but the war will also not last much longer. [He was, of course, wrong about the length of the war.]

I would so much like to be with you, but you know yourselves how it is and I think I have it better here. It's possible that things will also turn out well for you, at least so that you don't have only grain [corn] to eat, which I didn't enjoy.[29]

While the Civil War continued its devastating course, far to the west of Marshall County in Denver, where the gold seekers had been mining in the mountains, the war hardly existed. The pro-Union majority forced the few Southern sympathizers in the city to take down the Confederate flag they had hoisted, and the troops raised in the region were sent for action in Missouri.[30]

Meanwhile, Heinrich and Georg headed to Denver in the spring of 1863, some months before Quantrill's Raid. It had been five years since the start of the gold rush. Thousands of men, many of them jobless as a result of the Panic of 1857, had flocked to the area only to return, disappointed, to a nation at war. Some men from Marshall County had tried their hand at searching for gold, but Heinrich and Georg made the journey not to prospect but to seek other moneymaking opportunities.[31] Farming was hardly lucrative at the time, with no railway connections to markets in the East. In April 1863 Denver had suffered a devastating fire that destroyed the heart of the city, and it was the rebuilding effort that provided employment for Heinrich and Georg.[32] The flammable buildings constructed of pine were declared illegal and were being replaced with two-story brick ones.[33] Gottfried decided not to join them. Christina had just given birth to their fourth daughter, Rosa, in December 1862. He sought income locally that summer, helping George Guittard build a house and going to "the River" to bring back goods for a neighbor.[34]

Georg had been planning to go to Pike's Peak since the previous July, when he had corresponded with Friedrich about land. In addition to the funds Friedrich provided for the entire family, he had also lent money to Georg at various times, and as repayment, Friedrich was entitled to one-third of Georg's land. Georg's letter raises questions about his money management skills and perhaps about his truthfulness. He implies that he had gone into debt with someone else and put up his land as collateral, but there was no indication of any such encumbrance when his estate was probated some years later, at which time he still owed Friedrich the land. Georg could be a sly one. He wrote to his brother:

Your letter of 25th June, I received July 4th; and see there from that you desire for me to assign to you Property belonging to you for which I am indebted to you. Dear Brother, if the Land was paid for, I would deed to you the third thereof without delay, but since it is not paid for, I cannot do it. I will endeavor my upmost [sic] this summer to pay for it, or least to more even the indebtness [sic]. For this reason I contemplate to go to Pike's Peak to earn something as here Money can hardly be had for work.[35]

Georg's letter also contained the news that his wife had been sick and had gone to St. Louis "in the hope of finding relief there."[36] We know nothing of Wilhelmina's illness or when she returned, although we know she was home by July 1863.[37] They had no children, and Georg apparently did not object to her making the trip on her own; he was hardly being patriarchal, but he was making plans to do what he needed to do, irrespective of her illness.

Heinrich and Georg would be away from home for several months, during which time Anna Regina, Anna Maria, and Wilhelmina would have to manage on their own. For Anna Regina and Wilhelmina (assuming her condition had improved and she was home for at least part of the summer), this meant the usual chores such as milking the cows, churning butter, tending the garden, collecting the eggs, cleaning, hauling water, washing, sewing, and cooking. Presumably Heinrich and Georg had split enough logs for fuel, but if they ran out of wood, the women would have to scavenge for themselves. And, as the crops had been sown, the women had to keep an eye on them as well. They also had to protect themselves from coyotes and wolves, which were particularly active at night. Wilhelmina lived some distance from Gottfried's house, and Anna Regina had no relatives nearby. Although the women certainly must have known how to use firearms and axes, the absence of Heinrich and Georg made life considerably harder.

There were many routes to the gold fields in the roughly five hundred miles that separated Marshall County and Denver, including one that followed the Oregon Trail to Fort Kearny, where the various routes converged. Heinrich and Georg most likely joined the route that originated on the Missouri River at St. Joseph and turned northward along the Big Blue River Valley to the fort. From there, they would have taken the south fork of the Platte River Valley to reach Denver. They were hardly alone. Settlers were still heading to Oregon, California, and Utah. Prospectors were eager to reap the rewards of the silver and gold deposits found in Nevada in 1859 and Idaho in 1860. At Fort Kearny, these travelers split off from those heading to Denver and took the north fork of the Platte River Valley.

The heavy wagons—for a party of four prospectors, a load of about thirty-two hundred pounds—pulled by plodding oxen traveled eighteen to twenty miles a day. At that rate, it took roughly twenty-five days to reach Denver from Marshall County.[38] Heinrich and Georg did not expect to prospect and therefore did not need the equipment necessary for that enterprise, so it is highly likely that they traveled with just pack animals—each man riding one horse and packing their essentials on a second. Because they could not transport the spacious military-style tents (ten feet square with three-foot walls) that those with wagons could carry, they hazarded the elements, but riding horses made the trip much faster. They could cover twenty-five to thirty miles a day, thus cutting the travel time to Denver to fifteen or sixteen days.[39] Heinrich bought oxen and a wagon in Denver for his return trip, so the journey home took him longer.[40]

The men left after the spring planting and most likely took woolen clothing for the cooler temperatures in Denver's high altitude, blankets, guns, a few cooking utensils, and a small supply of coffee, beans, bacon, flour, and other nonperishables. They could hunt geese, ducks, and other game and maybe catch a fish or two along the way. In 1932, on the occasion of Heinrich's son John's sixty-sixth birthday, John told a reporter that his father had taken butter and eggs to Denver with an ox team and got good money for them.[41] This seems highly unlikely, as butter and eggs would certainly not travel well.[42]

Since the 1840s, when the first settlers headed to Oregon, trail conditions had become somewhat better as the numerous wagon trains made the road hard and smooth in many places. But it was not an easy journey. Attacks by Native Americans were rare, but nature put up many roadblocks. The greatest obstacle was unbridged streams, which had to be forded or crossed on rafts. In addition, Heinrich and Georg had to find grazing land for their animals and good water for both the animals and themselves—alkaline water with a high pH (normal drinking water is neutral) could fatally sicken the animals. They also needed fuel for cooking and to keep warm. None of these necessities were plentiful along the trails, leading to many problems for travelers.[43] Deaths of both people and animals were not uncommon. High on a bluff in the middle of nowhere, one hopeful prospector heading west found a grave marked by a headstone reading simply: L. W. Ramsey died May 21, 1859, 2 weeks.[44]

Based on William Byer and John Kellum's *Handbook to the Gold Fields of Nebraska and Kansas*, we can surmise where Heinrich and Georg might have found the best spots to camp.[45] The first leg of their journey, reaching Fort Kearny, was the easiest: at Small Creek, "one mile north of the road, plenty of wood and water," and at Little Nemaha River, "plenty of timber and good water; good camp." The major obstacle, according to Byer and Kellum, was the Blue River: "Should this stream be up you will have to build a raft to cross on. It is about fifty yards wide, has a very rapid current and abounds in excellent fish."[46] Heinrich and Georg probably swam their horses across.

But then the trail left the river valley, and the last thirty-four miles to Fort Kearny were bereft of good campgrounds: "Small Creek in the prairie—some timber, but the water is not good."[47] Fort Kearny was a welcome stopping place. It offered rest and protection to weary travelers and served as a mail depot for letters to and from the East. A stagecoach company charged 25 cents per letter and 10 cents per newspaper, in addition to standard postage, to transport mail between Fort Kearny and Denver.[48]

The last leg of Heinrich and Georg's journey started out with good prospects for camping. "Plum Creek—A good camp with wood, water and grass," and "Brady's Island—Good camp on bank of small channel of river—must bring fuel from island." But then came "Cedar Grove—In the bluffs south of the road. This is the last timber of any consequence for over 200 miles. Emigrants will do well to take fuel for six or seven days' travel." There was a stagecoach station and a trading post along the way, but also some sandy stretches that slowed travel and several places where the water was alkaline and unfit for the horses. Heinrich and Georg may have passed a startling sight: "The bodies of dead Indians are deposited on scaffolds in the tops of the trees. This is the mode of sepulture among many of the prairie Indians."[49] This practice was designed to help speed up the spirit's journey in the afterlife and kept the bodies from being eaten by prowling wildlife.

As Georg and Heinrich approached Denver, they had a spectacular view of the eastern Rocky Mountains, with Pike's Peak a conspicuous feature. Even coming from the Black Forest, Georg would have seen nothing like them. One traveler described his approach to Denver in the lush prose of the time:

> All my many and various wanderings in the European Switzerland, three summers ago, spread before my eye no panorama of mountain beauty surpassing, nay, none equaling, that which burst upon my sight at sunrise upon the Plains, when fifty miles away from Denver; and

which rises up before me now as I sit writing by the window in this city. From far south to far north, stretching around in huge semi-circle, rise the everlasting hills, one after another, tortuous, presenting every variety of form and surface, every shade of cover and color, up and on until we reach the broad, snow-covered Range that marks the highest summits, and tells where Atlantic and Pacific meet and divide for their long journey to their far distant shores. To the north rises the king of the range, Long's Peak whose top is 14,600 feet high; to the south, giving source to the Arkansas and Colorado, looms up its brother, Pike's Peak, to the hight [sic] of 13,400 feet. These are the salient features of the belt before us; but the intervening and succeeding summits are scarcely less commanding, and not much lower in hight.[50]

In its early years, Denver was a rip-roaring boomtown, full of shanties, tents, saloons, and prostitutes, but by 1863 it was beginning to settle down. The last duel was fought in 1860—with shotguns—and was fatal to the loser. The gang of ruffians who frequented the Criterion Saloon and loved nothing better than to take potshots at the local newspaper office had been run out of town.[51] Eastern money was beginning to pour in, buying up the small mining operations.

Georg and Heinrich went their separate ways once they arrived in Denver. Georg, the Lodholz who loved to travel, got work as a hauler. His job took him to Central City, forty miles west of Denver; it was the site of a major gold find and was known as the "Richest Square Mile on Earth." Georg bought a city lot there, hoping to sell it at a profit. In other words, he tried his hand at speculation, but in the end, his profit was small.[52] Heinrich presumably worked as a blacksmith and wheelwright. In Denver he wrote his only extant letter, revealing his deep love for his wife and son and expressing his confidence that she could manage things on her own—unlike the stereotypical image of the German patriarch:

> Dear Anna and mother-in-law, I am, thank God, still healthy. Work has stopped, I had to wait for 2 weeks before I received my pay, then I thought of you night and day. I bought myself a team of oxen and a wagon and want to get going on the journey back home tomorrow. I yearn to be back with you again. I will have your letter forwarded to me unless I receive it. So I want to write you once more, I can find plenty of work in Denver, my business too, but I will have no rest anymore until I see you again. I think I can earn enough at home to allow us to be

together, although I won't be bringing any money along, I paid for the bed; I can't think of much else new to write about. Everything is selling for a good price, grain is 5½, flour 6 dollars, eggs 1 dollar per dozen. I will keep my letter short, I trust in our dear father in heaven. He will guide everything as is best for us. When you receive these few lines, then write to me at Fort Kearney.

I send heartfelt greetings to you all and hope that these few lines find you in good health. Greet all the relatives and acquaintances for me.

You will perhaps want to know a great deal regarding what you should do, but I can't write it, you will have to do everything as you see fit.

Greet our loved ones for me. Tell Heinrich [his son] that I'm coming home again soon.

I remain your faithful Heinrich Reb.[53]

Georg returned from Pike's Peak at the beginning of the summer to haying and then went back to Denver and stayed for several more months. Heinrich returned separately and arrived home by October.

Today, it seems strange that two families living only twenty miles apart would not meet regularly face-to-face. But twenty miles was a fair distance for a horse and wagon to travel, entailing a good day's journey, an overnight stay, and the return trip—and that is assuming good weather. Thus, the exchanging of letters and getting news through the grapevine were important means of communication for the Lodholz and Reb families. Georg wrote to his mother and sister when he first returned from Pike's Peak: "I'm sorry to have waited so long to write to you. The cause is that I always thought I would come down to see you, but have not gotten around to that until now, and will hardly manage to do it for the time being, as now I'm working to get the haying done and am thinking of returning to road travel only after that." He added: "I'm glad that our dear brother Gottfried has already written to you of me, and I've also already heard about you through him."[54]

In January 1864 Gottfried wrote to Heinrich, explaining how he had learned of his brother-in-law's return and why he had been unable to visit:

Several times over I'd intended to come down and see how things are going with you, but was always prevented by bad weather. I wanted to look after you in early autumn, but when I learned coincidentally from your neighbor Mr. Barrett, whom I spoke to at that time in Marysville, that you had returned healthy and cheerful from Pike's Peak—this was during last October—I decided against the trip, partly because I had a great deal of work to do, and then I thought you would perhaps visit us before winter arrives. You must not have had the time, however, because this year we got cold weather very early, and it endured.

This is truly a hard winter. Like so many, I am not yet done with the corn husking, I have half of it lying in shocks covered thick with snow. My corn is quite good. The early frost did not damage much. My family continues to be quite happy, apart from the severe cold affecting us all right now. My house isn't warm enough for this weather, as I have no floor as of yet. The saw parts are in the mill for the year and I can't get them cut. The sawmill is worthless.

How is our dear mother doing? This cold weather will be trying for her. Is she not also considering visiting us again soon for a time?

Georg also recently returned back from P. P. I hope that we will soon be able to speak to each other in person.[55]

In that bitter cold winter of 1864, Christina gave birth to her and Gottfried's fifth daughter and last child, Sophia, on December 31.

As Gottfried feared, the harsh winter proved too much for Anna Maria. In April 1865 she died at the age of sixty-two, far from her native land. She left her daughter her precious books and her legacy of strength. There was no cemetery in Barrett until 1877.[56] Heinrich probably constructed a simple wooden coffin, and Anna Maria was most likely buried on the Reb property with the whole family (except for Friedrich) in attendance, along with neighbors and an abundance of prayers and hymns. Friedrich and his mother had always been close, and he was overcome with emotion at the thought that he would never see her again:

> Our dear brother Georg wrote me last week regarding the blessed passing of our eternally beloved mother. Oh what terrible pain is caused me by this news, when I must think that my dear mother's heart beats no more. . . . And oh, how the white satin shines again and again upon her gown, up on high on the crystal sea, there eternal bliss shines round her, for the Lord is her sun. And he is her alpha and omega.[57]

Although they considered it, neither Georg nor Heinrich returned to Pike's Peak. After Quantrill's Raid, the governor of Kansas ordered all persons subject to military duty to organize into local militias.[58] There is no record of Gottfried's or Georg's participation, but Heinrich joined Company E of the Seventeenth Regiment of the Kansas Home Guard on October 10.[59] His company was mustered into service to support Union troops defending Kansas from the raids of Confederate Major General Sterling Price, who was making a last-ditch effort to take deeply divided Missouri for the Confederacy. Heinrich apparently did not take part in any of the many skirmishes and battles involved in this campaign, which was carried out mainly to the south of Marshall County and ultimately won by the Union.

Another likely reason Heinrich and Georg did not return to Denver was the increasing hostility between Native Americans and the growing number of settlers heading farther west. Up until that time, despite occasional attacks and killings, the major problem overlanders encountered was theft.[60] And in fact, the Native Americans were often helpful, supplying the overlanders with food, clothing, equipment, horses, information, and much more.[61] That would soon change.

The Civil War allowed the passage of legislation long desired in the North but consistently opposed by congressional representatives from the South. The Homestead Act of 1862 provided free title to up to 160 acres of undeveloped public land west of the original thirteen colonies to anyone who had not borne arms against the United States and who was willing to live on the land for five years and improve it by growing crops and building a dwelling of minimal size. The act remained in effect until it was repealed and replaced in 1976, by which time 1.6 million homestead applications had been processed and 270 million acres had passed into applicants' hands.[62]

In the same year the Homestead Act was passed, Congress passed the Pacific Railroad Act, which chartered the Central Pacific and Union Pacific Railroads to construct a transcontinental rail line connecting East and West, following the northern route favored by politicians in the North rather than the southern route preferred by those in the South. Private railroad companies also began building shorter lines to connect important starting and ending points. In 1870 there were 1,124 miles of track in Kansas; by 1885, there were 4,181.[63] In Marshall County, one line ran north through the towns of Axtell, Beattie, Marysville, Herkimer, and Bremen, while another line in the southern part of the county ran through the towns of Vermillion, Frankfort, Barrett, Bigelow, Irving, Blue Rapids, and Waterville.

The resulting expansion of white settlements put greater pressure on the Native Americans living on the Great Plains, and the tribes fought back against what they must have perceived as an invasion. The Indian wars encompassed several isolated wars involving different tribes in different states from about 1847 to 1890. On the plains, with nowhere else to go, various tribes staged their last stand. There were atrocities and cruelty on both sides. The 1862 Sioux uprising in southern Minnesota was one of the bloodiest from the settlers' point of view. Confined to two small reservations, the desperate tribe was facing starvation as the money needed to purchase food—annuities promised by treaty—did not arrive. This was the catalyst for the Sioux going to war, led by Little Crow. In the end, there were some 450 casualties on both sides, and after their defeat, thirty-nine tribal leaders were executed.[64] In 1864 a group of Colorado volunteers under the command of Colonel John Chivington launched a surprise attack on a Cheyenne and Arapaho encampment and killed more than 160 women, children, and old men in what came to be known as the Sand Creek Massacre. As the troops approached, the inhabitants of the encampment had raised the US flag and a white flag as a signal that, under the treaties they had signed, they considered themselves at peace.[65]

Starting in the 1840s, the federal government built nine military forts in Kansas, starting with Fort Leavenworth, to protect settlers traveling west and, in the 1860s and 1870s, to both defend against and attack the Great Plains tribes. After the Civil War, a number of these forts were manned by the segregated African American regiments created by Congress in 1866—two cavalry and two infantry.[66] They became famous as the Buffalo Soldiers, so named by Native Americans because their hair resembled that of buffaloes. In the movies, when the cavalry comes to the rescue, the soldiers are portrayed as white. In real life, they were often black.

The Lodholzes and the Rebs experienced no violence by Native Americans, but fear was rampant in Marshall County. In his *History of the State of Kansas*, William Cutler states that Marshall County "was several times the seat of panics arising from depredations committed by the Indians. Emigrants and ranchmen in the overland road were often driven in, as were also the new settlers, who had taken up claims of Marshall County. At times apprehensions were felt that the Indians would extend their devastations to the older settlements, depleted as they were of able-bodied men, from enlistments in the army."[67]

According to Forter, a militia with arms furnished by the government was organized to protect against attacks by Native Americans, and it was sent to aid counties to the west that had suffered murderous attacks. The number of attacks, however, was relatively small. For the period 1857 to 1869, Forter mentions or describes only seven specific instances in the vicinity of Marshall County. Her treatment of these attacks varies, perhaps due to the fact that her history is actually a pastiche of information and stories, some firsthand and some culled from other sources, and they are not necessarily arranged in chronological order. When she first writes of Native American attacks, she gives detailed, often gruesome accounts and makes it sound like Marshall County itself was in great danger. But she later states, "Many minor skirmishes occurred . . . and the settlers suffered greatly from systematic pilfering and stealing by the Indians," but "thousands of Indians hunted, camped and traded in Marshall County, but singularly, few tragedies occurred."[68] It is thus not surprising that the Lodholzes and subsequently the Rebs never mentioned Native Americans in their letters. They seemed to have little or no fear, and it was nervous Friedrich in Terryville, reading about the Indian wars in the eastern newspapers, who worried the most.

Of greater concern to the families were more personal matters. In his July 1863 letter to his mother and sister, Georg mentioned that his "dear wife is thinking perhaps of going to St. Joseph next fall."[69] We do not know whether she actually went, but she disappeared from Georg's life. In the 1865 Kansas state census, Georg was listed as single.[70] What happened to Wilhelmina is a mystery. There is no death certificate for her among the official records for Marshall County or St. Joseph, Missouri; nor is she listed in the 1865 state census. One cryptic remark in a letter of Friedrich's points to her death: "I hope that George's sorrow will eventually lead to a better wife for him."[71] Georg and Wilhelmina had no children. He was away from home for months at a time, and she did not mingle easily with Gottfried's family, leaving her isolated and deeply lonely.[72] On top of this, she was responsible for the many heavy chores a pioneer wife had to perform. All this may have affected her health for the worse, or perhaps she simply left.

Meanwhile, all alone in Hartford, Friedrich, the most outwardly pious of the brothers, succumbed to the temptation of money. Sometime in 1864 he married a purportedly wealthy widow (we never learn her name) with a young son. He wrote to Anna Regina and Heinrich that his wife tried to cheat him, but he does not state how. Perhaps she misrepresented her circumstances and wanted Friedrich to support her and her child, when he expected otherwise. Whatever the reason, they quickly separated, and he returned to Terryville. When he learned of her death, he was relieved rather than saddened. Perhaps he thought it was just punishment. He harbored no ill will, however, toward the child and actually seemed to be fond of him. As he wrote to the Rebs:

The person who tried to cheat me in Hartford is no longer present. She met with a speedy end. On 8 September '64 at 9 o'clock in the evening she died from stomach cramps. Her son, a boy aged four years, is with his relatives in Bristol. Sometimes I visit him. He is with good people. Everything falls to the child. His caregiver is Mr. Luz from Hartford. That's how the entire story ended, and I am thus free. When I found out that she had died, a heavy burden was lifted from my heart, although I could do nothing about it.[73]

Friedrich was obviously not patriarchal, but this was no companionate marriage either.

Friedrich returned to Terryville not only to avoid his wife but also because on February 4, 1864, the Colt factory in Hartford burned to the ground. The cause of the fire is unknown, although there were suspicions that Confederate spies were responsible. The fire put Friedrich and some nine hundred other men out of work.[74] When the Colt factory was rebuilt and his old boss asked him to return, Friedrich was quite happy to remain in Terryville: "I'm doing very well. I like it better here in solitude than in the worldly turmoil in Hartford. . . . I'm very satisfied with these earnings ($9 per week)."[75]

There was a smallpox epidemic, but Friedrich got vaccinated, and his health was good. He had full-time work in the lock shop. He was boarding with a friend and enjoying a drink now and then. In January 1865 he wrote to Anna Regina and Heinrich: "Even though all drink is rare and expensive, I nonetheless and therefore bought myself a few kegs of hard cider last fall, and I feel cheerful as a result. I wish I could serve some to you."[76]

Friedrich was still the bean counter and, as always, was looking after his family in Kansas. In the same letter announcing his wife's death, he wrote that he had taken out a life insurance policy, something unheard of in Ebhausen:

> I must now make you aware of an object that could be very valuable to you at some point. It so happens I had myself insured on 30 December, 1864, with the Travelers' Insurance Company, Hartford, Conn., for a thousand dollars $1000. If an accident were to happen to me and I lost my life, whether on the railroad or any other way, my heirs would receive the above-named money. The most important document, the Policy, is always to be found in my chest, or you can refer yourselves to the agent with it, Travelers' Insurance Agent Josiah T. Peck, Bristol,

Conn. This insurance costs me six dollars per year. You will do well to keep the above in mind, as you three siblings up until this hour are my sole heirs.[77]

Within several months, however, Friedrich had a different beneficiary:

On 21 May I married again. My beloved wife comes from Kallstadt, near Türkheim [Bavaria]. She is 25 years old, and Protestant. She came only last September to this country. Dear sister, I consider it such a stroke of luck from God's hand to have found such a loving heart.

In earlier days I was looking more for money than sincerity and decency and for that I was punished severely. Therefore I took your advice. Our mother used to say that I should only be concerned with sincerity and I send my eternal gratitude into her grave, because she was right.

Sunday before our wedding, we had German Service here, it was there where we first met. Whoever meets that way—Love and loyalty can't help developing. I have a home now and don't need to live with strangers, which I like very much. We did not have a wedding celebration; if you could come we would be very happy.

Dear sister, thank God that the war which was raging for the last 4 years has been victoriously ended. Now there is peace again. God has saved us all.

My wife greets you. Her name is Anna Maria Hetterling.[78]

As Friedrich notes in his letter, by 1865, the Civil War was over. Given the number of volunteers and the heavy toll of casualties from Kansas, the war changed the face of the original territorial settlements to which the soldiers started to return in the summer of 1864.[79] The 1865 Kansas state census counted a population of 140,179, up 32,973 from 1860, with most of the increase coming in 1864.[80] Despite its title, the 1865 Kansas Non-Population Schedule did include population figures, and it reported a total of 2,349 inhabitants for Marshall County.[81] This was slightly less than the 2,426 reported in the 1860 federal census.[82] Twenty-eight soldiers had already returned to the county, the vast majority joining their families already settled there, and more Civil War veterans were to come.[83] This was encouraged by the Homestead Act, which allowed men who had served in the Union army to deduct their length of service from the required five-year occupancy of the land.[84]

War, Gold, Growth, Death, and Trouble, 1861–73

TABLE 4.1. Census Counts of Germans and Irish in Marshall County Townships, 1865

Township	1865 Kansas Non-Population Schedule		1865 Kansas State Census	
	German	Irish	German	Irish
Blue Rapids	1	6	2	6
Guittard	24	55	24	55
Marysville				
City	26	2	27	3
Township	94	6	93	6
Vermillion	5	0	9	46

Appendix F shows the distribution of Germans and other immigrants who had settled in significant numbers in the townships, according to the 1865 Kansas Non-Population Schedule. This is a potentially valuable resource because it provides detailed information on agricultural, manufacturing, and social statistics not presented elsewhere. The aggregate population figures it provides often, but not always, closely match the counts of individuals from the 1865 Kansas State Census, Schedule 1: Population (or simply the census). In Marshall County, although the overall population figures are in basic agreement, the counts of the foreign-born differ. Table 4.1 shows the two census counts of the German and Irish, the most numerous foreign-born groups in the county.

The Non-Population Schedule was apparently the basis, albeit amended, of the statistics J. Neale Carman cites from the Compendium of the Census of 1865 in volume 1 of his *Foreign-Language Units of Kansas*.[85] Carman voiced a concern about the accuracy of the compendium, as it was not based directly on counts of individuals.[86] Following his lead, I use the Non-Population Schedule for comparative purposes to give an overall picture of settlement, but I use the Schedule 1 figures for specific counts of the foreign-born.

The reason for the discrepancies between the two census schedules is unclear. We have no document specifying how the counts for the Non-Population Schedule were conducted. When the counts are off by just one or two individuals, it might be because the counts were carried out at different times. In addition, during this period, more townships were being formed and some of the counties were redrawn as well as renamed, so the difference might be a function of the exact areas covered by the counts. Or the data reported could simply be incomplete.

TABLE 4.2. Comparison of German-Born Inhabitants in the 1860 Federal Census and 1865 Kansas State Censuses

County	1860 Federal Census	1865 Kansas State Census Non-Population Schedule	1865 Kansas State Census
Anderson	48	17*	46
Chase	26	17	15
Coffey	31	16	27
Dickinson	88	67	70
Jefferson	109	84	45
Lyon**	34	17	17
Nemaha	85	63	51
Osage	37	14	25
Pottawatomie	153	136	147
Wyandotte	220	195	189

*Count error
**Formerly Breckinridge

In the broader picture of the entire state presented in appendix F, every county for which a census count is listed, except Marion, had German-born settlers. These include the two western counties of Saline and Ottawa and the southern county of Neosho. The count for Marion in the 1865 Kansas Non-Population Schedule is correct; that county lost the few German settlers it had in 1860. According to the 1865 Kansas state census, Marion had only four foreign-born in 1865. The state census likewise places German-born settlers in the newer counties, although the exact numbers differ slightly.[87]

A comparison of the figures from the 1865 Kansas Non-Population Schedule (appendix F) and those from the 1860 federal census (appendix B) reveals major fluctuations in the number of German-born residing in the counties. The counties of most interest are those that show a decline of at least ten individuals (nine in the case of Chase) in their German-born populations. There were ten such counties (table 4.2). Do the figures from the 1865 Kansas state census agree? Interestingly, as table 4.2 shows, it confirms the loss in seven of the counties. In fact, in four counties it reports a lower count than the Non-Population Schedule: Chase, Jefferson, Nemaha, and Wyandotte. In Lyon, the counts are the same. For Dickinson and Osage it reports higher counts, but they are still lower than the 1860 figures. In three of the counties, the 1865 state census count is close enough to the 1860 federal count to make little difference: Coffey, Anderson, and Pottawatomie.

So, it seems that German-born settlers, as well as the native-born, did not necessarily stay put. Even in those counties showing a gain, it was not always new arrivals adding to the population. The frontier in Kansas was still fluid.

In the four townships of Marshall County, one of the counties that gained German-born settlers but lost overall population, there was a massive turnover in the population at large.[88] This is reflected in the surnames of the inhabitants.[89] In 1860 in Blue Rapids, there was at least one individual residing there with one of 148 surnames; in 1865 only 41 of the surnames (28 percent) appeared in the state census for the township. Ten of those surnames appearing in the 1860 census belonged to German-born, but only one appeared in 1865. In Marysville, out of 157 surnames, 58 (37 percent) were still represented in the township in the 1865 census, including 10 of 24 German surnames. In Vermillion Township, out of 169 surnames, 50 (30 percent) were still represented there in 1865, including 2 of 6 German surnames (one of which was Heinrich's). The residents of Guittard, where the Lodholzes lived, were the most stable. Out of 59 surnames, 28 (47 percent) were still listed in the 1865 state census for that township, including 4 of the 8 German surnames. Unfortunately, we know very little about what happened to those who left. Of the 31 German-born individuals and heads of families with surnames that no longer appeared in township census data, only 3 could be identified with some confidence as living in other counties in Kansas.[90]

In the 1865 Kansas state census, Blue Rapids had a total population of 583 and no significant German-born population—or any other foreign-born, for that matter. This was a major decline from 1860. There were in fact only two Germans—both from Württemberg, one of them an elderly woman. Guittard's population of 362 included 24 German-born, an increase of 5 from 1860; they were greatly outnumbered by the 55 Irish settlers.[91] The Irish likewise dominated among the foreign-born in Vermillion, population 605; there were 46 Irish and only 9 German-born, a decrease of 6 from 1860.[92] In contrast, the city of Marysville and the surrounding township saw a remarkable increase in the number of Germans. In the city proper, there were 27 German-born among the population of 308, with only 3 each from Ireland, England, and Poland; 2 each from Scotland and Canada; and 1 each from Switzerland and Norway. In the rest of Marysville Township, there were 93 German-born, accounting for almost 20 percent of the 488 residents, along with 9 from Scandinavia, 7 from England, 6 from Ireland, and 5 from Scotland. Keeping in mind the discrepancies uncovered in the 1865 Kansas Non-Population Schedule, outside of the major cities, there were apparently only three other townships in Kansas that had 90 or more German-born: Eudora in Douglas County, Alma in Wabaunsee County, and Wyandotte in Wyandotte County. The initial density of German-born in Eudora and Alma—far greater at that time than in any of the townships in Marshall County—probably contributed to their staying power as a community.

The German-born who came to Marshall County in the early days after the Civil War represented the start of a second wave of settlers to Kansas. The majority settled in the northern part of the county, in Guittard and especially Marysville. This set the pattern of settlement for years to come. What do we know about the Lodholzes' new neighbors?

In every township in Marshall County, there were more single than married individuals in the population at large.[93] However, the majority of new German-born migrants to Marysville and Guittard were married with children—a total of thirty-two families. There were only nine new single males in the two townships, ranging in age from thirty to sixty-three, and only two of them were farming on their own. Most were working and boarding in the homes of German families. There were only four couples, two in which the spouses were younger than thirty and two in which the spouses were older than thirty-six.

The thirty-two families with children were in many ways similar to the families with children who had settled in the territorial days. Ten had started their families since arriving in Kansas. In three families, all the children present in Kansas had been born in Germany.[94] Ten of the remaining families had children born in Germany but added to their families once they arrived in the United States, and nine started their families after arriving in this country. These nineteen families were seasoned settlers, like their earlier counterparts. Ten initially resided in the North Midlands, six in the Northeast (Wisconsin in particular), and three in the Upper South (Missouri). The shortest documented stay was one year; the longest was twelve years. Of these nineteen families, three had moved twice before coming to Kansas.

Roughly half of the thirty-two families (15) had just one or two children; among the six families with five or more children, there were two with eight and one with eleven. Five of the male spouses had native-born wives.

Surprisingly, the 1860 federal census showed relatively few related German families settling next to or not far from one another, the exception being the settlement at Alma, which had a large number of related families (see appendix D). Most involved brothers, and the rest involved a parent and a son. There were several related families in Marshall County, including the Lodholz brothers. By 1865, the state census revealed that three of the new German-born settlers had family members living on farms around them. Whether these qualified as family compounds is questionable. It was still early in the settlement process, and this was not an exclusively German arrangement; ten of the native-born families had the same setup.

Apparently, 1865 was a fortuitous time to buy land. Judging from the list of properties sold for back taxes in the *Big Blue Union* published in Marysville in January 1864, land speculation was not paying off. In May 1862, 136 properties in the township, as well as numerous town lots in Marysville, had been sold off for back taxes, and the original owners were notified that they had until May 1864 to redeem their property or lose title to it.[95] These farms were extraordinary bargains; for example, 160 acres sold for $81, and 200 acres for $143.[96] At the time, Gottfried's 160-acre parcel was valued at $600.[97] The successful buyer of tax-delinquent property could presumably resell it at an attractive price and still make a profit. In addition, sheriffs' auction sales of land whose owners had defaulted on their mortgages continued to take place, as they had since territorial days.[98]

The Homestead Act opened up new possibilities. In 1865 there was still a lot of land left to settle, particularly toward the west, and homesteaders got a large share. They ultimately claimed approximately 25 percent of the land in Kansas.[99] In Marshall County, these homesteaders included Thomas and Eliza Howes from England:

> [The couple] had little to bring to their new home, as they brought only their bedding from their home in England. After their arrival in the county they homesteaded one hundred and sixty acres in Oketo township, but eighty acres of the tract was later taken away from them. They lived in the prairie schooner until Mr. Howes could cut the logs and build a one-room house, twelve by fourteen feet, and in this they lived for seven years. . . . The first year they were on the place, five acres of the tract was broken and a crop of buckwheat was raised. Their first year in their new home was a hard one, for they had been able to raise but little on their farm and they were without funds to buy.[100]

Civil War veteran David Heisse was fortunate to settle on land his future wife, Mary Wolfgang, had homesteaded in 1869.[101] The land available to many homesteaders in Marshall County was limited, however. Much of the land had already been secured with warrants by settlers such as the Lodholzes and Heinrich Reb, and it was difficult for newcomers to scrutinize plat maps to find vacant land. They often needed the help of professionals who were knowledgeable about locating such parcels. Even with the sale of tax-delinquent properties, much of the land was still in the hands of speculators. The railroads, which had been given loans and generous land grants as an incentive to lay track, also owned significant amounts of land alongside their roads.[102] The price of land in Marshall County was now a far cry from the $1.25 per acre charged by the federal government to preemptors before the Civil War. By 1870, Civil War veteran John Nichols was buying land at $5 an acre "and later had a most difficult time in keeping up the payments. The markets were far distant and the prices were low, and where there was grain or produce to sell, it brought but very little."[103] John McKee from Ireland bought railroad land at a similar price: $5.25 an acre.[104]

Like John Nichols, many of the new settlers were hard up for cash and needed to take other jobs to make money. When Perry Hutchinson needed a tunnel chiseled out to funnel water to power his flour mill in Marysville, he hired several grateful men, including Mathew Schumacher of Luxembourg. Schumacher's biographer stated: "Had it not been for the kindness of Mr. Hutchinson, our subject and many others would have been obliged to leave the country or starve."[105] Calvin Chesney taught school, and Fred Stohs, a native of Germany, become a farm laborer after his claim was "jumped" while he was working for the railroad.[106]

In some cases, small settlements of families eventually grew into towns later in the century. In others, settlers formed colonies in the fashion of Barrett and established towns mainly along existing or planned railroad routes. Among the most prominent in Marshall County was Irving, founded in 1859 by fourteen families from Iowa.[107] In 1869 residents from western New York purchased 287 acres of land near the junction of the Big and Little Blue Rivers; the considerable water power they provided allowed Blue Rapids to become a major manufacturing center.[108] Its main claim to fame was its high-quality gypsum rock, still mined today, which was used to make the plaster of Paris decorations on the temporary wooden structures at the Chicago and St. Louis World's Fairs.[109]

Frankfort (originally Frank's Ford) was deliberately founded to attract a railroad. The Frankfort Town Company was organized in Marysville and purchased land seven miles north of Barrett. The company offered half the town site to the Central Branch Railroad Company, also known as the

Atchison and Pike's Peak Railroad, in exchange for a station, a depot, and side track. When the railroad reached Frankfort in 1867, the town celebrated with a dance in the newly built depot.[110] Cattle, wheat, and flour immediately started to make their way to Chicago. The railroad was a boon to the fledgling town in other ways as well, providing work to laborers constructing the roadways and a market for local timber for the railway ties and fuel for the steam engines.[111]

Frankfort's generous offer to the railroad was bad news for the town of Barrett. There are two stories surrounding the decision by Atchison and Pike's Peak Railroad officials to bypass Barrett. One is that A. G. Barrett invited the railroad officials to dinner at his house, along with some of his African American workers, and the pro-slavery railroad men took offense.[112] The second and more plausible story is that A. G. Barrett did not offer as much land as the railroad desired, so the officials decided to locate the line in the more generously inclined Frankfort.[113] A. G. Barrett eventually provided the land and helped raise the money to build a railroad depot with a side track, but the town of Barrett never got out from under Frankfort's shadow.[114] Its earlier prominence was now much diminished.

In 1860 the total population of Kansas was 107,206; in 1870 it was 364,399, an increase of more than 300 percent.[115] Of the 1870 population, 298,041 were native-born whites; 48,336 were foreign-born whites; and 17,108 were African Americans, up significantly from the 627 living in Kansas in 1860 as ex-slaves made their way from the South.[116] The mostly poor African Americans received a cool welcome and lived mainly in segregated areas of cities.[117] Meanwhile, in the early 1860s the federal government made even more treaties with the local Native American tribes, eventually moving them out of Kansas and into Indian Territory (Oklahoma).[118]

After the Civil War, the Lodholzes, the Rebs, and their neighbors were focused on making a living from their land, and they were helped greatly by the railroads. In the 1865 Kansas state census, Heinrich's occupation was listed as blacksmith.[119] However, having brought oxen back with him from Denver, he was set to begin farming life in earnest. In 1869 he paid his neighbors Eli and Alvirada Putney $100 for five acres of timberland bordered by a creek to the west and the Black Vermillion River to the east.[120] This land is still owned by one of his descendants.

By the time of the 1870 federal census, Heinrich was listed as a farmer.[121] Of his reported 189 acres, 15 acres were woodland; 35 acres had been "improved" by erecting buildings, putting up fences, and plowing fields; and the remaining 139 acres were unimproved.[122] The relatively small size of the improved acreage is evidence of the difficulty of breaking the prairie sod and sowing and harvesting crops by hand. The value of the Reb farm was set at $3,780, higher than that of many neighboring farms, and the value of the farming implements was $50. Heinrich had paid wages of $50 to hired help. There were four horses, fourteen milk cows (a fairly large number), and fourteen other cattle, but no working oxen. The value of the livestock was $990.[123] This valuation of the Reb farm is an example of how increased migration in the wake of the Homestead Act and the end of the Civil War had pushed up land values.

The previous year, Heinrich had harvested 225 bushels of spring wheat, 500 bushels of Indian corn, and 40 bushels of oats.[124] Indian corn, so named because of its origins in Native American cultures, was the general term for almost any variety of corn. In addition to being a source of animal feed, once it was ground into cornmeal, corn was the staple grain for human consumption. The oats were used strictly for animal feed.

Heinrich and Anna (as Anna Regina will now be called) had a growing family. Young Henry was followed by Anna Mary (known as Mary) in 1865, John Frederick in 1866, Frederick C. in 1867, and William Gottfried (known as Will) in 1869. With five children, Anna had more clothes to sew and wash and more food to cook and preserve. And she had to do all this while still living in a log cabin. Anna's days were unending, even when some of the children were old enough to help with chores such as gathering eggs.

Meanwhile, Georg was corresponding with Friedrich about the land or its cash value that he still owed his brother. In May 1866 Georg explained, rather disingenuously, that since Friedrich did not need the money, Georg would be the best person to hold it for him. Once he learned that Friedrich was indeed in need of money, Georg urged him to come to Kansas immediately and buy land while there was still the chance to do so, so each brother would have 160 acres. Georg obviously did not want to give up any part of his property. The recently single Georg was also looking for a wife and was hoping that Friedrich's sister-in-law would come to Kansas too: "You should sell all of your Goods and things and come to us as soon as possible, if your dear Wife's sister is yet single and she should like to come here and she could Love me, it may be God's will, that she can become my Wife and Life-partner. . . . I have kept house long enough myself (alone)."[125] He was obviously looking for a housekeeper, sight unseen. Of the four men in the Lodholz-Reb family, Georg's attitude toward wives was the most utilitarian.

That pairing never materialized, as Friedrich was not eager to rush back to Kansas. By February 1867, however, Georg had found someone and was again married by a justice of the peace (not Gottfried this time). His new wife was Prussian-born Anna Rosina Genschoreck, who would prove to be feisty and was hardly self-effacing. Much later in life than Gottfried, Georg started a family in his early thirties. The 1870 federal census reveals that Georg and Rosina had two children: Mary, aged two, and Anna, aged eight months.[126]

The land of both Georg and Gottfried increased in value, but it was worth far less than Heinrich's. In 1865 Georg's land was valued at $600, and by 1870, its value had more than doubled to $1,600.[127] Gottfried's land also rose in value to $1,700.[128] Heinrich had more land than either of them and plenty of timber, which may account in part for its higher value.

Georg and his new family were certainly getting by. In 1870 he had 30 acres of improved land, 5 acres of woodland, and 125 acres of unimproved land. He had thirteen cattle, three horses, one mule (a particularly valuable draft animal), six milk cows, and one pig. The total value of the livestock was $460. Georg had harvested 190 bushels of spring wheat, 300 bushels of Indian corn, and 50 bushels of oats the previous year.[129] The family's house was simply furnished—one full bed (meaning the children probably slept with their parents), a table with five chairs, a clock, two trunks to store clothing, a kerosene lamp for light, and a wood-burning metal cookstove (no more cooking over an open hearth). Besides two Bibles, Georg possessed a copy of *History of the New World*, a natural for a man who loved to travel.[130]

Next door, Gottfried likewise had only thirty acres of improved land, but he was reaping more from his farm and branching out into a new endeavor. He grew more spring wheat (200 bushels) and Indian corn (400 bushels) than Georg, and his livestock included eleven cattle, five pigs, six milk cows, and ninety-eight sheep. The total value of the livestock was $750.[131] Others in Marshall County imported sheep to fatten up and ship to market elsewhere, but Gottfried focused on producing wool.[132] His decision may have been motivated by two considerations—the establishment of a woolen mill in Blue Rapids, and the relative ease of raising sheep.[133] Opened in 1872, the mill was a large facility, initially employing forty-five men. By 1883, the mill was running twenty-four hours a day, employing one hundred men, and using 300,000 pounds of wool annually to create yarns and various types of cloth.[134]

Gottfried had no sons, so he had to hire help, which was expensive, and rely on his wife and older daughters to pitch in with the farm chores. Although shearing sheep was hard, dirty work, it was only a once- or twice-a-year event, and raising sheep was less arduous than breaking sod, planting, cultivating, and harvesting in the erratic climate of the Great Plains. Sheep required no special feed; they foraged on whatever grasses were available—roots and all—even in winter, as long as the snow was not frost encrusted.[135] Sheep are fairly docile, even when being sheared, so Mary and Annie could tend them. The sheep were probably herded and guarded by the family dogs (in 1875 they had three), who alerted them when predators, such as wolves or other dogs, were nearby.[136]

Gottfried may have carded at least some of the wool—a skill he had probably learned many years ago in Ebhausen—so it could be spun into yarn for weaving. In November 1868 he ordered a $50 loom by mail—quite an investment.[137] It is unclear whether Gottfried considered weaving a possible commercial venture or an opportunity to teach his daughters the craft of their grandparents so they could make items for the family's personal use. There is no evidence that he sold any of the woven items.

In 1868, back in Terryville, Friedrich was still working in the lock factory and writing letters to the family. But like many factory workers in the East, he had grown bitter about how little he earned. "There is enough work in the shop. However, I am no longer liking it, because we Germans have to do all the work so the Yankees can earn a great deal without doing work. You were absolutely right when you wrote to us last year that one cannot rely on the shop business, farming is admittedly more certain. I will be happy when they get the railroad built up out your way." Friedrich was obviously feeling more and more distant from his relatives. In the same letter he wrote:

> As it has not yet been granted to us over these long years to see each other again in person, we are sending you our likenesses for Christmas, of my dear wife and me. You still recognize your brother, don't you? We wish that we could also have you and your dear children's [likenesses] sent to us and see you. It would make us very happy, but seeing each other personally soon is perhaps better. May our dear Lord only keep us in good health, so that we can reach that point.[138]

His weariness with the uncertainty of factory work and the loneliness of being separated from his birth family finally led Friedrich to visit Kansas in 1869 at the age of thirty-three. He traveled all the way by train and arrived at the newly built depot in Frankfort, where Heinrich picked him up—much different from his last trip to Kansas in an oxcart. The steam-driven trains, however, were still slow by today's standards. They had to stop periodically to refill their water tanks, rarely went faster than fifteen miles per hour, and were likely to confront wandering cattle on the tracks.[139] Friedrich's wife did not accompany him, perhaps because of cost.

It had been almost ten years since the siblings had seen one another, and there would have been much rejoicing at their reunion. Friedrich met for the first time Anna's husband and children, Georg's wife and children, and several of the new additions to Gottfried and Christina's home. They enjoyed meals and prayed together. Friedrich undoubtedly visited and prayed at his mother's grave, which must have been an emotion-filled moment. Always on the lookout for money, Georg and his wife took the opportunity to try to wheedle more of it out of Friedrich. The incident left a bad taste in his mouth, and he later asserted that they had used "trickery."[140]

After the visit, Friedrich returned to Terryville and his wife, and he never again set foot on the Great Plains. He had grown accustomed to the relative conveniences of city life, and faming must have seemed to him harder and more grueling than factory work. Friedrich wrote to Anna and Heinrich in November 1869:

> After we have seen each other again and I have taken many dear memories back from Kansas, it is time to write to you.
>
> I received your letter from August. You said not to stay too long in Conn., but come and see you again. I am sure that not many years will go by before we can do that, although we never know what fate has in store for us. Our brother Gottfried could have died easily when the wagon went over him but God's love kept him for us. Thanks and praise the Lord! May he be healthy and see some better days than the beginning of the sixties gave him. He is worth it!
>
> I found the word of God at your place, which pleased me.
>
> As far as we are concerned, we are healthy, business is strong in the factory. Farming is much healthier.
>
> I have heard that the St. Joseph railroad will be built where our brothers are. It is an Express Railroad and has an iron bridge across the Mississippi R.[141]

The year 1870 was one of great change and tragedy for the Lodholzes and the Rebs. The federal census showed that the number of families in Guittard Township had doubled in the past decade from 67 to 133. In Vermillion Township, the increase was even more dramatic—from 115 to 363, an increase of more than 300 percent.

Meanwhile, events in Germany were creating dramatic changes. Under Bismarck, Prussia had begun unification efforts. The small northern German states were now under Prussian control, but the southern German states such as Württemberg resisted. We do not know how this affected relations among German immigrants, but conflict between Prussia and the southern German states ended with the Franco-Prussian War, in which Baden and Württemberg sided with Prussia. In July 1870 Friedrich wrote to Anna and Heinrich: "Here is great excitement because of the war between Germany and France. It is too sad that wars have to happen. I hope that God will make Germany victorious."[142] The war ended in defeat for France and unification of the German states in the German Empire in 1871, with Prussia the dominant power. There was finally an actual country—of sorts. Unity, however, was not a given. Between 1872 and 1887, Bismarck and the Vatican waged a *Kulturkampf* over the formation of a secular state versus maintenance of the status quo in terms of who controlled the schools and ecclesiastical appointments. In addition, as Mack Walker points out, Prussia instituted conscription laws under which, for a considerable part of their lives, young men faced the prospect of being conscripted by lottery and serving for three years.[143] This was hardly appealing to many men.[144]

In the spring of 1870 Johannes Kempf, a cousin of Anna's from Ebhausen, visited the family.[145] The remainder of the year, however, brought no joy. In October thirty-seven-year-old Georg died of unknown causes. There is no death certificate and no mention of the cause of death in any extant letters. Possibilities include an accident, such as being thrown from a horse or falling off a wagon; "fever" contracted from mosquitoes swarming near the shady creeks; diseases such as tetanus, diphtheria, or typhoid; snakebite; food poisoning; and countless others. There were many ways to die on the tallgrass prairie.

Then Anna and Heinrich had more grief to bear. Shortly after Georg's death, their son Frederick, not quite three years old, likewise died of unknown causes. Anna certainly knew that her mother had also lost a young son named Friedrich in Ebhausen. Back in Terryville, Friedrich wrote a letter of condolence to his sister and brother-in-law:

How sad it is to hear that our dear brother Johann Georg has been taken from us so early. Georg has followed our deceased mother so early to heaven.

And the hurt for you to lose a little son so soon afterwards. It is hard for you, little Friedrich with his curly hair, closed his beautiful eyes as a child. Oh how pure will be his soul in paradise.[146]

Georg's death unleashed a bitter feud between his widow and Gottfried and Friedrich. Georg left no will, and under Kansas law, if a husband died intestate, his homestead, up to 160 acres, passed to his wife and children.[147] When Georg's estate was appraised, there was little of value among his personal effects. The most valuable property was the land, now worth $2,400; the livestock; one wagon; and twenty tons of hay.[148] The settlement should have been simple, but it was not.

For almost a year, Rosina retained full possession of all the property, which she and the children shared. But then she took up with a man named John Book and became pregnant in 1871. In August of that year, a John Book placed a legal notice in the *Marshall County News* seeking a divorce from Amanda Book.[149] It is likely that this was the same man. Rosina apparently married him sometime between 1871 and 1873, as court documents, family letters, and her own letters to family members referred to her as Rosina Book or variations thereof (Buch, Bok, and Buk).

The marriage, however, created a problem. With the birth of a child in the offing, Gottfried was concerned about the rights of Georg's children, and he intervened in October 1871. From his point of view, all Georg's land, so hard earned by the family as a whole, should not fall into the hands of the Books. He believed Georg's children should have their half of the inheritance. In addition, he and Friedrich thought Rosina should repay the money Friedrich had loaned Georg over the years.

Thus, almost a year after Georg's death, Gottfried persuaded (or more likely pressured) Rosina, who was still using the name Lodholz at the time, to file a court petition waiving her right to serve as administrator of her husband's estate and appointing Gottfried instead. He was also appointed the children's guardian. Immediately he took the proper probate actions—taking an inventory, getting an appraisal, posting a bond, placing a notice in the newspaper of his appointment as administrator, and the like. Gottfried devoted a great deal of time and energy to traveling to Marysville to file the necessary documents, attending to all the individuals involved in the inventory and appraisal, herding the children's share of the livestock (which Rosina had taken elsewhere) to his property, and even protecting the children's land from a prairie fire. He had legitimate expenses as the administrator of the estate, and his filing of papers related to that duty showed his command of the English language.

All seemed to be going smoothly. The land had been surveyed and divided, and Gottfried, as the children's guardian, had paid real estate taxes on their portion. In January 1872 Rosina wrote to Friedrich to ask "a little favor" regarding the money she owed him. Because she intended to raise the money by selling livestock, and prices were down, she asked if Friedrich could wait for prices to rise.[150] The following month, Gottfried leased the children's land to John Book and Rosina for a term of three years, and in March he paid Mr. Book to buy nails to fix fencing on the property. It was at this point that the Books' first child, Johanna, was born. By the time their second child, Charles, was born in 1874, the marriage had apparently fallen apart, or perhaps John Book had died, although there is no mention of that in family letters.[151] There is no record of a John Book under any possible spelling other than in the 1860 federal census, and he was never mentioned again.[152]

Rosina had apparently been abandoned and was on her own. If that were the case, she would have been frantic about how she would support herself and her children. She was dependent on Gottfried for the disbursement of funds from the estate and pestered him constantly. She was galled by his control and began to feel that she was being taken advantage of. Meanwhile, Gottfried was critical of her for selling property (which was not part of the estate) for what he considered too little. She had also sold a wagon that *was* part of the estate and had not shared with him the children's portion of the money.

In June 1873 Rosina hired a lawyer and filed a petition in court to remove Gottfried as administrator of the estate and guardian of Georg's children. She accused Gottfried of failing to faithfully administer the estate—specifically, selling the estate's property through private sales rather than public offerings and squandering the money. She further argued that Gottfried had been appointed guardian without her permission, which involved fraud and misrepresentation. She claimed that he was wasting the children's money and "is not a suitable person to be appointed Guardian of said children." These were serious charges.

Gottfried was dismayed at this public attack on his good name, and he sought the support of Heinrich and Anna. He appealed to Heinrich to attend the court session, set for July 28: "I could be happy if you, brother-in-law, could come to Marysville on that day. Our 'good name' is at stake, they want to rob us of our dignity."[153] Rosina also tried to enlist Anna's support and wrote a highly emotional, bitter letter to her:

> Since I have the honor of not having been insulted by you alone, I bid you my friendship....
>
> Who is in the right—I or Gottfried—who our money uses so that the children will not have much of it one day or I as mother. I have been

made to be bad, worse than Minna [short for Wilhelmina] which Georg himself admits that they did her injustice.

Friedrich insults me as well although I've never insulted him, probably Georg told him all those lies about me when he [Friedrich] was here.

Brother Gottfried can't be as holy if even your husband and all other take his side and say that I annoy him too much. I don't. You will remember the story of the brother who was selling his sister Dorthea—Gottfried would do the same if he could.[154]

Life in a small community can promote neighborly cooperation, but it can also generate vicious gossip and grievances. Rosina had obviously sought support from neighbors who disliked Gottfried and had told her about Wilhelmina, with whom Rosina identified.

The court date on July 28 did not result in a ruling in Rosina's favor, but she continued to avoid paying the money owed to Friedrich. Rosina wrote another bitter and wildly emotional letter to Anna on August 6, claiming that Anna was going to be called to testify.[155] Anna was thoroughly confused and wrote to Friedrich:

> There are the same difficulties. Georg's wife against Gottfried and you. I can't make it out what she means. She says that she doesn't owe you anything. I got a letter from her in which she invites me to the next Court Hearing in which they want to investigate my sincerity. Something about Georg owe [sic] you, or what he had paid to you. We don't know. He owed you, and he wanted to pay. Who would have thought that this old affair would be made public. Georg surely would have done right if he had known.[156]

In the end, Anna did not have to testify, and Rosina lost in court again. Friedrich got his money from the estate. In an accounting she provided to Anna, Rosina claimed that she had personally paid him $200.[157] Friedrich was hurting financially and felt that the whole family, not just Georg, owed him for the hard-earned money he had sent them in their early years on the prairie. He told Anna in November 1873, "you will probably remember that I was always promised land for the money that I handed over, but none has been ascribed to me, thus it is only proper to pay me."[158]

We do not know the details of the transaction, but certainly Gottfried, Anna, and Heinrich contributed money that allowed them to buy Friedrich sixty acres of the land that had belonged to Georg. As guardian of Georg's children, Gottfried could sell part of their land on their behalf. So Friedrich finally had a place to call his own if he ever chose to move to Kansas. But the ongoing economic depression left him with little in the way of funds to go west and start farming, even if he had wanted to. He must have counted on Gottfried to work the land or lease it to someone else.

Having faced hard times during the Panic of 1857, Friedrich's latest financial woes were the result of yet another economic downturn, the Depression of 1873, which would last for the rest of the decade. Corruption, runaway railway speculation, and overproduction led to a stock market collapse, bank closures, and falling farm prices. Unemployment rose to 14 percent.[159] Friedrich's May 1873 description of the depression was grim:

> As regards business, I have nothing good to report. For the past three months things have been very bad. Often there is no work and thus little in the way of earnings. So far people are just being let go, which is a bad sign. The gentlemen [at the lock factory] may want to employ me and a few others. Whether they can continue to do so, however, only time will tell.
>
> We will also soon begin to grow older, and it will soon be advisable to go to our homeland, where the bloodhounds are no longer causing desecration and torment in the factories.

He added later in the same letter: "For the past four weeks we've been working three days per week. No one knows if it will get worse yet. Thousands of men have no work at all in the cities. What will happen this next winter? In New York, the largest businesses are bankrupt. The prospects are bad."[160]

Whatever the family's feelings toward Rosina, there was nothing but kind concern for Georg's children. Friedrich wrote to Anna: "If you know anything of our dear brother Georg's children, then let me know it as well. We are obligated to protect them as long as we can."[161]

Rosina had another child in 1876—ironically, named George—in Colorado, where she had gone after losing her legal battles with Gottfried. We do not know her marital status at that juncture. From Colorado she tried one last time to wrest control of Georg's estate from Gottfried. Georg's probate file contains a petition from a probate judge in Elbert County, Colorado, asking for Rosina to be made administrator of the estate and guardian of her children. This may have goaded Gottfried into settling the estate once and for all.

According to the 1880 federal census, Rosina had left Colorado and settled permanently in St. Joseph, Missouri, with five children and seventy-four-year-old Thomas Balsam, listed as her father-in-law. She continued to use the surname Lodholz for both herself and all her children.[162] Later, on her death certificate, she was listed as the widow of John George Lodholz.[163] Rosina's path in life was hardly smooth, but once she left Marshall County, she could at least maintain a semblance of dignity.

CHAPTER 5

Change, Tragedy, and the Female Frontier in Marshall County, 1874–90

Kansas continued to experience tremendous growth and change between 1874 and 1890. The Kansas population was 343,866 in 1870, 984,300 in 1880 (an increase of more than 275 percent), and almost 1.5 million by 1890.[1] The vast majority of Kansans were native-born, but Germans accounted for a significant proportion of foreign-born settlers. Events from this era were memorably recorded in Howard Ruede's *Sod-House Days* and John Ise's *Sod and Stubble*.[2] Both works detail life among the mainly German settlements in Osborne County, located in the middle of the state, two counties south of Nebraska. In 1870 Osborne County had a population of 33; in 1878, it was 3,125.[3]

The 1870s also brought large groups of Volga and Black Sea Germans to Kansas. They established their close-knit communities, often with the help of a recruiting railroad agent, along the railroad lines in Ellis, Russell, McPherson, and Marion Counties, as well as others farther west.[4] In the late 1700s Prussian-born Catherine the Great, the empress of Russia, had recruited settlers in Germany to populate her country. Mennonites, Lutherans, Reformed (Calvinists), Moravians, and Catholics established self-contained villages along the Volga River and the Black Sea, where they continued to maintain their culture. She attracted these migrants by granting them various privileges, including exemption from military service. In the

1870s, under Tsar Alexander II, these privileges were eroded, contributing to the villagers' mass immigration to the United States.[5]

In Marshall County, according to the 1865 Kansas state census, the total population was 2,349; by 1880, it had reached 16,136 (an increase of almost 700 percent), and by 1890, it was 23,912.[6] In reviewing the biographies in Emma Forter's history and in *Portrait and Biographical Album of Marshall County*, it is apparent that much of the best land was quickly claimed, and the price made it unaffordable for many of the newcomers. Some purchased "raw" and "wild" prairie—railroad land selling for $4.37½ an acre.[7] Some of those who took up farming inherited, purchased, or rented family land.[8] However, many more reported working as farmhands before renting and later purchasing land—if they were lucky.[9] From 1880 to 1890, the number of cash renters in Kansas increased from 3.2 percent of all farms to 6 percent, and the sharecropper/tenant percentage increased from 11.1 to 22.2.[10] Decisions made decades ago by the Lodholzes and Heinrich Reb to stake their future on the soil of Marshall County had paid off.

There were several important factors that helped the Lodholzes be pioneers, and the absence of those factors likely hindered many other German immigrants in the early days. One was the men's decision to become US citizens, which allowed them to take advantage of preemption. Writing from Pittsburgh to his siblings in Germany in 1884, Christian Kirst compared the laws and customs in the United States with those in Germany and had this to say about citizenship: "There are many thousands here . . . who have been here 20–30 years already and still aren't citizens, and don't want to be, since a citizen has no more rights than someone who isn't a citizen, except he can vote for Congress or for President . . . you can also get a minor post like policeman, you have to know the English language though."[11] Clearly citizenship was more valuable in the Kansas Territory, where it could lead to landownership. Even by the time of World War I, many Germans immigrants still had not applied for citizenship, and once diplomatic relations with Germany were cut off, many rushed to begin the process.[12]

Second, the ability to speak English and being conversant with the basics of American laws and social norms contributed to their survival on the prairie. Without this facility, German immigrants heading west could be placed at a distinct disadvantage on the frontier.

A third factor was the amount of capital the Lodholzes were able to accumulate early on in the United States—at least enough to give them a start in farming. As we learned from the discussion of Georg's time in Chicago, it was too expensive for the average German immigrant to engage in agriculture, but that did not stop some of them from coming to the Kansas Territory, where they hoped to find work and earn the necessary funds.

The fourth factor was the family's determination to stick together, with each individual contributing in his or her own way. In particular, Friedrich's willingness to forgo some of life's pleasures to send money to his relatives on the prairie was crucial. It allowed the Lodholzes to obtain their land debt-free—a significant achievement.

Finally, there was their resilience in the face of hard times, wildfires, and all the other privations of the prairie. This is most apparent in the decisions made by Gottfried, the most ambitious of the Lodholz men, in response to market demands. He started raising sheep in the late 1860s, and by 1875, Gottfried's herd had increased to more than two hundred sheep that produced seven hundred pounds of wool a year.[13] As usual Christina and the couple's daughters also contributed to the family's income. By then, they had eleven "milch" cows and were churning out one hundred pounds of butter to sell each year. Gottfried had even devoted an acre to an orchard to satisfy the family's sweet tooth and perhaps earn a little extra cash. He also had two acres in rye, eighteen in spring wheat, forty in corn, and eight in oats.[14] So he was obviously not counting on grain sales to support them.

In stark contrast, in 1880 Gottfried's farm was valued at $6,176, much higher than that of his near neighbors.[15] He was no longer invested in sheep; the woolen mill would soon fold.[16] In the space of just five years, he and Christina had rethought the basis of their livelihood. In 1880 they harvested 1,800 bushels of Indian corn, 92 bushels of oats, 136 bushels of wheat, and 130 bushels of Irish potatoes. Their twenty-one milk cows produced 520 pounds of butter. They had forty-four other cattle and twenty-five swine, and their forty chickens produced 250 eggs for sale annually. Gottfried had made good on Georg's desire to grow fruit. His 75 apple trees and 111 peach trees produced far more fruit than the family needed for their own consumption and presumably provided another source of income.[17]

Agriculture was becoming mechanized, and the ox was being replaced by the much faster horse as the major source of power. The first riding plow, known as a sulky plow, was invented and manufactured by Linden Kirlin in the 1870s; he set up shop in Marshall County in the 1880s.[18] Machines such as the riding plow and the twine binder made farming tasks less arduous and less time-consuming. With a twine binder, two men and a team of horses could harvest and shock twenty acres of small grains, such as wheat and oats, in a day.[19] But machinery cost money, which made farming more expensive and led to more debt for many.

RESIDENCE OF GODFREY LODHOLZ, SEC. 26. RICHLAND TOWNSHIP

Etching of Gottfried's farm. In addition to his biography, Gottried was one of the few whose farms were depicted in *Portrait and Biographical Album of Marshall County* ([Chicago: Chapman Brothers, 1889], 317).

The ethnic composition of Marshall County was also changing. The Indian wars were still being waged farther west (the Battle of Little Big Horn took place in 1876), but in Marshall County, the peaceful Otoes had been moved to Indian Territory by 1881, as had other tribes before them.[20] Meanwhile, the town of Frankfort had gained enough of an African American population for them to have two churches of their own. Although their churches were segregated and the black residents were relegated to the edge of town for housing, their children attended the local public schools.[21]

In 1875 half the land of Marshall County—but probably not the better half—was still unsettled.[22] Native-born white settlers continued to make up the vast majority of those moving to Kansas and Marshall County, but Germans accounted for the greatest number among the foreign-born white population of both the state and the county. Marshall County became the site of a number of important German settlements, most of them in the northern part of the county.[23] With the advent of the railroad in 1871, Marysville continued to grow. At Horseshoe Creek, northwest of the city, the small German Lutheran settlement affiliated with the Missouri Synod now had its own church edifice and pastor, and by 1883, there were eighty families.[24]

According to the 1885 Kansas state census, which collected information not only about birthplace but also about where individuals lived before migrating to Kansas, the city of Marysville had a total of 1,932 inhabitants.[25] Of these, 286 were German-born, and more than half (153) had come directly from Germany. Marysville had become a destination; it was also continuing to attract German-born settlers who had settled elsewhere

Advertisement for the sulky plow, circa 1880s, which made it possible to farm sitting down and made oxen obsolete. (In the author's possession)

first and were now moving farther west. As in the past, the North Midland area provided the most settlers (92), followed by the Northeast (26, with 17 from Wisconsin) and the Upper South (14; all but one from Missouri). Illinois had not provided a particularly large number of German-born settlers to Kansas in the past, but now it did—a total of 75, or more than 80 percent of those from the North Midland area. More detailed research into Illinois history would be required to determine why these people left, but tenancy (rather than ownership) of farms had reached 31.4 percent in Illinois by 1880, and some Germans may have moved to less populated Kansas in the hope of obtaining land of their own.[26]

Representing 15 percent of Maryville's population, the German-born came from all social classes, including thirty-two laborers; many craftsmen, such as plasterers, carpenters, and butchers; one physician; eight merchants; and a banker, Charles Koester, whose elegant white mansion on the city's main street is a museum today. By the end of the century, some 90 percent of the businesses in Marysville were owned by Germans.[27] A German Evangelical church, affiliated with the German Evangelical Synod of the West, had been organized in 1868 and boasted an impressive edifice.[28] In 1874 the Marysville *turnverein*, a German gymnastic and cultural institution, was established.[29] By 1880, it had grown to thirty-seven members and had its own brick building, where physical education classes and cultural events were held.[30]

In Marysville Township the 1885 population was 3,042, with 616 German-born, representing 20 percent of the inhabitants.[31] Of the German-born, 256 (42 percent) had come directly from Germany. The remaining German-born were overwhelmingly from the North Midland area (287): 206 from Illinois and 51 from Nebraska. Forty-four were from the Northeast (thirty-three from Wisconsin), six from the Upper South, and four from the West. The remainder had moved from elsewhere in Kansas.

With such a large concentration of Germans in and around Marysville, it is not surprising that German was commonly spoken there. In fact, English did not become the dominant language among the Germans in Marysville until the 1920s.[32]

Forter described the Germans of Marshall County in the following terms: "There was never any spirit of revolution or anarchy among the Germans of Marshall county. They are peaceable, law-abiding and, in the main, religious."[33] This is not entirely accurate. In the period under discussion, there was a strong temperance movement in Kansas. In 1879 a constitutional amendment prohibiting the sale of alcohol was passed by the legislature and ratified by the voters, and it remained in force until 1947.[34] Many Kansans opposed the amendment, including many of the foreign-born in Marysville, reminiscent of the battle waged by German immigrants in Chicago many years earlier. A. G. Barrett was county treasurer at the time, and he was hardly appreciative of the ruckus made by "foreign elements," presumably meaning Irish and German immigrants. In a letter to his daughter dated June 21, 1881, he railed against them, believing they were being coddled by local politicians who wanted their vote.[35]

In Guittard and Vermillion Townships, the Lodholz and Reb families apparently stayed out of the fray. This may be because the German Evangelical Association was heavily influenced by Methodism, which forbade drinking.[36] In fact, all but one of the Reb children converted as adults to the Methodist Episcopal Church.

With so many Germans coming into the county, it is fortuitous for historians that the 1880 federal census recorded the locality of an individual's birth, as well as the birthplace of the individual's parents. Even though Germany was theoretically united in 1871, enumerators for the 1880 census were instructed not to list "Germany" but to record a specific birthplace (as they had been instructed to do in 1870, too).[37] As a result, some individuals gave the specific village where they were born. Thus, the 1880 census gives us a snapshot in time of the ethnic German environment in which the Lodholzes and Rebs now lived.[38]

In 1860 the German-born in Marshall County were evenly divided between northern and southern German states. Over the next twenty years, the balance shifted. The 1880 census reveals the distinct dominance of northern German immigrants. Of the 1,038 ethnic Germans in Marshall County,[39] only 14 percent were from the southern states of Württemberg (54), Bavaria (61), and Baden (29), the last two predominantly Catholic. Among the immigrants from the more northerly German states, those from Hanover have historically received a great deal of scholarly attention. They congregated in the area west of the Little Blue River in Marysville Township and, when combined with the Hanoverians in the neighboring townships in Washington County, constituted almost a quarter of the 1,812 inhabitants from Hanover in all of Kansas in the 1880 federal census.[40]

The most numerous ethnic Germans in both Marshall County and all of Kansas, however, were the Prussians.[41] A total of 417 individuals specified Prussia as their place of birth. They were found in every township, but the majority resided in Marysville, intermingled with the Hanoverians west of the Little Blue River. Together, these two northern states accounted for

58 percent of the ethnic Germans in the county (not counting second-generation German Americans).

In contrast, the much smaller number of Germans who came from Württemberg (54) were scattered among the townships. Like the Prussians, the largest number (32) lived in Marysville Township, but predominantly east of the Little Blue River, where they were likewise scattered. They tended not to form clustered groups of families. In Marysville, there were seventeen males born in Württemberg (three bachelors), thirteen females (one unmarried), and two children. Of the married men and women, only five couples were from the same German state; the rest were married to individuals from other German states, foreign countries, or native-born. In Guittard, there were six immigrants from Württemberg, counting Gottfried and Christina, who identified themselves as "German." The vast majority of Germans in Guittard were from Prussia (48), followed by Bavaria (14) and other areas of Germany (20). In 1880 in Vermillion Township, Anna was the only resident born in Württemberg.[42] The only other Germans were from Prussia (10), Baden (1), Bavaria (2), Hanover (1), and Darmstadt-Hesse (2).

The one "colony" formed in Kansas by immigrants from Württemberg was the settlement at Stuttgart in Mound Township in Phillips County, bordering Nebraska and several counties west of Marshall. These settlers had initially come to Marshall County and been directed to proceed to Phillips, perhaps because the intervening counties were filling up and Phillips still had a density ratio of less than five.[43] The 1880 federal census counted fifteen households headed by individuals from Württemberg; the majority of the settlers were native-born, with fifty-three heads of households. By 1890, however, the ratio had changed: twenty native-born heads of household, sixty-two heads of household born in Germany, and eight second-generation German Americans. Presumably, most of these people were from Württemberg.

Over time, the change in the ethnic composition of the population in the two townships of Guittard and Vermillion was dramatic. J. Neale Carman counted twenty-four German speakers in Guittard Township in 1865, but based on state census data, they represented only eight families.[44] At twenty-two families, the Irish almost matched the twenty-eight native-born families in the township. In the 1875 Kansas state census, the Irish continued to be the predominant foreign-born settlers, but not by much: Irish, 30 percent; German, 27 percent; Swedish, 19 percent; and English, 17 percent, with France, Norway, and Switzerland making up the difference. In Guittard, the small city of Beattie had a population of 476, 20 percent of whom were German. In Vermillion, out of 290 families, only 12 were German (4 percent of the foreign-born).⁴⁵ The majority of foreign-born (28 percent) were Irish.

Just ten years later, in 1885, the German population in Guittard Township far outnumbered the Irish (97 versus 30), and even the English residents (32) exceeded the Irish. Out of a total population of 1,498, German settlers represented 48 percent of the foreign-born but only 6 percent of the total. In Beattie, however, the number of Germans had dwindled to three, and Vermillion Township had only seven German families left. Although both townships had only a few Württembergers, the ethnic environments experienced by Gottfried and his family and Anna and her family were quite different and might have played a role in their assimilation (discussed in the epilogue).

In 1874 most of these developments still lay ahead for the Lodholz and Reb families. By now, the deep grief from the deaths of little Frederick and Georg had begun to ease into sad but fond remembrance, and the bitter feud between Gottfried and Rosina had subsided. Heinrich and Anna had six living children: Henry Jr., now twelve years old; Mary, nine; John, eight; Will, five; Helena Christina (known as Lena), four; and Louis Carl, just one year old. Then the unthinkable happened: forty-four-year-old Heinrich died of "fever" (malaria) at the beginning of the year. At thirty-six, Anna (like her mother) faced widowhood with young children to raise. Her experience had taught her that having a close-knit, supportive family was key to survival, and she fostered this closeness in her children. Her mother had been a remarkable model of how to deal with adversity. Friedrich reminded Anna of their mother's travails, about which he still seemed bitter:

> Remember that our blessed mother had a great struggle to endure when our blessed father died, because she gave up her possessions in order to rescue our father's good name [from debt], and had then to raise us in poverty. Admittedly it did us no harm, but if I had been grown back then, then it would no longer have happened that a poor widow should sacrifice her possessions to wealthy people.⁴⁶

Heinrich died intestate, and under the law, Anna and her children inherited the property. There was no probate. The farm was not split up into portions but was held communally. Given the age of the children, all decisions concerning the farm were Anna's to make. Gottfried lived too far from Barrett to be of any significant help with daily farm activities. Emotionally

Drawing of a grasshopper invasion in California, with an inset showing railroad workers removing carcasses that were blocking a train. (*Frank Leslie's Illustrated Newspaper*, July 4, 1885, 317)

high strung and impetuous at times, Friedrich pledged his help and wrote to Anna in March 1874: "I have firmly decided to come to you and support you as quickly as possible."[47] But Friedrich did not come, and that summer Anna faced a major drought and a grasshopper plague. Having first ravaged Minnesota, millions of grasshoppers appeared from the north in a hazy cloud; they stripped all the green vegetation and then started on the wooden fences and tool handles. They smothered the sides of buildings and attacked railroad ties in such numbers that the trains could not pass until the tracks had been sanded. Simply running them over made the tracks too slick for the locomotives to make the steep grades. In the end, the grasshoppers died off from disease. But as one local resident put it: "People were left greatly depressed."[48]

By September 1874, Friedrich was making excuses for changing his mind about coming to Kansas:

> It was admittedly my firm decision to come to you. But we are very far away from each other, and it costs a great deal to accomplish. I am constantly worried about you and how you are faring. . . . I never felt comfortable with it [life on the plains], and it's a miracle from God that the Indians did not attack us . . . in the first year, like they have now attacked the settlers farther out.[49]

In the bitterly cold winter, and with the economic depression still hanging over the country, Friedrich wrote from Terryville at the beginning of 1875:

> Here where we are things have not been the best for two years. We are admittedly healthy, for which we thank God. But business is no longer going well. Often there is no work. One rarely earns what one needs. Many houses here have been put up for sale, and many families must suffer want. It is no longer so good in America like it was before, and won't be good again anytime soon, as there is no longer any confidence.[50]

Friedrich's usual optimism had flagged, and he had every reason to feel discouraged. The Industrial Revolution was in full swing in the Northeast, manned by the increasing throngs of immigrants from eastern and southern Europe: Poland, Russia, Italy, the Balkan states, and the Austro-Hungarian Empire. Business interests generally encouraged immigration (except in the case of the Chinese) to help keep wages down. In 1870 the average

Gottfried and Christina—the only extant photograph of them. (In the family's possession)

workweek for a machinist in Connecticut was sixty hours, and the average pay was $2.66 an hour. By 1890, this had changed for the worse. Sixty hours was still the average workweek, but the average pay was only $2.06 an hour.[51] Friedrich could not get ahead financially.

Shortly after receiving Friedrich's letter, Gottfried and Christina traveled by wagon the twenty miles from Beattie to visit Anna. Getting to see one another face-to-face was a special treat, as it meant that Gottfried and Christina would be away from their farm for several days. Anna gave them some chickens and a rooster to take home, and as Christina related in her April 1875 letter, nearly everyone made it back safely:

> We arrived home safely. Only one misfortune happened to us. Of the chickens that we took along we lost the rooster, which saddened us both greatly. It was also a terrible storm. I was lying in the wagon, and so we didn't find out about it until we got to Beattie, and there the sun had gone down.
>
> At home we found everything well and happy, the cow had a calf the following Sunday. It passed successfully....
>
> Gottfried wrote to Friedrich. Last Saturday we received a letter from him. He writes that times are bad there, etc. Gottfried wrote to him that he should get out of there. He could also help you some. But of course the prospects are so variable, one would think it would be much better if he were here, he would have something to live from.[52]

Anna was basically on her own. In his second letter to her after Heinrich's death, Friedrich had written: "It is truly a great deal for you if you can take heart and remain steadfast."[53] Steadfastness—being firm in purpose and unwavering—is a trait the early pioneers shared in abundance. However, it was the steadfastness of the pioneer women of Marshall County that was most remarkable: "The privations and sacrifices and the loneliness of the pioneer life fell most heavily on the women. Business and necessity brought the men together occasionally, but the woman in the isolation of her prairie home often saw no friendly face for a month."[54] For the Lodholz and Reb families, this was particularly evident during Georg and Heinrich's time in Denver.

Many publications in recent decades have focused on pioneer women, several of which have been cited in this work. Here, the stories of Marshall County's pioneer women are of particular interest. On coming to Kansas from Iowa, Winifred Barrett Walker had to leave behind a walnut bureau made by her father. She subsequently spent three months driving an ox team and wagon back to Iowa to retrieve it.[55] With a husband wounded in the leg during the Civil War, another Mrs. Walker (no first name given) "plowed the land with her ox team and raised what crops she could."[56] Nora Pauley helped her husband in the fields while caring for two young children: "She fastened a box onto it [the cornstalk cutter she was driving] and in this box, she tucked the babies safely away, thus driving with them all day."[57] Widow Mary Lynch emigrated from Ireland with her four children in 1871 and bought eighty acres of land that she and her children developed.[58] The widow Robinson (no first name given) came to Marshall County with her children and settled on an undeveloped tract of 360 acres: "Their lives for the first few years were hard ones and it required a strong determination for a woman, with a family of children, to settle on an undeveloped prairie farm among strangers."[59] The Ockerman family settled in Vermillion Township but returned to Iowa. After the death of her husband, Polly Ockerman came back to the abandoned homestead, where "she effected good improvement on the place, carried on agriculture successfully, and reared her family."[60] On her husband's death, Emma Lann took "charge of the farm, and has proven herself a capable manager, being free from debt and prospering."[61] Harriet Gilchrist originally bought a sheep "ranch" for her son, but when he gave it up after two years, she stepped in. "When she first took charge . . . it had only a straw shed and a one-room shanty . . . she at once set about vigorously the improvement of the place. She has now a commodious residence of eleven rooms and on the lower level a well-equipped creamery."[62] Amanda Summers's husband was institutionalized after suffering mental trauma as a result of his service during the Civil War, but "since the misfortune of her husband, Mrs. Summers has conducted the farm in an admirable manner."[63]

So Anna was not alone in her steadfastness among the women of Marshall County. How did she manage? There is no evidence that she hired help or plowed the fields herself, although she and her older children would have cut and stacked hay to provide fodder for their horses, cows, and cattle. The 1880 federal census reported no acreage devoted to raising crops.[64] Most likely, Anna rented out whatever land she could. Otherwise, she focused on what she knew best and what she and her children could accomplish themselves: milking cows, raising chickens for their eggs, and raising cattle and swine for sale. By 1880, the family had seven horses, seven milk cows, seventeen other cattle with five calves, and fifteen swine.[65] They had produced 210 pounds of butter the previous year, and their one hundred chickens had provided three hundred eggs.⁶⁶ Anna sold some of the milk to a cheese factory in Frankfort.⁶⁷ She and older daughter Mary likely churned butter from the remainder and sold it, along with eggs, to neighbors or at a store in town. The family also would have planted a garden with potatoes, cabbage, tomatoes, and other vegetables to put food on the table. Anna even ordered fruit trees to create an orchard—an eventual source of delight and income.⁶⁸ Compared to Gottfried and Christina's farm, the Reb farm was hardly prosperous, but it was valued at $2,500, was not debt-ridden, and provided most of what they needed.⁶⁹ As the children grew, particularly the four boys, they would have been able to take on the heavier chores.

Anna occasionally sought Gottfried's help and advice. The severe drought in 1874 had lowered the water tables around Barrett, making life difficult for A. G. Barrett and his steam-powered gristmill. In 1876 he hoped to increase his mill's capacity and needed a greater water supply, so he approached Anna with the idea of building a dam on her property to divert water to his mill. Feeling pressure from her neighbors, Anna wrote to Christina to solicit Gottfried's thoughts. Because the land belonged to her and her children and had not been divided among them, she could not sell any part of the land but she could rent it. In the end, Gottfried left the decision up to his sister. His letter was typical of his clearheaded, unemotional approach and a strong endorsement of Anna's good judgment:

> As Christine told me that Barrett intends to get permission from you to build a new dam on your land, and you would gladly like to hear my opinion on the matter, I thought I would write you what I think about that. Admittedly I don't know what B. intends to do, whether he just wants to build a dam and then a canal from the dam to his mill, or whether he intends, once he has the water rights from you, to build a mill over there, as it's well suited there for a mill, since it has something of a fall, the place can become quite valuable over time, which is enough for B.
>
> I know well only two ways how it could be done. First of all, it will be necessary for you to find out how much land is needed for it and whether the water, when it is collected there, won't cause harm to your land, which it most likely will; that it should be to your advantage you must not blindly accept, first off it will wash away . . . land, and there is also a danger with the cattle, with that you can do what you like.
>
> The earth and the water belong to you to the extent that they are on your land, no one can force you. If you want to agree to it, then he

> should buy the land for it from you. However I don't know if you are allowed to sell the land, I don't believe so, or he should rent it for a certain number of years and pay a certain amount to you annually. That you would most likely be able to do.
>
> Dear sister, I believe that I have written my opinion about it for you just as well as I could tell it to you if I myself were there. . . . You shouldn't worry yourself so over such things, but rather get over them easily, and say according to your best knowledge what you want to do or not to do. One cannot always let others determine one's actions. It is probably good to ask for advice [from neighbors]. But with the dam issue, I think that they are more on B.'s side, because naturally it would be to the advantage of the entire neighborhood if the mill stays there and can be driven with water. One can't blame the people for that. But apart from that one must also take care of oneself.[70]

Anna did take care of herself. Gottfried's advice apparently strengthened her resolve, and she decided against having the dam on her property. Some years later the dam was built on the nearby Leavitt farm, after A. G. Barrett had sold the mill to a man named Rodoker. This was a major operation, as a tunnel four hundred feet long had to be dug from the dam to a branch of the Black Vermillion River so the water could reach the mill.[71]

After the drought, Anna finally had a good harvest. As fall approached, it was time to gather the hay to feed the cows and cattle over the winter. Then a new grasshopper plague came out of Nebraska, and in September 1876 Gottfried offered to come help her store the hay:

> As the time is once again approaching when it's necessary to prepare for the winter, and it's normally hard for you to bring in the hay, I thought I would help you out with that a bit, that is to say, if you have gotten a decent amount of hay cut and piled into haycocks, you can let us know. Then Willy and I will come with my hay wagon and help you bring it in.
>
> We are presently getting the hay done, the grasshoppers are doing a fair amount of damage here this fall. They've consumed all the corn foliage [which would have been used for fodder], therefore it's necessary to make more hay than usual. Write to us right away when we should come.[72]

Gottfried could not always make the trip to Barrett. Rainy weather and illness made life hard for everyone. In May 1877 he wrote to Anna:

We received yours from the 26th of last month. Admittedly it's a long ways for the boys to drive the cattle over here [apparently, Gottfried had suggested driving the cattle to pasture on his farm]. It was my intention to come out and help, but due to all the wet weather I've also gotten behind in my work. We are at the point of planting corn, but I still have some plowing to do.

Anna [his daughter] is not with us, and Millie is also away. And so we have plenty to do in order to get finished. . . . We learned from Blair and also from you that you were affected fairly seriously by the epidemic [probably influenza] that swept through, so it seems you have had a rough time.

If you can't rent out the "bottom," [low-lying land near the river] you're better off just to leave it lie—it's simply too much for you, and this year you never know what you'll get [in the way of harvest because of the wet weather].

Write back soon, so that we learn from time to time how things are going.[73]

Illnesses were endemic on the prairie—from cold and flu (the grippe) to more serious diseases such as measles and typhoid. It was one of the hardships not emphasized enough in histories of the Great Plains. With so much daily labor necessary to keep a farm running, settlers who were ill but not confined to bed would do their best to get the cows milked, the manure scraped up, and the crops planted and harvested.

That fall, Anna visited her brother after receiving the following letter from Christina:

As it's been such a long time that we've heard nothing from each other, I want to let you know how things are with us. Since we were together we've gone through certain things. My Sophie just had chicken pox, as did all the others, and Mary had it the worst. Just when it's harvest time again she's gotten a cold [as the oldest child, she apparently helped in the fields]. After being back 3 weeks Gottfried got the fever. It's not like usual, so much heat, always heat, the doctor gives him nothing, some quinine, and you know, dear sister-in-law, from Heinrich [who died of "fever"] that that is of no help. So we thought, if you have the fever medicine, from the doctor's book, and you could help him out with that, we would be very grateful to you. You know well how alone we are, one can't get everything in Beattie in regard to medicine, so it would be much appreciated by us if you knew of something for the fever. He also has a cough, and a red rash. I also don't feel at all well, I have diarrhea, so I hope to God that you and your children are all well, and perhaps you yourself could visit us, as your brother is badly off. I will close in the hope that these lines find you well. Forgive my bad writing, my arms are shaking with fever.[74]

That winter, Christina wrote again of Gottfried's poor health and their farm losses:

After you were at our place Gottfried became ill again. It was quite bad. We had two doctors. He could have succumbed, but to God be thanks and praise, he is doing better again now, he's gradually improving, and thank you, dear sister-in-law. And recently I myself was quite sick with a fever and sore throat. We're glad that your children are better again in this cold time of winter. . . .

I hope we will get better weather again . . . so much cattle have perished, they eat the dry feed. We ourselves lost one. Schmidts lost 7, and our uncle was recently burned out by a prairie fire.

We are quite happy that your wheat did not all go rotten and that there was yet something for your many cattle.[75] If it is God's will, perhaps we'll see you in the spring. I want to close in the hope that my letter finds you well. I remain sincerely your aunt and sister-in-law in Christ—and send greetings from everyone and we wish you a happy New Year.[76]

In July 1879 it was Anna's family dealing with illness and her sister-in-law offering advice:

We received your letter . . . and we see from that that things are not going well for you yet. We feel very badly for you. May our dear Lord stand by your side and strengthen you in your demanding service. . . . He is the Father of the widows and orphans and the sick. . . . I am sending the vermouth to you with this. . . . If you cook the tea for your Heinrich [Henry Jr.] make it weak at first, then gradually stronger. Perhaps he has gotten a cold. The doctor once prescribed turpentine for Anna [her daughter] to strengthen her stomach. One teaspoonful every morning. It has helped her.[77]

Added to the everyday challenge of illness on the plains was a massive tornado that struck Marshall County at the end of May 1879. It was a killer. When it entered the county it was a quarter mile wide, accompanied by rain and large hail. The roaring of the wind was described as "like the rumbling of a thousand train cars." It demolished buildings right and left and strewed their contents and inhabitants. It touched down just a mile and a half east of Gottfried and Christina's farm in Beattie, but the hardest hit was Irving, Kansas, which was practically obliterated.[78] At least thirteen people were killed in Irving, and many more were injured. In Frankfort, close to Anna, three people lost their lives.[79] Thankfully, neither family was harmed. Widespread reports of the tornado apparently inspired L. Frank Baum to write *The Wonderful Wizard of Oz*. As was commonly thought at the time, Friedrich described the tornado as an unexplainable punishment by God of the "brave and hardworking people of Marshall County."[80]

Family members were corresponding less and less with the passage of years. Certainly, the work of raising her family and keeping the farm going made it hard for Anna to find time to write. In June 1876 Friedrich lamented: "It is sad that we have not had news of each other in such a long time. But you are no doubt faring as we are, in our thoughts we are with you every hour, but one only seldom finds time to write." Still feeling guilty about not coming to Anna's aid after Heinrich's death, he added: "I am always sorry that I am so far away from you and can't stand by you in word and deed. If it weren't so expensive for this poor worker, I would have been at your side long ago. But my means are too meager."[81]

Friedrich's employment situation remained precarious, and in January 1877 he was forced to find work at a lock shop in Bridgeport, Connecticut, as "last year was bad in Terryville, little work and money."[82] Bridgeport was more than forty miles from Terryville, where his wife remained. When he wrote Anna in April, he had not seen his wife for ten weeks but was expecting a visit. Once more he was boarding among strangers and felt "homesick."[83] Friedrich stayed in Bridgeport until October 1877 and then returned to Terryville and his dear Maria. But in March 1878 he was off to Bridgeport again. "That made me feel bad. I stayed 7 weeks in a hotel but didn't like it. Last week I went home and brought [back] some household items with me and rented a room and live on my own now."[84]

Friedrich still dreamed out loud of going to Kansas, but no matter how hard his life as a factory worker was, he continued to endure it, despite complaining about the "coarse" language he heard there. He simply had no other financial prospects.

Dear sister, when will the day come when we can live in Kansas? If we can't do it fairly soon, our lives will be coming to an end. I will save as good as I can. I would like to see you all again and spend the rest of my life with you because a factory worker is so suppressed and the pay is so low that it just keeps you from starving. Many people in Terryville have to save on food and some of our old acquaintances are having a hard time.[85]

All the family had definitely endured a lot over the near decade since Georg's and Heinrich's deaths. Anna came through with her farm and family intact thanks to a great deal of hard work, resilience, and steadfastness. But it was not all dreary heroics to make ends meet and keep her children healthy; she truly delighted in them. And she made sure they attended school, as she herself had done so many years ago in Ebhausen. Theirs was not a church-run institution but public and secular. The school year was based on the agricultural cycle, with two terms—the winter term from November to April, and the summer term from May to August. This left the children free to help out during planting and harvesting, in addition to their chores before and after school. The small school building their father helped build had been replaced by a larger one-room schoolhouse presided over by Miss Elizabeth Mohrbacher, who "wielded the rod of correction in this humble school house."[86] Miss Mohrbacher lived a good distance away, near Marysville, and rode a pony "across the prairie wilderness" on faintly marked trails to the school, staying with Anna and her family during the week and returning home for the weekend.[87] This was probably a little intimidating for the children, as they would have to be on their best behavior. Miss Mohrbacher's father had emigrated from Bavaria, so she probably spoke German and could converse with Anna.[88] She was Catholic, but that seemingly made no difference to the Rebs.[89]

The school was not designed to prepare pupils for college, but the Reb children received an excellent education. Although they spoke German at home, the letters they wrote as adults show a mastery of English and, at least for Mary and Lena, beautiful handwriting (as evidenced by a copybook that survived). The Reb children's education lasted only through elementary school, but the curriculum was rigorous. They were schooled from the famous *McGuffey Readers*, which downplayed memorization and stressed speaking well, moral lessons, and comprehension based on a wide array of interesting stories and poems as well as illustrations. *McGuffey's Fourth Eclectic Reader*, which belonged to Louis (the youngest), had selections

FOURTH READER. 147

LIV   ROBINSON CRUSOE'S DRESS.

1 But had any man in England met such a man as I was, it must either have frightened him or raised a great deal of laughter; and, as I frequently stood still to look at myself, I could not but smile at the notion of my traveling through Yorkshire in such a dress.

Page from *McGuffey's Fourth Eclectic Reader*. Its discussion of *Robinson Crusoe* included information about the origin of the story: "It was founded on the adventures of Alexander Selkirk, a Scottish buccaneer, who was cast on the island of Juan Fernandez, west of South America in 1704, and remained there for more than four years before he was rescued." (*McGuffey's Fourth Eclectic Reader*, rev. ed. [Cincinnati: Van Antwerp, Bragg, 1879], 147; in the family's possession) from *Robinson Crusoe*, "The Wreck of the Hesperus" by Longfellow, the Sermon on the Mount, and a short story by Louisa May Alcott, as well as works by lesser-known writers with titles such as "Dare to Do Right," "Consequences of Idleness," and "Where There Is a Will There Is a Way." Louis sat on a hard-backed wooden bench and pored over the stories, which were followed by a list of vocabulary words, with their definitions and pronunciations, and a series of probing questions designed to make him think about what he had just read. For the selection from *Robinson Crusoe*, the words "fortification" and "egress" were defined, and the questions included "How did Robinson Crusoe make a house?" and "What does this lesson teach us in regard to perseverance?" Miss Mohrbacher would have tested Louis orally on what he had learned and corrected his pronunciation.

Outside of school and chores, Anna made sure the children received religious training. Both she and Heinrich were very active in the German Evangelical Association.[90] There was still no church building for this denomination near either Anna or Gottfried, so devotions were probably still held in people's homes. A letter from Christina alluded to this: "Last Sunday we had our last gathering at this year's conference, which prompted me to let Anna [Gottfried and Christina's daughter, who had been visiting her aunt Anna] know that the preacher, Geiser, left your sermon book here with us. I know that you will be in great demand for it, so you now know where you can pick it up."[91]

Even with school and church and chores, there was still time for the children to run in the woods and catch fish in the creek. All of them, including the boys, learned at least the rudiments of cooking and helped in the cleanup. The children collected wild fruit such as gooseberries, grapes, and blackberries. Anna scabbed and peeled tomatoes and set the slices out to dry in the sun. The children loved the natural sweetness of the sun-dried tomatoes and gobbled them up immediately, leaving none to be saved for the winter.[92] Anna also baked gingersnaps and gingerbread, based on her mother's recipes. Her cookies continued to be a favorite many years later.

[Gingersnaps]
- a teacup of molasses
- half a cup of sugar
- half a cup of butter
- half a cup of warm water

Melt the butter with a small teaspoon of "Salleretes" [saleratus: a type of salt or baking soda] and make it quite thin. Then a large spoonful of ginger and make the dough stiff and put it in the mold [most likely a cast-iron cookie mold].

White ginger bread! [made with white flour]
- a cup of flour
- a cup of butter
- 1½ cups molasses
- a cup of milk
- a big spoonful of "Saleretes" [saleratus]
- a small spoonful of ginger
- two eggs[93]

Gottfried's children attended school at Guittard Station, where sixteen pupils were enrolled. Sophia Lodholz in particular was a model student, not missing one day of school and never caught whispering without permission.[94] When Adam Volle arrived in 1876 and became Gottfried's neighbor, the area was still undeveloped. Beattie had only one store. Adam's son Jake and the Lodholz children made the five-mile trek to the school together, starting out while the stars were still shining and returning home at four o'clock.[95]

By the time of the 1885 Kansas state census, Anna's children were grown or nearly so. Henry was twenty-three; John, nineteen; Will, sixteen; and Louis, twelve. Mary and Lena, aged twenty and fifteen, respectively, helped with household chores and the garden. "The boys," as their sisters called them, helped out with housekeeping chores when needed—washing dishes, canning, and even baking bread.[96] By 1885, the family had started to raise grain—four acres in spring wheat, thirty in corn, and two in oats—along with a quarter acre in Irish potatoes. Their orchard was flourishing with forty apple, two hundred peach, one plum, and six cherry trees. They were no longer invested in cattle (having only three), but they still had eight milk cows, which produced three hundred pounds of butter annually. No mention is made of poultry or eggs in the census, but the women undoubtedly raised chickens.[97]

Although only two letters written to the Lodholzes from Ebhausen survive, the family's ties with their relatives and friends back in Württemberg continued throughout their lifetimes. In 1887 a relative in Germany died and left them an inheritance. Gottfried dealt with the matter, and in August 1887 he received a brief accounting of charges on the estate from Johann Martin Lodholz in Ebhausen, who had purchased 350 marks worth of dollars and sent the bill of exchange to Gottfried to be tendered at a bank.[98] It was worth approximately $83 at the time,[99] or a little over $2,000 in today's dollars.[100]

By this time, Gottfried had retired from farming, and in 1889 he embarked on a project that was close to his heart. In November of that year, Gottfried and two of his sons-in-law paid $50 on behalf of the Church of the Evangelical Association of North America for an acre of land in Richland Township, formerly part of Guittard Township, to build a church for the small number of adherents in Marshall County.[101] The church endured until 1930. The building must have been modest because it was eventually moved to property belonging to one of Gottfried's grandsons and became part of his house.[102]

Gottfried's generosity also extended to Friedrich, who was still working in the lock factory in Terryville. Business had taken another downturn, and his hours had been cut to three-quarters time. In June 1889 Friedrich told Anna of his good fortune in selling some of his land in Kansas to Gottfried (who had no real need for it):

> Because I had little use of my land [in Kansas] I wanted to sell 40 acres and wrote to Gottfried. He said that he would pay $15 per acre and I agreed. When he went to Marysville they told him that the U.S. patent for my land could not be found. I should go to Washington [DC]. I thought that all was lost. But the brave Americans listened to me and sent 3 letters to the Land Office to Commissioner Anderson and finally the patent arrived in February. You can imagine how pleased I was! Gottfried sent the money and I bought one of the best houses here, a 2-storey house, well built.[103]

So the land in Kansas finally did Friedrich some good, and he and his wife had a house of their own after many years of moving from one rented place to another. Friedrich was fifty-three and facing old age, and his wife was ill. Having the house must have been a godsend.

Only a fragment of the 1890 federal census exists, and it does not include data from Kansas, so we have no way to measure how well the farm in Vermillion Township was doing. However, judging from later letters in the possession of the Reb family, it was doing well. Like Gottfried, the Rebs had a large clapboard frame house. The log cabin days were over.

None of Anna's children were married at this time, but Gottfried's daughters were starting to marry and move to farms in Kansas with their spouses.

Mary, the eldest, never married, but her sister Annie married G. August Segenhagen in 1881, followed by Rosa's marriage to Peter Gürtler in 1884 and Christina's to Henry Seip in 1887.

Christina's 1889 letter to Anna brought news of the adventurous Sophie taking off for Denver. She was the last of the daughters to wed, marrying Peter Gürtler's brother John in 1893. Significantly, Christina complained about how densely settled the area was becoming:

> We received your much appreciated letter, and yet too late for Sophie, as she left on the 10th for Denver. We could not hold her back, and she also arrived there safely. . . . She is healthy and likes it there. How are things with you and your family? Are you all in good health? Winter has been nice so far. Today it is very cold. Thanks also for your nice apples. We got a new town in the north and they are talking of building another to the southeast. We're getting enough towns. Christine [and her husband] is moving three miles north to Mr. Simon's farm. . . . It's a miracle that they got one [a farm]. The plots are very rare. We are also happy.[104]

In 1890 the last confrontation between Native Americans and US government troops took place, known as the Battle (more accurately the Massacre) of Wounded Knee. That same year, the US Census Department declared that "practically the whole of Kansas has become a settled region," and the country as a whole was "so broken into by isolated bodies of settlement that there can hardly be said to be a frontier line."[105] The treaties and the prairie sod had been forever broken.

EPILOGUE

The Lodholzes, the Rebs, and the German Immigrant Experience

The Story Continues

Kansas (or, more accurately, the Kansas Territory) was the center of a raging conflict in the 1850s that helped determine whether slavery and democratic ideals could coexist. Ironically, it took its name from the Kansa or Kaw tribe, which purportedly "sold" the land to the US government in 1848.[1] The government promptly moved other eastern tribes to the area, only to break faith and allow white squatters to preempt land before new treaties with the tribes had even been ratified and the land surveyed. Thus, in many ways, Kansas became a special but integral part of the westward movement that characterized the last half of the nineteenth century. As we have seen, however, its settlement was extremely fluid: would-be pioneers, both native-born and German-born, came and left; moved from one place in the territory to another; or went off to war, many never to return. Only in the aftermath of the Civil War, the Homestead Act, and the extension of the railroads did the population of Kansas swell to fill the land. Compared to states in the North Midland and Upper South regions, from which Kansas drew most of its early settlers, Kansas had the largest percentage of its land occupied by homesteaders (25 percent). Illinois and Ohio had less than 1 percent; Iowa, 3 percent; and Missouri, 8 percent.[2]

Although not nearly as numerous as the native-born, German-born were present in the Kansas Territory from the beginning; in fact, they were the largest group of foreign-born. Early on, there was a large contingent of single males, but many families—couples, cohabiting relatives, and families with children—also moved there. Contrary to the depiction of German settlers as Johnny-come-latelies, we know from the ages and birthplaces of their children that many families came from other places in the United States where they had already tried to put down roots, thus becoming pioneers a second time. The migrating families tended to be small; they added more children once they settled, or couples started their families upon arrival in Kansas.

Some German-born supported abolitionism, helping the initially pro-slavery cities of Leavenworth and Atchison become part of the free-state cause.[3] Many, like the Lodholzes, were looking for cheap land. On his scouting trip, Georg priced land in Michigan, Illinois, and Iowa and found that it cost much more than the $1.25 per acre available to preemptors in Kansas.

The Civil War seriously disrupted settlement, but it resumed and increased afterward. Marshall County developed a distinctive settlement pattern: The northern area, centered in Marysville, attracted large numbers of German settlers directly from Germany, probably a case of chain migration, as well as from the Upper Midland region in particular. The southern area, encompassing Vermillion and Blue Rapids Townships, had few German-born. In the early days there were about equal numbers of German emigrants from northern and southern Germany, but after the Civil War Prussians became preponderant.

Although use of the term "German" masks the settlers' diversity, they were from many different German states, adherents of many different religious creeds, and speakers of many different dialects, and they adjusted to life in the United States in many different ways. They intermarried with individuals from other German states, with native-born, and with non-German foreign-born. Like members of other immigrant groups, some of the German-born settled in clusters of various sizes. In territorial days, however, these clusters were usually small and scattered, leaving them open to outside influences. They had many paths to assimilation, but some chose not to follow them and formed settlements that were averse to assimilation. There were several such settlements in Marshall County, largely based on religion, which survived and thrived after the Civil War.

The related terms "assimilation" and "acculturation" are beset with problems, not the least of which is their meaning. In *Assimilation in American Life*, sociologist Milton M. Gordon devotes a whole chapter to the complex definitions offered by sociologists and anthropologists.[4] The consensus seems to be that assimilation is a dynamic process occurring over time in which a minority group takes on the mores, cultural traditions, and institutions of a more dominant group while also influencing the more dominant group to a lesser or greater degree. This, however, presents a conundrum. The United States has distinct regional differences—from the Southwest, with its underlay of Catholic Spanish rule, to New England, with its strong history of English Protestant religious dissenters. When we speak of assimilation, what mores, cultural traditions, and institutions are we talking about? And into what social class are minority groups assimilating?

These issues are not explored in detail here; they are raised simply to provide context for the present discussion. We are dealing with a very small sample of four families—Friedrich and his wife in Terryville, Gottfried and Georg and their families in Guittard Township, and Anna and her family in Vermillion Township. They shared a common origin, religion, and dialect, as well as, to a certain extent, the German tradition of subordinating individual wants and needs to the survival of the family. Their circumstances changed, however, as a result of deliberate decisions they made about settlement and religious affiliation, and this influenced their assimilation into the larger societies of which they were a part: industrialized New England and the farmland of northeastern Kansas. Jon Gjerde has written about the concept of complementary identities, of German settlers maintaining dual loyalties—adopting the best America had to offer while adhering to the German language and traditions.[5] It is a useful construct for understanding the Lodholzes' and Rebs' experience as German immigrants.

Kathleen Neils Conzen has argued that the German immigrant's mind-set was "a colonizing vision" of "an America still ripe for cultural if not political colonization."[6] This was not the mind-set of the Lodholzes. They were not colonizers; nor were most of the others who came from Württemberg to Kansas, although small numbers may have clustered among Germans from other German states. Upon arriving in the United States, Gottfried looked for opportunities to make money; he did not seek out a German community. He was not part of a chain migration and did not make his way to Michigan, where numerous families from Ebhausen were then living. All the evidence points to his having no relatives or close friends in New York; he had to rely on John Strohm, a virtual stranger, to notify him when the ship carrying his mother, brother, and sister arrived, and when he was a day late meeting them at the dock, there was no one else to greet them. Although Georg wrote about founding a religious community in one letter sent during his land-hunting trip, nothing came of it. Interest in Kansas had waned in Terryville, and no relatives from Ebhausen followed the Lodholzes to Kansas. Georg spoke of Germans he met, but like Gottfried, he made no special effort to seek them out as neighbors. He abandoned his first choice of land simply because it was not worth the price. His letters repeatedly focused on the qualities of the land he was exploring as a potential homestead. The first federal census of the Kansas Territory showed that Guittard Township started out with many more Irish families than German, and in Vermillion Township, where Heinrich Reb lived, there were practically no ethnic Germans.

The Lodholzes and Heinrich, however, certainly thought of themselves as German. The Lodholzes referred to themselves as German in their letters (only one letter of Heinrich's survives), although we do not know precisely who was included in that term. They spoke German among themselves and wrote to one another in German; the newspapers and religious literature they read were written in German, and they chose to worship and engage in personal interactions with other German speakers. In this case, Friedrich and Gottfried had more opportunities to communicate in German than Anna did in the Vermillion. Paradoxically, perhaps, this did not make English her preferred language—just the opposite. All of her children except John, who was a wanderer and a bit of a maverick like his uncle Georg, learned to speak German well, but they mainly spoke English outside the home. Several German Evangelical churches in and near Marysville, none of which were affiliated with the German Evangelical Association, had their own parochial schools to ensure the teaching of German to the next generation.[7] There were none in Guittard or the Vermillion, however, so Anna presumably taught her children the language. Gottfried's children likely picked up German at home as well. Finally, all the Lodholzes married German immigrants and thus could communicate with their spouses in their native tongue.

It is clear, however, that the Lodholzes and Heinrich were committed to learning English to help them make their way in America. They could not have navigated so well in this country—working in the lock factory, dealing with the needs of those traveling on the Oregon Trail, journeying to Denver to find work—without knowing at least the rudiments of English. The documentary evidence from the probate proceedings related to Georg's estate clearly shows that Gottfried could not only speak English but also read and write it. We know from Jacob Lockridge's letter to Heinrich that he could both speak and read English. Although Anna preferred to speak German, she had to know some English to manage as a housekeeper for Mr. Gaylord

Anna Reb with her grandchildren. (In the family's possession)

in Terryville and at the Otoe Mission. There is even evidence from a later period that she could fitfully write in English, although her daughter Mary usually wrote letters in English for her. It is significant that both Gottfried and Anna expected their children to operate in an English-speaking society, as they sent their children to public school.

In terms of food and dress, there is little we can glean. Friedrich in Terryville enjoyed German fare when he was boarding with other Germans. In the early days on the prairie, the rest of his family was consuming what the native-born pioneers ate—strange new foods. We know that Anna continued the German tradition of making gingerbread cookies and cake. Both Gottfried and Anna maintained their love of fruit and ended up with good-sized orchards.

Chapter 3 includes a tintype of a young man, most likely Friedrich, dressed in the black clothing and domed, brimmed hat associated with formal occasions in Ebhausen. He closely resembles the description of his father in the *Wander-Buch*. We do not know when it was taken, but probably sometime in the 1860s. He most likely donned this ethnic apparel especially for the picture, as it was hardly appropriate wear for a factory worker. Whatever Anna may have worn when she first came to America, by the end of her life she was dressing in conventional American clothing.

Food and clothing are relatively minor matters of continuity and adaptation. More important is the degree of assimilation in the economic, political, and social life of the community. Although these major aspects of community life are treated more or less separately here, it is important to keep in mind that there is much overlap among them. In Connecticut, Friedrich was employed, except for a stint at the Colt factory, as a locksmith among many other locksmiths both native-born and foreign-born. That he was kept on at the factory, even during economic downturns, is a measure of his conformity to expectations. He purveyed news of economic opportunities for his relatives in Kansas—the building of railroads; the Pike's Pike gold rush, which he thought would send many would-be prospectors their way; and the possibility of free land. He took the initiative in finding out how financial institutions worked—using warrants to purchase land, buying life insurance, and creating a trust for his wife. And when he described economic conditions in the United States, he did so in terms of their general impact, not the specific impact on Germans. Thus, Friedrich was fairly sophisticated about the economic aspects of American life.

In Guittard, Georg may not have been a particularly successful farmer, but he took pains to learn about bank drafts and preemption, allowing him to register his land claims. He also tried his hand at speculation when he and Heinrich went to Denver.

Gottfried ended up a successful and well-respected farmer, as evidenced by his inclusion in *Portrait and Biographical Album of Marshall County*. He responded to market needs when he started to raise sheep and again when he ceased his operation. It is interesting to note that in his biography in the *Album*, he stressed how much he had paid in taxes to benefit the community.[8] In Vermillion, Heinrich initially went where his services as a blacksmith were in demand and then later started the farm, which Anna and their children kept on a sound financial footing after his death. They too knew how to navigate in the economic world, at least in Marshall County.

Politically, they all came from a monarchical society, but in Ebhausen, the king had been a distant figure. The local elite, one of whom had been Anna Maria's father, were largely in control. In the Palatinate, Heinrich experienced or at least witnessed the liberals' efforts to create a republic. Once in the United States, all the men in the family became citizens. Heinrich was a registered voter soon after he arrived in Barrett, and Friedrich voted as a Republican soon after obtaining citizenship. Neither man sought public office, but Gottfried, a Democrat, was elected township treasurer, assessor, justice of the peace, and school district clerk. Other ethnic Germans in Marshall County participated in local government, although few held as many positions as Gottfried did.[9] Being a Democrat, however, made Gottfried somewhat of a political outlier.[10] *Portrait and Biographical Album of Marshall County* includes the biographies of forty-five Democrats, with almost as many (forty-two) claiming membership in the very short-lived Union Labor Party. The remaining 310 were Republicans. We also know that Gottfried understood the probate laws. All three men were engaged politically, but Gottfried was more assimilated into the everyday workings of democracy.

Socially, assimilation is more complicated because it involves not only relations with native-born settlers but also relations with other German settlers. There was, in the words of Reinhard R. Doerries, a "lack of cohesion" among German immigrants, who were divided by regional, dialect, religious, and social class differences.[11]

Friedrich never mentioned a native-born acquaintance in his letters, although he must have interacted with them in the factory and elsewhere in his everyday life. He was friends with ethnic Germans and often boarded with them. Armbruster was from Baden; August Martinsen (aka Martins) was from Denmark, but Martinsen's wife was from Württemberg; and Friedrich's best friend, Friedrich Egan, was also from Württemberg. Friedrich mentioned no participation in community events. Given his work schedule, he probably had precious little leisure time. His main social activity seems to have been attending religious services conducted in German. In fact, he met his second wife at a church service. These religious services were apparently not associated with any particular Lutheran denomination, and there was no actual church building. He referred to his wife as "Protestant," probably to indicate to his family that she was not Catholic, which the majority of people from Baden were. Friedrich led a rather insular social life, and his letters often reflect his loneliness. The fact that he chose to remain in Terryville rather than returning to the Colt factory in Hartford seems to confirm that this was his preference. The outburst in his letter about the Germans doing all the work while the Yankees profited probably shows an underlying sense of difference from the native-born—as a German, not specifically as someone from Württemberg. In his early letters he is very conscious of the Irish, and his sense of being different from them may have reinforced his identity as German. He and his wife had no children, so the issue of continuity of culture to the second generation is not relevant.

Gottfried and his family mention no native-born acquaintances in their letters. Friedrich's letters mention relatives visiting them, as well as the few from Terryville who went west to explore Kansas. Both Emma Forter and *The Frankfort Story* describe the many types of entertainments the settlers organized—literary societies, singing schools, spelling schools, country dances, and corn husking bees, among others—some of which obviously depended on English-language skills.[12] The country dances were not ones the Germans would have been familiar with, such as the quadrille, Virginia reel, Bird in the Cage, polka and schottische (both Bohemian in origin), and waltz.[13] The directives of Methodism, whose doctrines were closely followed by the German Evangelical Association, proscribed "taking such diversions as cannot be used in the name of the Lord Jesus."[14] This may explain why neither Gottfried nor Christina ever mentioned attending such gatherings. But of course, this does not necessarily mean that they had no native-born friends or did not engage in social activities with the native-born. Such things were simply not central to their lives.

In fact, social life centered largely around religion, and a shared religious affiliation was sometimes more important than a similar cultural background. Anne Höndgen has explored this issue in detail and found that strong religious affiliations (Catholic versus Lutheran) overshadow similar origins and socioeconomic status. The two Ohio communities she studied created no common identity, and regional differences led the northwestern

Germans to reject the southern or southwestern German settlers.[15] J. Neale Carman found something similar in Marshall County, where different dialects and variants of Lutheranism kept the Bremen Germans and the East Frisian Germans apart, even though they lived near each other.[16]

The Germans in Marshall County came from many different German states and belonged to a wide variety of churches, particularly German Evangelical churches with different interpretations of Martin Luther's teachings. Gottfried's family belonged to a small non-Lutheran denomination within the confines of Marshall County. But in *Portrait and Biographical Album of Marshall County*, Gottfried identified himself as "Protestant."[17] No one else in the *Album* did so. The biographies denote religious affiliations, or not—for example, "freethinker," "not identified any denomination," and Catholic "but not a communicant."[18] The subjects were obviously candid in providing this information. Was Gottfried acting the politician and being vague? Was he very broad-minded with regard to faith? If so, why build the church for the German Evangelical Association?

Given the large number of Germans in the part of Marshall County where they lived, Gottfried and Christina had ample opportunity to interact with other German immigrants. However, there is no evidence that Gottfried had contact with any members of the German settlements discussed in this work, many of whom were from northern Germany and whose variants of Lutheranism derived from Prussia. He did not participate in the Marysville *turnverein*, which in 1880 included at least two members from Württemberg.[19] Nor was he a member of the many other social clubs and organizations, such as the very popular Masons, where he might have mixed freely with other ethnic Germans as well as native-born settlers. In Guittard Township, many of the Germans were Catholic and seemed to have more in common with the Irish than with German Evangelicals. The Catholic church organized in Beattie in 1879 included both ethnic groups.[20]

Gottfried's religious affiliation was passed on to his children.[21] Except for Mary, who remained single, all his daughters married ethnic Germans. Two of his sons-in-law helped purchase land for the German Evangelical Association of North America, so we can assume they too shared the faith. Thus, although Gottfried was obviously well respected among his neighbors (who elected him to various positions) and interacted with the community at large, like Friedrich, he and his family maintained a small social circle. Gottfried's political affiliation (Democrat) and the family's participation in a religion with a very small following in Marshall County meant they had fewer opportunities for social engagement than other ethnic Germans.

Wolfgang Helbich postulated that the ethnic German world consisted of concentric circles of increasingly less intense relationships: family; friends; individuals from one's hometown, from the vicinity of one's hometown, and from a general part of Germany; and finally the entire local German American community and, presumably, the larger society.[22] Certainly a number of these circles were not available to the Lodholzes.

Anna and her family represent a different degree of social assimilation. She spoke German within her family but had little opportunity to speak it with her neighbors. In her research on the lives of rural German-speaking women, Linda Pickle found that women like Anna—older, with small children, lacking close female family members (Christina lived some distance away)—were "especially susceptible to cultural alienation."[23] There is no indication that Anna devalued her German heritage; her display of items pertaining to Ebhausen shows a deep attachment to it. The fact that she received a photograph of the village from some cousins indicates that she was still in touch with relatives there, but neither she nor any of her brothers expressed a desire in their correspondence to return for a visit. It seems clear that they considered America their home. Friedrich even uses the term *heimat* (home) in reference to Kansas. Surrounded by native-born settlers, Anna's children learned English, and the whole family had much more social interaction with the native-born than Gottfried's did, particularly when almost all of them became Methodists (John chose a different Protestant denomination).[24] Their social life revolved around myriad church activities that they shared with neighbors. Anna's two daughters and one of her sons did not marry, but her other three sons all chose wives with little or no German heritage of the same religious persuasion as themselves. Anna's children attended community events held at the local schoolhouse, and one son became an avid baseball player—embracing the great American pastime.

None of the Lodholz brothers or Heinrich played the role of stern, unemotional patriarch. Georg's attitude came closest, in that he apparently regarded a wife as mainly a housekeeper. Even so, neither of his wives was subservient, and Rosina proved to be downright feisty in battling Gottfried. Given that Gottfried and Christina had only daughters, the female family members probably helped with the sheep and worked in the fields at least some of the time. The irrepressible Sophia was eventually allowed to take off on her own to Denver.

There is no evidence that Anna Reb worked in the fields, except at haying time. Once she was widowed, she did whatever was practical for her and her children—raising chickens, cattle, and milk cows. Though unusual for the time, Anna's sons took on household chores when called upon to do so and learned the rudiments of cooking.[25] Heinrich's letter from Denver reveals his great love for Anna and their son and his reliance on her judgment; Gottfried likewise told her to trust her own judgment about allowing the dam on her property. Friedrich made a bad marriage that did not last long, but then he chose a woman he loved deeply. Gottfried, Anna, and Friedrich all seemed to have companionate marriages.

Thus, family members showed different degrees of assimilation in different areas of everyday life, but they were no longer strangers in a strange land. The story continues far beyond 1890 for Friedrich and Anna. After 1890, Gottfried's health deteriorated; he died on April 25, 1892, at the age of sixty-two. He left his land and personal property to support his wife and unmarried daughters for Christina's lifetime, with provisions for the estate to be divided among his children upon her death.[26] Christina died ten years later, in 1902, after falling and breaking her hip.[27] With eldest daughter Mary serving as executrix, Gottfried's land was parceled out among his children.

The 1900 federal census for Connecticut shows that Fredrich and his wife had two young male German lodgers.[28] So the house they bought was providing an income as well as a roof over their heads. Probate documents from 1910 also show that he had additional income from renting out the land he still owned in Marshall County.[29]

Always trying to be farsighted, Friedrich prepared his will in 1892 and set up a trust for his wife in the event of his death.[30] But fate was not kind to him. Tragically, she died in a fire in 1901. Distraught by the death of a favorite nephew, she declined mentally and physically and was plagued by sleeplessness. Late one night she took a lantern downstairs, and it overturned and set her clothes on fire. Her screams wakened Friedrich, who put out the fire with a pail of water, but she died the next day.[31] His wife's death haunted him for the rest of his life. One of his nieces in Kansas, Mary Reb, wrote to her brother John: "Is it not sad that Aunt Mary, Uncle Fred's wife, met with such a terrible accident which caused her death and left him so alone? . . . He sees her before him all the time, sitting in the kitchen enveloped in flames, her arms out stretched to him calling for help. He wrote all his loved ones are gone, all he could do now was to weep at their graves."[32]

Friedrich reported to Anna in September 1907 that he had been very sick for two months in the spring but was feeling better.[33] He died two years later, on August 2, 1909, at the age of seventy-two and was buried in Plymouth, Connecticut, next to his beloved wife but far from his Kansas

Display of Ebhausen artifacts. Anna gave pride of place to the photograph of Ebhausen sent to her by her Swiss cousins. It clearly shows the tower of the church where Anna worshipped in her youth. (In the family's possession)

relatives, whom he had not seen in forty years.[34] He left an estate valued at roughly $3,600, not counting his land in Kansas. The bean counter managed to come out ahead in the end, and unlike his father, he left no debts.[35] Friedrich's heirs were his sister Anna; his nieces, including Georg's two children; and great-nieces and great-nephews.[36]

Now only Anna remained of the original family from Ebhausen. She and her children stayed on their farm, facing good times and bad. She lived to see her farm of several hundred acres flourish, with four orchards and timberland where the family cut wood and collected walnuts and gooseberries. They raised swine and Anna's beloved chickens (150 at one count) and had a large vegetable garden tended by the women of the household. The family kept some of the farm's bounty for their own use and sold the rest: corn and other grains not needed to feed livestock or provide seed, fruit, hogs, eggs, milk, and butter. They were largely, but not entirely, self-sufficient.[37] But theirs is another story.

Anna never forgot Ebhausen, which was a distant place to her children. Some Swiss cousins sent her a photograph of the village, with the tall white spire of the local church she had once attended rising above the houses. She lovingly displayed the photo with other mementos.

Obituaries at the time typically included background information on the individual, surviving relatives, and any special interests, much as they do today. But the obituary for Anna Regina Reb, who died in 1925 at age eighty-seven, was somewhat remarkable, for this rather florid prose was added at the end:

> Her six living children and five grandchildren speak her name in profound devotion, and knowing the history of the noble life makes us sure they have a right to do so. Being bereft of her companion, and helpmate, with six little children on her hands to provide for, and surrounded by a vast expanse of wild territory with neighbors far apart as were the conditions in the early pioneer days, she managed to keep her little flock with her, provide for them, give them all an education and to see them all lifted to a place of full grown manhood and womanhood. Surely she was a heroine of the highest order.[38]

That may have been putting it too strongly. But as her young friend told her so many years earlier when she was leaving Ebhausen, Anna was a "fire" woman.

APPENDIX A

Legal and Illegal Emigration

Emigration records were submitted to the state central repository by the *Oberamt* (district) in which the applicant lived. The *Oberamt* for Ebhausen was Nagold, and volumes 2 and 3 of *The Wuerttemberg Emigration Index* contain these records.[1] The compilers indicate that the records may not be complete, and in fact, they are not.

By emigrating, individuals forfeited their citizenship. If they left illegally, they sometimes later informed officials in Germany, renouncing their citizenship; that information was then entered in the official records.[2] It is apparent that there was a great deal of illegal emigration.[3] I have found no firsthand accounts or scholarly articles detailing how emigrants circumvented the seemingly stringent control over people's movement. There are, however, four situations that may have allowed or even encouraged illegal emigration. First, the entire territory of Württemberg could not be covered at all times by the horsed mobile forces of the state-controlled gendarmerie tasked with policing the areas not under local police control. In reality, they did little policing of these areas, as all such forces were centralized near the capital of Stuttgart.[4] Second, many emigrants traveled in groups, perhaps making them less subject to challenge. Third, passports were not necessarily needed to board a ship (only a ticket was required) or when arriving in the United States. Fourth and perhaps most importantly, the governments of the various German states, including Württemberg, were in disarray over how to handle the surge in emigration that started with the "Hunger Year" and continued in succeeding years. In Württemberg itself, emigration was officially forbidden, but the policy was not enforced.⁵ While the central administration did little in response, at the local level, officials who did not want to be burdened by the poor encouraged them to emigrate.⁶ The evidence shows that this was a distinct possibility in Ebhausen and its *Oberamt*.

Listed below are the names of emigrants from Ebhausen who are mentioned in the Lodholz family's letters and documents. Variants of names were considered, but as anyone who has done genealogical research on German names knows, numerous people, including relatives, may share the same name. Only individuals born in Ebhausen and applying at roughly the appropriate time were considered. The few names in boldface are listed in *The Wuerttemberg Emigration Index*, which was compiled from the official records. For Ebhausen as a whole, there is no listing of an applicant for emigration before 1853. Of the total number listed (85), 58 percent applied in 1860 or later. Obviously, individuals from Ebhausen had gone to the United States before 1853. In his May 14, 1857, letter Georg comments that some families had been there for fifteen years.⁷

Looking at the figures for the entire Nagold district, only a small number are listed before 1853 (each year represents one individual unless otherwise indicated): 1816 (several), 1817, 1826–27, 1837 (2), 1847 (family), 1838, 1844, 1845, 1847 (2), 1849 (3 and family), 1850 (2), 1851 (family), 1852 (12). By 1854, when Anna Maria and her two youngest children emigrated, although the central government was not enthusiastic about emigration, it licensed shipping agents such as the one who contacted Anna Maria.

Lodholz family:
Lodholz, Anna Maria
Lodholz, Gottfried
Lodholz, Johann Georg
Lodholz, Jakob Friedrich
Lodholz, Anna Regina

Letter from Anna Maria to Gottfried, August 8, 1848:
Christian Brenner of Waldorf
Konrad Kempf

Letter from Gottfried to Anna Maria, circa 1854:
Johannes Martin Kempf, cousin
Johannes Lodholz, cousin

Letter from Jakob Friedrich to Christian Killinger, circa 1854:
Hechelmacher's family (no Heckelmacher listed)

Letter from Christian Killinger to Gottfried Lodholz and family, October 26, 1854:
Christian Schöttle, heckle maker, along with his mother and family (No Christian Schöttle is listed, but two women and several children are listed as applying in September 1853, which is not necessarily the date the passport was approved. Approval could take some time.)
Müller Zimmermann, schoolteacher
Christian Nestle, school comrade
Peter Ensle, school comrade
Friedrich Braile
Gottlieb Lodholz, baker
Georg Lodholz, harness maker
Johann Georg Pfeihle
Christian Hauser, baker
Christian Kaufer, miller's assistant
Johannes Renz, shearer
Magdalena Schüttle
Christoph's Johannes (too little information)
Sara Lodholz, acquaintance, seamstress
Christian Killinger (There is a Christian Killinger, age eighteen, who was born in Enztel and applied in January 1855, but Enztel seems too far from Ebhausen to allow a definite identification.)
Iohannes Killinger Schmid

Letter from Johann Georg to family, May 14, 1857:
Jacob Spatholz (deceased at that time)
Beutler
Gottlieb Lodholz and wife (most likely the Gottlieb Lodholz from Christian Killinger's October 26, 1854, letter)
Magdalena Spaholz and husband

First letter from Johann Georg to family from Nebraska City:
Johannes Schmälzle (deceased at that time)
Tailor Zinweg's daughters (no Zinweg listed)
Johannes Lodholz (may be the cousin mentioned in Gottfried's letter circa 1854)
Schaalweather's Fritz

APPENDIX B

Total Population and German-Born by County

1860 Federal Census

The table that follows shows the relative relationships, but not the relative sizes, of the counties in the Kansas Territory at the time of the 1860 federal census. It is based on the 1860 map, with county names already updated from the 1860 census, from *Transactions of the Kansas State Historical Society, 1903–1904*.[1] I made two changes necessary to restore the locations and names of counties originally reported in the census.

The 1860 census collected information on each inhabitant's name, age, sex, "color," occupation, value of real estate owned, value of personal property owned (both values largely provided by the inhabitant), place of birth, if married within the year, school attendance, literacy, and whether the individual was "deaf and dumb, blind, insane, idiotic, pauper, or convict." The count is flawed mainly by omissions, including no data for a few counties with presumably little settlement and various pages lacking some of the required information, including birthplace. There are other flaws, such as obvious errors related to family members' birthplaces; for example, younger children were sometimes listed as being born in Germany, while their older siblings were listed as native-born. In cases in which a logical correction could be made, I did so. In addition, there are various pages, particularly for Riley County, where the writing is barely legible.

In Marshall County, Anna Regina Lodholz was counted twice, once when unmarried and a second time after her marriage and change of residence. The Lodholzes were also misidentified as being born in Hanover.

These errors have been corrected in my count, but they are indicative of other possible errors in the census.

The numbers in parentheses below the county names are the total population figures ("white," "free colored," and "Indian") for that county.[2] G denotes the number of German-born in the county (see page 276, note 1, for the definition of "German"). F denotes the number of German family groups, defined as couples, families with children, single-parent families, and siblings living together. A household might include more than one family, and a German-born individual might be married to a native-born or foreign-born spouse. S denotes single German-born individuals, including those living on their own in their own households (sometimes with others of the same sex with different surnames who are presumably not relations), those living in boardinghouses and hotels, and those serving or cohabiting in individual households. Five unorganized counties to the west were not included in the census.

Republic

	WASHINGTON (383)	MARSHALL (2,280)	NEMAHA (2,436)	BROWN (2,607)	DONIPHAN (8,083)
G	13	103	85	67	228
F	3	25	30	28	88
S	7	33	16	11	44

Shirley

	CLAY (163)	RILEY (1,224)	POTTAWATOMIE (1,529)	JACKSON (1,936)	ATCHISON (7,729)	LEAVENWORTH (12,606)
G	4	84	153	34	355	1,210
F	2	28	52	13	113	412
S	0	33	22	4	80	358

	JEFFERSON (4,459)	WYANDOTTE (2,609)
G	109	220
F	40	74
S	20	66

Ottawa

	DICKINSON (378)	DAVIS (Fort Riley) (1,163)	WABAUNSEE (1,023)	SHAWNEE (3,513)	DOUGLAS (Lawrence and Lecompton) (8,637)	JOHNSON (4,364)
G	88	126	181	56	355	129
F	26	47	52	21	126	42
S	9	35	36	21	88	47

(continued on the next page)

Total Population and German-Born by County

Ottawa

	MORRIS (770)
G	22
F	8
S	4

Saline

	MARION (74)	CHASE (808)	BRECKINRIDGE (3,197)	OSAGE (1,113)	FRANKLIN (3,030)	LYKINS (4,980)
G	3	26	34	37	35	48
F	1	7	11	12	17	19
S	1	5	14	12	9	15

	MORRIS (770)	MADISON (636)	COFFEY (2,842)	ANDERSON* (2,400)	LINN (3,336)
G	22	5	31	48	38
F	8	4	17	17	14
S	4	0	8	7	10

	OTOE (238)	BUTLER (437)	GREENWOOD (759)	WOODSON (1,488)	ALLEN (3,082)	BOURBON (6,101)
G	1	2	13	58	42	45
F	0	1	3	15	14	19
S	1	1	3	19	13	8

Irving

	HUNTER (158)	GODFROY (19)	WILSON (27)	DORN (88)	MCGHEE (1,501)
G	1	No data	None	4	14
F	1			0	8
S	0			4	2

* Only county in Kansas that still had slaves—two of them.

APPENDIX C

German-Born Place of Birth by County

1860 Federal Census

	WASHINGTON	MARSHALL	NEMAHA	BROWN	DONIPHAN
Germany			50	21	101
Baden	1	19		2	23
Bavaria	2	15		3	23
Hanover	9	22		4	15
Darmstadt-Hesse			23	19	2
Holstein		5			1
Prussia		18		3	47
Saxony		1		4	1
Württemberg	1	15	12	4	12
Hamburg				2	
"On Rhine"				5	
Rhineland-Palatinate					1
Bremen		8			
Brunswick*					2

211

	CLAY	RILEY	POTTAWATOMIE	JACKSON	ATCHISON	LEAVENWORTH	WYANDOTTE
Germany	3	49	132	34	331	933	153
Baden			1			78	5
Bavaria	1	4			4	40	8
Hanover					6	19	12
Hesse		2				4	
Holstein							
Prussia		12	19		12	96	38
Saxony		6			2	5	3
Württemberg						30	1
Bremen		1				1	
Westphalia		10					
Nassau							
Hamburg			1			1	

	JEFFERSON
Germany	47
Baden	3
Bavaria	4
Hanover	6
Hesse	10
Holstein	2
Prussia	16
Saxony	3
Württemberg	15
Westphalia	1
Hamburg	1
Brunswick	1

	DICKINSON	DAVIS	WABAUNSEE	SHAWNEE	DOUGLAS	JOHNSON
Germany	3	38	181	46	343	127
Baden		1			2	
Bavaria		8		1		
Hanover	1	5		1		
Hesse		2				
Holstein		2			1	
Prussia	84	54		6	9	2
Saxony		4		1		
Württemberg		5				
Mecklenburg		5				
Anhalt				1		
Nassau		1				
Gothers**		1				

	MORRIS
Germany	17
Baden	
Bavaria	
Hanover	2
Hesse	
Holstein	
Prussia	3
Saxony	
Württemberg	

	MARION	CHASE	BRECKINRIDGE	OSAGE	FRANKLIN	LYKINS
Germany	3	9	33	37	35	22
Baden		1				6
Bavaria						3
Hanover						2
Hesse						1
Holstein						
Prussia		15	1			11
Saxony						
Württemberg		1				
Palatinate						
Nassau						3

	MADISON	COFFEY	ANDERSON	LINN
Germany	5	31	4	25
Baden			2	
Bavaria			1	

(continued on the next page)

German-Born Place of Birth by County

	MADISON	COFFEY	ANDERSON	LINN
Hanover			13	1
Hesse				
Holstein				
Prussia			23	12
Saxony				
Württemberg			3	
Oldenburg			2	

	OTOE	BUTLER	GREENWOOD	WOODSON	ALLEN	BOURBON
Germany	1	2	13	22	33	29
Baden				6		
Bavaria				6	3	
Hanover				2	1	3
Hesse				3	1	
Holstein						1
Prussia				13	3	5
Saxony				1		1
Württemberg						6
Westphalia				5		
"Rhine"					1	

	Irving	GODFROY	WILSON	DORN	McGHEE
Germany		No data	None	4	13
Baden					1
Bavaria					
Hanover					
Hesse					
Holstein					
Prussia					
Saxony					
Württemberg					

	HUNTER
Germany	
Baden	
Bavaria	1
Hanover	
Hesse	
Holstein	
Prussia	
Saxony	
Württemberg	

*Presumably Braunschweig as opposed to New Brunswick.
**Presumably Gotha.

APPENDIX D

German-Born Population, County and Township Statistics by Category

1860 Federal Census

The counties are presented in six tiers moving from east to west (right to left), according to their positions on the 1860 map referred to in appendix B. Families are listed in the approximate order in which they appear in the census documents on Ancestry.com (in many cases, the beginning or ending pages were out of sequence). Census takers were instructed to number each township's inhabitants in the order in which they were visited.[1] In practice, this meant that households in a neighborhood were usually visited in order, as evidenced by the fact that "unoccupied" or "vacant land" is often noted, as are other buildings such as schools and churches located between the households. Thus, families listed near one another in the original census documents most likely lived in close proximity, but this is not necessarily the case, particularly if a township was sparsely settled.

In the absence of any spouse or children, individuals were considered "single," even though some may have had spouses (usually wives) who had not accompanied them to the Kansas Territory. In categorizing singles, a "mixed environment" means that the German-born individual was residing in a hotel or boardinghouse or was working for a family that had boarders or servants who were not German-born. "On own" denotes an individual living alone or an unmarried individual whose household included a servant or presumably unrelated individuals, often craftsmen, who may or may not have been German-born. Members of a household were presumed to be relatives when their last name was the same; in cases in which the surname was different and the individual was possibly a relative of a spouse, the determination was based on age, birthplace, and whether the person was identified as a servant. Note that in appendix B, siblings living or working together were counted as a family unit; in this appendix, they are counted individually under the rubric "with family."

The following markers were used to indicate the size of a township's total population:

More than 1,000: CAPITALIZED
500–1,000: regular typeface
300–500: **boldface**
Less than 300: *italic*

Within each county, townships are listed in alphabetical order. Note that township names may be repeated in different counties, and a county may have the same name as a township located in another county.

In families, the birthplace of the father is indicated first, with native-born and foreign-born spouses underlined. If children in a family were born in more than two states, those locations appear in the "Other state(s)" column. US states are indicated by their current two-letter abbreviations. German states are abbreviated as follows:

Bav = Bavaria
G = Germany
Ham = Hamburg
Han = Hanover
Hess = Darmstadt-Hesse
Hols = Holstein
Meck = Mecklenburg
Prus = Prussia
Sax = Saxony
Westp = Westphalia
Wurt = Württemberg

Whether a household was headed by a widow or widower was determined based on the age of the youngest child, the assignment of an occupation or property value to the widow or widower, and whether he or she was listed first or second in the entry with no individual of like age present. Boldfaced families for which additional information is provided indicate individuals sharing the same last name living on contiguous properties or, at most, two properties away from each other. If children's ages are doubled (e.g., 15/15), it indicates twins.

First Tier of Counties

Township	Families with children	# of children present	Ages of children	Where oldest or only child born	Where last child born	Other state(s)

DONIPHAN

Total couples, no children: 15 | From different German states: 0 | One spouse foreign-born: 6 | One spouse native-born: 1 | From same state: 8

Total singles: 50 | On own: 16 | With family members: 13 | Mixed environ.: 6 | G household: 5 | Native-born household: 7 | Foreign-born household: 3

Township	Families with children	# of children present	Ages of children	Where oldest or only child born	Where last child born	Other state(s)
Burr Oak	G/G	2	10, 6	G	MO	
	LA/Baden	3	8, 6, 3	MO	MO	
	Baden/Baden	10	20, 19, 17, 14, 12, 10, 6, 4/4, 5 mos.	OH	KY	
	Baden/Baden	1	8 mos.	KY		
	Baden/Baden	2	5, 1	IL	KY	
	G/G	3	4, 2, 1 mo.	MO	KS	
	Prus/Baden	4	13, 10, 4, 2	Pru	KS	
	Wurt/Wurt	1	20	Wurt		
	Wurt/Han	1	17	MO		
	Wurt/_Switz_	4	9, 8, 3, 2	MO	KS	
	Prus widower	3	20, 18, 16	Prus	Prus	
	G/Prus	3	12, 9, 4, 1	OH	IA	
	Han/Baden	3	7, 3, 6 mos.	OH	KS	
CENTER	G/_Switz_	4	12, 8, 6, 4	Switz	KS	MO
	G/G	3	8, 5, 3	MD	KS	MO
	Bav/_Switz_	2	5, 3	IA	IA	
	G/G	5	11, 7, 5, 3, 1	MO	KS	
	Bav/_England_	1	2	KS		
	Wurt/_MD_	4	7, 5, 3, 1	MD	MD	
	Prus/Prus	4	7, 5, 3, 1	Prus	KS	KY, MO
	G/G	5	9, 7, 5, 3, 1	Prus	MO	KY
ELWOOD	G/G	2	6, 4	IL	MO	
	G widower	2	18, 15	G	G	
	G widower	1	8	KY		
	Prus/Baden	1	2	MO		
	Prus/Prus	5	9, 7, 5, 3, 7 mos.	Prus	KS	MO

(continued on the next page)

(continued from the previous page)

Township	Families with children	# of children present	Ages of children	Where oldest or only child born	Where last child born	Other state(s)
			DONIPHAN			
ELWOOD	G/G	3	5, 3, 5 mos.	IL	NY	
	Hols widow	1	11	MO		
	G/G	1	1	KS		
	G/<u>OH</u>	8	15, 13, 11, 9, 7, 5, 2, 4 mos.	OH	MO	
	<u>MO</u>/G	2	3, 1	MO	MO	
	G/G	1	4	MO		
Highland	No families					
IOWA	No families					
Marion	G/G	5	25, 20, 18, 16, 14	G	G	
	G/G	3	4, 2, 1	KS	KS	
	Prus/Wurt	1	2	KY		
	Prus/Prus	4	21, 17, 15, 11	Holland	KY	
	G widower	5	25, 15, 11, 9, 4	G	OH	
	G/G	2	19, 18	G	G	
	G/G	2	8, 2	LA	KS	
	<u>OH</u>/Rhineland	3	7, 5, 1	IL	KS	
	Bav/Bav	3	8, 6, 4	MO	KS	
	G/Baden	2	2, 1	MO	KS	
	Baden/Baden (single male)	3	4, 2, 9 mos.	PA	KS	
	G/G	2	12, 3 mos.	G	G	
	Han/Bav	1	5	IL		
Troy	No families					
Washington	G/G	1	4	IA		
	G/G	1	3	MN		
	Han/Han	4	7, 5, 3, 5 mos.	MO	KS	
	Prus/Prus	6	22, 19, 15, 11, 4, 2	Prus	NY	MO
	Wurt/<u>OH</u>	2	10, 7	MO	MO	
	Unknown/G	1	4 mos.	KS		
	Han/Prus	5	15, 10, 5, 2, 5 mos.	Han	KS	MO

	OH/G	2	3 mos., 2 mos.*	IA	IA	
Wathena	Baden/MO	5	11, 10, 7, 5, 1	MO	KS	
	Prus/Switz	6	11, 8, 4, 2, 1, 1 mo.	MO	KS	
	Baden/Baden	4	7, 3, 1, 8 mos.	Baden	KY	MO
	Bav/KY	2	3, 1	MO	KS	
WAYNE	Hess/Hess	6	13, 11, 10, 8, 5, 3	PA	PA	
	Han/Han	3	14, 13, 5	Han	IL	LA
	Switz/Bav	2	15, 12	NY	OH	
	G/G	3	6, 3, 1	G	KS	IL
	G/PA	1	1		KS	
	Bav/Bav	2	2, 6 mos.	IL	KS	
	G/Han	2	2, 7 mos.	KS	KS	
	Bav/Bav	7	18, 16, 14, 12, 8, 6, 3	Bav	Bav	
	Bav/Prus	3	5, 3, 5 mos.	NY	KS	
	Prus widower	1	29	Prus		
	Bav/Bav	2	7, 2 mos.	CT	KS	
	G/G	1	6 mos.	KS		
	Han/Holland	2	3, 6 mos.	Vienna†	Vienna	
White Cloud	G/PA	3	10, 6, 3	MO	MO	
	Prus/Prus	2	3, 1	MN	KS	

BROWN

Total couples, no children: 1 | From different German state: 0 | One spouse foreign-born: 0 | One spouse native-born: 0 | From same state: 1

Total singles: 11 | On own: 3 With family: 5 | Mixed environ.: 1 | G household: 0 | Native-born household: 2 | Foreign-born household: 0

Clayton-ville	Hess/Hess	5	10, 8, 4, 2, 5 mos.	LA	KS	MO
	Baden/Hess	6	20, 17, 6, 4, 2, 3 mos.	MO	KS	
	Hess/Switz	6	10, 7, 5, 4, 2, 7 mos.	MO	KS	
	Hess/Hess	1	2	IL		
	Sax widower	2	9, 7	Sax	PA	

*An anomaly.
†Probably the township of Vienna in Pottawatomie County.

(continued on the next page)

(continued from the previous page)

Township	Families with children	# of children present	Ages of children	Where oldest or only child born	Where last child born	Other state(s)
			BROWN			
Clayton- ville	Wurt/Wurt	1	1	KS		
	Han/Han	1	12	Han		
	Hess/Hess	8	17, 15, 13, 11, 9, 7, 5, (?)	OH	OH	
	Hess/Hess	7	19, 17, 14, 8, 6, 2, 1 mo.	OH	KS	
Irving	Bav/Bav	9	20, 18/18, 17, 15, 13, 10, 7, 5	MO	IL	
	Ham/Ham	1	11	Wurt		
	Hess/OH	1	1	KS		
	Baden/OH	2	2, 3 mos.	KS	KS	
	Hess/Hess	4	13, 11, 8, 4	MO	MO	
	Hess/Hess	5	17, 15, 13, 8, 5	MO	MO	
Lockwin	G/G	4	24, 17, 14, 8	G	G	
	G widower	1	3	KS		
	G/G	1	3 mos.	KS		
	G/G	4	7, 4, 2/2	G	OH	
	G/G	3	11, 9, 5	WI	WI	
	G/G	2	3, 2	IL	IL	
	Ireland/G	1	4	MO		
Walnut	Hess/Prus	4	11, 9, 7, 2	LA	IL	KY
	Prus/Hess	3	5, 3, 8 mos.	IL	KS	
	On the Rhine/ On the Rhine	2	3, 2	KS	KS	
	On the Rhine/ On the Rhine	2	5, 1	IL	KS	
	Unknown/ On the Rhine	2	2, 9 mos.	IL	KS	

NEMAHA

Total couples, no children: 3 | From different German state: 0 | One spouse foreign-born: 0 | One spouse native-born: 1 | From same state: 2

Total singles: 17 | On own: 9 | With family: 6 | Mixed environ.: 0 | G household: 2 | Native-born household: 0 | Foreign-born household: 0

Capioma	Hess/Hess	1	8 mos.	KS		
	Hess/Hess	4	8, 6, 4, 2 mos.	IN	KS	
Clear Creek	G widower	1	6	G		
	G/G	9	20, 17, 15/15, 13, 10, 8, 4, 1	G	KS	WI
	Hess/Hess	2	7, 3	Hess	KS	
Granada	No families					
Home	G/G	2	6, 3	G	G	
Nemaha	Wurt/Wurt	5	23, 19, 12, 11, 8	Wurt	IA	
	Hess/Hess	5	18, 16, 11, 9, 7	Hess*	Hess*	
	G/G	1	2	KS		
	Hess/Hess	1	4	KS		
	Wurt/Wurt	1	16	IA		
	Wurt/Wurt	3	18, 15, 11	WI	WI	
	G/G	5	13, 9, 5, 3, 1	G	KS	WI
Red Vermillion	MD/G	1	1	KS		
Richmond	Hess/Hess	2	4, 1	KS	KS	
	Hess/OH	3	9, 6, 3	IN	KS	
	France/Hess	1	2	MO		
Rock Creek Valley	Hess/PA	2	17, 15	IN	IN	
	G/G	4	7, 5, 3, 7 mos.	IA	KS	
	G widow	1	16	G		
	G/G	3	20, 19, 17	G	G	
	G/G	2	3, 7 mos.	IL	KS	
	G/OH	4	17, 15, 12, 3	IL	IL	
	G/OH	4	7, 5, 3, 1	IL	KS	

*Presumed.

(continued on the next page)

(continued from the previous page)

Township	Families with children	# of children present	Ages of children	Where oldest or only child born	Where last child born	Other state(s)

MARSHALL

Total couples, no children: 3 | From different German state: 1 | One spouse foreign-born: 0 | One spouse native-born: 0 | From same state: 2

Total singles: 39 | On own: 26 | With family: 8 | Mixed environ.: 4 | G household: 0 | Native-born household: 1 | Foreign-born household: 0

Township	Families with children	# of children present	Ages of children	Where oldest or only child born	Where last child born	Other state(s)
Blue Rapids	Bremen/Bremen	1	1	MO		
	Bav/Bav	3	6, 4, 1	IL	IA	
	Hols/Hols	6	21, 18, 15, 13, 11, 8	Hols	WI	
	Han/Han	4	18, 6, 4, 2	Han	WI	
	<u>Belgium</u>/Prus	4	7, 5, 4, 1	WI	WI	
	Bav/Bav	11	23, 21, 18, 14, 12, 10, 8, 6, 5, 3, 1	Bav	WI	
Guittard*	Bremen/Bremen	1	2	MO		
	Bav/Bav	3	8, 6, 5	MO	MO	
	Wurt/Wurt†	3	5, 3, 11 mos.	CT	KS	
	Baden/Baden	1	5	WI		
	Bremen/Bremen	2	13, 11	WI	WI	
	Han/Han	3	16, 13, 9	IN	IN	
Marysville	Wurt/Baden	1	1 mo.	KS		
	<u>Poland</u>/Prus	8	14, 12, 10, 8, 6, 4, 2, 8 mos.	Prus	WI	
	Wurt widower	3	24, 16, 14	Wurt	Wurt	
	Baden/Wurt	3	4, 2, 2 mos.	IA	KS	
	Baden/Baden	1	1	KS		
	Baden/Baden	4	Not entered, 8, 6, 4	Baden	WI	
Vermillion*	Han/Han	3	15, 11, 9	Han	Han	
	Prus/Prus	2	3, 2 mos.	WI	KS	

*Corrected.
†Single male with mother—Lodholzes.

Prus/Prus	2	7, 2	IL	MO	
Han/Han	2	4, 2	IL	WI	

WASHINGTON

Total couples, no children: 1 | From different German state: 0 | One spouse foreign-born: 0 | One spouse native-born: 0 | From same state: 1

Total singles: 10 | On own: 0 | With family: 3 | Mixed environ.: 6 | G household: 0 | Native-born household: 1 | Foreign-born household: 0

Mill Creek	No families				
Washington	Han/England	4	13, 8, 6, 1	OH	IA

Second Tier of Counties

Township	Families with children	# of children present	Ages of children	Where oldest or only child born	Where last child born	Other state(s)

WYANDOTTE

Total couples, no children: 20 | From different German state: 1 | One spouse foreign-born: 4 | One spouse native-born: 3 | From same state: 12

Total singles: 68 | On own: 20 | With family: 7 | Mixed environ.: 14 | G household: 20 | Native-born household: 6 | Foreign-born household: 1

Township	Families with children	# of children present	Ages of children	Where oldest or only child born	Where last child born	Other state(s)
Quindaro	Prus/Canada	4	18/18, 15, 12	KS	KS	
	G/G	5	29, 18, 16, 14, 11	OH	OH	
	MD/G	3	8, 7, 6	OH	OH	KY
	G/KS	1	2	KS		
	Prus/NY	4	6, 4, 2, 3 mos.	NY	KS	
	G/G	6	11, 10, 6, 4, 2, 4 mos.	G	OH	
	G/G	4	10, 7, 5, 2	G	KS	NY, WI
	Baden/G	4	11, 7, 3, 6 mos.	OH	KS	
	G/G	4	14, 12, 11, 10	G	G	
	G/G	1	18	G		
WYANDOTTE	G/G	6	18, 15, 14, 7, 5, 4	G	MO	

(continued on the next page)

(continued from the previous page)

Township	Families with children	# of children present	Ages of children	Where oldest or only child born	Where last child born	Other state(s)
			WYANDOTTE			
WYANDOTTE	G/G	4	8, 6, 3, 3 mos.	MO	KS	
	G/G	2	10, 3	G	KS	
	G/G	4	10, 7, 4, 1	LA	KS	MO
	G/G	1	1	KS		
	KS/G	1	4*	KS		
	G/G	2	3, 1	MO	MO	
	France/G	1	11†	MO		
	G/Prus	1	4	PA		
	Prus/Sax	2	5, 2	IL	KS	
	G/OH	2	5, 2	OH	KS	
	G/G	3	12, 8, 4	G	NY	
	G/Sax	4	10, 7, 4, 2	IL	KS	
	G/PA	6	16, 12, 8, 5, 3, 1	IL	KS	IA
	G widower	5	28, 20, 18, 16, 13,	G	G	
	Bav/Bav	7	13, 11, 9, 7, 5, 3, 1	OH	OH	
	Prus/OH	2	4, 2	NY	KS	
	G/G	3	10, 7, 4	G	IL	
	G widow	7	29, 24, 22, 20, 18, 16, 14	G	G	
	Baden/Han	3	3, 2, 3 mos.	MO	KS	NE
	G/at sea	3	3, 1/1	KS	KS	
	G/Prus	2	12, 1	G	Kair (unk.)	
	G/G	1	1	IL		
	G/Prus	3	17, 13, 9	IL	MO	
	Prus widow	4	13, 11, 9, 4	Prus	Prus	
	Switz/G	1	2	KS		
	G/G	2	18, 16	G	G	
	Prus/Prus	1	4 mos.	KS		
	G/Holland	4	6, 5, 3, 7 mos.	OH	KS	WI
	Prus/Prus	1	2	KS		

*Also a six-mo-old with a different last name.
†Also a two-yr-old with a different last name.

Sax/Prus	2	5, 2	MO	MO	
G/AL	2	4, 2	MO	MO	
G/G	6	8/8, 5, 4, 2/2	OH	KS	KY
G/G	1	1	KS		
Prus/Bav	1	4	PA		
G/G	2	4, 3 mos.	MO	KS	
Han/Han	2	15, 13	Han	Han	
G/G	2	15, 5	G	KS	
G widower	1	12	G		
Prus/PA	1	35	Prus		
Prus/VA	3	9, 6, 2	MO	MO	
G/Baden	5	8, 7, 5, 3, 6 mos.	CT	KS	
G widower	5	19, 16, 14, 13, 8	PA	MO	OH

CITY OF LEAVENWORTH
(three pages contain no birthplace data)

The city of Leavenworth was a way station for many settlers planning to move to the interior. (See J. Neale Carman, "Continental Europeans in Rural Kansas, 1854–1861," in *Territorial Kansas: Studies Commemorating the Centennial* [Lawrence: University of Kansas Publications, Social Science Studies, 1954], 164.) The number of German-born residents in 1860 is too large to document here, but basic figures on the number of couples, single individuals, and families with children are provided. A breakdown by gender is included for singles because the numbers were large enough to reflect a significant difference. The figures do not include a contingent of Catholic priests from various European countries, including German states.

Total couples, no children: 63 | From different German state: 8 | One spouse foreign-born: 10 | One spouse native-born: 7 | From same state: 38

Total singles: 283 | On own: F, 6; M, 92 | With family: F, 10; M, 7 | Mixed environ.: F, 15; M, 68 | G household or establishment: F, 13; M, 35 | Native-born household or establishment: F, 14; M, 1 | Foreign-born household or establishment: F, 9; M, 13

Total families with children: 235 | From different German state: 16 | One spouse foreign-born: 20 | One spouse native-born: 25 | From same state: 149 | Widow/widower: 25

(continued on the next page)

(continued from the previous page)

Township	Families with children	# of children present	Ages of children	Where oldest or only child born	Where last child born	Other state(s)

LEAVENWORTH TOWNSHIPS OUTSIDE CITY OF LEAVENWORTH
(two pages contain no birthplace data)

Total couples, no children: 19 | From different German state: 3 | One spouse foreign-born: 1 | One spouse native-born: 4 | From same state: 11

Total singles: 89 | On own: 16 | With family: 18 | Mixed environ.: 39 (mainly teamsters serving Ft. Leavenworth and women, possibly prostitutes, living together) | G household: 7 | Native-born household: 7 | Foreign-born household: 2

Township	Families with children	# of children present	Ages of children	Where oldest or only child born	Where last child born	Other state(s)
Alexandria	G/G	3	7, 5, 3	WI	WI	
	G/G	3	15, 12, 6	G	IA	MO
	G/G	2	5, 2	WI	WI	
Delaware	G/G	3	9, 4, 1	IA	KS	MO
	G/G	2	5, 3	CT	CT	
	G/G	1	7	IA		
	G/G	5	13, 10, 8, 7, 5	G	IL	
	G/G	3	5, 3, 1 mo.	KS	KS	
	Switz/Baden	5	15, 13, 9, 7, 2	OH	KS	WI
	G/G	1	1	KS		
	G/G	1	6	KS		
	Wurt/Bav	1	10 mos.	KS		
	G/G	1	2	KS		
	G widow	4	16/16, 13, 4	G	IL	
	TN/G	4	11, 9, 4, 1	IL	KS	MN
	G widower	1	10	G		
	G/G	1	7	IA		
	G/G	1	8	IN		
Easton	G widow	1	7	KS		
	G/G	1	4	KS		
	G widower	1	20	G		
	G/G	1	9	G		
	G widow	1	1	KS		
	G/G	4	7, 4, 4 mos./4 mos.	MO	KS	
	G/G	3	6, 3, 1	OH	KS	
	G widow	1	21	MO		
	Prus/Wurt	1	1	KS		

	Prus/Prus	3	5, 2, 1	KS	KS	
	G/G	5	13, 11, 9, 3, 1	G	KS	
Ft. Leaven-	G widow	1	1	KS		
worth	G widow	4	9, 7, 3, 1	CA	RI	MI
	G widow	1	5	MD		
	G widow	1	4	PA		
	G widow	2	2, 10 mos.	KS	WI	
	G/G	5	16, 10, 9, 7, 6	MI	KS	Cherokee Nation, PA
	G widow	2	11, 7	G	G	
	G widow*	2	2, 6 mos.	KS	KS	
KICKAPOO	France/G	1	3	G		
	Bav/Bav	1	7	MO		
	G/G	2	3, 1	NY	KS	
	France/G	2	5, 2	MO	KS	
	G/G	4	13, 11, 6, 3	MO	KS	IA
	G/OH	2	3, 1 mo.	IL	KS	
	G/G	2	6, 11 mos.	G	KS	
	G/IN	2	2, 6 mos.	KS	KS	
	G/G	4	19, 13, 11, 7	MO	IA	
	G/G	2	5, 3	IA	KS	
	G/England	2	16, 1 mo.	England	KS	
	G/OH	1	1	KS		
	G/G	3	5, 2, 8 mos.	NE	KS	MO
	G/Hungary	2	2, 10 mos.	KS	KS	
	G/G	1	4 mos.	KS		
	Baden/Baden	1	11	MO		
	G/MO	2	2, 2 mos.	IL	KS	
	G/G	3	4, 2, 1 mo.	MO	KS	
	G/PA	1	12	IA		
	Baden/Baden	5	28, 25, 22, 21, 13	Baden	Baden	
	Ham/Prus	5	6/6, 4, 3, 1	IL	KS	
	G widower	2	2, 9 mos.	KS	KS	
	G/G	4	20, 12, 9, 5	G	IL	
	Bav/OH	4	7, 5, 3, 10 mos.	MO	MO	
	G/G	1	2	MO		
	G/Han	3	3, 2, 9 mos.	KS	KS	
	G/G	4	16, 14, 12, 7	IN	IA	

*All women without spouses were presumed to be widowed, but their true status is unclear.

(continued on the next page)

(continued from the previous page)

Township	Families with children	# of children present	Ages of children	Where oldest or only child born	Where last child born	Other state(s)
LEAVENWORTH TOWNSHIPS OUTSIDE CITY OF LEAVENWORTH						
KICKAPOO	G/G	5	13, 11, 7, 4, 2	MO	KS	
	G/G	3	4, 2, 9 mos.	IL	KS	
	G widow	3	7, 5, 9 mos.	MO	KS	
	G widower	5	19, 17, 13, 9, 5	MO	MO	
	G/G	8	20, 13, 11, 9, 7, 5, 2, 8 mos.	G	KS	
	G/G	1	1	KS		
	G/G	2	4/4	NE		
	G widow	1	3	KS		
	G/G	1	1 mo.	KS		
	G/G	4	11, 6, 3, 1	IL	KS	
Stranger	Prus/Prus	2	9, 6	Prus	Prus	
	France/G	3	13, 5, 3	G	MO	
	G/MO	6	12, 10, 8, 6, 4, 2	MO	KS	
	G/PA	2	15, 12	MO	MO	
	G/G	8	21, 18, 16, 14, 12, 10, 8, 6	IL	MO	
	G/G	1	3	MO		
	G/G	3	6, 4, 2	WI	WI	
	G/G	6	18, 16, 14, 10, 8, 3	MO	MO	
	G/G	1	1	IN		
	G/G	3	9, 2, 6 mos.	NY	KS	

ATCHISON

Total couples, no children: 19 | From different German state: 0 | One spouse foreign-born: 3 | One spouse native-born: 3 | From same state: 13

Total singles: 93 | On own: 31 | With family: 19 | Mixed environ.: 20 | G household: 9 | Native-born household: 10 | Foreign-born household: 4

Township	Families with children	# of children present	Ages of children	Where oldest or only child born	Where last child born	Other state(s)
ATCHISON	Han/Han	1	1	KS		
	G/G	2	14, 5 mos.	G	KS	
	G/PA	3	11, 9, 2	PA	PA	
	G/IL	1	2	IL		

G/Europe	1	3 mos.	KS		
Holland/Pru	2	2, 6 mos.	KS	KS	
G widower	2	4, 2	G	KS	
G widow	5	21, 10, 7, 5, 3	G	G	
Ireland/G	1	2	Ireland		
Sax/OH	2	4, 2	WI	WI	
G/G	4	16, 15, 14, 6	IA	IA	
Holland/G	3	12, 6, 4	OH	OH	
G/G	1	5 mos.	KS		
G/G	5	11, 7, 3, 2, 2 mos.	G	IA	
G widower	1	2 mos.	KS		
G/G	3	6, 2, 4 mos.	PA	KS	MD
Han/Han	3	8, 6, 3	Han	KS	MO
G/G	2	Unknown, 2	NY	KS	
G widower	2	24, 4	NY	NY	
G/G	1	2	IL		
G/G	2	12, 2	America	KS	
G/G	4	10, 4, 2, 11 mos.	G	MO	
G/G	1	12	MO		
G/G	1	2	KS		
G/G	2	2, 9 mos.	KS	KS	
G/G	2	3, 2	WI	WI	
G/G	1	1	KS		
G/Switz	1	3 mos.	KS		
G widow	1	20	G		
G/G	2	18, 16	G	G	
G/G	3	5, 3, 1	PA	KS	
G/G	5	11, 9, 5, 3, 8 mos.	G	KS	PA
G/G	2	5, 3	PA	PA	
G/G	1	7 mos.	KS		
G/G	2	4, 1	IL	KS	
G widower	2	4, 1	MO	MO	
G widow	1	12	G		
G/G	3	4, 3, 1	IL	KS	
G/G	1	5	WI		
G/G	2	4, 2	IL	IL	
G/G	1	2	MO		
G/G	2	2, 5 mos.	MO	KS	
MA/G	1	4	WI		
G/MS	1	4 mos.	Not indicated		

(continued on the next page)

(continued from the previous page)

Township	Families with children	# of children present	Ages of children	Where oldest or only child born	Where last child born	Other state(s)
			ATCHISON			
ATCHISON	G/G	2	3, 10 mos.	IL	IL	
	G/G	2	6, 2	G	KS	
	G/<u>NY</u>	1	1	IA		
	G/G	2	4, 2	IA	IA	
	G/G	3	4, 2, 1 mo.	MA	KS	IL
	G/G	2	11, 10	OH	OH	
Center	G/G	3	8, 4, 2	PA	KS	
	G/G	3	6, 4, 2	PA	PA	
	<u>MO</u>/G	4	18, 15, 12, 8	MO	MO	
	G/G	1	2	MO		
	G/G	1	7 mos.	NJ		
	G/G	2	18, 16	G	G	
	<u>IN</u>/G	6	18, 16, 12, 9, 4, 1	IN	KS	MO
Grass-hopper	G/widower	2	27, 19	G	Not indicated	
	G/<u>IN</u>	1	8 mos.	KS		
Kapioma	G/Europe	1	1	KS		
	G/G	6	15, 12, 10, 7, 4, 2	G	IA	
	G/G	5	15, 11, 7, 4, 1	KS	KS	IA
	G/G	1	1	KS		
Lancaster	G/G	5	15, 12, 11, 9, 4	WI	WI	
	G/G	1	7	OH		
	G/G	4	7, 5, 3, 4 mos.	OH	OH	
	G/G	2	5, 2	IL	IL	
MOUNT PLEASANT	G/<u>IN</u>	2	4, 2	IA	KS	
	G/G	1	2	KS		
	G/<u>WI</u>	3	7, 4, 2	MO	KS	
	G/G	5	10, 8, 5, 4, 2	IL	IL	
	G/G	1	2	KS		
Shannon	G/G	2	2, 6 mos.	MO	KS	
	G/G	3	5, 4, 1	MO	KS	
	G/<u>OH</u>	2	4, 6 mos.	KS	KS	
	G/G	2	3, 2	KY	KY	
	G/<u>Ireland</u>	2	2, 5 mos.	KY	KY	

WALNUT	G/G	1	2	KS			
	G/G	4	9, 5, 4, 2	OH	KS	IA, NY	
	G/G	2	5, 3	NY	NY		
	G/G	3	10, 3, 6 mos.	G	KS		
	G/G	7	21, 17, 15, 13, 11, 9, 6	G	VA	PA	
	G/G	2	3, 9 mos.	IL	IL		
	G/G	4	8, 6, 2, 6 mos.	MO	KS		
	G/G	2	3, 10 mos.	KS	KS		
	G/G	4	14, 11, 5, 3	G	KS	MO	
	G/G	4	6, 4, 2, 1	MO	KS		
	G/G	2	2, 1	IA	KS		
	G/G	3	15, 13, 9	G	PA		
	G/G	2	5, 3	G	KS		
	G/G	3	8, 2, 2 mos.	IN	KS		
	G/<u>OH</u>	1	3 mos.	KS			
	G/G	2	8, 6	G	G		
	G/G	2	4, 2	NY	KS		

JACKSON

Total couples, no children: 1 | From different German state: 0 | One spouse foreign-born: 0 | One spouse native-born: 0 | From same state: 1 Total singles: 4 | On own: 2 | With family: 1 | Mixed environ.: 0 | G household: 0 | Native-born household: 1 | Foreign-born household: 0

Douglas	G/<u>NY</u>	2	23, 21	NY	NY		
Franklin	G widow	5	16, 14, 12, 10, 7	G	G		
	G/G	4	7, 5, 3, 1	NY	KS		
	G/G	7	12, 10, 8, 6, 4, 2, 1	G	KS	NY	
	G/G	2	25, 18	IL	IL		
	G/G	3	6, 4, 2	NY	NY		
	G/G	2	4, 2	MO	KS		
	G/G	2	4, 2	KS	KS		
Holton	No families						
Jefferson	G/G	3	7, 5, 2	NY	KS		
	G/G	3	5, 4, 2	NY	NY		
	G/G	3	5, 3, 1	NY	KS		
	G/G	3	9, 7, 5	NY	IL		

(continued on the next page)

(continued from the previous page)

Township	Families with children	# of children present	Ages of children	Where oldest or only child born	Where last child born	Other state(s)

POTTAWATOMIE

Total couples, no children: 6 | From different German state: 0 | One spouse foreign-born: 0 | One spouse native-born: 0 | From same state: 6

Total singles: 30 | On own: 18 | With family: 11 | Mixed environ.: 0 | G household: 0 | Native-born household: 1 | Foreign-born household: 0

Township	Families with children	# of children present	Ages of children	Where oldest or only child born	Where last child born	Other state(s)
Blue	France/G	7	12, 10, 7, 6, 4, 2, 6 mos.	NY	KS	IN, PA
Louisville	G/G	2	3, 2	KS	KS	
	G/G	4	10, 8, 7, 5	G	PA	
	G/G	3	6, 3, 1	G	G	
	G/G	3	5, 3, 2	PA	PA	
Rockingham	G/G	5	18, 16, 14, 5, 2,	G	KS	
	G/G	4	21, 19, 18, 16	G	G	
	G/G	3	8, 6, 4	G	MO	
	G/G	5	14, 12, 9, 6, 3	G	MO	NY
	G/G	4	10, 7, 4, 1	G	KS	PA, MO
Shannon	No families					
St. George	G/Nassau	3	4, 2, 6 mos.	KS	KS	
	G/G	1	2	KS		
	G/MO	2	5, 10 mos.	KS	KS	
	G/G	1	1	KS		
	G/Baden	4	8, 6, 4, 2,	NY	KS	MO
	G/G	2	3, 1	KS	KS	
	Prus/Prus	2	15, 10	WI	WI	
	G widower	5	28, 18, 15, 3, 3 mos.	G	KS	IL
Vienna	G widow	2	22, 17	G	G	
	G/OH (single male)	2	2, 6 mos.	KS	KS	
	France/G	1	1	KS		
	G/G	3	5, 3, 1	KS	KS	
	G/G	2	4, 1	KS	KS	
	G/G	5	12, 11, 9, 4, 1	G	KS	WI
	G widow	2	16, 1	G	KS	
	G/OH	1	1	MO		

	Hungary/G	1	1	KS		
	G/G	1	1	KS		
	Prus/Prus	3	6, 3, 6 mos.	KS	KS	
	G/G	3	21, 12, 8	G	MD	
	G/G (couple)	1	6 mos.	KS		
	G/IN	1	1	KS		
	G widow	1	13	PA		
	Prus/Prus	1	4	KS		
	G/G	3	12, 4, 2	G	KS	
	G/G	2	4, 6 mos.	KS	KS	
	G/G	2	4, 2	KS	KS	
	G/G	3	10, 7, 2	G	KS	
	G/G	1	3	KS		
	G/G	3	12, 10, 9	G	G	
	G/G	4	18, 15, 12, 3	G	KS	
	G/G	2	5, 2	KS	KS	
	G widower	1	6	Not entered		

RILEY

Total couples, no children: 6 | From different German state: 2 | One spouse foreign-born: 1 | One spouse native-born: 1 | From same state: 2

Total singles: 33 | On own: 13 | With family: 2 | Mixed environ.: 4 | G household: 10 | Native-born household: 4 | Foreign-born household: 0

Manhattan	Hess/PA	3	11, 7, 6	PA	PA	
	G/G	4	16, 13, 7, 5	G	WI	
Not stated	Sax/MA	1	8	RI		
	Sax/Sax	1	7 mos.	MO		
	Westp/Westp (single male)	3	9, 7, 1	MO	KS	
	Westp/Westp	7	22, 17, 15, 13, 11, 3, 2 mos.	Westp	KS	IL
	G/G	2	12, 3	G	KS	
	G/G	1	4 mos.	KS		
	G/G	6	13, 9, 8, 6, 2, 1 mo.	MO	KS	
	G widower	3	19, 13, 10	G	G	
	G/G	1	4	WI		
	G widower	6	22, 18, 16, 12, 9, 2	G	KS	PA, WI
	Bremen/IL	2	2, 4 mos.	KS	KS	
	G/IL	5	9, 6, 4, 2, 1	IA	KS	

(continued on the next page)

(continued from the previous page)

Town-ship	Families with children	# of children present	Ages of children	Where oldest or only child born	Where last child born	Other state(s)
			RILEY			
NOT STATED	G/IL	5	9, 6, 4, 2, 4 mos.	IA	KS	TX, MO
	Prus/England	1	3	MA		
	G/NC	1	2	KS		
Ogden	Bav/Bav	1	3 mos.	KS		
	Prus/Prus	2	7, 2	Prus	KS	
	G/G	1	7	Ft. Louisiana*		
	Prus/Prus	1	14	Prus		
	G/G	2	3, 2	KS	KS	

CLAY

Total couples, no children: 0 | From different German state: 0 | One spouse foreign-born: 0 | One spouse native-born: 0 | From same state: 0

Total singles: 0 | On own: 0 | With family: 0 | Mixed environ.: 0 | G household: 0 | Native-born household: 0 | Foreign-born household: 0

Not stated	Bav widower	1	8	G		
	G/G	2	2, 1	IA	IA	

JEFFERSON (below Atchison)

Total couples, no children: 6 | From different German state: 1 | One spouse foreign-born: 2 | One spouse native-born: 3 | From same state: 0

Total singles: 25 | On own: 2 | With family: 7 | Mixed environ.: 3 | G household: 3 | Native-born household: 8 | Foreign-born household: 2

Grass-hopper Falls	Hess widower	5	25, 23, 19, 17, 13	Hess	Hess	
	Hess widower	2	5, 3	WI	WI	
	Switz/G	6	14, 12, 9, 6, 3, 1	MO	KS	
	Switz/G	5	17, 12, 11, 7, 5	G	KS	IL
	G widower	3	20, 12, 8	G	MO	
	G/G	2	17, 8	G	G	

*Probably Ft. Livingston, LA.

Jefferson	G/G	4	33, 18, 16, 14	G	IA	
	Han/Han	3	9, 5, 3	IA	KS	
	G widow	7	12/12, 9, 5, 3, 1/1	G	KS	PA
	G/G	4	5, 4, 3, 1	IA	KS	
	G/G	4	4, 3, 2, 1 mo.	MI	KS	IL
	Prus/OH	1	5 mos.	KS		
	France/Baden	3	7, 5, 4	VA	IL	
	France/G (French widow contiguous)	6	18, 15, 12, 10, 8, 6	IA	IA	
	G widower	2	30, 22	G	G	
	G/G	5	13, 12, 5, 4, 2	NY	KS	
Kaw	G/Han	3	5, 2, 1 mo.	MO	KS	
	Hess/Bav	4	29, 17, 11, 8	Hess	IL	
	G/OH	2	3, 7 mos.	OH	KS	
Kentucky	Wurt/Wurt	3	6, 4, 1	NY	NY	
	Prus/Prus	2	2, 4 mos.	KS	KS	
	Prus/Prus	3	8, 4, 1	Prus	KS	TX
	France/Prus	1	3	WI		
	Wurt/Wurt	1	1	NY		
	Prus/Sax	1	2	IL		
	Wurt/Wurt	1	11 mos.	KS		
Oskaloosa	Bav/Bav	3	9, 5, 2	LA	MO	
	Wurt/Switz	3	10, 3, 1	PA	KS	IA
	Luxembourg/Prus	3	19, 14, 11	Luxembourg	Luxembourg	
Ozawkie	Han/Prus	1	1	IL		
	Westp/Han	2	2, 1 mo.	IL	KS	
Rock Creek	Wurt/Wurt	4	11, 8, 5, 3	PA	IL	
	OH/Hess	7	16, 14, 9, 7, 6, 5, 2	OH	IL	

Third Tier of Counties

Township	Families with children	# of children present	Ages of children	Where oldest or only child born	Where last child born	Other state(s)

JOHNSON
(four pages contain no birthplace data)

Total couples, no children: 9 | From different German state: 0 | One spouse foreign-born: 0 | One spouse native-born: 1 | From same state: 8

Total singles: 47 | On own: 14 | With family: 4 | Mixed environ.: 14 | G household: 10 | Native-born household: 4 | Foreign-born household: 1

Township	Families with children	# of children present	Ages of children	Where oldest or only child born	Where last child born	Other state(s)
Aubry	No families					
DeSoto	OH/G	1	1	KS		
Gardner	G/KY	8	17, 16, 14, 12, 10, 8, 5, 1	KY	KS	
Lexington	Poland/G	1	7 mos.	KS		
	G/G	10	23, 21, 19, 18, 16, 14, 11, 6/6, 4	NY	KS	IL
	G/G	2	13, 8	MO	MO	
	G/G	5	14, 12, 11, 10, 6	LA	MO	
	G/G	4	6, 4, 3, 1	MO	MO	
McCamish	G/G	1	3	NY		
	G/IN	4	6/6, 4, 2	IN	KS	
	G/G	1	3 mos.	KS		
Monticello*	G/G	1	1	G		
	G/G	3	9, 3, 1	NY	MO	IL
Olathe	G/England	3	6, 4, 2	MO	KS	
	VA/G	1	3 (different surname)	MO		
Oxford	No families					
SHAWNEE	G widower	3	15, 7, 5	G	MO	
	Prus/Holland	1	2	WI		
	G/G	2	3, 8 mos.	MO	KS	
	G/MO	2	2, 1	MO	KS	
	G/G	1	2 mos.	KS		
	G/G	4	18, 7, 6, 3	G	PA	
	G/G	2	3, 1	KS	KS	

*Two G children, aged 7 and 3, in native-born household not counted.

	G widow	1	15	MO		
	G/Switz	1	2	OH		
	G widow	2	24, 10	G	G	
	G/IN	2	2, 1	IA	KS	
	G/G	3	5, 3, 7 mos.	MD	KS	MO
	G/G	3	3, 2, 1	MO	KS	
	G/G	5	8, 7, 5, 3, 5 mos.	MO	KS	
	G/G	4	6, 5, 3, 8 mos.	KS	KS	
	France/G	1	8	G		
	G/G	7	15, 14, 11, 9, 4, 2, 6 mos.	TN	KS	
Spring Hill*	G/PA	2	5, 2	MD	MD	
	G/G	1	1	KS		
Union	No families					

DOUGLAS

Total couples, no children: 22 | From different German state: 0 | One spouse foreign-born: 3 | One spouse native-born: 3 | From same state: 16

Total singles: 92 | On own: 21 | With family: 13 | Mixed environ.: 29 | G household: 15 | Native-born household: 13 | Foreign-born household: 1

Clinton	G/G	1	1	KS		
	G widow	4	22, 20, 18, 10	G	OH	
	G/G	5	15, 14, 11, 3/3	IN	IN	
	Polish widower	4	7, 6, 5, 1	G	G	
Eudora	G/G	1	2	KS		
	G/G	4	8, 6, 4, 2	MI	MI	
	G widower	1	30	G		
	G widower	4	15, 10, 6, 4	NY	IL	Canada
	G widower	1	19	Prus		
	G/G	4	10, 5, 3, 1	G	KS	NY, IL
	G/G	1	6 mos.	KS		
	G/IL	1	4 mos.	KS		
	G/G	2	3, 10 mos.	IL	KS	
	G/G	3	10, 8, 2	IL	KS	
	G/G	2	4, 10 mos.	IL	KS	
	G/G	6	11, 5, 3/3, 4 mos./4 mos.	G	KS	PA, IL

*Two G children, aged 2 and 1, in native-born household not counted.

(continued on the next page)

(continued from the previous page)

Township	Families with children	# of children present	Ages of children	Where oldest or only child born	Where last child born	Other state(s)
			DOUGLAS			
Eudora	G/G	1	1	MO		
	G/G	2	4, 1	IL	IL	
	G/G	4	12, 8, 5, 2	G	KS	
	G/G (couple)	1	3	IL		
	G/G	1	5 mos.	KS		
	G/G	2	3, 1	KS	KS	
	G/G	2	9, 6	G	G	
	G/G	2	4, 3 mos.	IL	KS	
	G/G	3	10, 3, 1	IL	KS	
	G/G	1	3	KS		
	G/G	3	5, 3, 8 mos.	IL	KS	
	G/G	5	11, 9, 8, 4, 1	France	KS	IL
	G/G	5	12, 10, 8, 5, 3 mos.	G	KS	IL
	G/G	3	8, 4, 2	IL	KS	
	G/G	1	13	G		
	G/<u>PA</u>	6	18, 10, 9, 7, 5, 2	PA	KS	IL
	G/G	1	3 mos.	KS		
Kanawaka	G/G	5	12, 10, 8, 4, 2	G	KS	OH, MO
	G/G	1	4	OH		
	G/G	3	7, ?, 3	OH	KS	
	G/G	2	28, 24	G	G	
	G/G	4	6, 4, 2, 6 mos.	KS	KS	
	G/G	1	2	KS		
	G/G	1	6	G		
LAWRENCE	G widow	3	25, 18, 14	NY	NY	
	G/G	2	2, 1 mo.	KS	KS	
	G/<u>Ireland</u>	3	4/4, 2	KS	KS	
	G/G	4	3, 2, 7 mos./ 7 mos.	IL	KS	
	Prus/Hols	2	2, 6 mos.	IL	KS	
	G/<u>France</u>	1	5 mos.	KS		
	G/G	2	8, 2	MO	OH	
	G/<u>MA</u>	4	6, 4, 2, 8 mos.	MA	MI	

	G/G	1	1	KS		
	G/PA	4	11, 7, 2, 10 mos.	CT	KS	
	ME/G	3	14, 12, 3	ME	KS	
	G/PA	1	6	NY		
	G/G	3	14, 13, 6	MD	MD	
	G/OH	1	2	KS		
	G/G	7	13, 12, 11, 8, 5, 4, 6 mos.	G	KS	
	G/G	1	6 mos.	KS		
	G/G	2	2, 2 mos.	KS	KS	
	G/G	1	6 mos.	KS		
	G widower	2	4, 2	IL	IL	
LECOMPTON	France/G	2	3, 1	IA	KS	
	G/G	1	2	KS		
	G widower	3	16, 12, 9	IN	IN	
	G widow	1	2	PA		
	G/G	1	13	G		
	G/G	1	1	KS		
	G/G	1	23	G		
	G/IL	3	6, 3, 2 mos.	MO	KS	
	G/G	5	13, 11, 9, 7, 3	MO	MO	
	G/G	1	5	IL		
	G/G	3	4, 3, 1	KS	KS	
	G/G	4	7, 5, 3, 6 mos.	G	KS	
	G/KS	1	3	IN		
Marion	G/G	4	8, 3, 2, 1 mo.	NY	KS	WI
	G/PA	1	7	OH		
	G/G	3	6, 4, 1	OH	OH	
	Prus/G	2	5, 3	IL	IL	
	G/G	4	7, 6, 3, 1	NY	KS	NJ, IA
PALMYRA	G/TN	2	3, 1	KS	KS	
	G/G	2	7, 4	G	OH	
	G/G	1	10	G		
	G/G	2	2, 1	KS	KS	
	G/AR	5	10, 8, 6, 4, 2	AR	KS	IN
	G/G	1	2 mos.	KS		
	G/G	1	33	G		
	G/G	1	2	WI		
	G/G	6	18, 16, 14, 12, 9, 7	G	WI	
	Switz/G	1	2	MO		
	G widow	1	13	TX		

(continued on the next page)

(continued from the previous page)

Township	Families with children	# of children present	Ages of children	Where oldest or only child born	Where last child born	Other state(s)
			DOUGLAS			
WAKARUSA	Baden/Baden	1	4	OH		
	G/G	4	19, 14, 12, 10	WI	MI	IL
	Prus/G	1	7	OH		
	G/G	1	8	NY		
	KS/G	1	6 mos.	KS		
	G/G	2	2, 6 mos.	KS	KS	
	G/G	3	8, 6 mos., 3 mos. (anomaly)	G	KS	
Willow Springs	G/G	7	20, 18, 15, 12, 10, 6, 4	Not indicated	IL	IA
	G/G	6	18, 15, 11, 8, 6, 2	KS	KS	
	G/G	3	6, 4, 2 mos.	OH	KS	
	G widower	2	3 mos./3 mos.	KS		
	G/PA	1	6 mos.	KS		
	G/PA	2	4, 1	PA	PA	
	G widow	3	20, 17, 14	G	G	

SHAWNEE

(one page contains no birthplace data)

Total couples, no children: 8 | From different German state: 0 | One spouse foreign-born: 0 | One spouse native-born: 2 | From same state: 6
Total singles: 21 | On own: 6 | With family: 1 | Mixed environ.: 3 | G household: 4 | Native-born household: 4 | Foreign-born household: 3

Auburn	G/G	4	11, 8, 6, 2	OH	KS	IN
	G/G	1	3 mos.	KS		
Monmouth	G/Switz	8	23, 22, 21, 19, 13/13, 10, 8	NY	NY	
Soldier	G/G	3	6, 4, 2	KY	KS	
	G/G	7	18, 16, 12, 8, 6, 3, 6 mos.	MO	KS	
Tecumseh	G/G	2	5, 2	OH	MO	
	Switz/G	5	11, 7, 5, 3, 1	MO	KS	

	G/G	5	18/18, 16, 14, 3	IN	KS	
TOPEKA	Prus/Bav	4	15, 9, 7, 4	MO	KS	
	NY/G	5	11, 7, 6, 2, 4 mos.	WI	KS	
	IN/G	1	3	MN		
	Prus/Anhalt	4	7, 5, 3, 2 mos.	IL	KS	IA
	G/OH	1	1	OH		
Williams-port	Scotland/G	1	4	IN		

WABAUNSEE

Total couples, no children: 12 | From different state: 0 | One spouse foreign-born: 1 | One spouse native-born: 0 | From same state: 11

Total singles: 39 | On own: 34 | With family: 3 | Mixed environ.: 1 | G household: 1 | Native-born household: 0 | Foreign-born household: 0

Alma	G/G	2	3, 1	KS	KS	
	G/G	1	1	KS		
	G/G	6	21, 19, 16, 13, 8, 3	G	KS	
	G/G (single male)	2	9, 4	G	G	
	G/G	2	2, 3 mos.	KS	KS	
	G widower	2	8, 5 mos.	MO	KS	
	G/G	3	12, 5, 2	G	KS	MO
	G/G	7	22, 18, 15, 13, 10, 4, 9 mos.	OH	KS	
	G/G (single male)	4	9, 7, 3, 2	G	KS	
	G/G	2	3, 8 mos.	MO	KS	
	G/G	2	14, 11	G	G	
	G/G	2	5, 2	G	MO	
	G/G	1	6 mos.	KS		
	G/G	3	9, 5, 1	G	KS	OH
	G/OH	1	4	OH		
	G/G	1	8 mos.	KS		
	G/G	3	21, 17, 11	G	IA	
	G/G	2	9, 6	NY	IA	
	G/G	2	7, 3	IL	MO	
	G/G	1	11	G		

(continued on the next page)

(continued from the previous page)

Township	Families with children	# of children present	Ages of children	Where oldest or only child born	Where last child born	Other state(s)
			WABAUNSEE			
Alma	G/G (single male)	3	6, 4, 1	G	KS	
	G/G	7	19, 16, 14, 12, 6, 4, 1	G	KS	MO
	G/G	2	14, 12	G	G	
	G/G	5	19, 17, 10, 6, 6 mos.	G	KS	MO
	G/G	1	1	KS		
	G widow (single male)	4	27, 25, 20, 18	G	G	
	G/G	4	14, 10, 7, 3	G	IL	MO
	G/G	1	2	KS		
	G/G	7	21, 18, 16, 14, 10, 8, 4	G	MO	
	G/G	3	8, 4, 9 mos.	G	KS	MO
	G/G	3	6, 4, 2	IL	MO	
	G widow	3	11, 7, 4	G	IL	
	G/G	3	22, 15, 10	G	OH	
	G/<u>OH</u>	3	5, 3, 1	IL	KS	MO
	G/G	4	8, 6, 3, 1	OH	KS	
	G/G	4	11, 9, 6, 3	G	MO	
Mission Creek	No families					
Wabaunsee	G/G	3	8, 4, 2	G	G	
	<u>Ireland</u>/G	1	17	NY		
Wilmington	No families					
Zeandale	OH/G	2	3, 1 mo.	KS	KS	
			DAVIS			

Total couples, no children: 10 | From different German state: 2 | One spouse foreign-born: 1 | One spouse native-born: 1 | From same state: 6

Total singles: 47 | On own: 22 | With family: 12 | Mixed environ.: 7 | G household: 3 | Native-born household: 3 | Foreign-born household: 0

Ft. Riley Reserve	G camp woman	2	6, 4	KS	KS	

	G camp woman	1	9	KS		
Junction	Han/PA	1	3	KS		
	OH/Prus	2	3, 1	MO	KS	
	OH/Bav	2	4, 1	OH	OH	
	Prus/Prus	2	3, 7 mos.	WI	KS	
	G/Prus	2	8, 4	IL	IL	
	Bav widow	2	4, 1	MO	KS	
Not stated	Hols/Hols	2	6, 3	OH	OH	
	G/G	2	9, 1	G	OH	
	Prus/Prus	2	3, 6 mos.	IA	KS	
	G/G	5	17, 15, 12, 10, 3	IN	IN	
	G/G	1	1	IN		
	G widower	4	11, 8, 6, 3	G	OH	
	Prus/Switz	2	6, 4	MO	MO	
	Prus/Prus	3	5, 3, 1	WI	KS	NE
	Prus/Prus	1	2	MI		
	G/G	3	6, 3, 3 mos.	MO	KS	
	Prus/Wurt	1	1	KS		
	G/TN	1	4	KS		
	Prus/Prus	1	1	KS		
	Sax/Wurt	1	7	OH		
	Baden/Gothers	2	4, 2	VA	VA	
	Meck widower	2	28, 21	Meck	Meck	
	Prus/Prus	1	16	Prus		
	Meck/RI	1	6 mos.	IL		
	G/G	2	6, 2	IL	KS	
	Prus/G	2	3, 2	KS	KS	
	G widower	2	15, 4	Sax	Sax	
	Prus/Prus	3	23, 20, 18	Prus	Prus	
	Prus/OH	6	14, 12, 9, 7, 3, 1	IL	KS	

DICKINSON

Total couples, no children: 3 | From different German state: 0 | One spouse foreign-born: 0 | One spouse native-born: 0 | From same state: 3

Total singles: 18 | On own: 6 | With family: 11 | Mixed environ.: 0 | G household: 1 | Native-born household: 0 | Foreign-born household: 0

Not stated	Prus/Prus	2	4, 1	Prus	KS
	Prus/Prus (couple)	1	1	KS	

(continued on the next page)

(continued from the previous page)

Township	Families with children	# of children present	Ages of children	Where oldest or only child born	Where last child born	Other state(s)
			DICKINSON			
Not stated	Prus/Prus	7	16, 13, 12, 10, 5, 3, 1	Prus	KS	WI
	G/<u>OH</u>	1	1	KS		
	Prus/Prus	2	29, 15	Prus	Prus	
	Prus widower	1	18	Prus		
	Prus/Prus	2	22, 13	Prus	Prus	
	Prus/Prus	1	13	Prus		
	Prus/Prus	1	6	Prus		
	Prus/Prus	2	4, 1	WI	WI	
	Prus widower	5	21, 8, 6, 4, 2	Prus	WI	
	Prus widower	3	8, 6, 5	Prus	Prus	
	Prus/Prus	4	14, 9, 7, 1	Prus	KS	
	Prus/Prus	1	1	WI		
	Prus/Prus	3	4, 3, 1	WI	WI	
	G/Prus	3	8, 6, 3	WI	WI	
	Prus/Prus	6	21, 19, 17, 13, 10/10	Prus	Prus	
	Prus/Prus	1	2	WI		
	Prus/Prus	1	8	Prus		
	Prus/Prus	3	22, 15, 6	Prus	Prus	

MORRIS
(below Davis County)

Total couples, no children: 1 | From different German state: 0 | One spouse foreign-born: 0 | One spouse native-born: 0 | From same state: 1 Total singles: 4 | On own: 3 | With family: 0 | Mixed environ.: 0 | G household: 1 | Native-born household: 0 | Foreign-born household: 0

Clarks Creek	G/G	2	4, 1	WI	KS	
	Han/Han	6	10, 8, 6, 5, 4, 1	OH	KS	
	Prus/Prus	1	1	KS		
	Prus/<u>Holland</u>	2	18, 4	G	WI	
	Prus/Prus	3	18, 9, 5	Prus	Prus	
Grove	G/G	1	2	KS		
	G/<u>IL</u>	1	1	KS		
Neosho	No families					

Fourth Tier of Counties

Town-ship	Families with children	# of children present	Ages of children	Where oldest or only child born	Where last child born	Other state(s)

LYKINS

Total couples, no children: 1 | From different German state: 0 | One spouse foreign-born: 0 | One spouse native-born: 1 | From same state: 0

Total singles: 15 | On own: 4 | With family: 1 | Mixed environ.: 5 | G household: 2 | Native-born household: 3 | Foreign-born household: 0

Town-ship	Families with children	# of children present	Ages of children	Where oldest or only child born	Where last child born	Other state(s)
Indianapolis	No families					
Leyar Creek	G/<u>MO</u>	5	11, 7, 5, 3, 6 mos.	MO	MO	
	Ireland/Baden	4	9, 7, 3, 1 mo.	VA	KS	MO
Marysville	Prus/G	3	6, 4, 1	NY	MO	
Miami	Ghent/G	2	6, 4	IA	IA	
	Prus widower	5	20, 18, 16, 14, 11	Prus	MO	
	Prus widower	2	12, 1	Prus	KS	
	Han/Han	1	1 mo.	KS		
Miami Ville	G/G	2	6, 4	IL	IL	
Middle Creek	No families					
Mound	G/G	6	17, 12, 10, 8, 6, 4	G	IL	NY
	Baden/Baden	2	3, 1	KS	KS	
	Baden/Baden	1	5 mos.	KS		
	G/<u>PA</u>	4	14, 12, 9, 5	PA	IA	
Osage	No families					
Osawato-mie	G/<u>PA</u>	2	2, 7 mos.	PA	KS	
Paola	<u>CT</u>/G	1	1	KS		
	<u>France</u>/Bav	2	2, 7 mos.	IA	KS	
	G widow	1	2	MO		
Richland	<u>NY</u>/G	4	6, 5, 3, 8 mos.	MI	KS	
Stanton	No families					
Wea	Nassau/Nassau	1	1	MO		

(continued on the next page)

(continued from the previous page)

Township	Families with children	# of children present	Ages of children	Where oldest or only child born	Where last child born	Other state(s)

FRANKLIN
(four pages contain no birthplace data)

Total couples, no children: 1 | From different German state: 0 | One spouse foreign-born: 0 | One spouse native-born: 1 | From same state: 0

Total singles: 9 | On own: 2 | With family: 3 | Mixed environ.: 1 | G household: 3 | Native-born household: 0 | Foreign-born household: 0

Township	Families with children	# of children present	Ages of children	Where oldest or only child born	Where last child born	Other state(s)
Centropolis	G/<u>OH</u>	1	1	KS		
	G/<u>KY</u>	3	14, 11, 4	MO	KS	
	G/<u>KY</u>	2	2, 1	KY	KS	
	G/<u>VA</u>	2	14, 11	VA	IN	
	G/G	4	17, 15, 12, 4	PA	OH	
	G/G	5	19, 14, 12, 9, 5	PA	PA	
Ohio	G/<u>MI</u>	1	6	KS		
	G/G	2	8, 1 mo.	KS	KS	
	G/G	1	2	KY		
	G/G	2	3, 1 mo.	WI	KS	
	G/G	2	3, 1	G	G	
Ottawa	G/<u>PA</u>	8	19, 17, 15, 13, 11, 5, 2, 5 mos.	PA	KS	
	<u>PA</u>/G	8	15, 14, 12, 9, 7, 6, 4, 9 mos.	PA	KS	
	G/<u>MI</u>	3	6, 4, 1	MI	KS	
	G/<u>MO</u>	1	5 mos.	KS		
Peoria	G/G	4	9, 6, 3, 3 mos.	MO	KS	
Pottawatomie	No families					

OSAGE
(two pages contain no birthplace data; three pages are repeated)

Total couples, no children: 1 | From different German state: 0 | One spouse foreign-born: 0 | One spouse native-born: 0 | From same state: 1

Total singles: 12 | On own: 3 | With family: 1 | Mixed environ.: 0 | G household: 4 | Native-born household: 4 | Foreign-born household: 0

Township	Families with children	# of children present	Ages of children	Where oldest or only child born	Where last child born	Other state(s)
RIDGEWAY	G/G	2	4, 1	MO	KS	

	G/G	1	7	NY		
	G/G	2	14, 9	KY	MO	
	G/OH	1	3 mos.	KS		
	G/G	5	22, 14, 13, 5, 2	G	MO	
	G/KY	2	3, 2	MO	KS	
	G/G	1	3	KY		
	G/G	1	3	IL		
	G/G	1	4	IL		
	G/G	2	12, 6	G	PA	
	G widow	1	11	PA		

BRECKINRIDGE

Total couples, no children: 2 | From different German state: 0 | One spouse foreign-born: 0 | One spouse native-born: 0 | From same state: 2

Total singles: 14 | On own: 4 | With family: 1 | Mixed environ.: 4 | G household: 2 | Native-born household: 3 | Foreign-born household: 0

Agnes City	No families					
Americus	G/G	3	14, 3, 1	MO	KS	IL
Cakola	No families					
Emporia	G/IN	5	11, 10, 6, 4, 2	IN	IN	
	NC/G	5	12, 11, 9, 7, 2	IN	IN	
	G/NY	1	1 mo.	KS		
	G/OH	3	8, 6, 8 mos.	IN	KS	
Forest Hill	G/G	4	10, 8, 6, 4	IL	IL	
Fremont	G/G	5	12, 10, 7, 4, 1	G	IL	
	G/IN	1	8	IN		
Pike	G/G	1	9 mos.	KS		
Waterloo	No families					

CHASE

Total couples, no children: 2 | From different German state: 0 | One spouse foreign-born: 0 | One spouse native-born: 1 | From same state: 1

Total singles: 5 | On own: 1 | With family: 0 | Mixed environ.: 2 | G household: 0 | Native-born household: 2 | Foreign-born household: 0

Bazaar	G/G	5	24, 15, 11, 8, 3	G	G	
Cottonwood	No families					
Diamond Creek	Prus widow	4	22, 20, 15, 11	Prus	WI	Atlantic Ocean

(continued on the next page)

(continued from the previous page)

Township	Families with children	# of children present	Ages of children	Where oldest or only child born	Where last child born	Other state(s)
			CHASE			
Diamond Creek	Prus/Prus	1	2	IL		
	Sohen (in Rheinland/Pfaltz)/Prus	8	11/11, 9, 7, 5, 4, 2, 1 mo.	WI	KS	
	Prus/Prus	3	13, 10, 7	Prus	Prus	
Falls	No families					
Toledo	No families					

MARION

Total couples, no children: 0 | From different German state: 0 | One spouse foreign-born: 0 | One spouse native-born: 0 | From same state: 0

Total singles: 3 | On own: 0 | With family: 2 | Mixed environ.: 0 | G household: 0 | Native-born household: 1 | Foreign-born household: 0

Marion	No families					

LINN
(below Lykins County)

Total couples, no children: 4 | From different German state: 0 | One spouse foreign-born: 1 | One spouse native-born: 3 | From same state: 0

Total singles: 12 | On own: 0 | With family: 3 | Mixed environ.: 4 | G household: 1 | Native-born household: 3 | Foreign-born household: 1

Township	Families with children	# of children present	Ages of children	Where oldest or only child born	Where last child born	Other state(s)
Centerville	No families					
Liberty	No families					
MOUND CITY	G widower	1	4 mos.	KS		
	G/G	1	11 mos.	KS		
PARIS	G/G	3	6, 5, 2	OH	KS	
	Prus/Prus	5	13, 10, 8, 3, 4 mos.	Prus	KS	
	Prus widower	5	20, 11, 8, 6, 4	Prus	IA	
POTOSI	G/<u>IL</u>	1	1	KS		
Scott	G widower	4	14, 12, 8, 4	G	WI	
VALLEY	G/Han	2	6, 1	IL	KS	
	G/G	5	8, 6, 4, 2, 5 mos.	TN	KS	AR

ANDERSON

Total couples, no children: 2 | From different German state: 1 | One spouse foreign-born: 0 | One spouse native-born: 0 | From same state: 1

Total singles: 12 | On own: 5 | With family: 5 | Mixed environ.: 1 | G household: 0 | Native-born household: 0 | Foreign-born household: 1

Garnett	Han/Han	1	2	KS		
	Prus/Prus	1	11 mos.	KS		
Greely	No families					
Jackson	No families					
Monroe	**Prus/Prus**	3	3, 2, 3 mos.	IL	KS	
	Prus/Prus	5	17, 15, 7, 5, 3	Prus	IL	
	Han/Han	6	16, 14, 10, 9, 7, 5	MO	KS	
	Prus/Prus	1	3	IL		
	Prus/Prus	1	6	IL		
	Prus/Prus	2	2, 1	IL	IL	
	Wurt/IL	2	3, 6 mos.	IL	IL	
	Wurt/OH	1	1	IL		
Ozark	No families					
Reeder	Han/Han	5	20, 14, 10, 7, 3	Han	NJ	
Walker	G/Baden	2	21, 19	OH	OH	
	Prus widower	4	23, 15, 12, 7	Prus	WI	
Washington	No families					

COFFEY

Total couples, no children: 4 | From different German state: 0 | One spouse foreign-born: 1 | One spouse native-born: 0 | From same state: 3

Total singles: 10 | On own: 2 | With family: 3 | Mixed environ.: 1 | G household: 2 | Native-born household: 2 | Foreign-born household: 0

Avon	G/G	1	10 mos.	KS		
	IL/G	2	6, 4	IL	IL	
	G/CT	3	18, 15, 10	CT	MA	
	IL/G	2	5, 2	IL	KS	
Burlington	No families					
California	G widow	4	16, 14, 13, 9	IL	IL	
	G/G	6	11, 9, 8, 6, 4, 1	IL	KS	MO
LeRoy	G/OH	3	4, 3, 1	IN	IN	
	G widower	1	8	G		
Neosho	G/G	4	9, 7, 5, 3	IA	IA	

(continued on the next page)

(continued from the previous page)

Township	Families with children	# of children present	Ages of children	Where oldest or only child born	Where last child born	Other state(s)
			COFFEY			
Ottuma	No families					
Pottawato-mie	G/G	5	8, 7, 5, 3, 1	IN	KS	WI
	G/G	4	8, 7, 6, 3	MD	OH	PA
	G/G	2	1, 1 mo.	KS	KS	
			MADISON			

Total couples, no children: 0 | From different German state: 0 | One spouse foreign-born: 0 | One spouse native-born: 0 | From same state: 0

Total singles: 0 | On own: 0 | With family: 0 | Mixed environ.: 0 | G household: 0 | Native-born household: 0 | Foreign-born household: 0

Elmendaro	No families					
Hartford	TN/G	2	6, 4	IA	IA	
	G/PA	1	2	IA		
	G/OH	4	9, 7, 4, 2	OH	IA	
	G/G	7	20, 18, 13, 11, 9, 6, 4	OH	IA	IN
Verdigris	No families					

Fifth Tier of Counties

Township	Families with children	# of children present	Ages of children	Where oldest or only child born	Where last child born	Other state(s)
			BOURBON			

Total couples, no children: 4 | From different German state: 0 | One spouse foreign-born: 0 | One spouse native-born: 1 | From same state: 3

Total singles: 10 | On own: 3 | With family: 3 | Mixed environ.: 2 | G household: 1 | Native-born household: 1 | Foreign-born household: 0

Fort Scott   No families

NOT STATED	Wurt/Wurt	1	15	SC	
	G/NY	4	10, 8, 6, 2	MI	IL
	Han/Han	7	9, 8, 7, 4, 3, 2, 5 mos.	IL	KS
	Han/Hols	1	1	IL	
	VA/G	3	6, 4, 1	IL	IL
	G/IL	4	4, 3, 2, 4 mos.	IL	KS
	G/KY	5	17/17, 5, 3, 6 mos.	MO	KS
	G/G	3	17, 15, 9	G	G
	G/IL	3	3, 2, 3 mos.	TX	TX
	G widower	2	11, 10	AR	AR
	Wurt/Wurt	3	7, 5, 3	SC	WI
	G/MO	8	17, 14, 13, 10, 7, 5, 3, 9 mos.	WI	KS
	Prus/Prus	3	10, 5/5	IL	IL

ALLEN

Total couples, no children: 3 | From different German state: 0 | One spouse foreign-born: 0 | One spouse native-born: 1 | From same state: 2

Total singles: 15 | On own: 3 | With family: 2 | Mixed environ: 0 | G household: 1 | Native-born household: 7 | Foreign-born household: 2

Not stated	PA/Prus	3	5, 3, 11 mos.	MO	KS	
	G widower	3	11, 9, 5	MO	MO	
	Bav/Bav	1	5	CT		
	G/G	3	28, 25, 22	G	G	
	G/G	2	11, 7	G	G	
	G/G	2	5, 3	MI	MI	
	Han/PA	7	24, 21, 18, 15, 14, 12, 10	OH	OH	
	Hess/Bav	2	3, 1 mo.	CT	KS	
	G/G	3	7, 3, 1	G	KS	CT
	G/G	4	18, 16, 15, 3	G	NY	

WOODSON

Total couples, no children: 2 | From different German state: 0 | One spouse foreign-born: 0 | One spouse native-born: 0 | From same state: 2

Total singles: 23 | On own: 13 | With family: 6 | Mixed environ.: 1 | G household: 2 | Native-born household: 1 | Foreign-born household: 0

Belmont   No families

(continued on the next page)

(continued from the previous page)

Township	Families with children	# of children present	Ages of children	Where oldest or only child born	Where last child born	Other state(s)
			WOODSON			
Liberty	Prus/Prus	3	12, 8, 4	Prus	IL	
Neosho Falls	G/Prus	1	3 mos.	KS		
	G/G	6	20, 18, 16, 10, 7, 2	G	IL	
	PA/G	2	5, 1	IL	IL	
	Prus widow	5	30, 14, 11, 10, 7	Prus	PA	
	Bav/Bav	7	26, 24, 21, 19, 18, 12, 2	Bav	IA	MD, OH, PA
Owl Creek*	Prus/Prus	3	3, 2, less than 1	IL	KS	
	Westp/Westp (couple)	2	9, 2	Westp	IL	
	Bav/Prus	2	3, 1	KS	KS	
	Hess/NY	3	5, 1, 1 mo.	IL	KS	
	Holland/Bav	6	12, 9, 5, 2/2, 3 mos.	IN	KS	
Verdigris	G/G	4	7, 6, 4, 2	OH	OH	
			GREENWOOD			

Total couples, no children: 2 | From different German state: 0 | One spouse foreign-born: 0 | One spouse native-born: 0 | From same state: 2

Total singles: 3 | On own: 3 | With family: 0 | Mixed environ.: 0 | G household: 0 | Native-born household: 0 | Foreign-born household: 0

Township	Families with children	# of children present	Ages of children	Where oldest or only child born	Where last child born	Other state(s)
Eureka	G/G (couple)	4	21, 18, 15, 12	G	G	
Greenfield	No families					
Pleasant Grove	No families					

*5 siblings, 3 male and 2 female, on contiguous properties.

BUTLER

Total couples, no children: 0 | From different German state: 0 | One spouse foreign-born: 0 | One spouse native-born: 0 | From same state: 0

Total singles: 1 | On own: 1 | With family: 0 | Mixed environ.: 0 | G household: 0 | Native-born household: 0 | Foreign-born household: 0

Chelsea	G/IA	3	6, 5, 1	MO	KS

OTOE

Total couples, no children: 0 | From different German state: 0 | One spouse foreign-born: 0 | One spouse native-born: 0 | From same state: 0

Total singles: 1 | On own: 1 | With family: 0 | Mixed environ.: 0 | G household: 0 | Native-born household: 0 | Foreign-born household: 0

Otoe	No families

Sixth Tier of Counties

Township	Families with children	# of children present	Ages of children	Where oldest or only child born	Where last child born	Other state(s)

McGHEE

Total couples, no children: 1 | From different German state: 0 | One spouse foreign-born: 0 | One spouse native-born: 1 | From same state: 0

Total singles: 2 | On own: 0 | With family: 0 | Mixed environ.: 1 | G household: 0 | Native-born household: 1 | Foreign-born household: 0

Township	Families with children	# of children present	Ages of children	Where oldest or only child born	Where last child born	Other state(s)
NOT STATED	G/G*	3	13, 9, 3	G	MO	
	G/G	2	7, 5	MO	MO	
	G/France	3	5, 3, 2	NY	NY	
	G/OH	1	1	OH		
	Switz/Baden	5	10, 9, 6, 4, 1	OH	MO	
	G/TN	6	15, 12, 10, 8, 3, 1	IL	MO	
	Ireland/G	5	17, 14, 12, 8, 6	OH	IN	

*Surnames of couple and children are different.

(continued on the next page)

(continued from the previous page)

Town-ship	Families with children	# of children present	Ages of children	Where oldest or only child born	Where last child born	Other state(s)

DORN

Total couples, no children: 0 | From different German state: 0 | One spouse foreign-born: 0 | One spouse native-born: 0 | From same state: 0

Total singles: 4 | On own: 0 | With family: 0 | Mixed environ.: 4 | G household: 0 | Native-born household: 0 | Foreign-born household: 0

Not stated   No families

WILSON*

Total couples, no children: 0 | From different German state: 0 | One spouse foreign-born: 0 | One spouse native-born: 0 | From same state: 0

Total singles: 0 | On own: 0 | With family: 0 | Mixed environ.: 0 | G household: 0 | Native-born household: 0 Foreign-born household: 0

Wilson   No families

*Wilson had a population of 27, with 8 dwellings.

GODFROY (no data)

HUNTER

Total couples, no children: 0 From different German state: 0 One spouse foreign-born: 0 One spouse native-born: 0 From same state: 0

Total singles: 0 On own: 0 With family: 0 Mixed environ.: 0 G household: 0 Native-born household: 0 Foreign-born household: 0:

Eldorado	Bav/PA	7	11, 10, 8, 7, 5, 3, 4 mos.	IN	KS	OH, MO

APPENDIX E

Number of German-Born by Page

1860 Federal Census

Each page of the federal census was designed to list forty names, but many do not. "Vacant" or "unoccupied" land was often interspersed among the names, or census takers might have completed the count in one area, leaving spaces blank, and started a new page to continue the count. Still, these pages graphically illustrate how dispersed most German-born settlers were. The following tables provide the number of pages in the census for each township and the number of pages on which German-born individuals were listed, according to the number present.

First Tier of Counties

Township	Total number of pages	*Number of pages with German-born*					
		0	1	2–3	4–5	6–9	10+*
DONIPHAN							
Burr Oak	21	9	3	3	2	0	2 (10,11)
Center	31	26	2	2	0	0	1 (10)
Elwood	15	5	4	4	0	2	0
Highland	3	1	2	0	0	0	0

(continued on the next page)

(continued from the previous page)

Township	Total number of pages	Number of pages with German-born					
		0	1	2–3	4–5	6–9	10+*
DONIPHAN							
Iowa	34	28	5	1	0	0	0
Marion	17	8	2	3	1	3	0
Troy	3	2	1	0	0	0	0
Washington	23	8	9	4	0	2	0
Wathena	5	3	0	1	1	0	0
Wayne	33	21	7	2	0	2	1 (12)
White Cloud	6	5	0	1	0	0	0
BROWN							
Claytonville	24	18	0	4	1	1	0
Irving	18	13	2	1	1	1	0
Lockwin	10	4	1	3	1	1	0
Walnut	18	15	0	2	1	0	0
NEMAHA							
Capioma	4	1	1	1	1	0	0
Granada	7	7	0	0	0	0	0
Home	5	4	0	0	1	0	0
Nemaha	6	2	0	1	1	1	1 (12)
Red Vermillion	7	6	1	0	0	0	0
Richmond	13	8	2	2	0	0	0
Rock Creek	10	9	1	0	0	0	0
Valley	10	7	2	0	0	0	1 (17)
MARSHALL							
Blue Rapids	16	13	1	0	0	1	1 (15)
Guittard	7	3	0	1	2	1	0
Marysville	13	6	2	0	1	1	2 (19, 15)
Vermillion	22	16	2	2	2	0	0
WASHINGTON							
Milk Creek	2	1	0	0	0	1	0
Washington	8	5	2	0	1	0	0

Second Tier of Counties

		Number of pages with German-born					
Township	Total number of pages	0	1	2–3	4–5	6–9	10+*
WYANDOTTE							
Quindaro	18	8	3	5	0	1	1 (16)
Wyandotte	48	15	5	7	5	9	7 (10, 19, 11, 11, 15, 11, 11)
LEAVENWORTH							
Alexandria	19	13**	2	4	0	0	0
Delaware	23	7	3	6	4	3	0
Easton	25	19	2	1	1	0	2 (10, 11)
Ft. Leavenworth	8	0	0	4	1	3	0
Kickapoo	39	15**	2	8	6	5	3 (11, 11, 15)
Leavenworth‡							
Stranger	25	9	5	10	0	1	0
ATCHISON							
Atchison†							
Center	23	14	4	4	0	0	1 (18)
Grasshopper	13	8	1	2	2	0	0
Kapioma	7	2	1	3	0	0	1 (10)
Lancaster	16	12	2	0	1	1	0
Mount Pleasant	28	23	1	2	2	0	0
Shannon	18	7	6	3	1	1	0
Walnut	33	18	3	5	2	1	2 (10, 12)
JACKSON							
Douglas	13	11	2	0	0	0	0
Franklin	13	8	1	1	0	3	0
Holton	4	3	0	1	0	0	0
Jefferson	20	16	0	4	0	0	0
POTTAWATOMIE							
Blue	5	2	2	1	0	0	0
Louisville	4	1	1	1	0	0	1 (14)

(continued on the next page)

Number of German-Born by Page

(continued from the previous page)

Township	Total number of pages	Number of pages with German-born					
		0	1	2–3	4–5	6–9	10+*
POTTAWATOMIE							
Rockingham	9	5	0	2	0	1	1 (13)
Shannon	3	3	0	0	0	0	0
St. George	6	2	0	0	3	0	1 (12)
Vienna	17	5	4	0	1	4	3 (17, 12, 16)
RILEY							
Manhattan	7	3	2	2	0	0	0
Not stated	24	9	4	6	2	2	1 (16, 11††)
CLAY							
Not stated	5	3	0	2	0	0	0
JEFFERSON (below Atchison)							
Grasshopper Falls	25	13	6	3	1	2	0
Jefferson	22	17	2	0	0	2	1 (13)
Kaw	8	3	3	2	0	0	0
Kentucky	16	8	3	4	1	0	0
Oskaloosa	25	21	3	1	0	0	0
Ozakie	11	9	1	0	0	1	0
Rock Creek	11	8	1	2	0	0	0

Third Tier of Counties

Township	Total number of pages	Number of pages with German-born					
		0	1	2–3	4–5	6–9	10+*
JOHNSON							
Aubry	8	7	1	0	0	0	0
DeSoto	4	2	2	0	0	0	0
Gardner	12	11	0	1	0	0	0
Lexington	10	5**	1	4	0	0	0
McCamish	12	9	0	1	2	0	0

Monticello	8	5	2	0	0	1	0	
Olathe	17	8	4	4	0	0	0	
Oxford	11	10	0	1	0	0	0	
Shawnee	26	13	3	3	3	3	1 (13)	
Spring Hill	10	7**	0	1	2	0	0	
Union	2	1	0	1	0	0	0	

DOUGLAS

Clinton	18	15	0	2	0	1	0
Eudora	16	5	3	1	2	1	4 (26, 17, 23, 25)
Kanawaka	19	12	4	0	1	1	1 (10)
Lawrence‡‡							
Lecompton	26	16	4	3	1	2	0
Marion	10	4	3	2	0	1	0
Palmyra	41	30	4	3	2	2	0
Wakarusa	36	25	3	8	0	0	0
Willow Springs	23	19	0	2	1	1	0

SHAWNEE

Auburn	15	10	4	0	0	1	0
Monmouth	8	7	1	0	0	0	0
Soldier	9	7	0	2	0	0	0
Tecumseh	18	13**	1	3	1	0	0
Topeka	36	21	6	8	1	0	0
Williamsport	5	4	1	0	0	0	0

WABAUNSEE

Alma	8	0	0	0	0	0	8†††
Mission Creek	4	3	1	0	0	0	0
Wabaunsee	8	4	2	1	1	0	0
Wilmington	6	5	0	1	0	0	0
Zeandale	5	4	0	1	0	0	0

DAVIS

Fort Riley Reserve	3	1	1	0	1	0	0
Junction	6	0	0	1	1	4	0
Not stated	22	10	1	3	3	1	4 (13, 11, 13, 12)

DICKINSON

Not stated	11	7	0	0	0	0	4 (20, 16, 30, 22)

(continued on the next page)

(continued from the previous page)

Township	Total number of pages	Number of pages with German-born					
		0	1	2–3	4–5	6–9	10+*
MORRIS (below Davis County)							
Clark's Creek	4	2	0	0	1	1	0
Grove	10	5	2	3	0	0	0
Neosho	6	6	0	0	0	0	0

Fourth Tier of Counties

Township	Total number of pages	Number of pages with German-born					
		0	1	2–3	4–5	6–9	10+*
LYKINS							
Indianapolis	1	1	0	0	0	0	0
Leyar Creek	10	8	2	0	0	0	0
Marysville	14	13	0	1	0	0	0
Miami	9	5	2	0	1	1	0
Miami Ville	3	2	0	1	0	0	0
Middle Creek	6	6	0	0	0	0	0
Mound	6	3	1	1	1	0	0
Osage	9	9	0	0	0	0	0
Osawatomie	23	20	3	0	0	0	0
Paola	19	13	3	3	0	0	0
Richland	12	10	2	0	0	0	0
Stanton	12	11	1	0	0	0	0
Wea	7	4	2	0	1	0	0
FRANKLIN							
Centropolis	20	16**	2	1	0	1	0
Ohio	15	10	0	3	2	0	0
Ottawa	14	11	1	2	0	0	0
Peoria	19	18	0	1	0	0	0
Pottawatomie	13	13	0	0	0	0	0
OSAGE							
Ridgeway	30	17***	4	6	0	3	0

BRECKINRIDGE

Agnes City	5	3	2	0	0	0	0
Americus	13	11	1	0	1	0	0
Cakola	4	3	1	0	0	0	0
Emporia	22	14	7	1	0	0	0
Forest Hill	14	11	1	2	0	0	0
Fremont	10	8	1	0	0	1	0
Pike	9	7	1	1	0	0	0
Waterloo	10	10	0	0	0	0	0

CHASE

Bazaar	4	3	0	0	0	0	0
Cottonwood	3	3	0	0	0	0	0
Diamond Creek	5	2	1	0	1	0	1 (11)
Falls	5	4	1	0	0	0	0
Toledo	5	5	0	0	0	0	0

MARION

Marion	2	0	1	1	0	0	0

LINN (below Lykins County)

Centerville	16	13	2	0	1	0	0
Liberty	4	4	0	0	0	0	0
Mound City	29	26	2	1	0	0	0
Paris	31	29	0	0	1	0	1 (10)
Potosi	29	27	2	0	0	0	0
Scott	25	21	2	2	0	0	0
Valley	26	23	0	3	0	0	0

ANDERSON

Garnett	6	4	0	2	0	0	0
Greeley	2	1	1	0	0	0	0
Jackson	8	8	0	0	0	0	0
Ozark	2	2	0	0	0	0	0
Reeder	9	8	0	1	0	0	0
Walker	15	11	2	1	1	0	0
Washington	6	6	0	0	0	0	0

COFFEY

Avon	13	9	3	1	0	0	0
Burlington	12	10	1	1	0	0	0
California	10	8	1	1	0	0	0
LeRoy	16	11	2	3	0	0	0
Neosho	9	8	0	1	0	0	0

(continued on the next page)

(continued from the previous page)

Township	Total number of pages	Number of pages with German-born					
		0	1	2–3	4–5	6–9	10+*
COFFEY							
Ottuma	9	8	0	0	1	0	0
Pottawatomie	4	2	0	1	1	0	0
MADISON							
Elmendaro	5	5	0	0	0	0	0
Hartford	5	3	0	2	0	0	0
Verdigris	7	7	0	0	0	0	0

Fifth Tier of Counties

Township	Total number of pages	Number of pages with German-born					
		0	1	2–3	4–5	6–9	10+*
BOURBON							
Fort Scott	7	4	2	1	0	0	0
Not stated	146	127	9	7	3	0	0
ALLEN							
Not stated	48	40	7	1	0	0	0
WOODSON							
Belmont	6	5	0	0	1	0	0
Liberty	5	4	0	0	1	0	0
Neosho Falls	14	7	3	3	0	1	0
Owl Creek	4	0	0	1	1	2	0
Verdigris	10	8	1	1	0	0	0
GREENWOOD							
Eureka	13	9	1	2	0	1	0
Greenfield	2	2	0	0	0	0	0
Pleasant Grove	5	5	0	0	0	0	0
BUTLER							
Chelsea	11	9	2	0	0	0	0

OTOE

Otoe	6	5	1	0	0	0	0

Sixth Tier of Counties

		Number of pages with German-born					
Township	Total number of pages	0	1	2–3	4–5	6–9	10+*
McGHEE							
Not stated	38	29	7	1	1	0	0
DORN							
Not stated	3	2	0	0	1	0	0
WILSON							
Wilson	1	1	0	0	0	0	0
GODFROY (no data)							
HUNTER							
Eldorado	4	3	1	0	0	0	0

*Number of individuals in parenthesis.
†All 3 wards had large numbers of German-born.
‡All 4 wards had large numbers of German-born.
**Including 1 page with no birth info.
††From North-Rhine-Westphalia.
‡‡German-born were scattered throughout the city.
***Including 2 pages with no birth info.
†††All 8 pages have more than 10 German-born listed.

APPENDIX F

Kansas State Census Non-Population Schedule 2

Foreign-Born by County and Township for Year Ending May 1, 1865

Kansas State Census Non-Population Schedule 2 is attached to the end of the Federal Non-Population Census Schedule for Social Statistics for Kansas compiled in 1860. It is entirely handwritten, and its tables are drawn by hand. The data cover agricultural, industrial/manufacturing, and social statistics as of May 1, 1865.[1]

Counties are listed alphabetically, and as they were in the 1860 federal census, Prussians and Bavarians were often counted separately from "Germans." There was seemingly no attempt to compile statistics on the number of residents from the various German states.

Figures on the origins of the foreign-born are often in essential agreement with the figures derived from the separate Kansas state census conducted in the same year (Schedule 1). However, there are significant deviations, as pointed out in the body of this book. Furthermore, data were not provided for all counties; thus, as the secretary of state indicated in January 1866 in the introduction to the report, the document is incomplete. But it still provides a general overview of who and where the foreign-born were at the close of the Civil War.

Many schedules have faded considerably, making them difficult to read. The names of some counties were changed when Kansas became a state, and several new counties were organized.

Township (Ts.)	Germany	Prussia	Ireland	England	Switzerland	Canada
ALLEN						
Deer Creek			1			
Geneva	1	2	4			
Iola	3		3			2
Cottage Grove	8	1				
Osage	1					
Humboldt	25	7	5			8

Other countries: France (6), Scotland (6), Denmark (2), Norway (1), Nova Scotia (1)

	Germany	Prussia	Ireland	England	Switzerland	Canada
ANDERSON						
Reeder			3			22
Ozark						1
Jackson						16
Walker						
Washington						
Monroe		17		4		

Other countries: Jamaica (1), Wales (1), Austria (5), Cherokee Nation (74), Scotland (18)

	Germany	Prussia	Ireland	England	Switzerland	Canada
ATCHISON						
City	223	35	49	17		16
Township	37	18	20	15		7
Lancaster	12	1	19	9		2
Walnut	48	1	1			7
Center	8		6	18		15
Mt. Pleasant	8	2	20	12		4
Kapiona	7	15	5			
Grasshopper			7			3

Other countries: Many different countries, particularly in the city

	Germany	Prussia	Ireland	England	Switzerland	Canada
BOURBON						
Osage			14	21		2
Freedom	8	1	14	2		2
Timber Hill	3		4	2	5	2
Franklin			8	1		
Marion	10	6	2		11	
Monahan	7		9	3		1
Scott	8	3	12	15	2	12
Ft. Scott City	30	18	25	15	5	7

Other countries: Bavaria (10), Scotland (27), Austria (27), Norway (41)

(continued on the next page)

(continued from the previous page)

Township (Ts.)	Germany	Prussia	Ireland	England	Switzerland	Canada
BROWN						
Walnut Creek	10	1		8	5	2
Lochnane	14	4	7	9		3
Irving	20	7	1	5	12	
Claytonville	34	10	13	12		

Other countries: Poland (1), Austria (11), Russia (1), Scotland (4), Sweden (2), Italy (4), Moravia (40), Wales (5), Norway (8)

	Germany	Prussia	Ireland	England	Switzerland	Canada
BUTLER						
Chelsea	1			1		1

Other countries: France (11), Scotland (6)

	Germany	Prussia	Ireland	England	Switzerland	Canada
CHASE						
Falls	1		5	1		
Diamond Creek	3	12	10	8		
Bazaar	1		4	2		
Toledo				3		
Cottonwood				2		

Other countries: Scotland (6), France (11), Austria (6)

	Germany	Prussia	Ireland	England	Switzerland	Canada
CLAY						
No township	7	1	2	6		2

Other countries: Isle of Ceylon (1)

	Germany	Prussia	Ireland	England	Switzerland	Canada
COFFEY						
Ottumwa		2	1	11	4	
Pottawatomie			14	5		
California	1	4				
Avon			4	4		11
Burlington	3		12	1		2
Leeroy	3		6	3		4
Neosho	3			2		3

Other countries: Cherokee Nation (70), Scotland (3), New Brunswick (25), Norway (3), France (6), Wales (6)

	Germany	Prussia	Ireland	England	Switzerland	Canada
DAVIS						
Junction City	10	14	7	3		3
Ft. Riley	9	3	25	3		1

Balance of county	35	32	46	8	1	13

Other countries: France (2), Poland (1), Scotland (14), Sweden (3), Wales (1), Nova Scotia (1), Mexico (2), Hungary (1)

DICKINSON

No township	32	35	41	2	17	8

Other countries: France (1), Scotland (2)

DONIPHAN

Troy Village	32	10	28	26	3	11
Marion	59	16	84	18	4	7
Wayne	9		28	19		7
Centre (Center)	41	21	16	21	7	6
Burr Oak	41	22	13	2		6
Washington	72	14	15	5	41	5
Wolf River	3		8	3		4
Iowa	2					
White Cloud	3					

Other countries: Wales (1), Scotland (15), Nova Scotia (1), Norway (38), France (45), Isle of Man (3), Austria (2), Italy (5), Sweden (2), New Brunswick (2)

DOUGLAS

Lawrence City	172	37	152	91	15	49
North Lawrence	10	5	28	14		13
Sarcoxie	2					2
Willow Springs	24	4	4	9		
Marion	1		11	7		
Clinton	2		5	2		3
Kanwaka	24	7	12	10	2	6
Lecompton City	10	4	31			
Leavenworth	3		7			
Wakarusa	17	12	22	25		13
Palmyra	44	11	19	24	6	19
Eudora	157	35	34	11	30	14

Other countries: Austria (2), Nova Scotia (15), Mexico (2), Denmark (6), New Brunswick (9), Poland (13), Wales (37), Scotland (52), France (73), Sweden (53)

FRANKLIN

Franklin	13	1	10	7	2	2
Centrapolis	2	1	2	9		5
Ohio	13		16	6		2
Pottawatomie	2		6	7		1

(continued on the next page)

(continued from the previous page)

Township (Ts.)	Germany	Prussia	Ireland	England	Switzerland	Canada
			FRANKLIN			
Peoria						
Ottawa	5		9	2		

Other countries: Scotland (1), France (2), Isle of Sumatra (1), Wales (2), Nova Scotia (1), Norway (5)

			GREENWOOD			
Janesville	7					
Madison						
Lane			8			1
Pleasant Grove	2		4			
Fall River	1	1	1	1		
Eureka		1				

Other countries: Scotland (5), France (1), Norway (21)

			JACKSON			
Jefferson	17	6	10	17	8	9
Franklin	14	14	20	8	7	7
Holton Village	6				2	1
Douglass	9			9	2	3

Other countries: Belgium (1), New Brunswick (4), France (2), Wales (1)

			JEFFERSON			
Oskaloosa	11	2	6	30		
Sarcoxie	1		2	1	1	9
Rock Creek	1		4	5		2
Kane	10		4		2	
Kentucky	11					
Ozarks	7		17	3		8
Grasshopper	8	3	3	7	6	8
Jefferson	24	3	12	4	1	1

Other countries: Poland (6), Scotland (21), France (3)

			JOHNSON			
Oxford	1		5	3		1
Town of Aubrey						
Aubrey Ts.	4		7			1
Town of Olathe		4	2	4		1

Olathe Ts.		5	24	6	3	5
Town of Spring-Hill				2		
Springhill Ts.			3	2	2	1
City of Gardner						
Gardner Ts.	2	2	18	4		5
Town of Monticello				2		
Monticello Ts.	2	1	3	5	2	1
Town of Desoto				3		
Livingston	24	8	3	5	3	5
Shawnee	29	3	13	21	4	6
Town of Shawnee	15	4	5	4		3
Town of McCamish						3
McCamish Ts.	12	7	39	7		
Town of Janesfield						

Other countries: Denmark (4), Sweden (2), France (24), Austria (2), Wales (1), Scotland (31)

LEAVENWORTH

City, Ward 1	417	397	77	26	17
City, Ward 2	345	271	57	4	25
City, Ward 3	245	296	70	5	25
City, Ward 4	429	623	65	10	39
Alexandria	42	167	8	2	10
Ft. Leavenworth	42	70	23	4	
Easton	27	123	19		
Steuben	83	103	13	8	15
Delaware	65	36	4		21
Stranger	40	84	23	5	24

Other countries: Many different countries, particularly in the city

LINN

Mound City	6	1	8		8
Centerville	2	2	3	1	1
Liberty					
Potosi					2
Valley	9		18		
Paris	13		4		
Scott	5		10		9

Other countries: New Brunswick (9), Scotland (1), Sweden (3)

(continued on the next page)

(continued from the previous page)

Township (Ts.)	Germany	Prussia	Ireland	England	Switzerland	Canada
\multicolumn{7}{c}{LYON (formerly BRECKINRIDGE)}
Americus	2		6	11		
Pike	1			1		
Fremont	12		6	3		
Agnes City				8		
Center			2			
Emporia	2		8	13		

Other countries: Sweden (1), Wales (56, all in Emporia)

Township (Ts.)	Germany	Prussia	Ireland	England	Switzerland	Canada
\multicolumn{7}{c}{MARION}
No township			1	2		

Other countries: Scotland (1), France (2)

Township (Ts.)	Germany	Prussia	Ireland	England	Switzerland	Canada
\multicolumn{7}{c}{MARSHALL}
City of Marysville	26		2	4	1	2
Marysville Ts.	94		6	5		4
Vermillion	5			7		2
Guittard	24		55	3		
Blue Rapids	1		6	8		1

Other countries: France (12), Sweden (1), Greece (1), Norway (3), Scotland (9), Poland (1), Nova Scotia (3)

Township (Ts.)	Germany	Prussia	Ireland	England	Switzerland	Canada
\multicolumn{7}{c}{MIAMI (formerly LYKINS)}
Mound	6		1	6		
Osawatomie	1		9	8		11
Osawatomie Village	1		4	3		10
Paola Ts.	24		9	14		
City of Paola	7		14	8		14
Osage	2		2	2		3
Stanton	7		5	3		
Richland	5		30	7		3
St. Marysville			4	5		
Wea	13		5	7		
Middle Creek			12			
Sugar Creek			6			
Miami	10		2	1		1

Other countries: Scotland (27), Wales (4)

MORRIS

Town of Council Grove	11	1	6	7	2	4
Council Grove Ts.			6	3		1
Neoscho	1	2	5	4	1	
Clark's Creek	20		3		3	

Other countries: Scotland (4)

NEMAHA

Clear Creek	2	10	22	5	1	
Nemaha	9	1	8	1	22	2
Richmond	5	13	5	2		11
Capioma		4				13
Granada	10		11	1		10
Red Vermillion			13	1	24	
Seneca	5		2	6		12
Home	1	2	3	9		2
Rock Creek			4	15	12	1
Valley	1		3	15	2	1

Other countries: France (20), Sweden (11), Norway (6), Scotland (16)

NEOSHO*

Neosho	2		1	4		
Big Creek						
Canville				1		
Mission						3

Other countries: New Brunswick (1), France (4), Denmark (2)
*Neosho County, south of Allen, was established in 1861.

OSAGE

Ridgeway	6		4	13		
Superior				13	3	1
Burlingame	8		20	12		7
Burlingame City			1	13	2	3
Sac/Fox Reserve						

Other countries: Wales (3), France (3), Austria (7), Sweden (5), Norway (6), Scotland (10), Hungary (4)

OTTAWA

No township	8	5	2	3	6	7

Other countries: Bavaria (2), Scotland (2), France (1)

(continued on the next page)

(continued from the previous page)

Township (Ts.)	Germany	Prussia	Ireland	England	Switzerland	Canada
POTTAWATOMIE						
St. George	8	2	1			
Pottawatomie	43	2	5	4		
Vienna	47	2	3	3		1
Shannon	13			7		
Louisville	18		30	6		
Blue	7	2	16	8		

Other countries: Sweden (35, 30 of whom were in Shannon), Norway (15), Denmark (6), Poland (1), Italy (2), France (18)

Township (Ts.)	Germany	Prussia	Ireland	England	Switzerland	Canada
RILEY						
Manhattan	5	24	8	8		6
Manhattan City	7	1	2	9		
Jackson	46	27	5	6		7
Ogden	3	2	15	4	1	
Ogden City	18	16	5			

Other countries: Scotland (4), Denmark (3), Wales (1), Sweden (32), France (1)

Township (Ts.)	Germany	Prussia	Ireland	England	Switzerland	Canada
SALINE						
Salina	1	5		1		
Elm Creek	18	8	17	2		3

Other countries: France (1), Scotland (10), Sweden (2), Belgium (4)

Township (Ts.)	Germany	Prussia	Ireland	England	Switzerland	Canada
SHAWNEE						
City of Topeka	25	2	18	5	2	16
Topeka Ts.			3	10		12
Tecumseh	17		18	6	1	1
Soldier	10		4	8		10
Williamsport			6	5		2
Auburn City			1	6	1	
Auburn Ts.	4	1	4	7	1	
Monmouth	2	1	6	9	2	

Other countries: Belgium (5), France (15), Italy (3), Norway (1), Scotland (23), Sweden (2), Sandwich Island (1), Wales (1)

Township (Ts.)	Germany	Prussia	Ireland	England	Switzerland	Canada
SOUTH OF BOURBON COUNTRY						
No township	—*		9	2		

Other countries: Norway (5)
*Unreadable.

WABAUNSEE

Mission Creek					
Fernsdale					
Wabaunsee	10		17		6
Wilmington	3	1	3		1
Alma	65	95	1	6	

Other countries: France (7), Wales (2), Scotland (3)

WASHINGTON

No return

WILSON

No return

WOODSON

Neosho Falls	11	3		6	2
Liberty	3	5	2	1	
Owl Creek	12	20	17	1	
Belmont	3	6	1		2

Other countries: France (4), New Brunswick (1)

WYANDOTTE

Wyandotte	168	150	21	20
Quindaro	27	34	17	62

Other countries: France (19), Scotland (12), Unknown (87)

Kansas State Census Non-Population Schedule 2

Notes

Epigraph

William Cronon, George Miles, and Jay Gitlin, "Becoming West: Towards a New Meaning for Western History," in *Under an Open Sky: Rethinking America's Western Past*, ed. William Cronon, George Miles, and Jay Gitlin (New York: W. W. Norton, 1992), 9.

Preface

1. Eleanor L. Turk, "Germans in Kansas," *Kansas History: A Journal of the Central Plains* 28, 1 (Spring 2005): 46–71, https://www.kshs.org/publicat/history/2005spring_turk.pdf.
2. Turk, 70.
3. Turk, 54–55.
4. Clara M. Fengel Shields, "The Lyon Creek Settlement," *Kansas Historical Collections* 14 (1918): 143–170, https://archive.org/details/collectionsofkan14kans/page/134/mode/2up?q=Shields.
5. John Ise, *Sod and Stubble: The Unabridged and Annotated Edition*, with additional material by Von Rothenberger (Lawrence: University Press of Kansas, 1996). To this list one could add Howard Ruede's *Sod-House Days: Letters from a Kansas Homesteader, 1877–1878*, ed. John Ise (1937; reprint, Lawrence: University Press of Kansas, 1983). Although Ruede and his parents were born in the United States, he grew up in a Moravian

community; he could not speak German but could apparently read it, and as an adult, he homesteaded amidst a German community. Thus, his letters provide much information about that community.

6. Turk, "Germans in Kansas," 46 (sidebar).

7. The entire corpus of letters and documents quoted or mentioned in *Once We Were Strangers*, both the originals and the translations from Old German, have been donated to Northern State University in Aberdeen, South Dakota, where much of the translation work was done. They have been digitized and are available to researchers.

Chapter 1. Coming to Amerika

1. Although inhabitants of the region used the terms "Germany" and "German," these terms were largely indeterminate and cultural and linguistic in nature, as discussed later in this book. Where I collected data on "Germans," the reference is to inhabitants of those states that eventually constituted Germany. Thus, the data do not include Austrians, Bohemians, Swiss, Luxembourgians, and Scandinavians.

2. Timothy Guinnane and Sheilagh Ogilvie, "A Two-Tiered Demographic System: 'Insiders' and 'Outsiders' in Three Swabian Communities, 1558–1914," *History of the Family* 19, 1 (2014): 80, fig. 2, http://dx.doi.org/10.1080/1081602X.2013.870491.

3. Sheilagh Ogilvie, Markus Küpker, and Janine Maegraith, "Community Characteristics and Demographic Development: Three Württemberg Communities: 1558–1914," Cambridge Working Paper in Economics 0910, March 2009, 153, 148, https://www.researchgate.net/publication/48915027_Community_Characteristics_and_Demographic_Development_Three_Wurttemberg_Communities_1558_-_1914.

4. Ogilvie, Küpker, and Maegraith, 29, 32, 101.

5. Unlike Catholicism, Lutheranism has no central dogmatic authority. Although the writings of Martin Luther were foundational, many reformers developed their own particular theological concepts and structure. One such reformer was Johan Brenz (Johannes Brentius), a contemporary and friend of Luther who counseled the ruler of Württemberg in establishing the church there. His catechism was used to prepare young people for confirmation, including one of the Lodholz children. See the article on Brenz in Samuel Macauley Jackson et al., eds., *The New Schaff-Herzog Encyclopedia of Religious Knowledge*, vol. 2 (Grand Rapids, MI: Baker Book House, 1952), https://www.ccel.org/ccel/schaff/encyco2.html?term=Brenz,%20Johann. See also *Das Königreich Württemberg: Eine Beschreibung von Land, Volk und Staat* (Stuttgart: Druck und Berlag von M. Rohlhammer, 1884; facsimile ed., Hanse Books, n.d.), 232, 237.

6. Guinnane and Ogilvie, "Two-Tiered Demographic System," 9.

7. Ogilvie, Küpker, and Maegraith, "Community Characteristics," 62–69.

8. Ogilvie, Küpker, and Maegraith, 169–170.

9. Ogilvie, Küpker, and Maegraith, 215, argue rather convincingly that it took only several weeks to learn the craft, but this assertion has been disputed by S. R. Epstein, "Craft Guilds in the Pre-Modern Economy: A Discussion," *Economic History Review* 61, 1 (2008): 162, http://www.jstor.org/stable/40057560. Sheilagh Ogilvie, email message to author, June 3, 2019.

10. Vagabonding and harassment were linked and were considered criminal offenses. In 1834–35, 375 individuals in Württemberg were arrested for *Vagabunditat uter Vetteln*; in 1835–36, the total was 40l. J. Memminger, *Württembergische Jahrbücher für vaterländische Geschichte, Geographie, Statistik und Topographie* (Stuttgart und Tübingen: J. G. Cotta'schen Buchhandlung, 1838; facsimile ed., Wentworth Press, n.d.), 48.

11. *Wander-Buch*, trans. Roberta Reb Allen, Lodholz/Reb Family Collection, South Dakota Germans from Russia Cultural Center, Williams Library, Northern State University, Aberdeen, South Dakota (hereafter, LRFC).

12. The comments about Josef were probably similar to those made years later about one of his sons who was attempting to start a career as a baker: "The below-signed certifies regarding the miller's assistant from Ebhausen, Johann Georg, that he worked for me from 16 November 1852 until 17 January 1853, and he carried himself in a faithful and hard-working manner, and nothing unseemly can be said about him. Certified, T. Georg Miller Walz." Work testimonials for Georg Lodholz, 1851–53, trans. Virginia L. Lewis, LRFC.

13. Ogilvie, Küpker, and Maegraith, "Community Characteristics," 78.

14. Ogilvie, Küpker, and Maegraith, 78, 43, 218, 221, 224.

15. Mack Walker, *Germany and the Emigration: 1816–1885* (Cambridge, MA: Harvard University Press, 1964), 2.

16. Eckart Shremmer, "The Textile Industry in South Germany: 1750–1850: Some Causes for the Technological Backwardness during the Industrial Revolution, Investment Approach and Structure Approach," *Textile History* 7, 1 (October 1976): 66.

17. Sheilagh Ogilvie, "Guilds, Efficiency and Social Capital: Evidence from German Proto-Industry," *Economic History Review* 57, 2 (May 2004): 308, https://www.jstor.org/stable/3698609; *Heiraten, Tote, Konfirmationen, Seelenregister u Familienbuch 1721–1924*, p. 63, no. 5, database with images, Ancestry.com, citing parish records of the Evangelische Kirche Walddorf (OA Nagold); Promissory note 1849/1853, trans. Inge von Pongracz, LRFC.

18. Sheilagh Ogilvie, *State Corporatism and Proto-Industry: The Württemberg Black Forest, 1580–1797* (Cambridge: Cambridge University Press, 1997), 95.

19. Wares Notebook, circa 1850, trans. Virginia L. Lewis, LRFC.

20. Memminger, *Württembergische Jahrbücher* (1838), 29.

21. R., "An Account of the Recent Progress and Present Extent of Manufactures in Prussia, and of the Trade of the Prussian Commercial Union in Manufactured Goods," *Journal of the Statistical Society of London* 2, 2 (March 1839): 155, https://www.jstor.org/stable/i315572.

22. *Taufen, Geburten u Heiraten 1609–1898*, p. 914, no. 9, database with images, Ancestry.com, citing parish records of the Evangelische Kirke Ebhausen (OA Nagold). At the ages of twenty-six and twenty-three, respectively, Josef and Anna Maria were slightly younger than the mean ages for a first marriage in Ebhausen in 1825, which were 27.02 for men and 25.71 for women. Guinnane and Ogilvie, "Two-Tiered Demographic System," 93, table 4.

23. Anna Maria Lodholz, list of children, January 28, 1845, trans. Freda Murray, LRFC.

24. *Tote, Konfirmationen, Seelenregister u Kommunionen 1600–1960*, 1829, p. 76,

no. 2, database with images, Ancestry.com, citing parish records of the Evangelische Kirke Ebhausen (OA Nagold).

25. Ogilvie, Küpker, and Maegraith, "Community Characteristics," 62–64.

26. Epstein, "Craft Guilds in the Pre-Modern Economy," 309.

27. The practice of feeding gruel to babies apparently arose because women had to engage in gainful employment to support their families. There was little time for breastfeeding, and wet-nursing was not practiced. Sophia Twarog, "Heights and Living Standards in Germany, 1850–1939: The Case of Württemberg," in *Health and Welfare during Industrialization*, ed. Richard H. Steckel and Roderick Floud (Chicago: University of Chicago Press, 1977), 308, fn. 18, https://www.nber.org/system/files/chapters/c7434/c7434.pdf.

28. Ogilvie, "Guilds, Efficiency and Social Capital," 98.

29. Guinnane and Ogilvie, "Two-Tiered Demographic System," 193.

30. Ogilvie, Küpker, and Maegraith, "Community Characteristics," 96–97.

31. Ogilvie, Küpker, and Maegraith, 210–211.

32. Ogilvie, Küpker, and Maegraith, 128, 130–132, 179.

33. Ogilvie, Küpker, and Maegraith, 44.

34. There are no published descriptions of conditions in Ebhausen, but just twenty-five miles away in Reutlingen, there were reports of inhabitants selling their furniture, slaughtering pets and livestock, and making hay soup. Linda Richter, "'Could You Not Turn Your Back on This Hunger Country?' Food in the Migration Process of German Emigrants, 1816–1856," 24, https://thestacks.libaac.de/bitstream/handle/11858/2464/aspeers_05-2012_03_Richter.pdf?sequence=1&isAllowed=y (accessed April 10, 2023). In Geradstetten, some thirty-eight miles from Ebhausen, mayor David Friedrick Lederer reported to the central government in August 1817 that some of the inhabitants had been reduced to eating boiled snails and making a cabbage-like dish out of the leaves of a common weed known as pig's ear. This caused people's feet and heads to swell, and some could no longer walk or work. "Report of the Famine and Hyperinflation of 1816 and 1817," https://www.asc.ohio-state.edu/palmer.2/Geradstetten/Report%20of%20the%20Famine%20and%20Hhe%20Hyper-Inflation%20of%201816%20and%201817.pdf (accessed April 10, 2023).

35. Ogilvie, "Guild, Efficiency and Social Capital," 207, 209, 198.

36. The relatives who backed Anna Maria pledged lands in other villages, including one located outside Württemberg in Hesse. Promissory Note 1849/1853, trans. Inge von Pongracz, LRFC.

37. Ogilvie, Küpker, and Maegraith, "Community Characteristics," 198–199.

38. The recording of Anna Maria's marriage to Josef indicates that her father was a member of the *Gemeinderath* (local council). *Taufen, Geburten u Heiraten 1609–1898*, 1825, p. 914, no. 9, database with images, Ancestry.com, citing parish records of the Evangelische Kirke Ebhausen (OA Nagold).

39. See, for example, "Christian History Chart: The Roots and Branches of Pietism," https://christianhistoryinstitute.org/magazine/article/roots-and-branches-of-pietism/ (accessed April 10, 2023). There is no evidence that the inhabitants of Ebhausen chose one form over another, except that they did not separate from the established church, as some pietists did.

40. See Peter Heltzel, "Phillipp Jakob Spener and the Rise of Pietism in Germany," in *The Boston Collaborative Encyclopedia of Modern Western Theology*, ed. Wesley J. Wildman, http://people.bu.edu/wwildman/bce/mwt_themes_410_pietism.htm (accessed April 11, 2023).

41. The adult members of the Ebhausen religious community referred to one another as brother and sister. A letter written by Anna Regina reveals that she and her girlfriends gathered twice a week for prayer. Draft letter from Anna Regina Lodholz at Otoe Mission to friends in Ebhausen, circa 1858. Georg's school work contains an 1848 essay on John Wycliffe praising his humility. A New Year's card from 1854 states: "We capture all reason beneath obedience to Christ. 2 Cor. 10, 5. A child of the light, who walks in simplicity (for it is this that provides counsel for us, and increases within us the same spiritual power through which one acts in an upright and proper manner), recognizes well the ways of our dear Savior, and learns also what he should do and avoid." When Anna Maria's fourteen-year-old goddaughter was confirmed, she wrote: "Now beloved godmother, for the kind deeds that you have done for me throughout my life, I thank you warmly and purely, and as I am too weak to thank you adequately, I ask God to reward you here in a timely fashion." Maria Rosina Schill to Anna Maria Lodholz, n.d. In a farewell letter to Anna Maria, the writer mentions sending her a song from Hiller. Unidentified writer to Anna Maria, July 2, 1854. Phillipp Friedrich Hiller (1699–1769) was a prolific and popular hymn writer who trained in Württemberg with the pietist J. A. Bengel. All the letters and documents cited in this note are from translations of the originals by Virginia L. Lewis and Freda Murray, LRFC.

42. Wares Notebook, circa 1850.

43. Gingersnaps recipe, trans. Virginia L. Lewis, LRFC.

44. In one of his school essays, Jakob wrote: "The Christmas tree on Christmas Eve offers a lovely appearance. The form alone of a young fir tree with its fresh greens makes a gratifying impression that is enhanced through the fruits of various kinds, and the glow of the candles it displays." Wares Notebook, circa 1850.

45. *Tote, Konfirmationen, Seelenregister u Kommunionen 1600–1960*, p. 176, no. 12, database with images, Ancestry.com, citing parish records of the Evangelische Kirke Ebhausen (OA, Nagold).

46. On the back of her list of confirmation gifts, Anna Regina (presumably) wrote in reference to her father on this important occasion: "We see now through a mirror etc. death where is your sting, hell where is your victory etc. patience, joy, innocence He is lord over life and death. It is he who calls those which are ours away from us. We shall not complain, if we lack wisdom, do we want to grumble when we don't know when the bad days come, the waves of evil come up and cover us in the slumber of security." Confirmation donations for Anna Regina, 1852, LRFC.

47. Walker, *Germany and the Emigration*, 50.

48. Guinnane and Ogilvie, "Two-Tiered Demographic System," 93, table 4.

49. Ogilvie, Küpker, and Maegraith, "Community Characteristics," 106.

50. Wares Notebook, circa 1850, LRFC. The Wares Notebook, which originally belonged to Jakob's father, contains a wide range of material written by Jakob, as well as copies of bills sent out. Paper was apparently at a premium, and many family documents and handmade books were written on the backs of bills and other paperwork.

51. At this time, the Kingdom of Württemberg lost about 1.5 percent of its population to emigration, split about equally between Russia and the United States. Walker, *Germany and the Emigration*, 8–9, 23, 35.

52. Walker, 14, 18, 29.

53. Frik and Reichert bill for Anna M, with religious material on the back, January 28, 1845, LRFC.

54. Ogilvie, "Guilds, Efficiency and Social Capital," 14, 220.

55. We know this because the backs of bills from Frik and Reichert were used as pages for various handmade books.

56. Eric Van Haute, Richard Paping, and Comac Ó Gráda, "The European Subsistence Crisis of 1845–1850: A Comparative Perspective," IEHC 2006 Helsinki, session 123: 11, http://www.helsinki.fi/iehc2006/papers3/Vanhaute.pdf.

57. Twarog, "Heights and Living Standards in Germany," 288.

58. Twarog, 318.

59. Unscanned partial letter from Gottfried to Heinrich, November 23, 1868, LRFC.

60. Walker, *Germany and the Emigration*, 54.

61. Walker, 63. There was also firsthand information from "circular migrants" who visited Germany and then returned to America. Jochen Krebber, "Creed, Class and Skills: Three Structural Limitations of Chain Migration," in *European Mobility: Internal, International, and Transatlantic Moves in the 19th and Early 20th Centuries*, ed. Annemarie Steidel, Josef Ehmer, Stan Nadel, and Hermann Zeithofer (Göttingen: V&R Unipress, 2009), 70. Anna Maria sent a letter to Gottfried via a circular migrant from a nearby village. Anna M. to Gottfried, with religious saying from Anna Regina, August 7, 1948, LRFC.

62. *Portrait and Biographical Album of Marshall County* (Chicago: Chapman Brothers, 1889), 489.

63. Promissory note, 1849/1853, LRFC.

64. Ogilvie, "Guilds, Efficiency and Social Capital," 7.

65. See appendix A. Despite government policies, illegal emigration was not uncommon. Walter D. Kamphoefner, Wolfgang Helbich, and Ulrike Sommer, eds., *News from the Land of Freedom: German Immigrants Write Home*, trans. Susan Carter Vogel (Ithaca, NY: Cornell University Press, 1991), 6.

66. Walker, *Germany and the Emigration*, 51.

67. Passenger list, Port of New York, *Samuel M. Fox*, August 17, 1854, database with images, Ancestry.com, citing *Passenger Lists of Vessels Arriving at New York, New York, 1820–1897*, microfilm publication M237, Records of the US Customs Service, Record Group 36, National Archives, Washington, DC, http://research.archives.gov/description/6256867.

68. Passenger list, Port of New York, *Splendid*, October 25, 1854, database with images, Ancestry.com, citing *Passenger Lists of Vessels Arriving at New York, New York, 1820–1897*, microfilm publication M237, Records of the US Customs Service, Record Group 36, National Archives, Washington, DC.

69. At the time, the regulation of immigration was left up to the states. Passenger lists were submitted quarterly to the secretary of state, who passed them on to Congress at each session. An Act Regulating Passenger and Shipboard Vessels (commonly known as the Steerage Act of 1819), Pub. L. No. 15-46, 3 Stat. 488 (chap. 46, sec. 1).

70. Gustav A. F. Steckfuss, *A German-American Tale: Memoir of a German Immigrant*, trans. Annika Romero (n.p.: Prussian Press, 2017), 90.

71. See Frederick W. Bogen, *The German in America or Advice and Instruction for German Emigrants in the United States of America*, 2nd ed. (Boston: B. H. Greene, 1851), 43–47, 53–54; Raymond L. Cohn, *Mass Migration under Sail: European Immigration to the Antebellum United States* (Cambridge: Cambridge University Press, 2009), 152.

72. Krebber, "Creed, Class and Skills," 74.

73. Advice by emigrants was published in local papers, as summarized in Bogen, *German in America*, 45–53.

74. Bogen, 51–52.

75. Cohn, *Mass Migration under Sail*, 169. In computing these data, Cohn considered the following states to be in the Midwest: Ohio, Michigan, Indiana, Illinois, Iowa, Wisconsin, and Minnesota.

76. Cohn, 168, table 7.4.

77. Cohn, 168, table 7.4.

78. *Portrait and Biographical Album*, 489.

79. Cohn, *Mass Migration under Sail*, 168, table 7.4.

80. In the mid-1850s, writing to her family in Württemberg, Anna Maria Schano commented on the difficulty of learning English: "It's not as easy to learn as you think, even now I don't know much, and there are many people here who don't even learn it in 6 to 8 years, but if you start off working for Americans then you can learn in one year as much as in 10 years living with Germans." Kamphoefner, Helbich, and Sommer, *News from the Land of Freedom*, 539.

81. Anna Maria Lodholz to Gottfried Lodholz, August 7, 1848, trans. Freda Murray, LRFC.

82. *Portrait and Biographical Album*, 489.

83. Cohn, *Mass Migration under Sail*, 168, table 7.4.

84. An Act to Establish an [sic] Uniform Rule of Naturalization and to Repeal the Acts Heretofore Passed on That Subject, Pub. L. No. 7-28, 2 Stat. 153 (chap. 28, sec. 2), commonly known as the Naturalization Act of 1802, https://govtrackus.s3.amazonaws.com/legislink/pdf/stat/2/STATUTE-2-Pg153a.pdf.

85. Tax Assessment Notice, July 1, 1850; draft letter from Friedrich Lodholz (Jakob) to the Killingers, circa 1854, trans. Virginia L. Lewis, LRFC.

86. Promissory note 1849/1853, LRFC.

87. Walker, *Germany and the Emigration*, 158.

88. Jakob discussed this in a November 22, 1849, letter to a friend in Baden. Wares Notebook, circa 1850.

89. Work testimonials for Johann Georg Lodholz, 1852–53, trans. Virginia L. Lewis, LRFC.

90. Wares Notebook, circa 1850.

91. Wares Notebook.

92. List of confirmation gifts for Jakob Friedrich Lodholz, 1850, trans. Virginia L. Lewis, LRFC.

93. List of confirmation gifts for Anna Regina Lodholz, 1852, trans. Virginia L. Lewis, LRFC.

94. The information about the neighbor growing and selling strawberries is related in a letter from Christian Killinger's father (also named Christian Killinger) to Anna Maria Lodholz et al., December 4, 1855, trans. Virginia L. Lewis, LRFC.

95. Walter D. Kamphoefner, *Germans in America: A Concise History* (Lanham, MD: Rowman & Littlefield, 2021), 169.

96. Walker, *Germany and the Emigration*, 157.

97. Walker, 169.

98. Shipping agent to Anna Maria Lodholz, January 22, 1854, trans. Virginia L. Lewis, LRFC.

99. The monetary system prevalent in southern Germany at the time was based on the gulden (also referred to as the florin), which equaled 60 kreuzers. According to the US consul in Stuttgart in 1857, one gulden equaled 40 cents. *Report on the Commercial Relations of the United States with All Foreign Nations*, vol. 3, prepared and printed under the direction of the secretary of state in accordance with resolutions of the House of Representatives (Washington, DC: A. O. P. Nicholson, Printer, 1857), 240, https://www.govinfo.gov/app/details/SERIALSET-00855_00_00-001-0047-0002. Assuming the average inflation rate between 1850 and 2023 as calculated by the Bureau of Labor Statistics (2.13 percent), 100 guldens would be worth approximately $1,500 today. Jakob and Anna Regina were presumably considered adults, so the fare for the three of them would have been the equivalent of $3,500, a hefty sum. See https://www.officialdata.org/us/inflation/1850?amount=40 (accessed April 10, 2023).

100. Raymond L. Cohn and Simone A. Wegge, "Overseas Passenger Fares and Emigration from Germany in the Mid-Nineteenth Century," *Social Science History* 41, 3 (2017): 401, 404, 405, https://www.jstor.org/stable/90017916.

101. The development of the remittance system was an important factor in promoting emigration. Cohn, *Mass Migration under Sail*, 65.

102. Le Havre was one of the major embarkation ports to New York City, along with Bremen in northern Germany. For the Lodholzes, Le Havre was closer and therefore less costly to reach. Cohn, *Mass Migration under Sail*, 134.

103. Gottfried Lodholz to Anna Maria Lodholz, circa 1854, trans. Virginia L. Lewis, LRFC.

104. Gottfried Lodholz to John Strohm, July 7, 1854, trans. Virginia L. Lewis, LRFC.

105. Walker, *Germany and the Emigration*, 153.

106. "The Germans in America: Chronology," www.loc.gov/rr/european/imde/germchro.html (accessed April 10, 2023).

107. J. G. D. Memminger, *Württembergische Jahrbücher für vaterländische Geschichte, Geographie, Statistik und Topographie, Jahrgang 1859, Erstes Heft* (Stuttgart: Karl Rue, 1861; facsimile ed., Wentworth Press, n.d.), 50, 43.

108. Passenger list, Port of New York, *Samuel M. Fox*, August 17, 1854.

109. The passport listed her as five feet four inches, but measurements can vary considerably across time and space. For example, an 1830 publication noted that 10 feet (*fuss*) was equivalent to 2.865 meters in the Kingdom of Württemberg, which meant that 1 foot equaled 11.26 inches. This would make Anna Maria a little under five feet tall. Friedrich Niemann, *Vollständiges Handbuch der Münzen, Masse, und Gewichte aller Länder der Erde* (Quedlingburg und Leipzig: Gottfried Basse, 1830), 286.

110. Emigration passport, trans. Roberta Reb Allen, LRFC (available digitally; original in the family's possession).

111. Ticket, back, Regulation No. 22, trans. Roberta Reb Allen (in the family's possession).

112. A document of this type was obtained by the Klinger family's eldest daughter in Württemberg. See Kamphoefner, Helbich, and Sommer, *News from the Land of Freedom*, 533–534.

113. Walker, *Germany and the Emigration*, 145.

114. The rules and regulations of Chrystie and Schlössmann forbade any member of the agency from assisting with visas and passports. Ticket, back, Regulation No. 24.

115. Jakob's description of the sea voyage, 1854, trans. Virginia L. Lewis, LRFC.

116. See, for example, *Königlich Württembergisches Hof-und-Staats-Handbuch berausgebeber von dem König. Statistisch-topographischen Bureau* (Stuttgart: Steinkopf, 1854), https://www.digitale-sammlungen.de/de/view/bsb10019624?page=5. It contains more than 830 pages detailing the court and state structure, along with the positions and names of major functionaries. See also the equally hefty Paul von Sick, *Beiträge zur Statistik der Landwirtschaft des Königreiches Warttemberg* (Stuttgart: Müller, 1853), https://www.deutsche-digitalbibliothek.de/item/GRMBSJCCM7NH5RUXJ5US5PGNSN4USF5H.

117. Ticket, front.

118. Ticket, back, Regulation No. 4.

119. Ticket, back, Regulation No. 9.

120. Robert Greenhalgh Albion, *Square-Riggers on Schedule: The New York Sailing Packets to England, France and the Cotton Ports* (Princeton, NJ: Princeton University Press, 1935), 315.

121. Maria Catherina Glaz to Anna Maria Lodholz, circa July 1854, trans. Virginia L. Lewis, LRFC.

122. Draft letter from [Jakob] Friedrich Lodholz to various friends and relatives in Ebhausen, circa 1854, trans. Virginia L. Lewis, LRFC.

123. Jakob's description of the sea voyage, 1854.

124. Christian Killinger to Jakob Lodholz, July 7, 1855, trans. Virginia L. Lewis, LRFC.

125. Christian to Jakob, July 7, 1855.

126. The description in this and the following paragraphs is from Jakob's description of the sea voyage, 1854.

127. Transportation Research Board, "Brief History of Railroad Speed Progress, Historique de la Vitesse Ferroviaire," https://trid.trb.org/view/13670 (accessed April 11, 2023).

128. Leo Schelbert, "On Interpreting Immigrant Letters: The Case of Johann Caspar and Wilhelmina Honegger-Hanhart," *Yearbook of German-American Studies* 16 (1981): 143.

129. "Le Havre: Une Ville Chargeé d'Histoire," https://www.lehavre.fr/ma-ville/une-ville-chargee-dhistoire (accessed April 11, 2023). See also Cohn, *Mass Migration under Sail*, 134.

130. Emigration passport, back.

131. Due to a number of factors, the United States could build ships for the transatlantic

commercial and passenger trade at half the cost incurred by Great Britain. Cohn, *Mass Migration under Sail*, 61.

132. Albion, *Square-Riggers on Schedule*, 284.

133. William R. Short and Reynir A. Óskarson, "Viking Ships," http://hurstwic.org/history/articles/manufacturing/text/norse_ships.htm (accessed April 11, 2023).

134. Albion, *Square-Riggers on Schedule*, 284. See also passenger list, Port of New York, *Samuel M. Fox*, August 17, 1854.

135. Fifteen hundred tons was the average tonnage of American-built ships in 1850, almost triple the size in 1830. Cohn, *Mass Migration under Sail*, 69.

136. An Act Regulating Passenger and Shipboard Vessels, 15th Cong., 2nd sess., chap. 46, secs. 1 and 2, https://govtrackus.s3.amazonaws.com/legislink/pdf/stat/3/STATUTE-3-Pg488a.pdf (accessed April 11, 2023).

137. Passenger list, Port of New York, *Samuel M. Fox*, August 17, 1854, p. 6, passengers 272, 273, 274. According to earlier passenger lists, the *Samuel M. Fox* arrived with 575 passengers in steerage in November 1851 and 630 in steerage in August 1852.

138. Thomas W. Page, "The Transportation of Immigrants and Reception Arrangements in the Nineteenth Century," *Journal of Political Economy* 19, 9 (November 1911): 742, https://www.jstor.org/stable/1820349.

139. Congressional Research Service, "U.S. Federal Government Revenues: 1790 to the Present," http://congressionalresearch.com/RL33665/document.php (accessed April 11, 2023).

140. James M. Bergquist, *Daily Life in Immigrant America, 1820–1870* (Westport, CT: Greenwood Press, 2008), 72.

141. Maldwyn A. Jones, "Transatlantic Steerage Conditions from Sail to Steam, 1819–1920," in *On Distant Shores: Proceedings of the Marcus Lee Hansen Immigration Conference, Aalborg, Denmark, June 29–July 1, 1992*, ed. Flemming Larsen, Henning Bender, and Karen Veien (Aalborg, Denmark: Danes Worldwide Archives in collaboration with Danish Society for Emigration History, 1993), 66.

142. Edwin C. Guillet, *The Great Migration: The Atlantic Crossing by Sailing-ship since 1770*, 2nd ed. (Toronto: University of Toronto Press, 1963), 11, https://archive.org/details/in.ernet.dli.2015.507500/page/n3/mode/1up.

143. Ticket, back, Regulation No. 5.

144. Ticket, back, Regulation Nos. 1 and 3.

145. Ticket, back, Regulation No. 5.

146. Passenger list, Port of New York, *Samuel M. Fox*, August 17, 1854.

147. Ticket, back, Regulation Nos. 10 and 21.

148. Johannes Killinger to Gottfried Lodholz, circa 1854, LRFC.

149. Ticket, back, Regulation No. 23.

150. "Farewell Poem," circa 1854, trans. Virginia L. Lewis, LRFC.

151. Albion, *Square-Riggers on Schedule*, 315.

152. Patrick Royce, *Royce's Sailing Illustrated*, vol. 2 (Inglewood, CA: ProStar Publications, 1997), 153. Nevertheless, in the fall of 1856, as the *Samuel M. Fox* was leaving Liverpool, it encountered a major storm and ended up stranded on the Great Burbo Bank. No lives were lost, but the ship's "back" was broken. It could not be towed back

to port and was put up for auction. See https://www.liverpool.ac.uk/~cmi/books/miscWr/threeUS.html (accessed April 11, 2023).

153. Guillet, *Great Migration*, 8.

154. Royce, *Royce's Sailing Illustrated*, 153. Also see Guillet, *Great Migration*, 66–80.

155. Passenger list, Port of New York, *Samuel M. Fox*, August 17, 1854.

156. Elfrieda Long, "Conditions of Travel Experienced by German Immigrants to Dubois County, Indiana," *Indiana Magazine of History* 41, 4 (December 1945): 331, https://scholarworks.iu.edu/journals/index.php/imh/article/view/7565/8844. The stipulation about cleaning was reported on a ticket issued in 1852 by Chrystie, Heinrich & Company, but it contains much the same wording as the regulations on the Lodholz ticket. In addition to the regulations listed on the ticket, the descriptions of conditions in steerage are based on numerous sources, including Royce, *Royce's Sailing Illustrated*, 153; Guillet, *Great Migration*, 66–80; National Museum of American History, "On the Water: Aboard a Packet," https://americanhistory.si.edu/on-the-water/maritime-nation/enterprise-water/aboard-packet (accessed April 11, 2023); and Maldwyn A. Jones, "Transatlantic Steerage Conditions from Sail to Steam, 1819–1920," in Larsen, Bender, and Veien, *On Distant Shores*, 59–71.

157. Draft letter from Jakob Friedrich Lodholz to the Killingers, circa 1855, trans. Virginia L. Lewis, LRFC.

158. The "Sandbank" refers to the sandbanks around the Atlantic coast of Newfoundland.

159. Jakob's description of the sea voyage, 1854.

160. Christian Killinger to Jakob Friedrich Lodholz, July 7, 1855.

161. In his letter, Christian lists all the members of the party from Ebhausen; see appendix A. There were quite a few Lodholzes in Ebhausen, and the exact relationship of Johann Georg Lodholz and Sara Lodholz to the Lodholzes in Connecticut is unknown. Christian Killinger to Gottfried Lodholz, October 26, 1854, trans. Virginia L. Lewis, LRFC.

162. Michigan State University, "Michigan Fever, Part 1," www.geo.msu.edu/extra/geogmich/michigan_fever.html (accessed April 11, 2023).

163. Jonathan Marwil, *A History of Ann Arbor* (Ann Arbor: University of Michigan Press, 1987), 6–7.

164. Buffalo, New York, had a substantial German presence. See H. Perry Smith, ed., *History of the City of Buffalo with Illustrations and Biographical Sketches of Some of Its Prominent Men and Pioneers*, vol. 1 (Syracuse, NY: D. Mason, 1884), https://archive.org/details/historyofcityofbo1smit/page/n8/mode/1up.

165. Christian Killinger to Jakob Friedrich Lodholz, July 7, 1855; "Norwich Mine (Essex Mine), Norwich, Ontonagon Co., Michigan, USA," https://www.mindat.org/loc-17100.html (accessed April 11, 2023).

166. Jochen Krebber, *Württemberger in Nordamerika: Migration von der Schwäbi-schen Alb im 19. Jahrhundert* (Stuttgart: Franz Steiner Verlag, 2014), 165.

167. The Statue of Liberty–Ellis Island Foundation, "The History of Ellis Island," https://www.statueofliberty.org/ellis-island/ (accessed August 15, 2023).

168. Gottfried Lodholz to John Strohm, July 7, 1854, trans. Virginia L. Lewis, LRFC.

169. Draft letter from Jakob Friedrich Lodholz to the Killingers, circa 1855.

170. Bogen, *German in America*, 47.

171. Draft letter from Jakob Friedrich Lodholz to the Killingers, circa 1855.

172. Draft letter from Jakob to the Killingers.

173. "Looking Back—Rollin' on the Connecticut River in the Great Steamers," https://www.ctinsider.com/opinion/article/Looking-back-Rollin-on-the-Connecticut-River-16959453.php (accessed August 17, 2023).

174. US Harbors, "Coastal News: Connecticut's Steamboat Past," https://www.usharbors.com/2017/08/connecticuts-steamboat-past/ (accessed April 11, 2023).

175. "Looking Back—Rollin' on the Connecticut River."

176. Draft letter from Jakob Friedrich Lodholz to the Killingers, circa 1855.

177. Christian Wolmar, *The Great Railroad Revolution: The History of Trains in America* (New York: Public Affairs, 2012), 1, 23, 68, 72.

178. Draft letter from Jakob Friedrich Lodholz to the Killingers, circa 1855.

179. Draft letter from Jakob to the Killingers.

180. "Population of Connecticut Towns 1830–1890," https://portal.ct.gov/SOTS/Register-Manual/Section-VII/Population-1830---1890 (accessed August 17, 2023). See also 1850 Federal Census, Litchfield County, Connecticut, Plymouth Township, Schedule 1, database with images, Ancestry.com, citing Seventh Census of the United States, 1850, microfilm publication M432, Records of the Bureau of the Census, Record Group 29, National Archives, Washington, DC.

181. Francis Atwater, *History of the Town of Plymouth, Connecticut* (Meriden, CT: Journal Publishing Co., 1895), 281, https://archive.org/details/historyoftownofp1895atwa/page/280/mode/2up.

182. 1850 Federal Census, Litchfield County, Connecticut, Plymouth Township, Schedule 1.

183. Draft letter from Jakob Friedrich Lodholz to the Killingers, circa 1855.

184. In his seminal essay on chain migration in Württemberg, Jochen Krebber found that Württemberg Protestants, as opposed to Catholics, preferred rural areas and small towns. Krebber, "Creed, Class and Skills," 71.

185. Booklet hours worked, back page, LRFC.

186. Draft letter from Jakob Friedrich Lodholz to the Killingers, circa 1855.

187. Draft letter from Jakob Friedrich Lodholz to friends in Ebhausen, circa 1855, trans. Virginia L. Lewis, LRFC.

188. It was not unusual for single women to emigrate. On the ship carrying Anna Maria, Jakob, and Anna Regina, 11 percent of the individuals from Württemberg were single females; their average age was twenty-three. Passenger list, Port of New York, *Samuel M. Fox*, August 17, 1854. In the 1900 federal census, which erroneously listed Christina as "Susan," she reported that she had emigrated in 1853. 1900 Federal Census, Marshall County, Kansas, Richland Township, Enumeration District 69, Schedule 1, sheet 9, dwelling 174, family 174, line 23, database with images, Ancestry.com, citing US Bureau of the Census, *Twelfth Census of the United States, 1900* (Washington, DC: National Archives and Records Administration, 1900). However, the only passenger arriving by ship near this time who might have been Christina was Christine Seid, from 1854 (Christina's maiden name was Seitz). Passenger list, Port of New York, *Isaac Belle*,

October 19, 1854, p. 8, database with images, Ancestry.com, *citing Passenger Lists of Vessels Arriving at New York, New York, 1820–1897*, microfilm publication M237, line 43, list number 1429, Records of the US Customs Service, Record Group 36, National Archives, Washington, DC, http://research.archives.gov/description/6256867.

189. In one of his letters, Jakob urged Christina to write to her sister, who was the widow of Johans Scheuring; she subsequently married Danish-born Augustus Von Martensen (Atwater, *History of the Town of Plymouth*, 243), referred to in the Lodholz letters as August Martins. [Jakob] Friedrich Lodholz to family, January 29, 1860, trans. Freda Murray, LRFC.

190. 1875 Kansas Territorial Census, Marshall County, Guittard Township, Schedule 1, p. 16, dwelling 127, family 128, lines 32 and 33, database with images, Ancestry.com, citing Kansas State Historical Society, *1875 Kansas Territory Census*, roll:ks1875_12.

191. Booklet hours worked, circa 1856–57, mainly untranslated, LRFC.

192. J. D. B. DeBos, Superintendent of the US Census, *Statistical View of the United States, Being a Compendium of the Seventh Census*, part 3, "Moral and Social Conditions" (Washington, DC: Beverley Tucker, Senate Printer, 1854), 164, table 175 (Average Wages, 1850), https://www.census.gov/library/publications/1854/dec/1850c.html.

193. Carrol D. Wright, Chief of the Bureau of Statistics of Labor, *Comparative Wages, Prices and Cost of Living from the Sixteenth Annual Report of the Massachusetts Bureau of Statistics of Labor for 1885* (Boston: Wright & Potter, 1889; facsimile ed., LeGare Street Press, 2022), 125 (Wages and Prices: 1752–1860), table (Prices: Fuel).

194. New York publisher to Jakob Friedrich Lodholz, November 22, 1856, trans., Virginia L. Lewis, LRFC.

195. Draft letter from Jakob Friedrich Lodholz to the Killingers, circa 1855. Between 1850 and 1854, foreign immigration increased the male labor force in the United States by more than 4 percent each year, leading to wage stagnation as the competition for jobs increased. Cohn, *Mass Migration under Sail*, 7.

196. There was a run on banks as depositors rushed to remove their funds. The global nature of the economic crisis was evidenced by the fact that British investors withdrew their money from American banks. Particularly unsettling was the potential failure of the New York branch of the Ohio Life Insurance and Trust Company because of widespread embezzlement. The market in land speculation that accompanied proposed new railroad routes collapsed. With the end of the Crimean War in Europe, Russia was again shipping grain for sale on the world market, and American farmers saw grain prices plunge. Even faith in the US government's credit was shaken. There was no federally issued paper money at this time, and the federal government dealt only in currency made of precious metals (species). The gold rush in California provided a lucrative source of gold for the government, but thirty thousand pounds of gold being shipped from San Francisco was lost in a hurricane off the coast of North Carolina. See http://www.americaslibrary.gov/jb/reform/jb_reform_goldlost_1.html and https://economic-historian.com/2020/07/panic-of-1857/ (accessed April 11, 2023). For a detailed analysis of how a feared decline in immigration affected western land values and railroad investments, see Charles W. Calomiris and Larry Schweikart, "The Panic of 1857: Origins, Transmissions, and Containment," *Journal of Economic History* 51, 4 (December 1991): 807–834, https://doi.org/10.1017/S0022050700040122. Piggybacking off the work of Calomiris and

Schweikart, Jenny Wahl links the panic to the Supreme Court's *Dred Scott* decision in March 1857, which declared the Compromise of 1820 unconstitutional, thereby opening up the possibility of slavery's expansion west. This slowed the westward movement of northerners who did not want to work alongside and compete with slaves, which in turn led to a lowering of land values, which had been subject to much speculation, as well as a decrease in the value of railroad securities as the need for railway expansion slowed. Jenny Wahl, "*Dred*, Panic, War: How a Slave Case Triggered Financial Crisis and Civil Disruption," in *Congress and the Crisis of the 1850s*, ed. Paul Finkelman and Donald R. Kennon (Athens: Ohio University Press, 2012), 159–200.

197. Atwater, *History of the Town of Plymouth*, 243.

198. Invoice (in the family's possession).

199. Walker, *Germany and the Emigration*, 57, 80. About 5 percent of the 1854 emigrants became discouraged and returned to Germany within the year, and more returned home in 1855. Walker, 173, fn. 62.

200. Kamphoefner, *Germans in America*, 137.

201. J. Neale Carman, "Continental Europeans in Rural Kansas: 1854–1861," in *Territorial Kansas: Studies Commemorating the Centennial* (Lawrence: University of Kansas Publications, 1954), 177, 193. Also see "Letter, F. M. Serenbetz to E. E. Hale, March 14, 1857," New England Emigrant Aid Company Collection no. 624, box 2, folder 1, item no. 101336, Kansas State Historical Society, Topeka; "Secretary, Kansas Society, Connecticut Kansas Colony Record Book, February 18, 1856 through June 26, 1857," Collection no. 569, item no. 100613, Kansas State Historical Society.

202. Georg Lodholz to Anna Maria Lodholz, March 12, 1857, trans. Virginia L. Lewis, LRFC.

Chapter 2. The Journey West

1. Under the ordinance, surveyors organized the land into townships six miles square; each township had thirty-six sections, each measuring one mile square and consisting of 640 acres. Sections could later be broken down into half, quarter (the ubiquitous 160 acres), and one-eighth sections. A minimum price per acre was set, and the land was put up for public auction, with the revenue going to the government. The section designated 18 was reserved to support public schools. See https://sdpb.sd.gov/EducationalServices Guide/etvprograms/pdf/18thDocuments/The%20Land%20Ordinance%20of%201785 .pdf (accessed April 11, 2023).

2. Benjamin Horace Hibbard, *A History of the Public Land Policies* (New York: Macmillan, 1924; facsimile ed., Gale, n.d.), 42. This pattern continued. During the Jackson administration, when the Indian Removal Act was passed, lands ceded by the tribes that had not yet been surveyed were almost immediately overrun by squatters, who staked claims and built cabins with no opposition from the federal or state government. Despite public outcry, land companies looking for speculative investments were not kept out either. In fact, many politicians and government officials, including Jackson and his friends, engaged in land speculation. Anthony Wallace, *The Long, Bitter Trail: Andrew Jackson and the Indians* (New York: Hill & Wang, 1992), 70. Likewise, some of the

hundreds of treaties with Native American tribes contain glimpses of the federal government's failure to control the white population's settlement. The following quotes are from Charles Kappler, *Indian Affairs: Laws and Treaties*, vol. 2, *Treaties* (Washington, DC: US Government Printing Office, 1904), https://www.govinfo.gov/app/details/GOVPUB-Y4 _IN2_11-1c227893bfbe1da6dd96b6883fd0205b; page numbers are given in parentheses:

Treaty with the Winnebago, etc., 1828, preamble: "in order to remove the difficulties which have arisen in consequence of the occupation by white persons of that part of the mining country which has not been heretofore ceded to the United States" (292–293).

Treaty with the Shawnee, 1825, article 4: "It appearing that the Shawnee Indians have various claims against the citizens of the United States to a large amount for spoliations of various kinds" (261).

Treaty with the Creeks, 1832, article V: Provides that there should be no intruders on ceded land until surveyed, "excepting however from this provision those white persons who have made their own improvements and not expelled the Creeks from theirs. Such persons may remain until their crops are gathered" (341). This statement indicates the presence of squatters.

Treaty with the Chickasaw, 1834, article III: "The Chickasaw are not acquainted with the laws of the whites, which are extended over them; and the many intruders which break into their country interrupting their rights and disturbing their repose, leave no alternative whereby restraint can be afforded, other than an appeal to the military force of their county, which they are unwilling to ask for, or see resorted to" (418).

In the first two chapters of *Fifty Million Acres: Conflicts over Kansas Land Policy, 1854–1890* (Ithaca, NY: Cornell University Press, 1954; reprint, Norman: University of Oklahoma Press, 1977), Paul Wallace Gates chronicles innumerable violations by squatters. In his 1854 annual report to Congress, Commissioner of Indian Affairs George Manypenny reported that on a portion of land ceded by the Delawares in the Kansas Territory, an association of settlers had illegally founded a town and sold lots with the "connivance" of the military; two military officers were members of the association. "US and Indian Relations," in *1855—Report of the Commissioner of Indian Affairs for 1854*, 19, https://digitalcommons.csumb.edu/hornbeck_usa_2_e/41.

3. There was hardly unanimity among politicians and members of the public on this issue. Many thought the Native Americans should not be removed and cited various reasons, including religious and constitutional. The vote on the act was 28 to 19 in the Senate and 102 to 97 in the House. Wallace, *Long, Bitter Trail*, 68–70.

4. Treaty with the Chickasaw, 1852, article III, in Kappler, *Indian Affairs*, 596.

5. It became clear that the land to be granted west of the Mississippi was not unlimited. Numerous boundary disputes arose among neighboring tribes, and some tribes were forcefully consolidated. Later treaties were vague about where the land granted to a particular Native American tribe would be. As a result, the Indian Territory became a mishmash. See the map of Indian Territory in 1850 in Clifford E. Trafzer, *As Long as the Grass Shall Grow and Rivers Flow: A History of Native Americans* (Belmont, CA: Thomson, 2000), 164. A particularly egregious example of the government's failure to fulfill its promises involved the Wyandot tribe, which signed a treaty in 1842 agreeing to move west of the Mississippi. The language of the preamble of the 1850 treaty with the Wyandot speaks for itself: "Among other stipulations it was agreed that the United States

should convey to said Indians a tract of country for their permanent settlement in the Indian Territory west of the Mississippi River, to contain one hundred an[d] forty-eight thousand acres of land: . . . said Indians never did receive the said one hundred and forty-eight thousand acres of land from the United States, but were forced to purchase lands from the Delaware nation of Indians, which purchase was agreed to and ratified by the United States." Kappler, *Indian Affairs*, 587.

6. Francis Paul Prucha, *American Indian Treaties: The History of a Political Anomaly* (Berkeley: University of California Press, 1994), 184.

7. When a woman married, her property became her husband's; thus, only widows who were citizens were mentioned in the law. Georg apparently misunderstood this aspect of the law, as he claimed land on behalf of his mother, who was a widow but had never declared her intention of becoming a citizen and thus was not entitled to claim land. This issue is discussed later in this book.

8. Hibbard, *History of the Public Land Policies*, 158, 167. The possibility of preemption actually seemed to embolden squatters.

9. Christian Killinger to Friedrich Lodholz, July 7, 1857, LRFC.

10. Frederick W. Bogen, *The German in America or Advice and Instruction for German Emigrants in the United States of America*, 2nd ed. (Boston: B. H. Greene, 1851; facsimile ed., Kessinger Legacy Reprints, n.d.), 47, 49.

11. Detroit Historical Society, "Boomtown Detroit 1820–1860," https://detroithistorical.org/learn/timeline-detroit/boomtown-detroit-1820-1860 (accessed April 11, 2023).

12. Georg Lodholz to family in Terryville, May 14, 1857, trans. Freda Murray, LRFC.

13. *History of Litchfield County, Connecticut* (Philadelphia: J. W. Lewis, 1881), 492, https://archive.org/details/historyoflitchfioojwle.

14. Detroit Historical Society, "Boomtown Detroit 1820–1860."

15. Georg Lodholz to family from Otoe City, Nebraska Territory, 1857, trans. Freda Murray, LRFC.

16. Georg to family in Terryville, May 14, 1857.

17. Georg to family in Terryville.

18. Georg to family in Terryville.

19. Georg to family from Otoe City, 1857.

20. Georg to family from Otoe City. In the 1840s Ann Arbor was poised to become a center for wool manufacturing. Jonathan Marwil, *A History of Ann Arbor* (Ann Arbor: University of Michigan Press, 1987), 18.

21. "State of Michigan, Table No. 1—Population by Age and Sex," in *Preliminary Report on the Eighth Census, 1860*, https://www2.census.gov/library/publications/decennial/1860/population/1860a-20.pdf (accessed April 11, 2023).

22. Marwil, *History of Ann Arbor*, 13.

23. Georg to family from Otoe City, 1857.

24. Office of the Illinois Secretary of State, "Early Chicago, 1833–1871," https://www.ilsos.gov/departments/archives/teaching_packages/early_chicago/doc23.html (accessed April 11, 2023).

25. Georg to family from Otoe City, 1857.

26. "Germans," in *Encyclopedia of Chicago*, http://www.encyclopedia.chicagohistory.org/pages/512.html (accessed April 11, 2023).

27. See the discussion in Humphrey J. Desmond, *The Know-Nothing Party: A Sketch* (Washington, DC: New Century Press, 1905; facsimile ed., Miami, FL: Hard Press, n.d.), 22–45, 50–51.

28. "Know-Nothing Party," in *Britannica*, https://www.britannica.com/topic/Know-Nothing-party (accessed April 11, 2023).

29. Desmond, *Know-Nothing Party*, 80–81, 54, 62–67, 69.

30. Desmond, 69.

31. "A Know Nothing Council Denouncing the Order," *Chicago Tribune*, June 29, 1855, 2; database with images, Newspapers.com.

32. Rudolf A. Hofmeister, *The Germans of Chicago* (Champaign, IL: Stipes Publishing, 1976), 55.

33. The trial testimony of the defendants, who were charged with intent to commit murder, indicated that the group numbered approximately forty. They were armed with clubs and about six muskets; one officer was shot. *Chicago Tribune*, June 20, 1855, 3.

34. Andreas referred to the affair as "sedition notoriously German." A. T. Andreas, *History of Chicago* (Chicago: R. R. Donnelley & Sons, 1884), 453–454, https://archive.org/details/historyofchicago01inandr/page/n3/mode/1up. See also Hofmeister, *Germans of Chicago*, 55; "Germans," in *Encyclopedia of Chicago*; Ron Grossman, "Chicago's Lager Beer Riot Proved Immigrants' Power," *Chicago Tribune*, September 25, 2015, https://www.chicagotribune.com/history/ct-know-nothing-party-lager-beer-riot-per-flashback-jm-20150925-story.html. The mayor's actions were roundly approved by the *Chicago Tribune*: "Another Quiet Sabbath," March 26, 1855, 3.

35. Hofmeister, *Germans of Chicago*, 54.

36. Statistics from 1870 indicate that immigrants from Württemberg made up 1.47 percent of the foreign-born population, compared to 17.25 percent from Prussia. Hofmeister, *Germans of Chicago*, 32, 33.

37. Alon Confino, *The Nation as a Local Metaphor: Württemberg, Imperial Germany, and National Memory, 1871–1918* (Chapel Hill: University of North Carolina Press, 1997), 17. The ruler of Württemberg changed sides midstream in the Napoleonic Wars.

38. The shared liturgy the king tried to impose was minute in its specifications about various practices and aspects of the religious culture, such as the design of altars, the manner of ecclesiastical dress, how to cross oneself, the number of hymns to be sung, and so on. The biggest bone of contention, however, involved the ambiguous treatment of Communion. The Reformed Church broke a loaf of bread and distributed bits meant to be symbolic of Christ's body. The Lutherans believed in the real presence of Christ in the wafers they used. Stan M. Landry, "German 'Worship Wars' and the 1830 Anniversaries of the Augsburg Confession," *Lutheran Quarterly* 26 (2012): 373–390.

39. Recall from chapter 1 that Catholics were not welcome in Ebhausen. During the devastating wars accompanying the Protestant Reformation, Ebhausen was burnt to the ground by Catholic forces, decimating the population and reducing the surviving inhabitants to eating roots. Sheilagh Ogilvie, Markus Küpker, and Janine Maegraith, "Community Characteristics and Demographic Development: Three Württemberg Communities: 1558–1914," Cambridge Working Paper in Economics 0910, March 2009, 29–34, https://www.researchgate.net/publication/48915027.

40. Andreas, *History of Chicago*, 294–295.
41. Andreas, 334, 348, 351.
42. Georg to family from Otoe City, 1857.
43. Bruce Levine, *The Spirit of 1848: German Immigrants, Labor Conflict, and the Coming of the Civil War* (Urbana: University of Illinois Press, 1992), 58.
44. Georg to family from Otoe City, 1857.
45. Iowa History Project, "Coming of the Railroads," chap. 36 of *Stories of Iowa*, http://iagenweb.org/history/soi/soi36.htm (accessed April 11, 2023).
46. Iowa Department of Transportation, "Historic Auto Trains: Diamond Trail," https://iowadot.gov/autotrails/diamondtrail (accessed April 11, 2023).
47. Georg to family from Otoe City, 1857.
48. Austin no longer exists. It is one of Iowa's ghost towns.
49. Georg to family from Otoe City, 1857.
50. Georg to family from Otoe City.
51. A. T. Andreas, "Otoe County Part 3: Ferries and Transfer Companies," in *Andreas' History of the State of Nebraska* (Chicago: Western Publishing, 1882), http://kancoll.org/books/andreas_ne/otoe/otoe-p3.html#ferry.
52. National Park Service, "Mapping the Great American Desert," https://www.nps.gov/foda/learn/education/upload/mappinggreatamericandesert.pdf (accessed April 11, 2023).
53. *1855—Report of the Commissioner of Indian Affairs for 1854*, 10.
54. Charles B. Bernhotz, Laura K. Weakly, et al., "As Long as Grass Shall Grow and Water Run: The Treaties Formed by the Confederate States of America and the Tribes in Indian Territory, 1861" http://treatiesportal.unl.edu/csaindiantreaties/ (accessed April 11, 2023).
55. There are too many examples to cite here. The following are representative: Treaty with the Western Cherokee, 1833, article I: "The United States agree to possess the Ceerokees [sic] and to guarrantee [sic] it to them forever, and that guarantee, is hereby pledged, of seven million acres of land to be bounded as follows." This was one of the first examples of the word "forever" being included in a treaty involving Native American land. Article II guaranteed them a "perpetual outlet" west—"a free and unmolested use of all the country lying west, of the western boundary of said seven millions of acres, as far west as the sovereignty of the United States and their right to soil extend" (Kappler, *Indian Affairs*, 396).
Treaty with the New York Indians, 1838, Article 2: "the United States agree to set apart the following tract of country, situated directly west of the State of Missouri, as a permanent home for all the New York Indians" (Kappler, 504).
Treaty with the Saux [sic] and Foxes, 1842, article II: "the President will as soon after this treaty is ratified on their part as may be convenient, assign a tract of land suitable and convenient for Indian purposes, to the Sacs and Foxes for a permanent and perpetual residence for them and their descendants" (Kappler, 546).
56. For example, see Treaty with the Menominee, 1848, article III, in Kappler, 572.
57. T. R. Fehrenbach, *Lone Star: A History of Texas and the Texans* (Boston: Da Capo Press, 2000), 153–158, 168–222.
58. Darlis A. Miller, "Cross-Cultural Marriages in the Southwest: The New Mexico

Experience: 1846–1900," *New Mexico Historical Review* 57, 4 (1982): 337, https://digitalrepository.unm.edu/cgi/viewcontent.cgi?article=2616&context=nmhr.

59. John D. Unruh Jr., *The Plains Across: The Overland Emigrants and the Trans-Mississippi West, 1840–60* (Urbana: University of Illinois Press, 1979), 122–123, 516 fn. 75.

60. Mack Walker, *Germany and the Emigration: 1816–1885* (Cambridge, MA: Harvard University Press, 1964), 83–85.

61. Lamberta Margarette Voget, "The Germans in Los Angeles County California: 1850–1900," 1933, http://files.usgwarchives.net/ca/losangeles/history/germans/chapter1.txt.

62. Carole Gosgrove Terry, "Die Deutschen in Kalifornien: Germans in Urban California 1850–1860" (doctoral thesis, University of Nevada–Las Vegas, 2012), http://dx.doi.org/10.34917/4332620. For a recounting of experiences from 1849, see Frederich Gerstaecker, excerpt from "Biography of Frederick Augustus Hihn (or Hühn)," and *California Gold Mines* (originally translated and published in English in London in 1854), https://library.ucsc.edu/speccoll/hihn/hihn-biographies/california-and-the-gold-fields-translated-from-the-german-of-frederic.

63. Roberta Lee Schmalenberger, "The German-Oregonians, 1850–1918" (master's diss., Portland State University, 1983), 17, *Dissertations and Theses,* paper 3430, https://doi.org/10.15760/etd.5316.

64. Tomas Jaehn, *Germans in the Southwest: 1850–1920* (Albuquerque: University of New Mexico Press, 2005), 29.

65. Frederick Merk, *Manifest Destiny and Mission in American History* (New York: Alfred A. Knopf, 1963; reprint, Cambridge, MA: Harvard University Press, 1995). Merk's book is largely devoted to an analysis of the propaganda churned out by those in favor of expansion. It should be pointed out that the impetus for expansion was not limited to the late 1840s. Both John Quincy Adams and Andrew Jackson tried to buy Texas from Mexico.

66. John O'Sullivan, "Annexation," *United States Magazine and Democratic Review* 17 (1845): 5–6, 9–10.

67. See Merk, *Manifest Destiny and Mission.* He discusses these options throughout the book.

68. Merk, xii–xiii. In the foreword written for the 1995 reprint, John Mack Faragher presents the views of various later historians, who were in agreement on this matter.

69. Merk, 35–38.

70. The first line of the last stanza of the poem "On the Prospect of Planting Arts and Learning in America" by English philosopher George Berkley (1685–1753)—"Westward the course of empire takes its way"—became associated with Manifest Destiny. It is the title of a huge mural painted for the Capitol in 1861 by Emmanuel Gottlieb Leutze, who was born in Württemberg and is perhaps more famous for painting *Washington Crossing the Delaware.*

71. Prucha, *American Indian Treaties,* 241–242.

72. Gates, *Fifty Million Acres,* 21.

73. Georg to family from Otoe City, 1857.

74. *Historical Statistics of the United States, Colonial Times to 1970,* pt. 1 (Washington, DC: US Bureau of the Census, 1975), series A119–135, Population by Age, Sex, Race and Nativity: 1790 to 1970.

75. Andreas, "Otoe County Part 4: Nebraska City: Early Settlement," in *Andreas' History of the State of Nebraska*.

76. Andreas, "Otoe County Part 4: Nebraska City: Early Settlement, Selling Town Lots," in *Andreas' History of the State of Nebraska*.

77. Andreas, "Otoe County Part 4: Nebraska City: Early Settlement"; "Part 5: Nebraska City: Transportation and Telegraphs, Education"; "Part 6: Religion"; "Part 8: Manufacturing Interests," in *Andreas' History of the State of Nebraska*.

78. Georg to family from Otoe City, 1857. Although trained as a baker, Georg apparently never sought a job as one. On his journey he worked as a laborer.

79. Georg to family from Otoe City.

80. John Arkas Hawgood, *The Tragedy of German-America* (New York: Arno Press, New York Times, 1970), 27.

81. While visiting the United States in 1831, Frenchman Alexis de Tocqueville, author of the classic *Democracy in America*, described traveling with the mail in the frontier: "I traveled along a portion of the frontier of the United States in a sort of cart, which was termed the mail. Day and night we passed with great rapidity along the roads, which were scarcely marked out through immense forests; when the gloom of the woods became impenetrable, the coachman lighted branches of pine, and we journeyed along by the light they cast. From time to time we came to a hut in the midst of the forest, which was a post-office. The mail dropped an enormous bundle of letters at the door of this isolated dwelling, and we pursued our way at full gallop, leaving the inhabitants of the neighboring log houses to send for their share of the treasure." See https://www.gutenberg.org/files/815/815-h/815-h.htm (accessed April 11, 2023). Georg sent and received his mail via steamboat up the Missouri River, but as he probed beyond its shores, Tocqueville's description of isolated post offices became the norm.

82. Georg Lodholz to family, July 4, 1857, trans. Virginia L. Lewis, LRFC.

83. Andreas, "Early History, Part 7, Indian Tribes and Treaties," in *Andreas' History of the State of Nebraska*.

84. Georg was referring to square hectares, a metric measurement of land. One square hectare is equal to ten thousand square meters, which in turn is equal to approximately two and a half acres.

85. Georg was referring to the garrison at Fort Leavenworth, established in 1827 and still in operation today. It was roughly 130 miles south of Nebraska City in the Kansas Territory.

86. Georg to family, July 4, 1857.

87. George L. Anderson, "Some Phases of Currency and Banking in Territorial Kansas," in *Territorial Kansas: Studies Commemorating the Centennial* (Lawrence: University of Kansas Publications, 1954), 105.

88. Hawgood, *Tragedy of German-America*, 31.

89. Anderson, "Some Phases of Currency and Banking," 112.

90. Georg Lodholz to family from Otoe City, n.d. (second letter), trans. Virginia L. Lewis, LRFC.

91. J. George Lodholz to friends from Gage County, Nebraska Territory, November 3, 1857, trans. Gottfried Lodholz, in probate records for John George Lodholz, Marshall County District Court, Marysville, KS. After Georg's death, there was a contentious legal

battle between his widow and Gottfried and Friedrich. The probate records contain copies of letters that were originally written in German.

92. Paul W. Gates, *Landlords and Tenants on the Prairie Frontier* (Ithaca, NY: Cornell University Press, 1973), 49, 51.

93. Gates, 49, 51,73, 171.

94. See Gates, 48–71.

95. Georg Lodholz to family, n.d., circa fall 1857, trans. Virginia L. Lewis, LRFC.

96. CPI Inflation Calculator, https://www.officialdata.org/us/inflation/1855?amount =270 (accessed April 11, 2023).

97. J. George Lodholz to friends from Gage County, November 3, 1857.

98. Georg Lodholz to family, December 10, 1857, trans. Freda Murray, LRFC.

99. Georg to family, December 10, 1857.

100. See W. Heiss, *The Census of the Territory of Kansas, February, 1855 with Index and Map of Kansas Election Districts in 1854* (Knightstown: Eastern Indiana Publishing Co., 1967), map insert between pp. 15 and 16. When it was officially organized, Marshall County was located at 39° 57' N and –96° 30' W. Although voter censuses were conducted every year up to 1859, the 1855 census was the only one that included, in some districts and for some individuals, the voter's country of origin. Thus, this census gives an indication but hardly a complete picture of the foreign-born residents in Kansas at the time.

101. 1855 Kansas Territory Census, District 10, database with images, Ancestry.com, citing microfilm reel K-1, Kansas State Historical Society.

102. Ute Planert, "International Conflict, War, and the Making of Modern Germany, 1740–1815," in *The Oxford Handbook of Modern German History*, ed. Helmut Walser Smith (Oxford: Oxford University Press, 2011), 109.

103. 1855 Kansas Territory Census, District 10. This is the only district where the census taker summarized his findings, indicating how quickly migrants were coming to Kansas: "There are in this District 53 farmers; 2 physicians; 2 lawyers, 1 clergyman; 1 mason; 1 cooper; 1 painter. There are *forty-five* persons between 21 and 30 years of age; *twenty-seven* between 30 and 40; *eleven* between 40 and 50; *four* between 50 and 60; *three* over 60; and *sixty-one* minors [younger than 21]. There are 56 persons last from Missouri; 17 from Maine; 14 from Illinois; 12 from Massachusetts; 12 from Bavaria; 8 from Indiana; 8 from New Brunswick; 7 from Ohio; 5 from Iowa; 2 from Kentucky; 2 from Pennsylvania; 2 from Louisiana; 1 from Rhode Island; 1 from Michigan; 1 from New York; 1 from Oregon; 1 from California."

104. 1855 Kansas Territory Census, District 11, database with images, Ancestry.com, citing microfilm reel K-1, Kansas State Historical Society.

105. Georg Lodholz to family, December 26, 1857, trans. Virginia L. Lewis, LRFC. The papers to which Georg referred were undoubtedly Friedrich's initial application for citizenship—his Declaration of Intent.

106. Eleanor L. Turk, "Germans in Kansas," *Kansas History* 28 (Spring 2005): 56.

107. Emma Forter, *History of Marshall County: Its People, Industries and Institutions* (Indianapolis: B. F. Bowen, 1917), 549, https://archive.org/details/historyofmarshaloofost.

108. William G. Cutler, "Marshall County, Part I: Topography and Geology," in *History of the State of Kansas* (Chicago: A. T. Andreas, 1883), http://www.kancoll.org

/books/cutler/marshall/marshall-co-p1.html; plat of Richland Township (formerly part of Guittard Township), sections 25 and 26, http://www.kansasmemory.org/item/209410/page/29 (accessed April 11, 2023); plat of the estate of John George Lodholz, deceased, as divided by order of the commissioners, probate records for John George Lodholz, Marshall County District Court, Marysville, KS.

109. "Milestone Documents: Missouri Compromise (1820)," National Archives, https://www.archives.gov/milestone-documents/missouri-compromise (accessed April 11, 2023). The greater part of Missouri is north of 36° 30', which is why it had to be specifically designated a slave state.

110. Oregon Secretary of State, "Black in Oregon 1840–1870: National and Oregon Chronology of Events," https://sos.oregon.gov/archives/exhibits/black-history/Pages/context/chronology.aspx (accessed April 11, 2023).

111. Christopher Childers, *The Failure of Popular Sovereignty: Slavery, Manifest Destiny, and the Radicalization of Southern Politics* (Lawrence: University Press of Kansas, 2012), 102–103.

112. "A Century of Lawmaking for a New Nation: U.S. Congressional Documents and Debates, 1774–1875," *Statutes at Large*, 31st Cong., lst sess., chap. 49, sec. 2, p. 447, https://memory.loc.gov/cgi-bin/ampage?collId=llsl&fileName=009/llsl009.db&recNum=474; chap. 51, sec. 1, p. 443, https://memory.loc.gov/cgi-bin/ampage?collId=llsl&fileName=009/llsl009.db&recNum=480 (both accessed April 12, 2023).

113. Utah State Department of Cultural and Community Engagement, "I Love Utah History: Utah Statehood," https://ilovehistory.utah.gov/utah-statehood/; New Mexico Museum of Art, "New Mexico Art Tells New Mexico History: Statehood," https://online.nmartmuseum.org/nmhistory/people-places-and-politics/statehood/history-statehood.html (both accessed April 13, 2023).

114. "A Century of Lawmaking for a New Nation," *Statutes at Large*, 33rd Cong., 1st sess., chap. 59, sec. 14, p. 283, https://memory.loc.gov/cgi-bin/ampage?collId=llsl&fileName=010/llsl010.db&recNum=304 (accessed April 12, 2023).

115. F. I. Herriott, "The Germans of Chicago and Stephen A. Douglas in 1854," *Deutsch-Amerikanische Geschichtsblätter* 12 (1912): 381, 388, 399.

116. Hofmeister, *Germans of Chicago*, 102.

117. Nicole Etcheson, *Bleeding Kansas: Contested Liberty in the Civil War Era* (Lawrence: University Press of Kansas, 2004), 28, 57–58, 95, 148.

118. Etcheson, 50, 67–68, 91–92, 131, 143, 158–159.

119. Lecompton Constitution, November 7, 1857, Kansas State Historical Society, https://www.kansasmemory.org/item/207409/text.

120. Etcheson, *Bleeding Kansas*, 31.

121. Daniel Wilder, *Annals of Kansas, New Edition, 1541–1885* (Topeka: T. Dwight Thacker, Kansas Publishing House, 1886), 48, 49, https://archive.org/details/annalsofkansasoowild. The town of Atchison was named after US senator David Rice Atchison from Missouri, one of the most vocal pro-slavery advocates. He led pro-slavery troops, encouraged Missourians to enter Kansas and vote illegally, and sought money and pro-slavery settlers from the South. See https://www.kshs.org/kansapedia/david-rice-atchison/16725 (accessed April 12, 2023).

122. Etcheson, *Bleeding Kansas*, 94, 119, 93.

123. Oretha Ruetti, *It Happened Here: Stories from Marshall County Kansas*, comp. Marshall County Historical Society (Hillsboro, KS: Print Source Direct, 2002), 67.

124. Etcheson, *Bleeding Kansas*, 153–155, 52–53, 56–57, 164.

125. Etcheson, 31, 43.

126. Etcheson, 59, 66, 72–75, 78.

127. Etcheson, 101, 126.

128. Biased toward the Free Staters, Daniel Wilder nevertheless provides a graphic daily account of the chaos in his *Annals of Kansas*, 41–310.

129. Etcheson, *Bleeding Kansas*, 104–105.

130. Etcheson, 108–109.

131. James Hanway's account of the Pottawatomie massacre, James Hanway Collection, no. 372, manuscript vol. 1856, https://www.kansasmemory.org/item/90225 (accessed April 12, 2023).

132. Ruetti, *It Happened Here*, 63.

133. Forter, *History of Marshall County*, 65.

134. Forter, 66.

135. The description is based on a scale model displayed at the Marshall County Historical Society in Marysville, KS.

136. Ruetti, *It Happened Here*, 65.

137. Cutler, "Marshall County, pt. 4," in *History of the State of Kansas*, http://kancoll.org/books/cutler/marshall/marshall-co-p4.html#MARYSVILLE.

138. Ruetti, *It Happened Here*, 67.

139. "Kansas Meeting," *Cadiz Sentinel*, March 14, 1855, 3, database with images, Newspapers.com.

140. Ruetti, *It Happened Here*, 111; George Schiller, foreword to "The Abolitionist: A Saga of the Albert Gallatin Family in Early Kansas," http://www.kancoll.org/books/schiller2/gws_foreword.htm (accessed April 12, 2023).

141. Ruetti, *It Happened Here*, 111.

142. Schiller, foreword to "The Abolitionist."

143. Schiller, "The Abolitionist," 56, http://www.kancoll.org/books/schiller2/gws_ch05.htm.

144. *The Frankfort Story: A History of Frankfort, Kansas and Surrounding Communities Honoring Frankfort's Centennial in 1967*, comp. Maynie Shearer Bush assisted by Winifred Shearer (n.p., sponsored by Frankfort Chamber of Commerce in cooperation with Frankfort Centennial Inc., n.d.), 119.

145. Paul Kessinger, "Kansas' Birthday a Reminder of Marshall County's Role in Earliest Days," *Marysville Advocate*, January 31, 2018, https://www.marysvilleonline.net/news/kansas-birthday-a-reminder-of-marshall-county-s-role-in-earliest-days/article_2b7200a2-06a7-11e8-a3fa-975c74c76112.html. The article reports on a presentation by Beth Skinner of the Marshall County Historical Society on January 17, 2011. See also Schiller, "The Abolitionist," 61, http://www.kancoll.org/books/schiller2/gws_ch06.htm.

146. Etcheson, *Bleeding Kansas*, 141–142, 147–150, 153–156.

147. "F. J. Marshall," http://kansasboguslegislature.org/members/marshall_f_j.html (accessed April 12, 2023).

148. Cutler, "Marshall County," in *History of the State of Kansas*.

149. Wilder, *Annals of Kansas*, 13. See also "Census of Another Ruffian Stronghold," *Weekly News-Democrat* (Emporia, KS), March 6, 1858, 2, database with images, Newspapers.com.

150. Helmut Walser Smith, ed., introduction to *Oxford Handbook of Modern German History*, 4.

151. CT Humanities Project, "Slavery and Abolition—Connecticut History," https://connecticuthistory.org/topics-page/slavery-and-abolition/ (accessed April 12, 2023).

152. 1840 Federal Census, Connecticut, Litchfield County, Plymouth Township, census summary, 39–40, database with images, Ancestry.com, citing *Sixth Census of the United States*, 1840, microfilm publication M704, Records of the Bureau of the Census, Record Group 29, National Archives, Washington, DC.

153. "F. J. Marshall," http://kansasboguslegislature.org/members/marshall_f_j.html (accessed April 12, 2023).

154. Etcheson, *Bleeding Kansas*, 163–165, 184, 205–206, 224.

155. 1859 Kansas Territory Census, Marshall County, Vermillion Township, p. 1, database with images, Ancestry.com, citing microfilm reel K-1, Kansas State Historical Society.

156. Rev. A. Stapleton, *Annals of the Evangelical Association of North America and History of the United Evangelical Church* (Harrisburg, PA: Publishing House of the United Evangelical Church, 1895), 333, https://www.lycoming.edu/umarch/books/ANNALS.htm.

157. William D. Keel, "Deitch, Däätsch, Düütsch and Dietsch: The Varieties of Kansas German Dialects after 150 Years of German Group Settlement in Kansas," in *Yearbook of German-American Studies*, supplemental issue 2, *Preserving Heritage: A Festschrift for C. Richard Beam* (Lawrence, KS: Society for German-American Studies, 2006), 27–48, https://doi.org/10.17161/ygas.v2i.

158. Wilder, *Annals of Kansas*, 160–161.

159. Heiss, *Census of the Territory of Kansas*, map insert between pp. 15 and 16, 23–26.

160. Etcheson, *Bleeding Kansas*, 110.

161. See Voting Districts 2, 3, 4, 12, 13 and 15 (combined), and 16 in 1855 Kansas Territory Census.

162. Etcheson, *Bleeding Kansas*, 190–206.

163. J. George Lodholz to friends, November 3, 1857.

164. Lodholz to friends, November 3, 1857.

165. Eleanor L. Turk, "Selling the Heartland: Agents, Agencies, Press and Policies Promoting German Emigration to Kansas in the Nineteenth Century," *Kansas History* 12, 3 (Autumn 1989): 156.

166. Georg to family, December 10, 1857.

167. Georg to family, December 26, 1857.

168. Forter, *History of Marshall County*, 1010.

169. "Guittard Station, Kansas," https://legendsofkansas.com/guittard-station-kansas (accessed April 12, 2023).

170. Unfortunately, Georg's application no longer exists. Records of the Kickapoo Land Office and those of several other land offices were consolidated at the Topeka Land

Office, which suffered a fire in 1869. Any records from the Kickapoo Land Office that might still exist would be archived at the US Department of the Interior, and research into its holdings shows no records from the relevant period.

171. See Samuel J. Reader, watercolor of his staking a claim, July 26, 1855, https://www.kshs.org/kansapedia/portrait-of-a-pioneer-staking-a-claim/10246.

172. Louise Barry, *The Beginning of the West: Annals of the Kansas Gateway to the American West 1540–1854* (Topeka: Kansas State Historical Society, 1972), 1227; *Portrait and Biographical Album of Marshall County* (Chicago: Chapman Brothers, 1889), 375, https://archive.org/details/portraitbiograph20chap. Thomas Waterson reported to his biographer that he made a preemptive claim "by driving a clapboard in the ground and writing his name upon it, and laying the foundation of a home by crossing four poles." It appears that this was the convention.

173. J. Butler Chapman, *History of Kansas and Emigrants' Guide* (Akron, OH: Teesdale, Elkins, 1855), 41, https://archive.org/details/GR_647.

174. Kansas Kickapoo Tribe, "History and Language Resources: Treaties," https://www.ktik-nsn.gov/history/treaties/ (accessed April 12, 2023); Treaty with the Kickapoo, 1832, article 1, in Kappler, *Indian Affairs*, 365.

175. Forter, *History of Marshall County*, 47.

176. At a 1916 meeting of the Old Settlers and Pioneer Association (organized in 1870), the principal speaker described settlers' attitudes: "During those years, when the white men were traveling through Kansas, they were not making settlements here. The country remained in the undisputed possession of the Indians; the white men did not want it as yet. They looked upon these vast prairies not as a resource, but as so much land to be crossed in reaching places further west. But changing conditions in the states east of the Mississippi river made people begin to look upon Kansas in a different light. The country there was becoming thickly settled and people wanted the lands of the Indians. As the Indians had all been removed to these western plains, the white man could not settle on these reservations without the consent of the Indians. According to the treaties, the Indians were promised their land so long as grass should grow or water run. But it soon developed that the white man wanted Kansas land. Also, in the year 1854, we find the tribes being transferred to the Indian territory, now Oklahoma, where the remnants of various tribes still remain." Forter, *History of Marshall County*, 57.

177. Hibbard, *History of the Public Land Policies*, 141–142.

178. Barry, *Beginning of the West*, 1196.

179. In preparing this book, I reviewed all 500 biographies in *Portrait and Biographical Album of Marshall County* (published in 1889), the 291 biographies in Forter's *History of Marshall County* (published in 1917), and the few biographies in *The Frankfort Story*. There is little overlap; only twenty-two individuals have biographies in more than one of these works. The population of Marshall County was 23,912 in 1890 and 22,730 in 1920, so the percentage of the population represented by these biographies is small. Even so, the biographies are extremely detailed, giving background information about the individual (almost invariably male) from birth, his parents or sometimes even earlier ancestors dating back to the Revolutionary War, his wife from birth, and her parents and other ancestors. So each biography can cover a considerable number of people. The population samples are skewed toward those who survived and prospered to a greater or

lesser degree, but inclusion depended on many factors. Publishers of the *Album* sent out a "corps of writers" to personally interview individuals, but some refused, some were indifferent, some could not be found, and some declined to cooperate because a family member objected (*Portrait and Biographical Album*, 9). It seems that Forter included people she personally knew or knew about. Many important individuals mentioned elsewhere in her history who were still alive when she published the book did not get a biography. Godfrey Lodholz has a biography in the *Album*; Henry Reb, who will be introduced shortly, is included in Forter.

180. *Portrait and Biographical Album*, 243.
181. *Portrait and Biographical Album*, 375.
182. *Portrait and Biographical Album*, 254.
183. Forter, *History of Marshall County*, 882.
184. *Portrait and Biographical Album*, 552.
185. Georg Lodholz to family, partial letter, circa fall 1857, trans. Virginia L. Lewis, LRFC.
186. Forter, *History of Marshall County*, 10.
187. C. A. Weslager, *The Log Cabin in America: From Pioneer Days to the Present* (New Brunswick, NJ: Rutgers University Press, 1969), 19, 86, 210.
188. Joanna Stratton, *Pioneer Women: Voices from the Kansas Frontier* (New York: Simon & Schuster, 1981), 86.
189. Stratton, 61.
190. Weslager, *Log Cabin in America*, 14.
191. Weslager, 14.
192. This type of construction was used for the log cabin I viewed at Blackberry Farm in Aurora, Illinois, which is operated by the Fox Valley Park District.
193. Forter, *History of Marshall County*, 59.
194. Weslager, *Log Cabin in America*, 16, 17.
195. Weslager, 14–15.
196. Stratton, *Pioneer Women*, 50–51.
197. See the descriptions in Hannah Anderson Ropes, *Six Months in Kansas* (Boston: John P. Jewett, 1856; facsimile ed., Wentworth Press, n.d.), 51, 61.
198. Georg to family, December 26, 1857.
199. Georg Lodholz to family from Atchison, circa 1859, trans. Virginia L. Lewis, LRFC.
200. Statement of account by Friedrich Lodholz to Gottfried Lodholz, circa 1871, trans. Gottfried Lodholz, probate records for John George Lodholz, Marshall County District Court, Marysville, KS, letter 6.
201. *Portrait and Biographical Album*, 489.
202. Forter, *History of Marshall County*, 1010.
203. *Portrait and Biographical Album*, 489.
204. Sandra L. Myres, *Westering Women and the Frontier Experience: 1800–1915* (Albuquerque: University of New Mexico Press, 1982), 141.

Chapter 3. Life in Kansas and Connecticut, 1859–61

1. J. Neale Carman, *Foreign-Language Units of Kansas*, vol. 1, *Historical Atlas and Statistics* (Lawrence: University of Kansas Press, 1962), 4.

2. John D. Unruh Jr., *The Plains Across: The Overland Emigrants and the Trans-Mississippi West, 1840–60* (Urbana: University of Illinois Press, 1979), 260.

3. Birthplace of father, Helena C. Rebb, Standard Certificate of Death 583845, filed May 4, 1931, State of Kansas, Office of Vital Statistics.

4. Emma Forter, *History of Marshall County: Its People, Industries and Institutions* (Indianapolis: B. F. Bowen, 1917), 1010–1011, https://archive.org/details/history ofmar.

5. Walter F. Willcox, *International Migrations*, vol. 2, *Interpretations* (Cambridge, MA: National Bureau of Economic Research, 1931), 347, https://www.nber.org/books-and-chapters/international-migrations-volume-i-statistics.

6. Kaiserslautern was the main center of revolutionary activity in the Palatinate. Though hardly in favor of the 1849 revolution that temporarily created an independent government, Otto Fleischmann provides a detailed timeline of events in *Geschichte des Pfälzischern Aufstandes im Jahre 1849* (Kaiserslautern: Buchdruckeri von Emil Thieme, 1899), 110, 113, 121, 340–341, https://archive.org/details/geschichtedespfo1fleigoog. For a more recent and more objective account of the uprisings in the Palatinate, see Jonathan Sperber, *Rhineland Radicals: The Democratic Movement and the Revolution of 1848–1849* (Princeton, NJ: Princeton University Press, 1991).

7. R. R. Palmer, *A History of the Modern World*, 2nd ed., revised with the collaboration of Joel Colton (New York: Alfred A. Knopf, 1964), 512–513.

8. Heinrich arrived in February 1858, too late to participate in the census of voters conducted earlier that year. 1859 Kansas Territory Census, Marshall County, Vermillion Township, p. 1, database with images, Ancestry.com, citing microfilm reel K-1, Kansas State Historical Society.

9. Forter, *History of Marshall County*, 159, 281.

10. E. M. Putney, "Echoes of '56 and '57 and the Drought of '60," *Frankfort Index*, September 8, 1913, 6, database with images, Newspapers.com.

11. W. C. Martin, *History of Warren County, Iowa: From Its Earliest Settlement to 1908* (Chicago: S. J. Clarke, 1908), 360.

12. Letter from Jacob Lockridge to Henry Rebb, July 10, 1865, in the family's possession.

13. Oregon-California Trails Association, "Outfitting for the Trail," https://www.octa-trails.org/articles/outfitting-for-the-trail/ (accessed April 9, 2023).

14. Randolph Marcy, *The Prairie Traveler: A Handbook for Overland Expedition* (New York: Harper & Brothers, 1859), chaps. 1, 3.

15. *The Frankfort Story: A History of Frankfort, Kansas and Surrounding Communities Honoring Frankfort's Centennial in 1967*, comp. Maynie Shearer Bush assisted by Winifred Shearer (n.p., n.d.), 119, sponsored by Frankfort Chamber of Commerce in cooperation with Frankfort Centennial Inc.

16. *Portrait and Biographical Album of Marshall County* (Chicago: Chapman Brothers, 1889), 319, https://archive.org/details/portraitbiograph20chap.

17. *Frankfort Story*, 125.

18. Forter, *History of Marshall County*, 1010.

19. John Arkas Hawgood, *The Tragedy of German-America* (New York: Arno Press, New York Times, 1970), 22, 23. Hawgood is hardly the only scholar to emphasize this point. See, for example, Linda Pickle, *Contented among Strangers: Rural German-Speaking Women and Their Families in the Nineteenth-Century Midwest* (Urbana: University of Illinois Press, 1996), 8.

20. This figure does not include ten who were Catholic missionaries serving at a school. 1855 Kansas Territory Census, database with images, Ancestry.com, citing microfilm reel K-1, Kansas State Historical Society.

21. Walter D. Kamphoefner, *Germans in America: A Concise History* (Lanham, MD: Rowman & Littlefield, 2021), 200.

22. Marian L. Smith, "'Any Woman Who Is Now or May Hereafter Be Married . . .': Women and Naturalization, ca. 1802–1940," *Prologue* 30, 2 (Summer 1998), https://www.archives.gov/publications/prologue/1998/summer/women-and-naturalization-1.html.

23. Carman, *Foreign-Language Units of Kansas*, 1:4.

24. Lockridge to Rebb, July 10, 1865. Although the letter was written in 1865, it is not clear when Lockridge left Nebraska, given that Heinrich arrived in Kansas in 1857.

25. "Jacob G. Lockridge," https://ancestors.familysearch.org/en/2ZS4-SJV/jacob-g-lockridge-1837-1924 (accessed April 12, 2023).

26. Horse stealing was common at this time. A Lawrence, Kansas, newspaper reported: "Ordinarily, whenever a horse is stolen in the country, it is the habit of the local press to make mention of the same, but horse stealing has become the rule rather than the exception in Kansas, and to mention them all would be an impossibility." *Kansas Herald of Freedom*, July 17, 1858, 3, database with images, Newspapers.com.

27. Kansas Historical Society, "Bleeding Kansas," https://www.kshs.org/kansapedia/bleeding-kansas/15145 (accessed April 12, 2023).

28. Map of Douglas County, Kansas, July 4, 1857, item no. 217187, Kansas State Historical Society, https://www.kansasmemory.org/item/display.php?item_id=217187&f=.

29. Wakarusa was chosen as an example because its boundaries remained substantially the same in 1860 as in 1857.

30. Allan G. Bogue, *From Prairie to Corn Belt: Farming on the Illinois and Iowa Prairies in the Nineteenth Century*, 2nd ed. (Lanham, MD: Ivan R. Dee, 2011), 21, 25.

31. Paul W. Gates, *The Farmer's Age: Agriculture 1815–1860* (New York: Holt, Rinehart & Winston, 1960), 23–30, 42–43. Interestingly, the Pennsylvania Dutch—descendants of German emigrants from the 1600s—followed good farming practices, including spreading manure and rotating crops, and thereby maintained the productivity of their soil (Gates, 43). Settlers in Kansas, in contrast, showed a general lack of care for the land, and decades later, soil depletion became a problem in the state. See George E. Putnam, "The Land Credit Problem," *Bulletin of the University of Kansas Humanistic Studies* 2, 2 (1916): 16, https://kuscholarworks.ku.edu/handle/1808/6489.

32. Bogue, *From Prairie to Corn Belt*, 16.

33. This categorization of German demographics covers almost all situations, but there were cases in which a particular individual, couple, or family fit more than one

category, such as a couple serving in the house of a native-born. In these cases I chose the category that seemed the most salient for purposes of this discussion.

34. Individuals not identifiable as spouses or other relatives, but similar in age and with the same last name, were considered to be siblings.

35. The oldest couples were aged sixty-five and sixty in Pottawatomie County and fifty-seven and sixty-five (the wife being older) in Davis County. The couple in Pottawatomie was living next door to a son, which was rare among couples at this time.

36. "Average Number of Children per U.S. Family (Historic)," https://populationeducation.org/wp-content/uploads/2020/04/average-number-children-per-us-family-historic-infographic.pdf (accessed April 12, 2023).

37. In a negligible number of cases, the birthplace of the first child was missing from the census records or the child was born in a foreign country.

38. James R. Shortridge, *Peopling the Plains: Who Settled Where in Frontier Kansas* (Lawrence: University Press of Kansas, 1995), 10–11, table 1.1. The distribution of German families whose first child was born in America mirrors the distribution by collection unit/culture area of all residents included in the state census of 1865.

39. The Northeast collection unit/culture area consists of Connecticut, Maine, Massachusetts, Michigan, Minnesota, New Hampshire, New York, Rhode Island, and Wisconsin; the North Midland consists of Delaware, Illinois, Indiana, Iowa, Nebraska, New Jersey, Ohio, and Pennsylvania; the Upper South consists of Arkansas, District of Columbia, Kentucky, Maryland, Missouri, North Carolina, Tennessee, Virginia, and West Virginia (in 1860 West Virginia had not yet split off from Virginia); the Lower South consists of Alabama, Florida, Georgia, Louisiana, Mississippi, South Carolina, and Texas; and the West consists of California, Colorado, Idaho, Nevada, New Mexico, Oregon, and Utah. Shortridge, *Peopling the Plains*, 10–11, table 1.1.

40. Jochen Krebber, *Württemberger in Nordamerika: Migration von der Schwäbischen Alb im 19. Jahrhundert* (Stuttgart: Franz Steiner Verlag, 2014),137, 179–182, 233, 263.

41. "Im März verbreitete sich auch über Würtemberg die Grippe, von welcher ganz Deutschland heimgesucht wurde," in *Württembergische Jahrbücher für vaterländische Geschichte, Geographie, Statistik und Topographie* (1838), 22.

42. Christian Jansen, "The Formation of German Nationalism, 1740–1850," in *The Oxford Handbook of Modern German History*, ed. Helmut Walser Smith (Oxford: Oxford University Press, 2011), 239.

43. Bernhard Mann, *Die Württemberger und die deutsche Nationalversammlung 1848/49* (Düsseldorf: Droste Verlage, 1975), 9, https://archive.org/details/diewurttembergeroooomann/page/n3/mode/2up.

44. See the minutes of the major debate that took place on October 26, 1848. Mitchell Allen and Michael Hughes, eds., *German Parliamentary Debates, 1848–1933* (New York: Peter Lang, 2003), 31–99.

45. US Department of the Interior, "Eighth Census, U.S., Instructions," https://www2.census.gov/programs-surveys/decennial/technical-documentation/questionnaires/1860/1860-instructions.pdf (accessed April 12, 2023).

46. In a few townships, the entries specified Germany but the state of birth was written too small to decipher, even under magnification.

47. Jansen, "Formation of German Nationalism," 236.

48. Eleanor L. Turk, "Germans in Kansas," *Kansas History* 28 (Spring 2005): 47.

49. Roughly, this was a division between Low German and High German dialects. The Lodholzes spoke one of the latter (Swabian), but they would have been taught standard High German in school, as it was considered the lingua franca for communication between individuals whose native dialects differed. It was also used in formal writing and other written communications. Pickle provides examples of the conflicts caused by linguistic, religious, and class differences in *Contented among Strangers*, 8.

50. See Kamphoefner, *Germans in America*, 75–88; J. Neale Carman, "Continental Europeans in Rural Kansas: 1854–1861," in *Territorial Kansas: Studies Commemorating the Centennial* (Lawrence: University of Kansas Publications, 1954), 176–193.

51. James M. Estes, ed. and trans., *Godly Magistrates and Church Order: Johannes Brenz and the Establishment of the Lutheran Territorial Church in Germany, 1524–1558* (Toronto: Centre for Reformation and Renaissance Studies, 2001), 4–5.

52. The Lutheran Church–Missouri Synod, "History," https://www.lcms.org/about/lcms-history (accessed April 12, 2023). See also Stan M. Landry, "German 'Worship Wars' and the 1830 Anniversaries of the Augsburg Confession," *Lutheran Quarterly* 26 (2012): 390.

53. Mack Walker, *Germany and the Emigration: 1816–1885* (Cambridge, MA: Harvard University Press, 1964), 78.

54. United Church of Christ, "The German Reformed Church," https://www.ucc.org/about-us_short-course_the-german-reformed-church (accessed April 12, 2023).

55. Its history is a microcosm of the mergers, disagreements, and splitting off that characterized Lutheranism in the United States. See Frederick Bente, *American Lutheranism*, vol. 2, *The United Lutheran Church (General Synod, General Council, United Synod in the South)* (St. Louis: Concordia Publishing House, 1919), 2–21, https://archive.org/details/americanluthera02bent.

56. The Reverend Richard Rhoades, First Evangelical Lutheran Church, Galveston, TX, email to author, December 22, 2021. The church is still very much in existence.

57. "Report of the Preacher Wendt in Galveston in Texas Regarding the General Synod in Winchester," trans. Virginia L. Lewis, LRFC.

58. In 1858 the German Evangelical Association reported a membership of thirty-two thousand. W. W. Orwig, *History of the Evangelical Association*, vol. 1, *From the Origin of the Association to the End of the Year 1845*, trans. from German (Cleveland, OH: Charles Hammer for the Evangelical Association, 1858), 401, https://archive.org/details/EVwmHistoryOfTheEvangelicalAssociationByWWOrwig/.

59. *Encyclopedia Britannica*, 11th ed., vol. 9, s.v. "Evangelical Association" (Cambridge: Cambridge University Press, 1910), 960, https://archive.org/details/encyclopaediabrit09chisrich; "Albright Brethren," in *Catholic Encyclopedia*, vol. 1 (New York: Encyclopedia Press, 1913), https://ecatholic2000.com/cathopedia/vol1/volone387.shtml.

60. In J. Neal Carman and associates, *Foreign-Language Units of Kansas*, vol. 2, *Account of Settlement and Settlements in Kansas* (Lawrence: University Press of Kansas, 1974), both denominations are classified as pietistic, with the only difference being language. Copy of original manuscript, 96, https://kuscholarworks.ku.edu/handle/1808/7160?show=full (accessed April 12, 2023).

61. W. Harrison Daniel, "Wilhelm Nast (1807–1899): Founder of German-Speaking

Methodism in America and Architect of the Methodist Episcopal Church Mission in Europe," *Methodist History* 39, 3 (April 2001): 154–156, https://archives.gcah.org/bitstream/handle/10516/6506/MH-2001-April-Daniel.pdf.

62. Kamphoefner, *Germans in America*, 80.

63. Although Forter took great pains to discuss the many churches in Marshall County, the only mention of the German Evangelical Association is in the biography of Henry Reb. Forter, *History of Marshall County*, 1012. The association, however, recruited adherents across the country. Many nineteenth-century newspaper archives begin in the early 1880s (later than the arrival of the Lodholzes and Heinrich Reb), but they indicate a vigorous outreach. Congregations existed in Brooklyn, New York, where the association had 1,806 members in 1893 ("In Convention," *Standard Union*, June 28, 1893, 2); in Kansas City ("Town Topics," *Leavenworth Post*, March, 17, 1911, 6); in Streator, Illinois ("Decided to Build," *Streator Free Press*, March 8, 1906, 4); in San Bernardino, California ("The Churches," *San Bernardino County Sun*, April 21, 1907, 10); in Pittsburgh ("In Annual Conference," *Pittsburgh Daily Post*, March 10, 1899, 2); in Indianapolis ("The Church Workers," *Indianapolis Journal*, September 6, 1891, 8); and in Green Bay, Wisconsin ("Quarterly Meeting of Association to Be Held," *Green Bay Press-Gazette*, March 17, 1910, afternoon ed., 5). The German Evangelical Association also had adherents in other Kansas towns; the closest was in Hanover in Washington County, just west of Marshall, where a class was organized in 1870 and, after a bit of a struggle, a church was built in 1879. The association also built a church in Leavenworth in 1861, and in 1882 it had forty members. Carman, *Foreign-Language Units of Kansas*, 2:461, 466, 600. The association was gaining in popularity elsewhere in Kansas too, including Salina ("A New Pastor," *National Field*, August 14, 1891, 5), Eudora ("Eudora and Vicinity," *Eudora Weekly News*, March 21, 1895, 3), and Peach Grove ("New Church at Peach Grove," *Randolph Enterprise*, August 29, 1912, 1).

64. Orwig, *History of the Evangelical Association*, 157, 161, 277.

65. Orwig, 401.

66. Krebber, *Württemberger in Nordamerika*, 125.

67. *Fifty Years in the Kansas Conference, 1864–1914: A Record of the Origin and Development of the West of the Evangelical Association in the territory covered by the Kansas Conference* (Cleveland, OH: Press of Evangelical Association, n.d.), 14–19, 65, https://archive.org/details/fiftyyearsinkansooevan. The letters sent by the missionaries for printing in one of the Association's organs give vivid descriptions of the primitive conditions at the time.

68. "Nobody seems to want to go to Kansas." Friedrich Lodholz to family, partial letter, November 1858, trans. Freda Murray, LRFC.

69. Carman, "Continental Europeans in Rural Kansas," 190–191.

70. Carman, 178–179.

71. See Linda Schelbitski Pickle, "Rural German-Speaking Women in Early Nebraska and Kansas: Ethnicity as a Factor in Frontier Adaptation," *Great Plains Quarterly* 9, 4 (Fall 1989): 248, https://www.jstor.org/stable/23531115.

72. 1860 Federal Census, Brown County, Kansas Territory, Lockwin Township, Schedule 1, p. 61, dwelling 487, family 445, line 22, database with images, Ancestry.com, citing *Eighth Census of the United States, 1860*, microfilm publication M653, vol. 1, roll 347.

73. 1860 Federal Census, Wyandotte County, Kansas Territory, Wyandotte Township, Schedule 1, p. 18, dwelling 129, family 140, line 5.

74. 1860 Federal Census, Riley County, Kansas Territory, Township Not Stated, Schedule 1, p. 24A, dwelling 234, family 200, line 6.

75. 1860 Federal Census, Jefferson County, Kansas Territory, Jefferson Township, Schedule 1, p. 27, dwelling 218, family 181, line 23.

76. 1860 Federal Census, Atchison County, Kansas Territory, Atchison, Schedule 1, p. 8, Peter Young, dwelling 527, family 496, line 8.

77. 1860 Federal Census, Leavenworth County, Kansas Territory, Leavenworth, Schedule 1, p. 8, George Ernstein, dwelling 72, family 74, line 17.

78. 1860 Federal Census, Leavenworth County, Kansas Territory, Leavenworth, Schedule 1, p. 29, Charles Soongood, dwelling 279, family 264, line 37; p. 113, Mise Fresburg, dwelling 1122, family 1012, line 1; p. 116, Augustus Connor, dwelling 1161, family 1045, line 36.

79. 1860 Federal Census, Leavenworth County, Kansas Territory, Leavenworth, Schedule 1, p. 176, John Schous, dwelling 1741, family 1525, line 30.

80. 1860 Federal Census, Leavenworth County, Kansas Territory, Leavenworth, Schedule 1, p. 27, A. M. Sattig, dwelling 257, family 246, line 35.

81. 1860 Federal Census, Davis County, Kansas Territory, Ft. Riley Reserve, Schedule 1, p. 79, dwelling 733, family 622, line 3.

82. By the time of the 1880 federal census, the birthplaces of an individual's parents were listed, showing that, more often than not, a native-born spouse had German-born parents.

83. In one instance, a mother was present.

84. 1860 Federal Census, Davis County, Kansas Territory, Junction Township, p. 52, William Becker, M. Helsburg, F. Flatz, dwelling 493, family 415, lines 37–39.

85. 1860 Federal Census, Davis County, Kansas Territory, Junction Township, Kansas Territory, p. 52, P. Schoenthaler, H. Nurce, F. Slumff, dwelling 487, family 410, lines 17–19.

86. 1860 Federal Census, Johnson County, Kansas Territory, Desoto Township, p. 20, J. H. Jacobs, E. Phillipps, dwelling 118, family 124, lines 14, 15.

87. 1860 Federal Census, Leavenworth County, Kansas Territory, Leavenworth, p. 10, John Brandon, Henry Gotater, John Storms, dwelling 90, family 92, lines 38–40.

88. 1860 Federal Census, Leavenworth County, Kansas Territory, Leavenworth, p. 39, Sophia Prisitz, dwelling 374, family 344, line 10; p. 173, Bridget Kalmers, Emma Kalmers (?), Mary Burchman, dwelling 1707, family 1492, lines 16–18.

89. Carman, "Continental Europeans in Rural Kansas," 176–193. Other Germans who settled at the same time as the Lodholzes traveled much farther west than Marshall County. For example, there was a settlement along Lyon Creek in Davis (now Geary) County, almost halfway across what is now the state of Kansas. The settlement did not start out as an exclusively German colony, but Germans gradually became the predominant ethnic group beginning in the late 1850s. The earliest German settler, Herman Oesterreich, was born in Prussia and came to Kansas from Watertown, Wisconsin, in 1856. In describing his search for a place to claim, he stated: "I could not get through along the creek on account of the grass, as high as my head, and the tangle of grape and hop

vines." Clara M. Fengel Shields, "The Lyon Creek Settlement," ed. William E. Connelley, *Collections of the Kansas State Historical Society* 14 (1918): 143, 146, https://archive.org/details/collectionsofkan14kans/page/134/mode/2up?q=Shields.

90. Walker, *Germany and the Emigration*, 51.
91. Forter, *History of Marshall County*, 455.
92. *Portrait and Biographical Album*, 469.
93. Forter, *History of Marshall County*, 455.
94. Carman, "Continental Europeans in Rural Kansas," 186; Shortridge, *Peopling the Plains*, 33.
95. Forter, *History of Marshall County*, 170. In the 1860 census, H. Lenker's name is given as "Henry Lumbes." 1860 Federal Census, Marshall County, Kansas Territory, Marysville, p. 52, dwelling 443, family 443, line 31.
96. Carman, "Continental Europeans in Rural Kansas," 186–187.
97. Forter, *History of Marshall County*, 170. In 1860 Hepperman was living with Herman Karst, another immigrant from Hanover, and close to three other single men from the same German state: Emil Hoeffer, George Detrich, and Martin Gillets. 1860 Federal Census, p. 52, dwellings 439 and 440, families 439 and 440, lines 16–20.
98. *Portrait and Biographical Album*, 516. In the 1860 census, only William Raemer and his family appear, and they are listed as coming from Baden. 1860 Federal Census, Marshall County, Kansas Territory, Marysville Township, pp. 52–53, dwelling 446, family 446, lines 38–20, 1–3. This is a case in which the settlers reported on the same page probably lived some distance from each other.
99. 1860 Federal Census, Marshall County, Kansas Territory, Marysville Township, p. 47.
100. 1860 Federal Census, Marshall County, Kansas Territory, Marysville Township, p. 55, Thomas McCoy, John Boardman, dwelling 468, family 468, lines 29–30; p. 58, Edward Kirch, dwelling 487, family 487, line 11.
101. 1860 Federal Census, Marshall County, Kansas Territory, Blue Rapids Township, pp. 7–8.
102. *Portrait and Biographical Album*, 491, 703, 268; *Frankfort Story*, 119.
103. 1860 Federal Census, Marshall County, Kansas Territory, Guittard Township, p. 42, dwelling 352, family 352, line 20, and dwelling 349, family 349, line 9.
104. The census marshals were instructed to obtain the figures from local tax assessments and then "add the proper amount to the assessment, so that the return should represent as well the true or intrinsic value as the inadequate sum generally attached to property for taxable purpose." From Report of the Eighth Census (1860), quoted in *Compendium of the Eleventh Census:1890*, pt. 3 (Washington, DC: US Government Printing Office, 1897), 947, https://babel.hathitrust.org/cgi/pt?id=iau.31858019288772&view=1up&seq=7&skin=2021&size=125&q1=real%20estate%20mortgages.
105. Bogue, *From Prairie to Corn Belt*, 21, 25.
106. *Portrait and Biographical Album*, 490.
107. In 1860, in addition to the population count, census takers collected information about agriculture, manufacturing, and social statistics. The only extant agricultural schedule for Marshall County is for Blue Rapids, which shows a heavy investment in livestock—oxen, horses, milk cows, and other cattle—as well as corn (the grain grown

almost exclusively) and Irish potatoes (as opposed to sweet potatoes). 1860 Federal Census, Schedule 4, Marshall County, Kansas Territory, Blue Rapids Township, database with images, Ancestry.com, citing *1860 Non-Population Schedules for Kansas, 1850–1880*, microfilm publication T1130, rolls 1–2, 5, 8–41, Records of the Bureau of the Census, Record Group 29, National Archives and Records Administration, Washington, DC.

108. North Carolina State Extension, "Helianthur maximiliani," https://plants.ces.ncsu.edu/plants/helianthus-maximiliani/ (accessed April 12, 2023).

109. Report of the Commissioner of Indian Affairs for 1854: US and Indian Relations, 11, https://digitalcommons.csumb.edu/hornbeck_usa_2_e/41.

110. The description of the night sky is based on a quotation from one of the female diarists and letter writers in Sandra L. Myres, *Westering Women and the Frontier Experience: 1800–1915* (Albuquerque: University of New Mexico Press, 1982), 29. The remainder is based on personal experience.

111. Xavier Guittard, the youngest son of George Guittard, recalled that when the whole family settled in the fall of 1857, their nearest neighbors were seventeen and twenty-two miles away. *Portrait and Biographical Album*, 617.

112. Anonymous, "Tallgrass Prairie, Fire and Grazing in the Prairie," National Park Service, https://www.nps.gov/tapr/learn/nature/fire-and-grazing-in-the-prairie.htm (accessed April 10, 2018).

113. The descriptions of farming techniques are based on myriad sources, including firsthand accounts in Forter, *History of Marshall County*; *Portrait and Biographical Album*; and *Frankfort Story*. For example, Daniel Leavitt, whose family settled near Barrett in 1855, described farming as follows: "The first reaper was a scythe and seeding was done by hand. The mother made a seed bag from either canvas or an old sheet and fastened around the father so as to make a bag in front to hold grain and seed was thrown from the bag. Right hand throwing to the left, and left hand throwing toward the right. Later standing grain was cut with a cradle which dropped it evenly." *Frankfort Story*, 124–125.

114. The earliest prairie plows were made of cast iron, but they quickly became dull and often broke apart. The heavy soil clung to parts of the plow it came in contact with, necessitating frequent stops to scrape it off. By 1849, the John Deere Company had a booming business in steel moldboard plows that were stronger and more efficiently designed.

115. Georg may have used German words to direct the oxen, but as he had bought them locally, the animals were probably used to the conventional terms used by native-born farmers.

116. Clarence W. Taber, *Breaking Sod on the Prairies: A Story of Early Days in Dakota* (Yonkers-on-Hudson, NY: World Book, 1927), 43.

117. J. Butler Chapman, *History of Kansas and Emigrants' Guide* (Akron, OH: Teesdale, Elkins, 1855), 77, https://archive.org/details/GR_647.

118. Chapman, 78.

119. Joanna Stratton, *Pioneer Women: Voices from the Kansas Frontier* (New York: Simon & Schuster, 1981), 59.

120. *Frankfort Story*, 5.

121. See Forter, *History of Marshall County*, 514, 541 (biographies of John Ellenbecker and Peter Stroyer).

122. *Frankfort Story*, 72.

123. *Frankfort Story*, 10.

124. *Frankfort Story*, 72.

125. The original missionaries to the Otoes were Baptist, but the Presbyterians later established a presence. *Nebraska: A Guide to the Cornhusker State*, comp. Federal Writer's Project, Works Progress Administration, sponsored by Nebraska State Historical Society (New York: Hastings House, 1937; reprint, St. Clair Shores, MI: Scholarly Press, 1976), 268, 278, https://digitalcommons.unl.edu/nebraskianapubs/2/. In *Portrait and Biographical Album*, Byron Hill's biographer states that Hill's residence was on land formerly occupied by the Presbyterian Mission to the Otoes (267).

126. Forter, *History of Marshall County*, 267.

127. Anna Regina to girlfriends in Ebhausen, circa 1856, trans. Freda Murray, LRFC. She listed her friends at the end of the letter: Margaretha Barbara Lodholz, Christiana Kempf, Magdalena Hauser, Maria Katharina Glatz, Carolina Dengler, Katharina Barbara Pfeifte, Rosina Katharine Lodholz, Barbara Kempf, Heinerita Gutekunst, Katharine Gutekunst, Anna Maria Lodholz.

128. Meaning someone who could instill enthusiasm and strength. The full text reads: "We must remain watchful, so when the Lord comes at midnight he will find us awake! Also pray for me and for Bärbele, that we also receive abundant blessings from our study and from the weekly school, from our teacher—when we listen to him, we get so sleepy. You are a fire woman; therefore, you must heat us up—especially me." Christina Killinger to Anna Regina Lodholz, circa 1854, trans. Virginia L. Lewis, LRFC.

129. Descriptions are based on myriad sources, including several major studies of female pioneers on the Great Plains, especially Myres, *Westering Women*, chap. 6; Stratton, *Pioneer Women*, chap. 3; and the unnumbered chapters "A Home in the West: Pioneer Women Settling In" and "The Work of Women's Hands: Pioneer Women in Action," in Linda Peavy and Ursula Smith, *Pioneer Women: The Lives of Women on the Frontier* (Norman: University of Oklahoma Press, 1996).

130. "Historian Tells of More Early-Day Settlers in the Beattie Community," *Marshall County News*, August 4, 1949, 5, database with images, Newspapers.com.

131. Forter, *History of Marshall County*, 206.

132. Friedrich Lodholz to family, October 20, 1859, trans. Virginia L. Lewis, LRFC.

133. Forter, *History of Marshall County*, 220.

134. Forter, 60–61.

135. See Marjorie Sackert, "Kansas Pioneer Recipes," *Western Folklore* 22, 2 (April 1963): 103–104, https://doi.org/10.2307/1497875.

136. *Frankfort Story*, 4.

137. William H. Ukers, *All About Coffee* (New York: Tea and Coffee Trade Journal Company, 1922), 47, https://archive.org/details/allaboutcoffeeooukeruoft/page/47/mode/1up.

138. Ukers, 105, 113.

139. Martin Hall, who came to Marshall County in 1858 and married there, reported

to his biographer: "The first winter spent here after his marriage he and his wife lived for three months on corn coffee and hominy." *Portrait and Biographical Album*, 315.

140. Many years after the Lodholzes had already settled in Marshall County, Mary Jones, who came from Kentucky, wrote to her daughter (who had married a Reb) about the effects of the wind: "The wind blew so hard and the dust was so bad a boddy [sic] couldn't see. The dust was a half a inch deep on the floor and ain't any better today again." Letter in the family's possession.

141. For example, "Wells held the plow to break the prairie while Mrs. Wells drove the oxen, leaving their baby at the end of furrows." *Frankfort Story*, 122. Additional examples are cited in chapter 5.

142. Jon Gjerde, *The Minds of the West: Ethnocultural Evolution in the Rural Middle West 1830–1917* (Chapel Hill: University of North Carolina Press, 1997), 149–158.

143. Pickle, "Rural German-Speaking Women in Early Nebraska and Kansas," 239–251; Pickle, *Contented among Strangers*, 75, 201.

144. Kamphoefner, *Germans in America*, 165–166.

145. Gjerde, *Minds of the West*, 170–173.

146. Gjerde, 149.

147. Kamphoefner, *Germans in America*, 166. In addition, their employers might provide their room and board, thus relieving their own families of the expense.

148. Gjerde, *Minds of the West*, 167; Pickle, *Contented among Strangers*, 59.

149. Jon Gjerde, "The 'Would-be Patriarch' and the 'Self-made Man': Marcus Lee Hansen on Native and Immigrant Farmers in the American Middle West," in *On Distant Shores: Proceedings of the Marcus Lee Hansen Immigration Conference, Aalborg, Denmark, June 29–July 1, 1992*, ed. Birgit Flemming Larsen, Henning Bender, and Karen Veien (Aalborg, Denmark: Danes Worldwide Archives in collaboration with Danish Society for Emigration History, 1993), 39.

150. Gjerde, *Minds of the West*, 163; Pickle, *Contented among Strangers*, 181.

151. Pickle, *Contented among Strangers*, 81.

152. *Portrait and Biographical Album*, 490.

153. Forter, *History of Marshall County*, 159, 400.

154. Note that the role of domestic was not always gendered. Censuses list some males as domestics.

155. 1860 Federal Census, Marshall County, Kansas Territory, Vermillion Township, p. 20, Eliza Waller, dwelling 178, family 178, line 32.

156. 1860 Federal Census, Marshall County, Kansas Territory, Vermillion Township, p. 24, Emily Lathrop, dwelling 210, family 210, line 32.

157. Friedrich Lodholz to family, partial letter, November 1858, trans. Freda Murray, LRFC.

158. Friedrich to family, November 1858.

159. Richard Cordley, *Pioneer Days in Kansas* (New York: Pilgrim Press, 1903), 31, 32.

160. Friedrich to family, November 1858.

161. Friedrich Lodholz to family, circa January 1859, LRFC.

162. Friedrich Lodholz to family, September 2, 1859, trans. Virginia L. Lewis, LRFC.

163. Friedrich to family, November 1858.

164. Friedrich to family, circa January 1859.

165. Linda Richter, "'Could You Not Turn Your Back on This Hunger Country?' Food in the Migration Process of German Emigrants, 1816–1856," 25–26, https://thestacks.libaac.de/bitstream/handle/11858/2464/aspeers_05-2012_03_Richter.pdf?sequence=1&isAllowed=y (accessed April 12, 2023).

166. Friedrich to family, November 1858.

167. Friedrich Lodholz to family, March 28, 1859, trans. Freda Murray, LRFC.

168. Friedrich Lodholz to family, January 4, 1859, trans. Freda Murray, LRFC.

169. Friedrich Lodholz to family, partial New Year's greeting, circa January 1859, LRFC.

170. Friedrich Lodholz to family, January 30, 1859, trans. Freda Murray, LRFC.

171. Friedrich Lodholz to family, February 27, 1859, trans. Freda Murray, LRFC.

172. Friedrich to family, September 2, 1859.

173. Friedrich to family, September 2, 1859.

174. Friedrich to family, New Year's greeting, circa January 1859.

175. Friedrich Lodholz to family, circa spring 1859, LRFC.

176. Francis Atwater, *History of the Town of Plymouth, Connecticut* (Meriden, CT: Journal Publishing, 1895), 45–67, https://archive.org/details/historyoftownofp1895atwa.

177. It was customary to refer to individuals by their last name in the plural, thus, in effect, referring to the individual's whole family.

178. Atwater, *History of the Town of Plymouth*, 281.

179. Friedrich to family, New Year's greeting, circa January 1859.

180. Friedrich to family, November 1858.

181. Friedrich Lodholz to family, partial letter, circa January 1859 or 1860, LRFC.

182. Friedrich Lodholz to family, partial New Year's greeting, circa 1859–60, trans. Virginia L. Lewis, LRFC.

183. Friedrich to family, New Year's greeting, circa 1859–60.

184. Friedrich to family, November 1858.

185. Friedrich to family, New Year's greeting, circa January 1859.

186. Friedrich Lodholz to family, February 27, 1859, LRFC.

187. Friedrich to family, February 27, 1859.

188. Friedrich to family, February 27, 1859. There is a bit of snobbery here in the insistence on white flour, which was more expensive because it requires extra processing. The bran and germ must be removed, and the endosperm has to be softened with water to break its dark outer casing, which is then removed by sieving. White flour became the gold standard for baking. Today in the United States white flour may be further processed by bleaching.

189. Friedrich to family, September 2, 1859.

190. Friedrich to family, September 2, 1859.

191. Friedrich Lodholz to family, January 29, 1860, trans. Freda Murray, LRFC.

192. Friedrich Lodholz to family, January 9, 1859, trans. Freda Murray, LRFC.

193. Friedrich Lodholz to family, January 20, 1859, LRFC.

194. Friedrich to family, November 1858.

195. Friedrich to family, March 28, 1859.

196. Friedrich to family, January 4, 1859.

197. "The Mountain Meadows Massacre," *The American Experience*, https://www.pbs.org/wgbh/americanexperience/features/mormons-massacre/ (accessed April 12, 2023).

198. Friedrich to family, February 27, 1859.

199. George A. Root and Russell K. Hickman, "Pike's Peak Express Companies, Part 2," *Kansas History: A Journal of the Central Plains* 13, 4 (November 1944): 217–218, https://www.kshs.org/p/pike-s-peak-express-companies-2/12981.

200. My count is based on the 1860 federal census, at which time Arapahoe County (later in the Colorado Territory) was still considered part of Kansas, although counts from Arapahoe were not included in summaries of population figures for Kansas. 1860 Federal Census, Arapahoe County, Kansas Territory, database with images citing *Eighth Census of the United States*, 1860, microfilm copy no. 653, vol. 1A, roll 348.

201. Benjamin Horace Hibbard, *A History of the Public Land Policies* (New York: Macmillan, 1924; facsimile ed., Gale, n.d.), 165–166, 170.

202. Paul Wallace Gates, *Fifty Million Acres: Conflicts over Kansas Land Policy, 1854–1890* (Ithaca, NY: Cornell University Press, 1954; reprint, Norman: University of Oklahoma Press, 1977), 83.

203. Friedrich to family, January 4, 1859.

204. *Kansas Herald of Freedom* (Lawrence), July 17, 1858, 3. See also *Atchison Union*, April 21, 1860, 2; *Kansas Weekly Herald* (Leavenworth), September 19, 1857, 4, database with images, Newspapers.com.

205. 1860 Federal Census, Atchison County, Kansas Territory, Atchison, p. 43, Joseph Challys (NJ), dwelling 353, family 332, line 1; p. 68, George Challys (NJ), dwelling 536, family 505, line 11; p. 30, Michael Hampton (Ireland), dwelling 231, family 218, line 10; p. 57, W. H. Hyde (NH), dwelling 451, family 412, line 14; p. 34, H. B. Sacket (NY), dwelling 275, family 260, line 1; p. 51, William Martin, presumed (identification as a speculator is on the line above, listing a seven-year-old child [KY]), dwelling 418, family 369, line 38.

206. 1860 Federal Census, Leavenworth County, Kansas Territory, Leavenworth, p. 88, R. R. Gist (Poland), dwelling 881, family 799, line 24.

207. 1860 Federal Census, Douglas County, Kansas Territory, Lecompton, p. 167, R. McLackay (IN), dwelling 1360, family 1271, line 16.

208. 1860 Federal Census, Douglas County, Kansas Territory, Lawrence, p. 9, Charles Williamson, dwelling 68, family 72, line 38.

209. The value of small investors' real estate might not identify them as speculators. In contrast, large investors, who were often prominent individuals in their communities, can be identified as speculators based on the value of their landholdings. For example, the surveyor general of Kansas and Nebraska possessed $15,000 in real estate. 1860 Federal Census, Leavenworth County, Kansas Territory, Leavenworth, p. 56, Ward Bennett, dwelling 546, family 493, line 15. Likewise, the sheriff of Atchison had $10,000 worth of real estate. 1860 Federal Census, Atchison County, Kansas Territory, Atchison, p. 43, R. S. McCullen, dwelling 394, family 344, line 35.

210. Gates, *Farmer's Age*, 81.

211. Bogue, *From Prairie to Corn Belt*, 43.

212. Bogue, 43.

213. "The conveyance of the public land to settlers in the various methods prescribed

by law has incidentally led to the incurring of a considerable proportion of the mortgage debt in the states and territories concerned. The settlers have commonly been poor, and often have needed to borrow money with which to pay the fees and charges incidental to obtaining their titles. They have also to a great extent borrowed money with which to equip their farms and to begin the cultivation of the soil." This had consequences for years to come. In 1890 Kansas had "more mortgages in force on acre tracts [farms] than any other state." *Compendium of the Eleventh Census: 1890*, pt. 3 (Washington, DC: US Government Printing Office, 1897), 1003, 1007, https://babel.hathitrust.org/cgi/pt?id=iau.31858019288772&view=1up&seq=7&skin=2021&size=125&q1=real%20estate%20mortgages.

214. For example, *Weekly Leavenworth Herald*, March 10, 1860, 5; *Western Home Journal* (Lawrence, KS), January 5, 1860, 3, database with images, Newspapers.com.

215. William G. Murray, "An Economic Analysis of Farm Mortgages in Story County, Iowa 1854–1931," Iowa State College of Agriculture and Mechanic Arts, Research Bulletin 156 (January 1933), 364, https://dr.lib.iastate.edu/server/api/core/bitstreams/58507c8c-8c09-4cdd-a2bd-5848d53dedf5/content.

216. *Weekly Leavenworth Herald*, March 10, 1860, 3–5; *Topeka Tribune*, September 29, 1860, 2, database with images, Newspapers.com.

217. *Weekly Leavenworth Herald*, March 10, 1860, 1.

218. Gates, *Farmer's Age*, 81.

219. "West of the Mississippi river and north of Arkansas and Texas mortgage contracts, as commonly drawn, do not permit partial payments [on the principal], one of the chief reasons being that a large portion of the lenders are resident in the east, their loans are made for investment, and neither partial nor entire payment is desired as long as the interest is paid." *Compendium of the Eleventh Census: 1890*, pt. 3; Putnam, "Land Credit Problem," 34.

220. Bogue, *From Prairie to Corn Belt*, 37.

221. Friedrich to family, March 28, 1859.

222. Hibbard, *History of the Public Land Policies*, 121.

223. Hibbard, 127.

224. Friedrich to family, January 4, 1859.

225. Friedrich to family, January 9, 1859.

226. Senator Andrew Johnson from Tennessee would later become vice president and then president of the United States after Lincoln's assassination. On the public lands issue, he was one of the few southern politicians to favor cheap land for settlers.

227. Friedrich to family, January 30, 1859.

228. This person was probably Hezckea Gillert of New Haven, Connecticut. He is listed as an agent in the 1850 federal census, which may mean he acted for investors as well as for himself in loaning money to purchase land. He obviously thought land in the West was too risky at the time. 1850 Federal Census, New Haven County, Connecticut, City of New Haven, p. 466, dwelling 1387, family 2092, line 1, database with images, Ancestry.com, citing *Seventh Census of the United States, 1850*, microfilm publication M432, Records of the Bureau of the Census, Record Group 29, National Archives, Washington, DC.

229. Friedrich Lodholz to family, May 17, 1859, trans. Freda Murray, LRFC.

230. Friedrich Lodholz to family, May 24, 1859, trans. Virginia L. Lewis, LRFC.

231. Friedrich to family, September 2, 1859.

232. Gottfried (Godfrey) Lodholz, https://glorecords.blm.gov/results/default.aspx?searchCriteria=type=patent|st=KS|cty=|ln=Lodholz|fn=Godfrey|lo=18|sp=true|sw=true|s adv=false (accessed April 13, 2023); John G. (Georg) Lodholz, https://glorecords.blm.gov/results/default.aspx?searchCriteria=type=patent|st=KS|cty=|ln=Lodholz|fn=John|lo=18|sp=true|sw=true|sadv=false (accessed April 13, 2023).

233. Friedrich to family, January 29, 1860.

234. George W. Glick, "The Railroad Convention of 1860," ed. George W. Martin, *Transactions of the Kansas State Historical Society* 9 (1905–6): 468, https://archive.org/details/collectionsofkan09kans.

235. Friedrich Lodholz to family, October 30, 1859, trans. Virginia L. Lewis, LRFC.

236. Friedrich to family, October 30, 1859.

237. Friedrich to family, January 29, 1860.

238. Friedrich to family, October 30, 1859.

239. Friedrich to family, October 30, 1859.

240. Friedrich Lodholz to family, November 10, 1859, trans. Virginia L. Lewis, LRFC.

241. Friedrich to family, January 29, 1860.

242. George W. Glick, "The Drought of 1860," ed. George W. Martin, *Transactions of the Kansas State Historical Society* 9 (1905–6): 482–483, https://archive.org/details/collectionsofkan09kans.

243. Friedrich Lodholz to family, August 26, 1860, trans. Virginia L. Lewis, LRFC.

244. Friedrich Lodholz to family, December 8, 1861, trans. Virginia L. Lewis, LRFC.

245. Forter, *History of Marshall County*, 73.

246. Gottfried Lodholz to Heinrich Reb, January 8, 1864, trans. Virginia L. Lewis, LRFC.

247. Friedrich to family, August 26, 1860.

248. "News of the Day," *New York Times*, July 19, 1860, 4.

249. Marriage records of John George Lodholz and Wilhelmina Gertrude Wender and Anna R. Lodholz and Heinrich Reb, September 13, 1860, Marysville County Courthouse, Book O, p. 21. At the time, most couples were married by a justice of the peace, which was an elected office. In Ebhausen, church weddings had been the norm.

250. J. George Lodholz to friends, November 3, 1857, Probate Records for John George Lodholz, Marshall County District Court, Marysville, KS.

251. Friedrich Lodholz to family, January 14, 1861, trans. Freda Murray, LRFC.

252. Document no. 99654, accession no. MW-0942-222, Military Warrant, issue date October 1, 1860; document no. 13551, accession no. MW-0438-004, Military Warrant, issue date April 1861, https://glorecords.blm.gov/details/patent/default.aspx?accession=0438-004&docClass=MW&sid=xppppazb.lk1#patentDetailsTabIndex= (accessed April 13, 2023).

253. This description is based largely on Judith Walzer Leavitt, *Brought to Bed: Child-Bearing in America, 1850–1950* (New York: Oxford University Press, 1986), 37–38. Unfortunately, most women did not write about the experience of giving birth.

254. Stratton, *Pioneer Women*, 86–87.

255. Leavitt, *Brought to Bed*, 25.

256. Michael Haines, "Fertility and Mortality in the United States," https://eh.net/encyclopedia/fertility-and-mortality-in-the-united-states/ (accessed April 13, 2023).

257. Friedrich to family, October 30, 1859.

258. "Whig Party," in *Britannica*, https://www.britannica.com/topic/Whig-Party (accessed April 13, 2023).

259. Friedrich Lodholz to family, April 6, 1860, trans. Virginia L. Lewis, LRFC.

260. The Godfrey Lathrop who became a naturalized citizen in Plymouth was presumably Gottfried. Heinrich and Georg were listed as citizens in the 1870 federal census.

261. Friedrich to family, August 26, 1860.

262. Friedrich to family, January 14, 1861.

263. CT Humanities, "Workers at the Colt Armory, Hartford 1867," https://connecticuthistory.org/workers-at-the-colt-armory-hartford-1867/ (accessed April 13, 2023).

264. Friedrich to family, April 6, 1860.

265. Friedrich to family, August 26, 1860.

266. Friedrich Lodholz to Anna Maria and Anna Regina Lodholz, December 8, 1861, trans. Virginia L. Lewis, LRFC.

Chapter 4. War, Gold, Growth, Death, and Trouble, 1861–73

1. PBS, *This Far by Faith, 1776–1865: From Bondage to Holy War*, https://www.pbs.org/thisfarbyfaith/journey_2/p_5.html (accessed August 19, 2023).

2. Mark Granquist, "American Lutherans and the Civil War," https://metrolutheran.org/2011/03/american-lutherans-and-the-civil-war/ (accessed August 19, 2023).

3. "Kansas and the Centennial of the Civil War," *Kansas History: A Journal of the Central Plains* 31, 1 (Spring 1965): 62–66, https://www.kshs.org/p/kansas-and-the-centennial-of-the-civil-war/13173. See also, Kansas Historical Society, "Civil War," https://www.kshs.org/kansapedia/civil-war/14565#:~:text=Before%20the%20war%20ended%2C%20the%20federal%20government%20issued,regiments%20and%20four%20batteries%20to%20the%20Union%20forces (accessed April 13, 2023).

4. National Park System, "First to Serve—1st Kansas Colored Infantry Regiment," https://www.nps.gov/articles/1stkansas.htm (accessed April 24, 2018).

5. John A. Martin, "The Progress of Kansas," *North American Review* 142, 353 (April 1886): 348–349, https://www.jstor.org/stable/25118607.

6. Oretha Ruetti, *It Happened Here: Stories from Marshall County Kansas*, comp. Marshall County Historical Society (Hillsboro, KS: Print Source Direct, 2002), 76.

7. Emma Forter, *History of Marshall County: Its People, Industries and Institutions* (Indianapolis: B. F. Bowen, 1917), 70, https://archive.org/details/historyofmar.

8. Ruetti, *It Happened Here*, 77.

9. Forter, *History of Marshall County*, 263.

10. Forter, 264.

11. Ruetti, *It Happened Here*, 77.

12. Forter, *History of Marshall County*, 266–267. Despite their loyalty, the Otoe tribe was moved in 1881 to Indian Territory in what would soon become the state of Oklahoma.

13. Albert Castel, *Civil War Kansas: Reaping the Whirlwind*, authorized ed. with new preface (Lawrence: University Press of Kansas, 1997), 37–64; originally published as *A Frontier State at War: Kansas, 1861–1865* (Ithaca, NY: Cornell University Press, 1958).

14. Oklahoma Historical Society, "Quantrill's Raiders," in *The Encyclopedia of Oklahoma History*, https://www.okhistory.org/publications/enc/entry.php?entryname =QUANTRILL%27S%20RAIDERS; Kansas Historical Society, "Quantrill's Raids," https://www.kshs.org/kansapedia/quantrill-s-raids/18335 (accessed April 13, 2023).

15. Castel, *Civil War Kansas*, 130–132.

16. Richard Cordley, *Pioneer Days in Kansas* (New York: Pilgrim Press, 1903), 178–179, 217–218.

17. Castel, *Civil War Kansas*, 142–144, 152.

18. Forter, *History of Marshall County*, 340–341.

19. Forter, 498.

20. "Civil War Conscription Laws," https://blogs.loc.gov/law/2012/11/civil-war-con scription-laws/ (accessed August 19, 2023).

21. The full text of the law was printed by the *New York Times*: "The Conscription Act," February 19, 1863, 8, database with images, Newspapers.com.

22. Kansas Historical Society, "Civil War."

23. Forter, *History of Marshall County*, 170.

24. Max Kade Institute for German-American Studies, University of Wisconsin–Madison, "German Americans in the Civil War Era," https://mki.wisc.edu/research/immigra tion-communities/german-americans-in-the-civil-war-era/ (accessed April 13, 2023). See also Joseph George Rosengarten, *The German Soldiers in the Wars of the United States*, 2nd ed. (Philadelphia: J. B. Lippincott, 1890), 193–197.

25. "The Mob in New-York," *New York Times*, July 14, 1863, 1; "Another Day of Rioting, *New York Times*, July 16, 1863, 1, database with images, Newspapers.com.

26. John Oliver, "Draft Riots in Wisconsin during the Civil War," *Wisconsin Magazine of History* 2, 3 (March 1919): 336, https://content.wisconsinhistory.org/digital /collection/wmh/id/28403/rec/5.

27. In the North there was a cadre within the Democratic Party, derisively called "copperheads" by pro-Unionists, who opposed the war and advocated for peace with the Confederate states.

28. Arnold Shankman, "Draft Resistance in Civil War Pennsylvania," *Pennsylvania Magazine of History and Biography* 101, 2 (April 1977): 197, 200–201, https://www .jstor.org/stable/20091147.

29. Friedrich Lodholz to Anna Maria and Anna Regina Lodholz, September 1, 1863, trans. Virginia L. Lewis, LRFC.

30. William B. Vickers, *History of the City of Denver, Arapahoe County and Colorado* (Chicago: O. L. Baskin, 1884), 197–199, 206, https://archive.org/details/historyof cityofdooinolba/page/n10/mode/1up.

31. Only one man, Van White, reportedly made any significant money from it, enough to start a business. *Portrait and Biographical Album of Marshall County* (Chicago: Chapman Brothers, 1889), 251, https://archive.org/details/portraitbiograph2ochap.

32. Ovando J. Hollister, *The Mines of Colorado* (Springfield, MA: Samuel Bowles, 1867), 129.

33. Vickers, *History of the City of Denver*, 201.

34. Gottfried Lodholz to Heinrich Reb, partial letter, circa fall 1863, trans. Virginia L. Lewis, LRFC.

35. George Lodholz to his brother Fredrich, July 9, 1862, trans. Gottfried Lodholz, Probate Records for John George Lodholz, Marshall County District Court, Marysville, KS.

36. George to Fredrich, July 9, 1862.

37. Georg Lodholz to Anna Maria and Anna Regina Lodholz, July 19, 1863, trans. Virginia L. Lewis, LRFC.

38. William N. Byer and John Kellum, *Handbook to the Gold Fields of Nebraska and Kansas: Being a Complete Guide to the Gold Regions of the South Platte and Cherry Creek* (Chicago: D. B. Cooke, 1859), 26, 27, https://www.kansasmemory.org/item/4535/page/1.

39. Byer and Kellum, 26–27.

40. Heinrich Reb to Anna Regina Reb and Anna Maria Lodholz, August 22, 1863, trans. Virginia L. Lewis, LRFC.

41. "Irving Vicinity Is Visited by Our Roving Correspondent," *Marshall County News*, April 8, 1932, 7, database with images, Newspapers.com.

42. Heinrich reported to Anna Regina and Anna Maria that eggs were $1 a dozen, the same figure given by John. Heinrich to Anna Regina and Anna Maria, August 22, 1863. However, the impracticality of transporting eggs and butter to Denver makes John's story improbable. Georg reported in one of his letters from Denver that a pound of butter was just 15 cents and a dozen eggs 18 cents. Georg to Anna Maria and Anna Regina, July 19, 1863.

43. See David Lindsey, ed., "The Journal of an 1859 Pike's Peak Gold Seeker," *Kansas Historical Quarterly* 22, 4 (Winter 1956): 305–320, https://www.kshs.org/p/the-journal-of-an-1859-pike-s-peak-gold-seeker/13129.

44. Lindsey, 305–320.

45. There were numerous such guidebooks published at the time. See LeRoy R. Hafen, ed., *Pike's Peak Gold Rush Guidebooks of 1859 by Luke Tierney, William B. Parsoons and Summaries of the Other Fifteen*, Southwest Historical Series, vol. 9 (Glendale, CA: Arthur H. Clark, 1941; facsimile ed., n.p., 2021).

46. Byer and Kellum, *Handbook to the Gold Fields*, 69.

47. Byer and Kellum, 69.

48. Hollister, *Mines of Colorado*, 100.

49. Byer and Kellum, *Handbook to the Gold Fields*, 50–52.

50. Hollister, *Mines of Colorado*, 13–14.

51. Vickers, *History of the City of Denver*, 197–199.

52. Georg to Anna Maria and Anna Regina, July 19, 1863.

53. Heinrich to Anna Regina and Anna Maria, August 22, 1863.

54. Georg to Anna Maria and Anna Regina, July 19, 1863.

55. Gottfried Lodholz to Heinrich Reb, January 8, 1864, trans. Virginia L. Lewis, LRFC.

56. *The Frankfort Story: A History of Frankfort, Kansas and Surrounding Communities Honoring Frankfort's Centennial in 1967*, comp. Maynie Shearer Bush assisted by

Winifred Shearer (n.p., n.d.), 121, sponsored by Frankfort Chamber of Commerce in Cooperation with Frankfort Centennial Inc.

57. Friedrich Lodholz to Anna Regina and Heinrich Reb, May 9, 1864, trans. Virginia L. Lewis, LRFC.

58. "The State to Be Placed upon War Footing," https://www.kshs.org/index.php?url=km/items/view/213261 (accessed April 13, 2023).

59. Results of query: surname Reb, given name Henry, Kansas State Historical Society, "Civil War Militia, 1861–1865," https://www.kshs.org/kmi/kmi_civwarmilitias/search/surname:Reb/fname:Henry/sndx:yes/regiment:/submit:SEARCH (accessed April 13, 2023).

60. John D. Unruh Jr., *The Plains Across: The Overland Emigrants and the Trans-Mississippi West, 1840–60* (Urbana: University of Illinois Press, 1979), 180–181.

61. Unruh, 156–160.

62. Lee Ann Potter and Wynell Schamel, "The Homestead Act of 1862," *Social Education* 61, 6 (October 1997): 359–364, https://www.archives.gov/education/lessons/homestead-act.

63. Carroll D. Clark and Roy L. Roberts, *People of Kansas* (Topeka: Kansas State Planning Board, 1936), 45.

64. Clifford E. Trafzer, *As Long as the Grass Shall Grow and Rivers Flow: A History of Native Americans* (Belmont, CA: Thomson, 2000), 208–209. See also Kenneth Carley, *The Sioux Uprising of 1862*, 2nd ed. (St. Paul: Minnesota Historical Society Press, 1976), 3–6.

65. Trafzer, *As Long as the Grass Shall Grow*, 212–213. See also Ohio State University, ehistory, "Sand Creek (Chivington) Massacre," https://ehistory.osu.edu/battles/sand-creek-chivington-massacre (accessed April 13, 2023).

66. National Park Service, "Buffalo Soldiers," https://www.nps.gov/chyo/learn/historyculture/buffalo-soldiers.htm (accessed April 13, 2023).

67. William G. Cutler, "Indian Outrages, Marshall County, Part 2," in *History of the State of Kansas* (Chicago: A. T. Andreas, 1883), https://www.kancoll.org/books/cutler/marshall/marshall-co-p1.html.

68. Forter, *History of Marshall County*, 266, 52–54, 73, 78, 52–54, 266.

69. Georg to Anna Maria and Anna Regina, July 19, 1863.

70. 1865 Kansas State Census, Marshall County, Guittard Township, dwelling 29, family 20, line 8, database with images, Ancestry.com.

71. Friedrich Lodholz to Anna Regina and Heinrich Reb, January 31, 1865, trans. Virginia L. Lewis, LRFC.

72. Georg's second wife feuded with Gottfried after Georg's death and stated in a letter to Anna Regina: "I have been made to be bad, worse than Minna which George himself admits that they did her injustice." Rosina Buk to Anna Regina Reb, circa July 1873, trans. Freda Murray, LRFC.

73. Friedrich to Anna Regina and Heinrich, January 31, 1865.

74. CT Humanities, "Colt Armory Burns—Today in History: February 4," https://connecticuthistory.org/colt-armory-burns-today-in-history/ (accessed April 13, 2023).

75. Friedrich to Anna Regina and Heinrich, January 31, 1865.

76. Friedrich to Anna Regina and Heinrich, January 31, 1865.

77. Friedrich to Anna Regina and Heinrich, January 31, 1865.

78. Friedrich Lodholz to Anna Regina and Heinrich Reb, June 14, 1865, trans. Freda Murray, LRFC.

79. Martin, "Progress of Kansas," 351.

80. Martin, 351.

81. Non-Population Census Schedules for Kansas, 1850–1880, microfilm publication T1130, rolls 1–2, 5, 8–41, Records of the Bureau of the Census, Record Group 29, National Archives and Records Administration, Washington, DC.

82. J. Neale Carman, *Foreign-Language Units of Kansas*, vol. 1, *Historical Atlas and Statistics* (Lawrence: University of Kansas Press, 1962), 4.

83. My count is from the 1865 Kansas State Census, Marshall County, database with images, Ancestry.com, citing microfilm reels K-1–K-8, Kansas State Historical Society.

84. Martin, "Progress of Kansas," 350.

85. Carman, *Foreign-Language Units of Kansas*, 1:5–8. The compendium is archived at the Kansas State Historical Society. The figures in the two documents are precisely the same for twenty-four of the thirty-six counties enumerated and within just a few inhabitants in eight others. In the three where they disagree substantially, the reasons seem clear. In Anderson County, the figure in the Non-Population Schedule includes only the number of Prussians listed in the compendium. In Leavenworth County, the figure does not include the number of inhabitants in the city itself, while the compendium does (1,735 versus 3,149). In Jefferson County, there was apparently an error in addition (81 versus 91).

86. Carman, *Foreign-Language Units of Kansas*, 1:5. At the time he was writing, he apparently did not have access to the actual 1865 state census.

87. My count is from the 1865 Kansas State Census, Saline, Ottawa, and Neosho Counties.

88. In appendix F, Marshall County is listed as having 150 German-born residents, up from 100 in 1860. Based on my count from the 1865 Kansas State Census, there were 155.

89. The following figures are based on my counts from the censuses referenced. In making the comparison, I considered that the spelling of surnames may have been phonetic. For example, I matched "Frazure" in the 1860 census with "Frazier" in the 1865 census, and I matched "Rains" with "Raines."

90. 1885 Kansas State Census, Schedule 1, Leavenworth County, City of Leavenworth, Fourth Ward, p. 429, Henry Sellers, dwelling 431, family 229, line 8; Washington County, Hanover Township, p. 76, Jacob Gundlefinger, no dwelling no., family 130, line 17, database with images, Ancestry.com, citing microfilm reels K-1–K-8, Kansas State Historical Society; 1880 Federal Census, Schedule 1, Ness County, Kansas, Township 16, Range 22, p. 12, William Bunzell, dwelling 11, family 11, line 26, database with images, Ancestry.com, citing U.S. Federal Population Census, 1880, microfilm publication series T9, Records of the Bureau of the Census, Record Group 29, National Archives and Records Administration, Washington, DC.

91. To this were added three from Nova Scotia, three from England, nine from France (six of whom were George Guittard's family), and one from Scotland.

92. Again, as in Guittard, there were few other foreign-born: five from England, three from France, two from Canada, and one from Scotland.

93. Database with images, Ancestry.com, citing Non-Population Census Schedules for Kansas, 1850–1880, microfilm publication T1130, rolls 1–2, 5, 8–41, Records of the Bureau of the Census, Record Group 29, National Archives and Records Administration, Washington, DC.

94. Two of these "children" were men in their twenties whose parents were in their late fifties and sixties. Only one family with two children, the youngest of whom was one year old, likely came directly from Germany.

95. Multiple properties and particularly multiple town lots were owned by one individual, clearly a sign of land speculation.

96. "List of Land Sold for Taxes, May 6th 1862," *Big Blue Union* (Marysville, KS), January 2, 1864, 3, database with images, Newspapers.com.

97. 1865 Kansas State Census, Schedule 1, Marshall County, Guittard Township, Kansas, p. 5, Gottfried Lodholz, dwelling 28, family 29, line 1.

98. Sheriff sale notices, *Big Blue Union*, January 2, 1864, 3.

99. Richard Edwards, Jacob K. Friefeld, and Rebecca S. Wingo, *Homesteading the Plains: Toward a New History* (Lincoln: University of Nebraska Press, 2017), fig. 1.3, 10. The land records for Marshall County are incomplete. See https://www.kshs.org/government/landsrvy/pdfs/kansas_tract_book_guide.pdf (accessed April 13, 2023).

100. Forter, *History of Marshall County*, 751.

101. *Portrait and Biographical Album*, 545.

102. Paul Wallace Gates, *Fifty Million Acres: Conflicts over Kansas Land Policy, 1854–1890* (Ithaca, NY: Cornell University Press, 1954; reprint, Norman: University of Oklahoma Press, 1977), 231–231.

103. Forter, *History of Marshall County*, 876.

104. Forter, 909.

105. *Portrait and Biographical Album*, 732. Hutchinson himself knew the hardships facing new settlers. When he came to Kansas in 1859, he made money by husking corn and got one bushel out of every fifty as his pay. *Portrait and Biographical Album*, 156.

106. *Portrait and Biographical Album*, 440, 526.

107. William G. Cutler, "Marshall County, Part 9, Irving," in *History of the State of Kansas*, https://www.kancoll.org/books/cutler/marshall/marshall-co-p9.html#IRVING.

108. William G. Cutler, "Marshall County, Part 8, Blue Rapids," in *History of the State of Kansas*, https://www.kancoll.org/books/cutler/marshall/marshall-co-p8.html#BLUE_RAPIDS.

109. Forter, *History of Marshall County*, 39.

110. William G. Cutler, "Marshall County, Part 10, Frankfort," in *History of the State of Kansas*, https://www.kancoll.org/books/cutler/marshall/marshall-co-p10.html#FRANKFORT.

111. *Frankfort Story*, 5, 7.

112. *Frankfort Story*, 6–7.

113. *Frankfort Story*, 6–7.

114. *Frankfort Story*, 5–6.

115. Clark and Roberts, *People of Kansas*, table 8, 50.

116. Clark and Roberts, table 8, 50.

117. Kansas Historical Society, "African American Residents in Kansas," https://

www.kshs.org/kansapedia/african-american-residents-in-kansas/17878 (accessed August 20, 2023).

118. Francis Paul Prucha, *American Indian Treaties: The History of a Political Anomaly* (Berkeley: University of California Press, 1994), 275–276.

119. 1865 Kansas State Census, Marshall County, Vermillion Township, p. 11, Henry Rebb, dwelling 81, family 81, line 27.

120. Warranty Deed and Abstract of Title, in the family's possession.

121. 1870 Federal Census, Schedule 1, Marshall County, Vermillion Township, Kansas, p. 43, Henry Reb, dwelling 347, family 355, line 27, database with images, Ancestry.com, citing 1870 US Census, Population Schedules, microfilm publication M593, National Archives and Records Administration, Washington, DC.

122. 1870 Non-Population Schedules, Schedule 3: Productions of Agriculture, Marshall County, Vermillion Township, Kansas, p. 5, Henry Reb, line 13, database with images, Ancestry.com, citing Non-Population Census Schedules for Kansas, 1850–1880.

123. 1870 Non-Population Schedule 3, Marshall County, Kansas, Vermillion Township, p. 5, Henry Reb, line 13.

124. 1870 Non-Population Schedule 3, p. 5, Henry Reb, line 13.

125. John George Lodholz to Friedrich Lodholz, May 13, 1866, trans. Gottfried Lodholz, Probate Records for John George Lodholz, Marshall County District Court, Marysville, KS.

126. 1870 Census of the United States, Schedule 1, Marshall County, Kansas, Guittard Township, p. 7, dwelling 45, family 52, lines 15–19.

127. 1865 Kansas State Census, Marshall County, Guittard Township, p. 5, dwelling 29, family 30, line 8; 1870 Non-Population Schedule 3: Productions of Agriculture, Marshall County, Guittard Township, p. 2, line 39.

128. 1870 Non-Population Schedule 3, Marshall County, Guittard Township, p. 2, line 40.

129. 1870 Non-Population Schedule 3, Marshall County, Guittard Township, p. 2, line 39.

130. This information is from probate documents. The listed *History* was most likely in German. "Personal Property," Probate Records for John George Lodholz, Marshall County District Court, Marysville, KS.

131. 1870 Non-Population Schedule 3, Marshall County, Guittard Township, p. 2, line 40. The number of horses is unreadable.

132. Ruetti, *It Happened Here*, 7.

133. William G. Cutler, "Marshall County, Part 1, General Products," in *History of the State of Kansas*, http://www.kancoll.org/books/cutler/marshall/marshall-co-p1.html#GENERAL_PRODUCTS.

134. Cutler, "Marshall County, Part 8, Blue Rapids."

135. Cornell University, College of Agriculture and Life Sciences, Cornell Small Farms Program, "Considerations for Winter Grazing Your Sheep," https://smallfarms.cornell.edu/2015/01/considerations-for-winter-grazing-your-sheep/.

136. 1875 Kansas State Census, Schedule 2: Productions of Agriculture, Marshall County, Guittard Township, p. 8, line 5, database with images, Ancestry.com, citing 1875 Kansas State Census, microfilm reels K-1–K-20, Kansas State Historical Society.

137. Gottfried Lodholz to Heinrich Reb, November 23, 1868, trans. Freda Murray, LRFC.

138. Friedrich Lodholz to Anna and Heinrich Reb, November 22, 1868, trans. Virginia L. Lewis, LRFC.

139. *Frankfort Story*, 8.

140. Friedrich Lodholz to Anna and Heinrich Reb, November 12, 1873, trans. Virginia L. Lewis, LRFC.

141. Friedrich to Anna and Heinrich, June 14, 1865.

142. Friedrich Lodholz to Anna and Heinrich Reb, July 25, 1870, trans. Freda Murray, LRFC.

143. Mack Walker, *Germany and the Emigration: 1816–1885* (Cambridge, MA: Harvard University Press, 1964), 180. Walker provides no evidence supporting this motive for immigration.

144. Emigrating to escape military service was probably not something a man wanted to dwell on. Forter, however, profiles a son who admitted that his father did so before the unification. Andrew Hurt said of his father, Joseph, who was born in Germany (most likely Prussia): he emigrated "in 1840 in order to escape military service." But Joseph Hirt was no coward; he fought in the Civil War. Forter, *History of Marshall County*, 806.

145. Friedrich to Anna and Heinrich, July 25, 1870.

146. Friedrich Lodholz to Anna and Heinrich Reb, November 13, 1870, trans. Freda Murray, LRFC.

147. Charles Frederick William Dassler, *Compiled Laws of Kansas, 1879* (St. Louis: W. J. Gilbert, 1879), 378, chap. 33 (2102), sec. 2.

148. The details of the probate proceedings are recorded in a multitude of documents in the probate file for John George Lodholz, Marshall County District Court, Marysville, KS. The narrative that follows is based on these records.

149. *Marshall County News*, August 10, 1871, 2.

150. Rosina Book to J. F. Lodholz, January 2, 1872, trans. Gottfried Lodholz, Probate Records for John George Lodholz, Marshall County District Court, Marysville, KS.

151. 1880 Census of the United States, Buchanan County, Missouri, St. Joseph Enumeration District 051, p. 8, Charles Lodholz, dwelling 31, family 37, line 42, database with images, Ancestry.com, citing Tenth Census of the United States, 1880, microfilm publication T9, Records of the Bureau of the Census, Record Group 29, National Archives and Records Administration, Washington, DC.

152. John and Amanda Book, with two young children, were listed in the 1860 federal census in Atchison County, Mount Pleasant Township, p. 44, dwelling 1023, family 1040, line 9, database with images, Ancestry.com, citing Kansas Territory, Census of Population, Eighth Census of the United States, 1860, microfilm publication M653, vol. 1, roll 346, National Archives and Records Administration, Washington, DC.

153. Gottfried Lodholz to Anna and Heinrich Reb, July 15, 1873, trans. Virginia L. Lewis, LRFC.

154. Rosina Book (presumed) to Anna Reb, unsigned, circa 1873, trans. Freda Murray, LRFC.

155. Rosina Book to Anna Reb, August 6, 1873, trans. Virginia L. Lewis, LRFC.

156. Anna Reb to Friedrich Lodholz, draft, circa 1873, trans. Virginia L. Lewis, LRFC.

157. Rosina to Anna, August 6, 1873.

158. Friedrich to Anna and Heinrich, November 12, 1873.

159. "The Panic of 1873," Library of Congress Research Guides, https://www.loc.gov/rr/business/businesshistory/September/Panic1873.html; PBS, *American Experience: The Panic of 1873*, https://www.pbs.org/wgbh/americanexperience/features/grant-panic/ (accessed April 13, 2023).

160. Friedrich Lodholz to Anna and Heinrich Reb, May 24, 1873, trans. Virginia L. Lewis, LRFC.

161. Friedrich Lodholz to Anna Reb, June 5, 1876, trans. Virginia L. Lewis, LRFC.

162. 1880 Census of the United States, Buchanan County, Missouri, St. Joseph Enumeration District 051, p. 8, dwelling 31, family 37, lines 37–42, database with images, Ancestry.com, citing 1880 US Census, Population Schedules, microfilm publication M593, National Archives and Records Administration, Washington, DC.

163. Death certificate of Rosina Lodholz, St. Joseph, Buchanan, Missouri, November 29, 1926, File No. 30909, Registered No. 1051, database with images, Ancestry.com, citing Missouri Death Certificates, Missouri Secretary of State.

Chapter 5. Change, Tragedy, and the Female Frontier in Marshall County

1. J. Neale Carman, *Foreign-Language Units of Kansas*, vol. 1, *Historical Atlas and Statistics* (Lawrence: University Press of Kansas, 1974), 9.

2. Howard Ruede, *Sod-House Days: Letters from a Kansas Homesteader: 1877–78*, ed. John Ise (New York: Columbia University Press, 1937; reprint, Lawrence: University Press of Kansas, 1983); John Ise, *Sod and Stubble: Unabridged and Annotated Edition*, with additional material by Von Rothenberger (Lawrence: University Press of Kansas, 1996).

3. Kansas State Board of Agriculture, First Biennial Report, "Osborne: 1878," http://www.ksgenweb.org/archives/1878/osborne.html (accessed April 13, 2023).

4. Carman, *Foreign-Language Units of Kansas*, 1:58.

5. Norman E. Saul, "The Migration of the Russian-Germans to Kansas," *Kansas Historical Quarterly* 40, 1 (Spring 1974): 38–62, https://www.kshs.org/p/kansas-historical-quarterly-the-migration-of-the-russian-germans-to-kansas/13242.

6. Carman, *Foreign-Language Units of Kansas*, 1:46, 198.

7. *Portrait and Biographical Album of Marshall County* (Chicago: Chapman Brothers, 1889), 173, 388, https://archive.org/details/portraitbiograph20chap.

8. See, for example, *Portrait and Biographical Album*, 192, 202, 368.

9. See, for example, Emma Forter, *History of Marshall County: Its People, Industries and Institutions* (Indianapolis: B. F. Bowen, 1917), 665, 739, 758, 822, 927, 986, https://archive.org/details/historyofmarshal00fost. Carl Weber from the "Rhine country" offers a glimpse of the immigrants' financial circumstances. He arrived in Marshall County with only $25 to his name and was among those who rented. Forter, 752.

10. Fred S. Shannon, *The Farmer's Last Frontier: Agriculture, 1860–1898*, vol. 5 of *Economic History of the United States* (New York: Harper & Row, 1945), 418.

11. Walter D. Kamphoefner, Wolfgang Helbich, and Ulrike Sommer, eds., *News*

from the Land of Freedom: German Immigrants Write Home, trans. Susan Carter Vogel (Ithaca, NY: Cornell University Press, 1991), 482.

12. "Rush for Citizenship," *Salina (KS) Daily Union*, February 13, 1917, 4.

13. 1875 Kansas State Census, Schedule 2: Productions of Agriculture, Marshall County, Guittard Township, pp. 7–8, line 5, database with images, Ancestry.com, citing 1875 Kansas State Census, microfilm reels K-1–K-20, Kansas State Historical Society.

14. 1875 Kansas State Census, Schedule 2, Marshall County, Guittard Township, pp. 7–8, line 5.

15. 1880 Federal Non-Population Schedule 2, Marshall County, Guittard Township, p. 13, line 5, database with images, Ancestry.com, citing Non-Population Census Schedules for Kansas, 1850–1880, microfilm publication T1130, rolls 1–2, 5, 8–41, Records of the Bureau of the Census, Record Group 29, National Archives and Records Administration, Washington, DC.

16. Forter, *History of Marshall County*, 143–144.

17. 1880 Federal Non-Population Schedule 2, Marshall County, Guittard Township, p. 13, line 5.

18. Forter, *History of Marshall County*, 720.

19. Shannon, *Farmer's Last Frontier*, 135.

20. Forter, *History of Marshall County*, 51.

21. *The Frankfort Story: A History of Frankfort, Kansas and Surrounding Communities Honoring Frankfort's Centennial in 1967*, comp. Maynie Shearer Bush assisted by Winifred Shearer (n.p, n.d.), 44, sponsored by Frankfort Chamber of Commerce in cooperation with Frankfort Centennial Inc.

22. J. Neal Carman, *Foreign-Language Units of Kansas*, vol. 2, *Account of Settlement and Settlements in Kansas* (Lawrence: University Press of Kansas, 1974), 96, copy of original manuscript, https://kuscholarworks.ku.edu/handle/1808/7160?show=full (accessed April 11, 2023).

23. Carman, *Foreign-Language Units of Kansas*, 1:46.

24. William G. Cutler, "Marshall County, Part 6, Herkimer," in *History of the State of Kansas* (Chicago: A. T. Andreas, 1883), https://www.kancoll.org/boos/cutler/marshall/marshall-co-p6.html#HERKIMER.

25. Based on a local count for City of Marysville, Marshall County, 1885 Kansas State Census, p. 61, database with images, Ancestry.com, citing 1885 Kansas State Census, microfilm reels K-1-K-146, Kansas State Historical Society.

26. Ernest Ludlow Bogart and Charles Manfred Thompson, *The Centennial History of Illinois*, vol. 4, *The Industrial State* (Springfield: Illinois Centennial Commission, 1920), 220, https://archive.org/details/centennialhistor04illi/page/n9/mode/1up.

27. Oretha Ruetti, *It Happened Here: Stories from Marshall County Kansas*, comp. Marshall County Historical Society (Hillsboro, KS: Print Source Direct, 2002), 83–84.

28. Forter, *History of Marshall County*, 320. See also "German Evangelical Synod of North America," in *Kansas: A Cyclopedia of State History, Embracing Events, Institutions, Industries, Counties, Cities, Towns, Prominent Persons, etc.*, vol. 1, ed. Frank W. Blackmar, http://www.ksgenweb.org/archives/1912/g/german_evangelical_synod.html (accessed April 14, 2023).

29. In some parts of the country, including Kansas, and particularly Atchison during

the territorial period, *turnvereins* played a political role in opposing slavery, supporting Lincoln, and defending their communities against Sabbath laws. The *turnverein* in Marysville, however, was strictly devoted to physical education and cultural events. It held an Easter Ball in its hall in 1883 (advertisement, *Marshall County Democrat*, March 23, 1883, 2); presented two plays in 1900 (*Marysville Advocate*, March 23, 1900, 5); and, on the occasion of its thirty-first anniversary, its members staged singing and exercise performances at the fairgrounds, with about a thousand in attendance ("The Turner Anniversary," *Marshall County News*, August 25,1905, 1). The organization also held occasional beer gardens.

30. Forter, *History of Marshall County*, 122–123.

31. The total population is based on a local count in 1885 Kansas State Census, Marysville Township, Marshall County, p. 95, database with images, Ancestry.com, citing 1885 Kansas State Census, microfilm reels K-1–K-146, Kansas State Historical Society. The German-born population is based on my own count.

32. William D. Keel, "Deitch, Däätsch, Düütsch and Dietsch: The Varieties of Kansas German Dialects after 150 Years of German Group Settlement in Kansas," in *Yearbook of German-American Studies*, supplemental issue 2, *Preserving Heritage: A Festschrift for C. Richard Beam* (Lawrence, KS: Society for German-American Studies, 2006), 27–48, https://doi.org/10.17161/ygas.v2i.

33. Forter, *History of Marshall County*, 222.

34. Constitution of the State of Kansas, Article 15, sec. 10: Intoxicating Liquors, History, pp. 38–39, https://www.kssos.org/other/pubs/KS_Constitution.pdf (accessed April 14, 2023).

35. George Schiller, "The Abolitionist: A Saga of the Albert Gallatin Family in Early Kansas," chap. 14, http://kancoll.org/books/schiller2/gws_ch14.htm (accessed April 14, 2023).

36. "The General Rules of the Methodist Church," https://www.umc.org/en/content/the-general-rules-of-the-methodist-church (accessed April 14, 2023).

37. US Census Bureau, "1870 Census Instructions to Enumerators," https://www.census.gov/programs-surveys/decennial-census/technical-documentation/questionnaires/1870/1870-instructions.html (accessed April 14, 2023). Despite the instructions, 126 inhabitants were still classified as coming from Germany, 81 of them in Franklin Township, one of the new townships in Marshall County.

38. Except where otherwise noted, the following discussion is based on my count from Ancestry.com, citing Tenth Census of the United States, 1880, microfilm publication T9, Records of the Bureau of the Census, Record Group 29, National Archives and Records Administration, Washington, DC.

39. Carman, *Foreign-Language Units of Kansas*, 1:198.

40. Numbers of settlers from the "German Empire" in Kansas and, specifically, from Prussia and Hanover are from Jacob C. Ruppenthal, "The German Element in Central Kansas," *Collections of the Kansas State Historical Society* 13 (1913–14): 516, https://archive.org/details/collectionsofkan13kans_0/page/513/mode/1up?q=Volume+XIII&view=theater.

41. Ruppenthal, 516.

42. Friedrich faced the same situation in Terryville. Although the first German to arrive in the village was born in Württemberg, he died within a few years and apparently attracted

no others except for Gottfried and his family. Francis Atwater, *History of the Town of Plymouth, Connecticut* (Meriden, CT: Journal Publishing, 1895), 281, https://archive.org/details/historyoftownofp1895atwa. In the 1870 federal census, only 3 out of 129 Germans were from Württemberg: Friedrich, Friedrich's best friend Fredrich Egan, and a woman married to a Prussian. By 1880, the number had increased by only two.

43. James R. Shortridge, *Peopling the Plains: Who Settled Where in Frontier Kansas* (Lawrence: University Press of Kansas, 1995), 98; Carroll D. Clark and Roy L. Roberts, *People of Kansas* (Topeka: Kansas State Planning Board, 1936), 34–35.

44. Carman, *Foreign-Language Units of Kansas*, 1:7.

45. The figures include one from Bavaria and one from Prussia.

46. Friedrich Lodholz to Anna Reb, March 28, 1874, trans. Virginia L. Lewis, LRFC.

47. Friedrich to Anna, March 28, 1874.

48. *Frankfort Story*, 9.

49. Friedrich Lodholz to Anna Reb, September 23, 1874, trans. Virginia L. Lewis, LRFC.

50. Friedrich Lodholz to Anna Reb and Christina Lodholz, February 22, 1875, trans. Virginia L. Lewis, LRFC.

51. Estelle May Steward and Jesse Chester Bowen, *History of Wages in the United States from Colonial Times to 1928* (Washington, DC: US Government Printing Office, 1928), 299, 302, https://fraser.stlouisfed.org/title/history-wages-united-states-colonial-times-1928-4126.

52. Christina Lodholz to Anna Reb, April 4, 1875, trans. Virginia L. Lewis, LRFC.

53. Friedrich to Anna, September 23, 1874.

54. Forter, *History of Marshall County*, 59.

55. Forter, 77.

56. Forter, 78.

57. Forter, 817.

58. Forter, 787.

59. Forter, 1022.

60. *Portrait and Biographical Album*, 273.

61. *Portrait and Biographical Album*, 422. She was given her own biography.

62. *Portrait and Biographical Album*, 647. She was given her own biography.

63. *Portrait and Biographical Album*, 714. She was given her own biography.

64. 1880 Federal Non-Population Schedule 2: Productions of Agriculture, Marshall County, Kansas, Vermillion Township, p. 1, line 10, database with images, Ancestry.com, citing Non-Population Census Schedules for Kansas, 1850–1880, microfilm publication T1130, rolls 1–2, 5, 8–41, Records of the Bureau of the Census, Record Group 29, National Archives and Records Administration, Washington, DC.

65. The herding of cattle was often assigned to young children. Jon Gjerde, *The Minds of the West: Ethnocultural Evolution in the Rural Middle West 1830–1917* (Chapel Hill: University of North Carolina Press, 1997), 152–153.

66. 1880 Federal Non-Population Schedule 2: Productions of Agriculture, Marshall County, Vermillion Township, p. 1, line 10.

67. Friedrich Lodholz to Anna Reb, February 22, 1875, trans. Virginia L. Lewis, LRFC.

68. Order receipts, in the family's possession.

69. 1880 Federal Non-Population Schedule 2: Productions of Agriculture, Marshall County, Vermillion Township, p. 1, line 10.

70. Gottfried Lodholz to Anna Reb, June 23, 1876, trans. Virginia L. Lewis, LRFC.

71. *Frankfort Story*, 123.

72. Gottfried Lodholz to Anna Reb, September 14, 1876, trans. Virginia L. Lewis, LRFC.

73. Gottfried Lodholz to Anna Reb, May 10, 1877, trans. Virginia L. Lewis, LRFC.

74. Christina Lodholz to Anna Reb, September 28, 1879, trans. Virginia L. Lewis, LRFC.

75. Anna may have rented out land on a sharecrop basis. Schedule 2 of the 1880 federal census recorded no grains planted.

76. Christina Lodholz to Anna Reb, December 30, 1878, trans. Virginia L. Lewis, LRFC.

77. Christina Lodholz to Anna Reb, July 21, 1879, trans. Virginia L. Lewis, LRFC.

78. "The Irving Tornado(es)," http://www.kansas.net/~rjherman/Irving%2C%20Kansas%20Tornado.htm (accessed June 13, 2019).

79. Forter, *History of Marshall County*, 429–431.

80. Friedrich Lodholz to Anna Reb, June 5, 1879, trans. Freda Murray, LRFC.

81. Friedrich Lodholz to Anna Reb, June 6, 1876, trans. Virginia L. Lewis, LRFC.

82. Friedrich Lodholz to Anna Reb, April 22, 1877, trans. Freda Murray, LRFC.

83. Friedrich Lodholz to Anna Reb, April 22, 1877, LRFC.

84. Friedrich Lodholz to Anna Reb, May 28, 1878, trans. Freda Murray, LRFC.

85. Friedrich to Anna, May 28, 1878.

86. Forter, *History of Marshall County*, 159, 400.

87. "Barrett School Historic Landmark," *Frankfort Index*, April 5, 1973, 1, database with images, Newpapers.com.

88. Forter, *History of Marshall County*, 583.

89. Forter, 490–491.

90. Forter, 1017.

91. Christina Lodholz to Anna Reb, February 10, 1882, trans. Virginia L. Lewis, LRFC.

92. Mary Reb to John and Lulu Reb, July 22, 1899, in the family's possession. Mary was describing how her mother sun-dried tomatoes when they were children.

93. Gingerbread recipe, circa 1860s, trans. Virginia L. Lewis, LRFC.

94. "Guittard Items," *Marshall County News*, June 20, 1874, 2, database with images, Newspapers.com.

95. "Jake Volle Writes of His Early School Days at Guittard," *Marshall County News*, October 3, 1949, 5.

96. Doing such chores is described in a second series of family letters written in English and spanning the 1890s to the 1960s, in the family's possession.

97. 1885 Kansas State Census, Schedule 2, Marshall County, Vermillion Township, p. 17, line 20, database with images, Ancestry.com, citing 1885 Kansas State Census, microfilm reels K-1-K-146, Kansas State Historical Society.

98. John Martin Lodholz to Gottfried Lodholz, August 30, 1887, trans. Virginia L. Lewis, LRFC.

99. "Historical Dollar-to-Marks Currency Convertor," https://marcuse.faculty.history.ucsb.edu/projects/currency.htm (accessed April 14, 2023).

100. CPI Inflation Calculator, https://www.in2013dollars.com/us/inflation/1899?amount=1 (accessed April 14, 2023).

101. The fact that only Gottfried and his sons-in-law contributed to the church's establishment indicates that the number of adherents was small. When other churches were founded in the county, several unrelated community members unusually served as the initial trustees. Forter, *History of Marshall County*, 300–347.

102. Oretha Ruetti, "German Evangelical Church Existed for 41 Years," *Marysville Advocate*, October 21, 1999, 19, database and images, Newspapers.com.

103. Friedrich Lodholz to Anna Reb, June 10, 1889, trans. Virginia L. Lewis, LRFC.

104. Christina Lodholz to Anna Regina, February 27, 1889, trans. Virginia L. Lewis, LRFC.

105. Robert Porter, Superintendent, US Census Bureau, *Compendium of the Eleventh Census: 1890*, pt. 1, *Population* (Washington, DC: US Government Printing Office, 1892), xlvii, xlviii, https://www.census.gov/history/pdf/1890statisticalcompendium.pdf. Also see https://www.census.gov/dataviz/visualizations/001/ (accessed April 14, 2023). The Census Bureau considered the frontier line to be fewer than six people per square mile, based on county data. This statement did not mean there was no more land to settle; however, the bureau intended to stop tracking the frontier line in subsequent censuses.

Epilogue

1. Emma Forter, *History of Marshall County: Its People, Industries and Institutions* (Indianapolis: B. F. Bowen, 1917), 47, https://archive.org/details/historyofmar47.

2. National Park Service, "Homestead: State by State Numbers," https://www.nps.gov/home/learn/historyculture/statenumbers.htm (accessed April 15, 2023).

3. James R. Shortridge, *Peopling the Plains: Who Settled Where in Frontier Kansas* (Lawrence: University Press of Kansas, 1995), 32.

4. Milton M. Gordon, *Assimilation in American Life: The Role of Race, Religion, and National Origins* (New York: Oxford University Press, 1964), 60–83.

5. Jon Gjerde, *The Minds of the West: Ethnocultural Evolution in the Rural Middle West 1830–1917* (Chapel Hill: University of North Carolina Press, 1997), 59–62.

6. Kathleen Neils Conzen, "Phantom Landscapes of Colonization: Germans in the Making of a Pluralist America," in *The German-American Encounter: Conflict and Cooperation between Two Cultures, 1800–2000*, ed. Frank Trommler and Elliott Shore (New York: Berghahn Books, 2001), 11.

7. Forter, *History of Marshall County*, 320, 322, 324. The German Evangelical church in Marysville had a parochial school to teach German and provide religious training. The Evangelical churches in Hermansburg (a few miles from Bremen) and Herkimer went further. Hermansburg had two parochial schools that taught all subjects up to the eighth grade; likewise, the curriculum of the school in Herkimer included all the subjects taught in the public schools. In both cases, instruction was presumably provided in German.

8. *Portrait and Biographical Album of Marshall County* (Chicago: Chapman Brothers, 1889), 489–490, https://archive.org/details/portraitbiograph20chap.

9. See, for example, the biographies of the Raemer brothers, Hugo Rohde, Joseph Totten, Adam Sachs, and Louis Hanke in *Portrait and Biographical Album*, 192–193, 195, 201, 209, 223, 244.

10. Members of the Democratic Party in Marshall County cut across ethnic and religious lines.

11. Reinhard R. Doerries, "Immigrants and the Church: German-Americans in Comparative Perspective," in *German-American Immigration and Ethnicity in Comparative Perspective*, ed. Wolfgang Helbich and Walter Kamphoefner (Madison, WI: Max Kade Institute for German-American Studies, 2004), 4.

12. Forter, *History of Marshall County*, 61–62.

13. *The Frankfort Story: A History of Frankfort, Kansas and Surrounding Communities Honoring Frankfort's Centennial in 1967*, comp. Maynie Shearer Bush assisted by Winifred Shearer (n.p., n.d.), 33, sponsored by Frankfort Chamber of Commerce in cooperation with Frankfort Centennial Inc.

14. "The General Rules of the Methodist Church," https://www.umc.org/en/content/the-general-rules-of-the-methodist-church (accessed April 15, 2023).

15. Anne Höndgen, "Community versus Separation: A Northwest German Emigrant Settlement Region in Nineteenth-Century Ohio," in Helbich and Kamphoefner, *German-American Immigration and Ethnicity*, 29, 41.

16. J. Neal Carman. *Foreign-Language Units of Kansas*, vol. 2, *Account of Settlement and Settlements in Kansas* (Lawrence: University Press of Kansas, 1974), 1254, copy of original manuscript, https://kuscholarworks.ku.edu/handle/1808/7160?show=full.

17. *Portrait and Biographical Album*, 489.

18. See the biographies of Andrew Shearer, A. G. Barrett, and John Hazlett in *Portrait and Biographical Album*, 495, 450, 268.

19. In 1947 the cornerstone of the old Turner Hall was opened. It contained a list of the members in 1880. "Cornerstone Reveals Early Turnverein Members," *Marysville Advocate*, May 8, 1947, 11, database with images, Newspapers.com. I identified the two members from Württemberg from census records.

20. Forter, *History of Marshall County*, 334.

21. The obituary for Gottfried's daughter Rosa Gürtler specifically mentioned that she had accepted the faith early in her life. Obituary, *Axtell Standard*, May 4, 1950, 1.

22. Wolfgang Helbich, "The Letters They Sent Home: The Subjective Perspective of German Immigrants in the Nineteenth Century," *Yearbook of German-American Studies* 20 (1987): 13.

23. Linda Pickle, *Contented among Strangers: Rural German-Speaking Women and Their Families in the Nineteenth-Century Midwest* (Urbana: University of Illinois Press, 1996), 182.

24. Doerries states: "Faith and the organizational church are, therefore, of considerable importance in the immigrant's life, and changing them is likely to be one of the more significant aspects of the acculturation experienced by the second generation." Doerries, "Immigrants and the Church," 5.

25. Pickle, *Contented among Strangers*, 75. Years later, when Louis had a problem

with his lungs, he and his brother Will went to New Mexico, where Will did the housekeeping. He also did all the housekeeping when he took his wife and young son to California in the hope of curing her tuberculosis. Louis sometimes baked bread, and his future wife once commented how strange it seemed to see the brothers washing dishes. Letters in the family's possession.

26. Probate file for Godfrey Lodholz, Marshall County District Court, Marysville, KS.

27. "Another Death," *Beattie Eagle*, January 17, 1902, 1.

28. 1900 Federal Census, Litchfield County, Connecticut, Plymouth, Dist. 0248, Connecticut, p. 13, lines 87–90, database with images, Ancestry.com, citing Twelfth Census of the United States, 1900, T623, National Archives and Records Administration, Washington, DC.

29. Friedrich Lodholz, "Administration Account," Connecticut Probate Court (Plymouth District), vol. 22, pp. 102–103, digitized microfilm images, FamilySearch, citing Connecticut State Library, film 007626510, Probate Records 1833–1925, vol. 20 (p. 330–end), vol. 22 (p. 1–530), 1906–14.

30. Probate file for Frederick Lodholz, Marshall County District Court, Marysville, KS. As Friedrich still had property in Kansas, his will had to be probated in both Connecticut and Kansas.

31. "Terryville Woman Burned to Death," *Hartford Courant*, July 15, 1901, 2.

32. Mary Reb to John Reb, September 30, 1901, in the family's possession.

33. Mary Reb to John and Lulu Reb, September 9, 1907, in the family's possession.

34. Database with images, Ancestry.com, citing Charles R. Hale Collection, Hale Collection of Connecticut Cemetery Inscriptions, Connecticut State Library, Hartford.

35. Friedrich Lodholz, "Administration Account," Connecticut Probate Court (Plymouth District), vol. 22, pp. 102–103.

36. Probate file for Frederick Lodholz, Marshall County District Court, Marysville, KS.

37. In addition to the letters in German, several hundred letters in English between Reb family members are in the family's possession. They chronicle life on their farm from the 1890s through the 1960s.

38. Obituary, *Frankfort Index*, July 13, 1925, 3, database with images, Newspapers.com.

Appendix A

1. Trudy Schenk and Ruth Froelke, comps., *The Wuerttemberg Emigration Index*, vols. 2 and 3 (Salt Lake City, UT: Ancestry Incorporated, 1986, 1987). There are a total of six volumes.

2. *Wuerttemberg Emigration Index*, 1:ix.

3. Mack Walker, *Germany and the Emigration: 1816–1885* (Cambridge, MA: Harvard University Press, 1964), 143.

4. Zef M. Segal, *The Political Fragmentation of Germany: Formation of German States by Infrastructures, Maps and Movement, 1815–1866*. (Chaim, Switzerland: Palgrave Macmillan, 2019), 29, 32.

5. Mack, *Germany and the Emigration*, 13.
6. Mack, 18, 19–20.
7. Georg Lodholz to family in Terryville, May 14, 1857, trans. Freda Murray, LRFC.

Appendix B

1. *Transactions of the Kansas State Historical Society, 1903–1904*, ed. Geo. W. Martin, vol. 8 (Topeka, KS: Geo. A. Clark, 1904), cited in http://www.ksgenweb.org/archives/county/map3.html.
2. 1860 Federal Census, table 2, https://www2.census.gov/library/publications/decennial/1860/population/1860a-14.pdf.

Appendix D

1. US Census Bureau, "Measuring America: The Decennial Censuses from 1790 to 2000," Report POL/02-MA(RV), September 2002, 9, https://www2.census.gov/library/publications/2002/dec/pol_02-ma.pdf.

Appendix F

1. 1865 State Non-Population Schedules, database with images, Ancestry.com, citing Non-population Census Schedules for Kansas, 1850–1880, microfilm publication T1130, rolls 1–2, 5, 8–41, Records of the Bureau of the Census, Record Group 29, National Archives and Records Administration, Washington, DC.

Index

Page numbers in *italics* refer to figures.

abolitionism, 68, 69, 84, 193
acculturation. *See* assimilation
African-Americans, 137, 156, 170
  buffalo soldiers, 146
  See also slavery
agriculture
  capital required, US, 52
  Ebhausen, 6, 110–111
  farming practices, poor, US, 302n31
  frontier, on Kansas, 103
  mechanization, 169
  See also farming
Anna Maria and children's voyage to America
  actual length of, 34
  average length, 28
  conditions in steerage, 34–35
  food requirements, 25, 28
  narrative, (Jakob) Friedrich's notebook, 29, 30–31, 33, 34–35
  railroad travel, France, 30–31
  weight and size of trunks allowed, 25
  See also Lodholz, Anna Maria
Armbruster, 117, *118*
assimilation, 3, 18, 23, 97–98, 193
  definition, 193–194
  English, learning, 19, 41–42, 195, 281n80
  government service, 99
  intermarriage, native-born, 99
  life insurance policy, purchase of, 148
  preemption, knowlege of, 65
  religion, role of, 329–330n24
  single Germans, opportunities for (1860), 100
  surname, anglicization of, 99
  See also names of individual family members
Association for Lutheran School, 15
Atchison, David Rice, 296n121
Atchison, KS, 92
  free state, change to, 193
  Lodholz meeting site, 74, *75*, 76, 77, 81
  pro-slavery, founded as, 68
  supplies, source of, 86, 124, 126
Austria, 93, 100

Baden, 21, 30
  settlers from, Kansas (1860), 94
banking, Kansas frontier, 63, 64
Barrett, A. G., 71–72, 83, 86, 156, 173.
  See also dam proposal

333

Barrett, KS
  Civil War, participation in, 134
  railroad, extension of, to, 156
  territorial period, 70, 71, 84, 86
Bavaria, 64, 84, 88, 94
Beattie, KS, 76, 124, 174–175, 189, 200
Beuttler, Daniel Friederich, 9, 17, 21
"Bleeding Kansas," 68, 70
Blue Rapids (city and township), 193
  agricultural schedule (1860), 307–308n107
  manufacturing center, 155, 158
  population: 1860, total, 100; ethnic composition, 101–102, 150t, 152; turnover of, during Civil War, 152
  settlement, German (1860), 101–102
Book, John, 162, 163, 322n152
Book (Bok, Buch, Buk), Rosina. See Lodholz, (Anna) Rosina
"Border Ruffians," 68, 69, 72
Brenz, Johan, 95, 276n5
Brown, John, 70, 74
Buffalo, NY, 37, 47
Bureau of Indian Affairs, 57
Bushwackers, 134, 136

California, 55, 56, 66
Calw Worsted Trading Association, 8, 9
Carmen, J. Neale, 97, 150, 174, 200, 319n85
cash renters, 168
chain migration, 18, 37, 59, 92, 193, 194, 286n184
Chicago, 47, 49, 50
  German-speaking population, 49, 51; political affiliation, 49–50, 67–68; religious affiliations, 51–52
childbirth, 129
Chrystie and Schlössmann, 24, 25, 31, 32
citizenship
  attitude towards by some Germans, US, 168
  Ebhausen, 7, 11–12, 205
  female participation, US, 87

Lodholz males participation, US, 130, 168
United States, 20–21, 87, 130, 290n7, 295n105
Colt pistol factory, 131, 148
complimentary identities. *See* Gjerde, John
Compromise of 1850, 66
Connecticut
  German settlement in, 40
  Hartford, 38, 43, 44, 131–132, 147–148
  slavery in, 73
  Terryville (Plymouth), 20, 38, 41, 59, 118, 126, 148
Conscription Act of 1863, 136
  opposition to, 137
craft guilds, 6–7, 276n9. *See also* worsted weaving
Civil War
  border warfare, Kansas/Missouri, 134
  Conscription Act of 1863, 136: opposition to, 137
  divisiveness, religious, 133
  German participation in, 137
  Kansas participation in, 133
  Marshall County participation in, 133–134
  Reb, Heinrich, support of and participation in, 134, 145
  settlement, disruption of, in Kansas, 136, 149, 193

dam proposal
  of Barrett, A. G., 181
  Reb, Anna, decision by, 181–182
Darmstadt-Hesse, 94, 98
deaths
  Lodholz, Anna Maria (Friedrich's wife), 202
  Lodholz, Anna Maria (mother), 144
  Lodholz, Christina, 202
  Lodholz, Friedrich, 202–203
  Lodholz, Georg, 161
  Lodholz, Gottfried, 202

Lodholz, Josef Friedrich, 14
Lodholz, Rosina, 323n163
Lodholz, Wilhemina, 147
Reb, Anna Regina, 204
Reb, Friederick C., 161
Reb, Heinrich, 175
declarants, 64, 65, 87
Denver, 138, 142
   Rocky Mountains, decription of, 141–142
   trip, Heinrich Reb and Georg Lodholz's, 138, 139, 140–142, 143
   See also Pike's Peak Gold Rush
Der Chrisliche Botschafter, 52, 96
dialects, German, 304n49
diet
   coffee, 110
   cornbread (cornpone), 109
   Ebhausen, lack of calories, 16
   Friedrich's in Terryville, 115
   frontier, on, 103, 109–110, 309–310n139
   gingersnaps and gingerbread recipe, 188–189
   Oregon Trail, on, 84–85
   tomatoes, sun-dried, 188
   white flour, 311n188
Douglas, Stephen A., 49, 67, 130
Douglas County, Wakarusa Township in, 88
draft. *See* Conscription Act of 1863
drought, 126, 177, 181

Eagle Lock Company, 20, 23, 40
   wages, 42, 43, 131, 148, 159
Ebhausen, 5, 6, 203, 204
economic conditions
   Civil War, during, 136
   Depression of 1873, 165, 177, 179, 186
   Ebhausen, 6, 9, 14, 17
   frontier, Kansas, on, 62–63, 64, 81, 107, 120–121
   Marshall County, post–Civil War, 155

Panic of 1857, 43, 64, 81, 90, 287–288n196
Terryville, 131
education
   Ebhausen, 114–115
   females, German, 112
   Lodholz, Gottfried and Christina, children of, 189
   parochial schools, German, Marshall County, 195, 327–328n7
   Reb, Anna Regina, children of, 186, 187, 188,
Egen, Friedrich, 129, 131
1848 revolutions in Europe, 17, 21, 84, 93, 94
1855 Kansas Territory census, 64, 71, 74, 87
   foreign-born settlers, comparison numbers of, 86–88
1860 federal census, 88, 151t
   couples, German, 89, 97, 99, 100, 303n35
   families with children, German, 89–92, 97, 99, 100
   flawed, 89, 208–209
   German emigrants: families, as defined, number of by county, 209–210; German states of birth, by county, 93–94, 211–214; individuals, number of by county, 209–210; number per page in census, 98–99; population, by county, 92, 209–210; US states from which emigrated, 91–92
   intermarriage: German states, spouses from different, 97–98; native-born, with, 99; non-German foreign-born, with, 99
   population, total of, Kansas, 149, 156
   settlement pattern, 92, 94
   sibling groupings, German-born, 89, 303n34
   single individuals, German, 89, 100, 209–210
   summary, 92, 193
   widows and widowers, German, 90

1865 Kansas Non-Population Schedule, 150, 150t, 151
population, foreign-born, by county and township, 264–273
population, Marshall County, total of, 149
1865 Kansas State Census, 150t, 151, 156
population total of state, 149, 168
See also names of individual Marshall County townships
1870 Federal Census, 156, 160, 167
1875 Kansas State Census. See names of individual Marshall County townships
1880 Federal Census, 167, 168, 173
1880 Federal Non-Population Schedule 2, 169
1885 Kansas State Census. See names of individual Marshall County townships
Ellis Island, 17, 37
emigration, German
fares, traveling to US, 23
female, single, 286n188
first and second waves, 15, 17, 205–206
illegal, 17, 205–206, 280n65
impact work force, US, 287n195
Killinger, Christian, 17, 29–30, 36–37
Lodholz, (Johann) Georg, 22, 39
Lodholz, Anna Maria, Jakob Friedrich, and Anna Regina, 30–31
Lodholz, Gottfried, 17
passport, emigration, 24–25, 26–27, 30, 205
policy, Württemberg, 15, 22, 24–25, 205–206
records, official: to US from Ebhausen, 206; to US from *Oberamt* of Nagold, 206
returnees, 288n199
statistics, Württemberg, 22, 24, 280n51; gender and age, 17, 286n188; marital status, 286n188

ticket, 28, 33
See also Anna Maria and children's voyage to America
Erie Canal, 37, 47

family compounds, 154
family size, US (1860), 89
famine, Germany, 11, 16
"Farewell Poem for the Trip to North America," 33–34
farming
capital required, US, 52
disparities, economic, US, 102, 307n104
Ebhausen, 10–11
farmland, productivity of, US, 88
female labor: butter and eggs production, 110–111, 169; Ebhausen, 10–11; field work, US, 108, 111, 112–113, 180, 183, 201, 310n141; household, 108–109, 139, 157
German immigrants, percentage engaged in, 44, 52
Lodholz, (Jakob) Friedrich, attitude towards, 113
Lodholz, Georg, 158
Lodholz, Gottfried, 144, 170, 182, 183; sheep raising, 158–159, 169; livelihood, change in basis, 169
marketing, problems before arrival railroad, 107, 114, 138
mechanization, 169, 171
Reb, Anna Regina, 175, 180–181, 182, 183, 184, 189, 201–202, 203
Reb, Heinrich, 156–157
soil management, poor practices, 302n31
tenants/sharecroppers/cash renters, increase of, 168
tools and techniques, early frontier, 105–107, 308n113–114
"fire woman," 108, 204, 309n128
Forter, Emma, 65–66, 168, 172, 299–300n179

Native American land, rational for taking, 78, 299n176
Fort Kearny, 107, 139, 140, 141
Fort Leavenworth, 70, 294n85
Franco-Prussian War, 161
Frankfort, KS, 155–156, 170, 185
Free Soil Party, 123
Free State Party, 69, 70, 72, 74
French Revolution, 7, 8, 29
Frik and Reichart, 9, 15, 21
frontier, 52, 54, 89,
    females in Marshall County, 179–180, 310n141
    fluidity, pre- and post–Civil War, Kansas, 88, 152
    US Census Bureau announcement of frontier end, 191, 328n105

Gaillert, 123–124, 313n228
Genschoreck, Anna Rosina, 158, 162–166
German, 92–93
    definition used, 276n1
    identity, Lodholzes, 93, 195
German Evangelical Association, 188
    church construction, Marshall County, 190
    Lodholz, decision to join, 95–96
    membership, 304n58, 305n63
    missionaries in Kansas, 97
    slavery, opposition to, 74
German Evangelical Church Society (Synod) of the West, 95, 101, 172
German Methodist Church, 96
Germany, 5
    conscription laws, 161
    Palatinate, 83–84, 301n6
    regional differences, 94–95
    unification, 93, 161
    See also names of individual states
Gjerde, John, 2–3, 111, 194
Golden Swan, 38, 39
grasshopper invasion, 176, 177, 182
Great American Desert, 54, 55, 56
Greeley, Horace, 120, 123

guilds, 6. *See also* craft guilds; worsted weaving
Guittard, George, 76, 308n111
Guittard Township, 100
    demographics of German emigrants, post–Civil War, 153
    families, increase in number (1870), 160
    German states, settlers from (1880), 174
    occupations (1860), 101
    population composition, ethnic, 102, 150, 150t, 152, 174–175
    turnover of population, during Civil War, 152

Hanover, KS, 101
Hanover (German state), 94, 98, 101, 173
Havre, 17, 23, 30, 31
Hawgood, John, 59, 62, 86, 88, 89, 113
Helbich, Wolfgang, 201
Herkimer (city and township) 101
Hetterling, Anna Maria, 158, 162–166, 189. *See also* Lodholz, Anna Maria
Homestead Act (of 1862), 123, 149, 154, 157, 192
    Civil War veterans, provision for, 145
homesteaders, 154–155, 192
Humbolt, KS, 44, 97
"Hunger Year," 11, 15, 16, 277n34
Hutchinson, Perry, 155, 320n105

Illinois, 56, 88, 97, 172. *See also* Chicago
illness and disease, 183
    Ebhausen, 10, 11
    Lodholz, Anna Maria, 114
    Lodholz, Christina, 184
    Lodholz, Friedrich, 115–116, 131, 148
    Lodholz, Gottfried, 183, 184
    Lodholz, Wilhelmina, 139
    Lodholz children, 183
    Reb, Heinrich, 175
    Reb, Henry (son), 184
    remedies, 118, 183, 184
    tuberculosis, 119

Indian Removal Act of 1830, 46, 54,
    289n3. *See also* Native Americans
"Indian territory," 54, 156, 170, 289n5
infant mortality
    United States, 129
    Württemburg, 10, 277n27
inheritance
    from relative in Ebhausen, 189–190
    laws, Ebhausen, 11
    laws, Kansas, 162, 178
Iowa, 52–53, 88
    Austin, 53
    Greenbush, 84
    Iowa City, 52
Irish immigrants, 19, 34, 40, 87
    Eagle Lock Company, work at, 116
Irving, KS, 155, 185

Jayhawkers, 134
Johnson, Andrew, 123, 313n226

Kansas (state) population
    by decade (1870–1890), 156, 167
    1865, 149
    loss during Civil War, 151–152, 151t
Kansas-Nebraska Act, 67, 68, 71,
    129–130
    German reaction, Chicago, 49, 67
Kansas Territory, 57, 68
    admission as state, 74
    crime, 88, 302n26
    demographics, German pioneers, 92, 94
    departure of settlers, reasons for, 88–89
    1855 territorial census, 69, 74, 86–87,
        295n100, 295n103
    emigration to, reasons for, 88–89
    extent, 68, 312n200
    Free State Party, formation of, 69
    Free State Party, position and strategies, 69, 72
    government, lack of control, 68, 69
    Native Americans, presence of, 78–79
    percentage of Germans, counties with largest, 92

population: 1860, 88
pro-slavery position and strategies, 68, 69, 72
voter fraud, Marysville, 72–73
Kansa tribe, 78, 192
Kaw Nation (tribe), 78, 192
Kehl, 25, 30
Kickapoo (*Kickaapol*), 2, 78, 79
Kickapoo Land Office, 77, 298–299n170
Killinger, Christian, 42, 46, 48–49, 131.
    See also emigration
Kleindeutchland, 18
Know-Nothing Party
    Chicago, 49–50, 51
    Connecticut, 50
Krebber, Jochen, 2, 92

Lager Beer Riot, 51, 291n33–34
Land Act of 1785, 45, 62, 288n1
land speculation, 62–63, 65–66, 120–121,
    155, 288n2, 312n209
    absentee landlords, 121
    back taxes, sale of land for, 154
    disregard of treaties, 288–289n2
    foreclosures, 121, 154
    loan contracts and debt, 122, 312n213, 313n219
    loans, interest rate of, 121
land values
    frontier, Kansas, 60
    Iowa, 53–54
    Marshall County, 155, 156, 157, 168
    Michigan, 48, 158, 162
land warrants, military, 122–123, 124, 129
Lawrence, KS, 69
    1856 attack, 70
    1863 attack, 134–136, 135
    Order No. 11, 136
Leavenworth, KS
    slaves escaping to, 113–114
    territorial period, 68, 74, 92, 193, 225
Lecompton Constitution, 68, 72, 74
Le Havre, 17, 23, 30, 31
Lincoln, Abraham, 68, 130

Lockridge, Jacob, 84, 88
Lodholz, (Anna) Rosina, 158, 162–166, 189
Lodholz, (Jakob) Friedrich, 2, 10, 22
   assimilation, degree of, 195, 197, 198
   Bridgeport factory, work in, 185
   business, helping mother with, 22
   citizenship, 130, 295n105
   Colt pistol factory, work in, 131
   confirmation gifts, 22
   Eagle Lock factory, work in, 116, 125, 165
   land in Kansas, 164–165, 190
   loans to Georg Lodholz, 138, 157, 160, 162
   reaction to Anna Regina's widowhood, 177, 185
   visit to Kansas, 159–160
   See also under death; farming; illness and disease
Lodholz, (Johann) Georg, 2, 10, 19, 20
   apprenticeship, Ebhausen, 20, 21
   assimilation, degree of, 63, 195, 197–198
   money, borrowing, from Friedrich, 138, 157
   travels as journeyman, Württemburg, 21–22, 57, 58–65
   travels to find land, US, 46–49, 52–54
   See also under deaths; emigration, German; farming
Lodholz, Anna Maria, 2, 9–10, 14–16, 19–20, 21–22
   bankruptcy, 21
   physical description, 24, 282n109
   See also Anna Maria and children's voyage to America
Lodholz, Anna Regina, 2, 10, 22, 40, 107
   assimilation, degree of, 201
   Reb family, 175
Lodholz, Christina, 178, 179, 183–184, 191
Lodholz, Gottfried, 2, 10, 18–21, 39, 178
   assimilation, degree of, 162, 194, 195, 198, 199
   Eagle Lock factory, work in, 20
   land, purchase of, from Friedrich, 190
   Massachusetts factory, work in, 19
   See also under deaths; emigration, German; illness and disease
Lodholz, Josef Friedrich, 7, 8, 9
Lodholz, Sophia, 189, 191, 201
Lodholz and Reb families, children born by
   Lodholz, George and Rosina, 158
   Lodholz, Gottfried and Christina, 42, 138, 144, 190–191
   Lodholz, Rosina and John Book, 163
   Reb, Anna and Heinrich, 131, 157, 175
Lodholz family
   capital accumulation, 168
   cohesiveness, 40–41, 107, 111, 169
   financial support, Anna Regina's, 40, 107, 113
   financial support, Friedrich's, 113, 117–118, 123, 124, 148, 168
   mutual support, 168
   stability, desire for, 44, 62
Lodholz/Reb Family Collection, 3
log cabin, 82, 109, 157
   conditions in winter, 125, 127, 144
   construction, 79–80
Lutheran Church-Missouri Synod, 95, 101, 170
Lutheranism, 6, 95, 276n5, 304n55
Lutheran School, Association for, 15
Lyon Creek settlement, xi, 306–307n89

Madison County, 99
Manifest Destiny, 56, 58
Manypenny, George W., 57, 79
marriage
   companionate marriage, 11, 148, 202
   Lodholz, Anna Regina and Heinrich Reb, 128–129
   Lodholz, Georg, and Anna Rosina Genschoreck, 158
   Lodholz, Georg, and Wilhelmina Wender, 128, 157–158

marriage, *continued*
  Lodholz, Gottfried and Christina Seitz, 42
  Lodholz, (Jakob) Friedrich and unnamed widow, 147–148, 149
  Lodholz, Josef and Maria Schill, 9
  Lodholz, Rosina and John Book, 162
  Lodholz daughters, Gottfried and Christina, 190–191
  mean age for marriage, Ebhausen, 277n22
  mean age for remarriage, Ebhausen, 14
Marshall, Frank, 70, 71, 72, 74, 133–134
Marshall County, KS, 64, 65, 75
  demographics, second wave of settlement, 153–154
  description, physical, 66
  population, German, 65, 92, 94, 152, 170
  population total (1860), 83, 149; 1865, 149, 168; comparison German and Irish counts, 150, 150t
  population total (1880), 168
  population total (1890), 169
  turnover, post–Civil War, 152
  settlement pattern, German, post–Civil War, 153
  southern vs. northern German states, 94, 173–174
  Württemburg, percentage emigrants from (1860), 94
  See also names of individual townships
Martins (Martinson), August, 117, 130
Marysville (city)
  business ownership, German, 172
  demographics, German emigrants, post–Civil War, 152–153
  ethnic composition, 100, 150t, 152–153, 170–171, 193
  German-born, locations emigrated from (1885), 170–171
  German settlers, increase in, 152
  population total (1885), 170
  social classes, German (1885), 172
  territorial period, 70, 71, 72–73
  turnverein, 172, 329n29

Marysville Township
  Civil War, participation in, 134
  Civil War, turnover of population, during, 152
  demographics, German emigrants, post–Civil War, 153
  ethnic composition, 101, 150t, 152–153
  German-born, locations emigrated from (1885), 172
  German settlement pattern, post–Civil War, 193
  German settlements, pre–Civil War, 101
  German settlers, increase in, 152–153
  population total (1885), 172
  Württemberg, settlers from, 174
Methodist (Episcopal) Church, 96, 173
Michigan
  Ann Arbor, 37, 46, 47, 48–49
  Detroit, 47, 87
  Fredonia, 47–48
  Norwich Falls, 37
  Ypsilanti, 48
military land warrants, 122–123, 124, 129
Missouri, 66, 68, 87
Missouri Compromise of 1820, 66, 67
Mohrbacher, Elizabeth, 186
Mormons, 55, 119
mourner's bench, 96. *See also* pietism

Nagold
  administrative center, 24, 205
  river and valley, 5–6, 8, 18
Napoleon, 7, 8, 21, 51, 64, 93
Native Americans, 45, 78
  annuity payments, 62, 64, 146
  Lodholz family, reaction to, 59, 61, 78–79, 127, 147
  Marshall County, fear of, 79, 146–147
  Native American land, white settlers attitude regarding, 78, 299n176
  Indian wars, 145–146, 170
  treaties: US government's breaking faith

of, 56–57, 156, 192, 289–290n5;
Kickapoo, with, 78; squatters,
disregard of, 288–289n2; wording,
54, 292n55
nativism, 49
naturalization. *See* citizenship
Naturalization Act of 1802, 20–21, 130
Nebraska City, 54, 57–58, 60
New England Emigrant Aid Company, 69
New Mexico, 54, 56, 66–67
northern German states, list of, 94
Northwest Ordinance, 45, 288n1

"Old Lutherans," 95
Ordinance for Ascertaining the Mode of
Disposing of Lands in the Western
Territory, An, 45, 288n1
Oregon, 55–56, 66
Oregon Trail, 55, 70, 71, 81, 139, 140
supplies needed, settlers, 84–85
Otoe City, NE, 58, 59
Otoe mission, 107, 309n125
Otoe tribe, 108, 109, 134, 170

packet ship, 31, 34, 35
Palmetto, 69, 71
Panic of 1857, 43, 64, 81, 90,
287–288n196
passport, 24–25, 26–27, 30, 205
patriarchal family, German
Lodholz/Reb family comparison, 112,
142–143, 148, 157, 201
Pickle, Linda Schelbitski, 2–3,
111–112, 201, 302n19
versus native-born, 111–112
Pawnee Indians, 127–128
pietism, 12–13, 15, 95–96, 278n39,
279n41
Pike's Peak Gold Rush, 119–120, 138
prospectors' kit, 140
See also Denver
pioneers, Germans as, 2–3, 86–87, 89,
193
Lodholz and Reb, factors promoting
as, 168–169

Plymouth. *See* Connecticut
political
Ebhausen, organization of, 6–7, 11–12
Lager Beer Riot, 51, 291n33–34
political party affiliations, German, 49,
50, 67–68
temperance movement, Kansas,
172–173
Württemberg, organization of, 24–25
popular sovereignty, 66–67, 68
population, age of, US (1850), 57
Pottawatomie Creek raid, 70, 74
prairie fire, 126–127
preemption, 46, 57, 60, 87, 120, 192, 193
Barrett, in founding, 71
females, by, 290n7
Lodholzes, by, 65, 77–78, 168
staking claim, 76–77, 299n171–172
probate, Friedrich's estate, 203
probate, Georg's estate, 162–166
Prussia, 84, 93, 94 161
Marshall County, preponderance post–
Civil War, 193
population: Chicago, 51–52; Kansas
(1860), 94
religious diversity, 51; liturgy, attempt
at unifying by government, 291n38
See also settlements, major, by German
state of origin/Russia

Quantrill, William, 134. *See also*
Lawrence

railroads, US, 38–39, 47, 49, 53, 160
accident, Friedrich's train, 114
Iowa, 52
Kansas, 124
land grants, 120, 155
Marshall County, 145, 155–156, 160,
170
settlements along, 155, 167
transcontinental, 119, 130, 145
Reb, Anna (Regina). *See* Lodholz, Anna
Regina
Reb(b), Heinrich, 74, 83

Reb(b), Heinrich, *continued*
   assimilation, degree of, 84, 195, 198
   Barrett, settlement in, 83
   blacksmithing, 84, 85, 85–86
Reb and Lodholz families, children born by
   Lodholz, George and Rosina, 158
   Lodholz, Gottfried and Christina, 42, 138, 144, 190–191
   Lodholz, Rosina and John Book, 163
   Reb, Anna and Heinrich, 131, 157, 175
religion
   Catholicism, shared German and Irish, 200
   Chicago, diversity in, 51–52
   Ebhausen, 7, 12–13, 95
   Germans, divisiveness among, US, 94–96, 199–200
   Lodholz, choice of, 96, 97
   missionaries on frontier, 97, 107–108
   Prussia, 51, 291n38
   slavery, divisiveness of denominations over, 133
   Terryville, 41, 116–117
Republican Party, 66–68, 129–130

Samuel M. Fox, 33, 34, 38, 284–285n152
   description of, 31
   passengers, number of, 31–32
   safety, 34
   tonnage, 31, 32
   Württemburg, demographic of passengers from, 17, 33
Sand Creek Massacre, 146
schools, public, 84. *See also* education
Seitz, Christina, 42
settlement, German (general)
   clusters, small, 98–99, 100, 101–102, 193
   fluidity, 52, 88
   nationally, 19, 52, 87
settlements, German, other than Kansas
   Chicago (1870), 291n36
   Ebhausen emigrants, 37, 46, 47, 48, 49
   Oregon, 55–56
   southwest, 55–56
   See also settlement, German (general)
settlements, location of discrete German, by county
   Anderson, Monroe Township, 97
   Brown, Claytonville Township, 98
   Chase, Diamond Creek, 97
   Davis, 94
   Dickinson, Not Stated Township, 97
   Douglas, Eudora (city), 97, 153
   Marshall, Marysville Township: Hanover (town), 101; Horseshoe Creek, 101, 170; Raemer's Creek, 101
   Nemaha, 94
   Osborne County, 167
   Phillips, Mound Township, 174
   Riley, 94
   Waubausee, Alma Township, 97, 153, 154
   Wyandotte, Wyandotte Township, 153
settlements, major, by German state of origin/Russia
   Black Sea Germans, 167–168
   Darmstadt-Hesse, 94, 98
   Hanover, 173–174
   northern German states (1880), 173
   Prussia, 94, 97, 101, 173–174
   southern German states (1880), 173
   Volga Germans, 167–168
   Westphalia, 94
   Württemburg, 173, 174
sheep raising, 158–159, 169
Sioux uprising, Minnesota, 146
slavery
   Barrett, A. G., attitude towards, 72
   Connecticut, in, 73
   German attitude towards, 67, 74
   Kansas Nebraska Act, 67
   Lodholz attitude towards, 73
social divisions, 102
southern German states, 11, 173, 193
   list of, 94
   monetary system, 283n99

speculation, land. *See* land speculation
squatters, 45, 46, 192, 288–289n2, 290n8
steamboat travel, 38, 47, 74–75, 114
steerage, 32–33, 34–35
Steerage Act of 1819, 31–32
step migration, 92
Strohm, John, 37–38, 194
Sttuttgart, KS, 174
sulky plow, 169, 171. *See also* farming
Switzerland, 98, 99–100

tallgrass prairie, 103, *104*, 104–105
temperance movement, Kansas, 172–173
tenant farmers, 168, 172
Terryville, CT, 20, 38, 41, 59, *118*, 126, 148
Texas, 54–55, 56, 66
tornado, 185
town company, 57–58, 71, 97, 155, 289n2
Turk, Eleanor, xi–xii, 65, 94
turnverein, 172, 325n19

United Lutheran Church General Synod, 95
United States, sections defined, 91, 303n39

US Postal Service, 59, 62, 294n81
Utah, 66–67, 119

Vermillion Township, 100, 193
   Civil War, participation in, 134
   Civil War, turnover of population during, 152
   ethnic composition, 102, 150, 150t, 152, 175
   families, increase in number of, 160
   occupations (1860), 102–103
   work expectations of teenage native-borns, 112–113

Wabaunsee County, 92, 97
Wakarusa Township (Douglas County), 88
Wander-Buch, 7–8, *8*, 277n11
Washington County, 101, 173
Wender, Wilhelmina, 128, 139, 147, 164
Wendt, Pastor, 95
Westphalia, 94
Whig Party, 50, 130
Wöllhausen, 5–6. *See also* Ebhausen
worsted weaving, 7, 8, 9, 276n9. *See also* craft guilds
Württemburg, 5, 6, 10, 12, 18, 21, 25, 51, 94, 98

www.ingramcontent.com/pod-product-compliance
Lightning Source LLC
Chambersburg PA
CBHW030519230426
43665CB00010B/687